CHILDREN'S
EMERGENT LITERACY

CHILDREN'S EMERGENT LITERACY

From Research to Practice

Edited by David F. Lancy

Foreword by James Moffett

Westport, Connecticut
London

Library of Congress Cataloging-in-Publication Data

Children's emergent literacy : from research to practice / edited by
    David F. Lancy ; foreword by James Moffett.
        p.   cm.
    Based on papers originally presented at a conference held at the
University of Toledo in 1991.
    Includes bibliographical references and index.
    ISBN 0–275–94589–8 (alk. paper)
    1. Reading—Congresses. 2. Reading—Parent participation—
Congresses. 3. English language—Composition and exercises—Study
and teaching—Congresses. 4. Socially handicapped children—
Education—Language arts—Congresses. 5. Literacy—Social aspects—
Congresses. I. Lancy, David F.
LB1050.C46   1994   93–23475
372.4—dc20

British Library Cataloguing in Publication Data is available.

Library of Congress Catalog Card Number: 93–23475
ISBN: 0–275–94589–8

First published in 1994

Praeger Publishers, 88 Post Road West, Westport, CT 06881
An imprint of Greenwood Publishing Group, Inc.

Printed in the United States of America

The paper used in this book complies with the
Permanent Paper Standard issued by the National
Information Standards Organization (Z39.48–1984).

10 9 8 7 6 5 4 3 2 1

For Leslie and all those who love to read with children.

Contents

viii   Contents

Tables and Figures

TABLES

FIGURES

Foreword
James Moffett

Perhaps because packaging and marketing guide attention in our society, how you name something becomes excessively important. Thus we may not recognize familiar things because they are not labeled as expected, or we assume a new name betokens a new reality when it may merely re-label the familiar. I worry about this problem in regard to "emergent literacy," which—whatever else it means—refers to learning activities I heartily endorse. But, precisely, I have been advocating most of them since the 1960s, and indeed many are practices old before my time. Likewise, "whole language" renames activities long familiar to at least some parents, children, and teachers, many of which, in fact, re-occur in discussions of emergent literacy.

To exemplify the problem—a reviewer (and a much valued colleague) concluded that my co-author and I do not deal with emergent literacy in our teaching methods book, apparently because we did not use this term, even though in chapter after chapter we detail our recommendations for all the literacy-related activities now gathered under the rubric of emergent literacy, including not only general ones such as play, drama, task and topic talk, and independent writing but, specifically, reading to small children, taking down their dictations, and fostering their invented spelling. We were unpolitic enough to title the chapter most focusing on all this "Becoming Literate" instead of "Emergent Literacy." This same reviewer praised my work for pioneering from the 1960s what is now called "whole language" and took to task contemporary whole language proponents for not acknowledging this leadership.

Part of the renaming problem concerns role. This reviewer specializes in emergent literacy, whereas I work across the whole language curriculum for all ages. Also, he was thinking as a researcher and scholar, a university professor obliged to situate discussion in ongoing academic forums, to cite previous contributions, and to cast it all in the accepted currency of such forums, whereas I was thinking more like the curriculum developer, school troubleshooter, and inservice workshop leader that I am. My co-author and I are communicating with classroom teachers, not with colleagues and competitors. We just want schools to sponsor these activities. We don't care what they call them. But for advancement and funding, researchers and professors face the practical problem of having to carve out and guard something distinctive with which they can be associated. At its worst, renaming becomes a way of trying to copyright something already in the public domain. At its best, however, renaming may help us see something familiar in a new light. "Emergent literacy" partakes of both and hence is at once confusing and useful.

I have played the renaming game myself. When I was trying in the 60s to get schools and "reading specialists" to honor reading to children as a major way to teach literacy I called it the "lap method." By this renaming, I meant to dignify this folksy home activity as a method so that teachers would acknowledge and use it as such, even though reading research of that time never compared its efficacy with that of other methods because it simply wasn't in the repertory of reading pedagogy and research. I hoped by this also to make reading to children one example of my claim that the home can be an excellent model for language learning generally. We all learned to talk at home by its naturally individualized, interactive, and integrated way of incorporating a new person into the culture.

By calling out-of-school ways of learning language "emergent literacy," we risk actually dissociating them from what we really have in mind. One is apt to think, "This must be unfamilar to me because I've not heard these terms before." Schoolbooks and curricula chronically do this to students by labeling familar experience with the technical terms of professionals. This dissociation prevents students from building on what they already know. Having students learn formal grammar is an example. Most language arts teachers today may understand the term "invented spelling," which is just a handy name researchers made up to designate the make-shift writing that generations of pre-school children who know the alphabet have done at home for fun. But how many parents would recognize in it the activity their own children are doing or have done? As pointed out in several chapters in this book, parents and children seldom think of their oral language exchanges or bedside storytime sessions as "education".

Nevertheless, and at the risk of seeming to announce some new technical and therefore possibly threatening matters, calling these familiar and familial activities "emergent literacy" can notify parents and teachers to take them seriously and to cultivate them as real ways for children to learn to read and write.

As investigation, "emergent literacy" does refer to some new phenomena, namely, a body of research projects such as this book contains that show how certain activities like perusing a picture book or storytelling or conversing about a topic, not traditionally associated with literacy proper, and certainly not with "reading instruction," represent, in fact, stages of successively approximating reading and writing. Some of this research may register ethnographically how parents and children of different socioeconomic classes interact verbally and how this abets or aborts the acquisition of literacy. Some research consists of experimental intervention projects in and out of school designed to prove the value of familiar home practices or to determine if other intergenerational or communal activities can also act in effect as curricula.

This research is helping to validate for schools some old folk ways of learning that were not heretofore regarded as pedagogical—at least not by the educational establishment. I must ask why we needed this research to tell us that certain kinds of family atmospheres and human relating and play and natural language activites not only manifest an emerging literacy but indicate a pedagogy for schooling? I think most of this was known before and would have been understood as we understand it now, and applied in school, had not some jealous professionalism, a guild mentality, combined with commercialism to fend off such perception.

Renaming folk practices "emergent literacy" has indeed served an important purpose—to legitimize these unacknowleged ways of learning to read and write that many educators have long had powerful reasons to deny. The research underlying this reconceptualization challenges a lot of reading instruction and materials in which schools have heavily invested for generations. The fact is that the pedagogy indicated by this research and by "whole language" approaches can unsettle teachers because it doesn't necessarily require professionals except to direct the processes. Once oriented by professionals, virtually any literate person who is willing can midwife the emergence of another's literacy. As a number of studies herein demonstrate, communities can arrange for literacy to ripple among its members with only limited guidance from educators. And, as several of these also mention, school people have often ignored or declined to cooperate with such projects. Family, folk, or communal pedagogy seems to threaten teachers with loss of employment or at least with a drastic change in role from being the star of one's own classroom to becoming some sort of roving consultant extending from the school out into the community.

And such a pedagogy certainly unsettles the educational-industrial complex, because it doesn't require all those commercial materials—worksheets, basals. and "skill-building" programs—that the chronic failure of reading instruction has made into a flourishing business. The main problem with rippling is that it costs too little. All you really need is people, trade books, and paper. It is too cheap for our economy, which requires expensive solutions to self-perpetuating problems. "Emergent literacy" rightly implies a certain naturalness to learning to read and write in that it extends not only speaking but other physical and social activities essential to human being. The research indicates how much literacy depends on patterns of human relating and how these may be altered to favor it.

Since human resources include peers and elders available in numerous circumstances, they are inexhaustible. The only cost—and initial only—is in running the sort of experiments needed to pilot this educational conversion, as reported by some authors in this collection, Though "emergent" may suggest that literacy will always occur spontaneously somehow and only needs to be awaited and signaled, the emphasis that the emergent literacy movement places on deliberately arranging the necessary human relations should effectively offset this misleading connotation. Literacy emerges in individuals only when they are immersed in a community of literacy, which may often have to comprise more than their family, or may have to emerge in their family first. The costs for running a communal pedagogy, once it is established, should be less than now spent on literacy, but shifting learning from materials to people will shunt money away from the educational-industrial complex, which no doubt will redouble the pressure it has always exerted on schools.

I'm personally cheered, finally, to see the literature of emergent literacy bring out how inseparable reading and writing are from the rest of human functioning. Part of why literacy specialists can sometimes frustrate their own efforts is that any specialization tends to encourage isolating the object of one's focus—a problem serious enough for pure research but potentially catastrophic for a pragmatic enterprise like public education. Literacy is at once physical, mental, interpersonal, and cultural. The participating body, mind, people, and culture all have other business and purposes than literacy, which may indeed be peripheral. If literacy plays a significant role in the culture, then it will be linked in myriad ways with these other things, which will naturally provide myriad occasions to learn and practice literacy. The authors collected here seem to me to be saying that literacy emerges in many ways and places that we have not suspected and have therefore not regarded as learning circumstances. Crawlng and drawing, chatting and imitating, teach literacy. Whether literacy actually emerges may be determined more by social customs, family habits and attitudes, than by what schools do.

Like any other human activity, reading and writing partake of what I call a sacred matrix, a primal unity with the world that individuals gradually differentiate themselves from as we grow up. Oneself and others, inner and outer, body and mind, senses and muscles, all gradually distinguish themselves from each other as they develop their own characteristics and specialize into their own natures. For the infant, speech only gradually separates itself from other sounds and becomes a means of communication different from other physical and social activity. Since literacy presupposes acculturation and external instrumentalities, it will with much more difficulty become a distinct activity to cultivate, especially as the child already avails itself of a very satisfactory means of communication in speech. As the main mission of schooling, literacy tends to be conceived far too much as a discrete action or function, stripped of the multiple contexts that alone ensure its emergence. By definition, an individual is indivisible. In trying for institutional reasons to disembed one aspect of total human being from this primal unity, we feel the violence we do and the poverty of results. It seems time now to honor this sacred matrix from which literacy, like all else, emerges.

Preface

Although the term *emergent literacy* (EL) was first used by Marie Clay (1966) in her doctoral dissertation, it has only recently come into widespread use and acceptance. Undoubtably, Teale and Sulzby's (1986) edited volume *Emergent Literacy: Writing and Reading* must be seen as a second benchmark in this evolving field. Emergent Literacy provides a refreshing change from decades of work on children's literacy that fragmented the process into myriad skills and denigrated the importance of out-of-school literacy experiences and the value of real literature and real writing.

The contributions in this book aim to enrich the field but also sharpen its focus. That is, all the chapters in the first section part company to some extent with prevailing orthodoxy. Data are presented that suggest a degree of qualification may be needed for some of the EL theorists' bolder claims—Kenneth Goodman's that "learning to read is natural in a literate society" (cited in Teale & Sulzby 1986, xvii), for example.

On the contrary, we argue that even in a literate society, it may not be natural or easy for children to become literate in the conventional sense. Hence, the second part of this book reviews a variety of intervention strategies aimed at children who are at risk. These strategies are all informed by recent research and theory in EL. Some of these strategies focus on the pivotal role of parents, others focus on children's fantasy play, and still others examine the teacher's role.

Our aim, then, is to foster a reciprocal relationship between basic research on the social, cultural, and cognitive roots of literacy and applied research on programs that attempt to create or recreate environments that are supportive of children's EL. In the process we believe that both theory and practice will advance. It should be made clear at the outset, however, that none of our findings suggests a return to the bad old days of skill and drill—of teaching children to blend rather than helping them to become readers and writers.

This volume had its origin in an emergent literacy conference I organized—ably assisted by my colleague Eileen Carr—at the University of Toledo in May 1991. Both the UT Foundation and the Center for Applied Cognitive Science played instrumental roles. All presenters at that conference—except Chris McCormick, who had made a previous commitment—agreed to submit chapters based on their work. Later I invited scholars whose work was complementary to the work presented at the conference to submit chapters and the collection grew. It should be obvious from these varied contributions that emergent literacy has become an extremely fruitful avenue for studying and promoting children's understanding and use of print.

Finally, without the typing and editorial assistance provided by Kathy Daugherty, Greg Parker and, especially, J. J. Green, this book would not have appeared during the present century.

David F. Lancy
Logan, Utah

Part One

The Emerging Field of Children's Literacy

1

The Conditions that Support Emergent Literacy

David F. Lancy

A PERSONAL FOREWORD

It was 1980 and three events came together to bring about my own baptism in the religion that was to be called emergent literacy. I had just started writing up the "Indigenous Mathematics Project," a comparative study of culture, cognition, and education undertaken earlier in Papua New Guinea (Lancy 1983) and was, hence, attuned to the sorts of issues we will be talking about here.

I also had two young daughters who feasted on books and stories like some kids gobble down Halloween candy. Nadia confounded the school authorities because she did not know her alphabet, yet read at a "fourth-grade level." Sonia, two years her junior and in nursery school, was chafing at the bit. At the dinner table after Nadia had shared the day's school stories, Sonia used her turn to complain about how much math homework she had to do! Since her school experiences didn't seem as academic as Nadia's, she made them up. A master storyteller, she, too, learned to read as easily as she had learned to talk (see Baghban 1984; Lass 1982).

Then there was Dorothy, the girls' mother, who was enrolled in reading courses at Arizona State University (ASU) to complete qualifications for an Arizona teaching credential and her school stories were grim. She struggled to make sense of a curriculum worthy of nuclear physics. These courses presented literacy acquisition as an extremely complex process, like a delicate watch that must be hand-crafted by experts and could be damaged by the slightest deviation from standard procedure.

Like a moth, I was drawn to the flame sparked by these apparently contradictory views of children's literacy. ASU in the early 1980s was a fortuitous place to begin such a personal odyssey as it contained, within the education faculty, some of the leading proponents of what became opposing schools of thought on the subject of reading acquisition—Nick Silvaroli and Carole Edelsky, to name but two. It was at ASU, also, that I initiated—with Kelly Draper—the study reported in Chapter Five.

The deeper I probed, the more convinced I became that emergent literacy represented both an accurate theory of how most children become literate, and, contrariwise, also explained illiteracy. Likewise, I have become very excited by the promise that emergent literacy holds as a wellspring of ideas for intervention with at-risk children and curricular reform.

WHAT IS EMERGENT LITERACY?

Adherents of emergent literacy are concerned with an old and well-studied question—how do children become literate? But Teale and Sulzby (1986) indicate that emergent literacy must be viewed as a "paradigm shift" (Kuhn 1970) where aspects of children's literacy that formerly seemed central—letter-naming—are now seen as peripheral, and aspects that were seen as trivial, or even dysfunctional—invented spelling—are seen as critical. The old paradigm, of course, is still alive and kicking (see, e.g., Adams 1990) and, indeed, the majority of parents, educators, policy makers, publishers, and even educational researchers still adhere to it. But there are signs of defection, *en masse*, to the new paradigm.

Emergent literacy places the onset of literacy at shortly after birth—even earlier if babies are read to in the womb (De Casper & Spence 1986). Becoming literate, in this view, occupies every waking moment throughout childhood. This contrasts with the view that literacy begins with reading instruction, in the first grade, or that, prior to first grade, pupils should receive training in pre-reading and reading readiness skills such as learning to identify letters or phonemes. Storybook reading by the teacher in preschool has not necessarily been seen as making a direct contribution to the child's literacy. Likewise, Head Start was developed to remedy the problem of poor academic performance—of which reading is the linchpin—by providing "compensatory" education. Yet, literacy in any guise is (or was, until recently) virtually absent from the Head Start curriculum. In Sweden (Chapter Six, this volume) this disjunction is even sharper than it is in the United States. Swedes believe that young children benefit from exposure to storybooks, rhymes, and conversations, but that this has nothing to do with learning to read, which they must be taught to do but no earlier than age seven when they begin formal schooling.

At least part of the reason for the assertion that literacy begins at an early age is that it follows from a second fundamental assertion—that reading, writing, and speaking are interrelated (Hiebert 1981). The child who will, eventually, become literate is exposed to and uses language in ways that are distinctive (Bernstein 1971). In Dickinson and Snow's research (Chapter Three, this volume) children who experience regular family talk around the dinner table and who have opportunities to use narrative and explanatory speech patterns are advantaged in learning to read. This contrasts with the prevailing view that separates learning to talk from learning to read. EL also challenges the notion that learning to write must *follow* learning to read.

It follows then, that children probably acquire the use of literate forms like story-telling, letter-writing, and menu reading from telling stories, writing letters and reading menus, not from "training" in skills far removed from real literacy, like "matching opposites" (c.f. Moffett & Wagner 1992).

Also, those who are expert in the uses of literacy—parents and older siblings as opposed to reading teachers—model and introduce these uses to children. They create situations—dinner table conversations, interactive bedtime story rituals—where children can flap their stubby little literacy wings without fear of crashing to the ground (see Vygotsky 1978).

If literacy is influenced by conversations a child has participated in, by being read to, by opportunities to enact stories in play, and so on, it follows that his or her literacy will be dynamic. It will grow and change. It will emerge.

So what do we offer, in this volume, that advances beyond these generalities? Strickland and Cullinan (1990, 427), in a recent defense of EL, argue: "Rather than classify children as readers or non-readers, we believe it is more accurate to consider their literacy development as being on a continuum of increasing competence." But, as Kamberelis and Perry (Chapter Seven, this volume) show in their study of nine first-graders, there is an evident discontinuity that occurs during the transition to "conventional literacy." This stage-like process is not a theorist's invention, it is grounded in the data obtained during a probing microgenetic study.

Another discontinuity occurs, according to Pellegrini and Galda (this volume, see also Figure 13.2), between reading and writing. Although obviously related, their research shows that reading is promoted primarily through joint storybook reading—where children learn to attend to metalinguistic verbs, whereas writing is driven by the child's growing capacity for symbolic representation—a capacity nurtured in verbal interaction with one's mother and symbolic play with peers.

Again we hear from Strickland and Cullinan (1990) that, "Unlike many early researchers, most contemporary researchers talk about what children *can* do rather than what they *cannot* do" (p. 430). We must not let our commitment to seeing literacy as emerging blind us to some unpleasant realities. As several chapters in Part One show, there is enormous variation in where any two children of the same age fall along the EL continuum. In the Kamberelis and Perry study (Chapter Seven), for example, they dropped from their sample children who made the transition early in first grade and those who hadn't made it by the end of the year. Similarly, in the study reported in Chapter Five, there were children—from the same school—who were reading fluently in kindergarten while others still weren't reading fluently by the end of first grade. Further, we know from Connie Juel's (1988) massive study that children who are behind in first grade don't catch up, they fall further behind. Donny, the main subject in Purcell-Gates's case study (Chapter Four), already shows signs of developing various coping mechanisms that will permit him to "pass" in school even though he is a nonreader.

Purcell-Gates's work also shows quite clearly that, contrary to the Goodmans' assertion (Goodman & Goodman 1979), the presence of environmental print and the wide availability of print material in a literate society is no guarantee that children will naturally become readers and writers. All through these research reports (Bergin, Lancy, and Draper, Chapter Five; Dickinson & Beals, Chapter Three; Svensson, Chapter Six), we read sobering stories of children growing up with limited exposure to books, to decontextualized speech (see Snow 1983), to assisted performance (see Tharp & Gallimore 1988) and to fantasy play (Smilansky 1968) with predictable consequences for their acquisition of literacy. Hence, although the United States and, by extension, the industrialized world may be a literate society in a statistical sense and in the sense that to fully participate in this society requires a level of literacy never before associated with "the masses" (Resnick & Resnick 1977), emergent literacy is more consistently found within the cultural mainstream than outside it—a topic we will take up shortly.

The major contribution we make to the corpus of material supporting EL is a series of studies of programs aimed at changing the environments—home, preschool, kindergarten, primary classrooms—where emergent literacy occurs. Teale and Sulzby's (1986) collection includes but a single "rare example of an intervention study that takes an emergent literacy perspective" (p. 90). In Part Two, "The Design of Emergent Literacy Environments," we offer case studies of ten such interventions.

LITERACY IN CULTURE

Ultimately, emergent literacy occurs within specific cultural contexts, so we must first consider these contexts. For centuries, scholars have been drawn to the study of the origins of writing (Schmandt-Besserat 1978) and to theorizing about the impact this invention has had on society. Havelock's (1976) analysis of the impact of alphabetic literacy on Greek society is but one example. Goody (1987) and Olson (1984) have carried these arguments further: "It is now generally agreed that literacy is associated with both a distinctive form of social organization, a *literate society,* and with a distinctive form of thought and talk, a *literate mind* " (Olson 1984, 185). In particular, Goody (1977) discusses the vastly expanded information store that writing and numbers make available to us. Postulation on the transformative effects of literacy on individuals and societies has been the inspiration for national literacy campaigns in the Third World (Freire 1970).

However, recent research suggests that these claims may be overstated. Stock (1983) shows the profound effect that print had on European society as, for example, in the church, such issues as sainthood and heresy were increasingly examined in light of written documents, rather than resorting to torture and scapulamancy (a form of divination). But this process took several centuries. Similarly, Reder and Green (1983), in their study of the Seal Bay Eskimo community, show how conservative society is with respect to the adoption of literacy. While public school instruction in English has been available locally for at least 50 years, levels of academic literacy remain low. In this fishing and hunting community, literacy is of little value. Only recently, with the growth of a social service bureaucracy, has the lure of paid employment provided sufficient incentive to induce some community members to become literate. On the other hand, there remain individuals able to recite in Slavonic from Cyrillic sacred texts 125 years after the end of Russian sovereignty because the Orthodox church is still active in the area.

Historians (Graff 1986; Resnick & Resnick 1977) have also documented how few individuals could actually read and write in so-called literate societies. In a landmark study in Liberia, Scribner and Cole (1981) showed how the cognitive effects of literacy can more appropriately be credited to prolonged exposure to formal education. In a society with an indigenous script but no tradition of school-based literacy, literacy is used to a very limited extent and, consequently, its practice does not confer the sort of general abilities associated with the term "literate mind." Also, Heath (1986a) in a comparative study of three distinct but neighboring communities, found that literacy seems to have few of the effects claimed for it.

> In both Trackton and Roadville, the patterns of uses of literacy and the presumed benefits of literacy do not match those predicted from the general literature. . . Neither group has the receptive and productive skills and values surrounding reading and writing that fit those described for "modern" communities. Written materials are not a major source of new information for either community, and neither group writes to distribute ideas beyond their own primary group. In neither community does literacy bear any direct relationship to job status or chances for upward mobility. (p. 225)

Heath (1982, 1983) has led us away from the literate/oral dichotomy toward the view that there is a gradation from communities where literacy plays a valuable but very limited role to those that are saturated with literacy, where literacy functions not only as a tool but where reading and writing become ends in themselves (Nell 1988). Even more important, for the goals of this chapter, Heath shows how literacy in culture also includes a complex of beliefs and routines about how adults and children should interact vis-à-vis literacy and connects these patterns to the varied experiences that children from these communities face when they encounter academic literacy in school.

Heath's three communities of Maintown (middle-class white), Roadville (working class white), and Trackton (impoverished—in the view of outsiders, not of the residents themselves—black) reflect three points along this continuum. Literacy is present in all three communities but, as she says of the seven uses of literacy in Trackton, "It is significant that these types do not include those uses—critical, esthetic, organizational, and recreational . . . usually highlighted in school-oriented discussions of literacy uses" (1986b, 22). A fourth possibility, that of a community in which literacy is absent, is identified in Purcell-Gates's (Chapter Four, this volume) research. A parallel gradation has been found by Carraher (1987) in Brazil and by Wagner, Messick, and Spratt (1986) in Morocco, where the elite are literate in French and send their children to schools where the language of instruction is French, through communities where scribes are available, for a fee, in the marketplace to perform literacy services for their illiterate clients. In Morocco, we also see a widespread form of literacy primarily for "...communication to or about God . . . . [which] . . . was a restricted literacy." (Goody 1987, 139). That is, individuals laboriously *memorize* lengthy passages in order to "read" the Quran.

Literacy in the Home

The other night Ellie [7] and I bought a copy of *Peter Rabbit* in French for Hannah [11], to put in her stocking (for Christmas) because we wanted to have a toy or something. And Hannah has always loved *Peter Rabbit*, so we had it out here and we were looking at it trying to decide whether Ellie should have it because she just started taking French or whether we should really give it to Hannah. Hannah came in from dancing class and said, "Oh my goodness, French *Peter Rabbit*" and picked it up and we both said to her, "Well, Merry Christmas to you". . . and she sat down with it and she opened it up and began looking through it and she said, "Look, the pictures are exactly the same." We always keep *Peter Rabbit* right here, so we got the English and we read a page and then she read a page and the next thing we knew we were going through all the *Peter Rabbit* books . . . it was twenty minutes to eleven and we were reading *Peter Rabbit*, curled up on the couch, the three of us. What a marvelous evening that was, to go back all the way back to the age of three or four, and it was just a wonderful time (Taylor 1983, 82-83).

This passage epitomizes the culture of literacy in mainstream, middle-class homes. It is taken from a study of six stereotypical "All-American" families: fathers all professionals, mothers well educated but working at home, with 2 or 3 children; their lives permeated by literacy. Here a mother describes an episode that illustrates the critical role that literacy and literature play in bonding family members. Heath (1982) similarly shows how, in Maintown, adult-child interaction pivots around books or "book-talk." She notes the large libraries of picture books, of bedroom furnishings patterned with literary characters and themes, and the complexity of the bedtime story ritual. The field of emergent literacy has its origin in studies like these.

Parent-child interaction in reading has attracted a great deal of attention from scholars (Teale 1984a). Ninio and Bruner (1978) observed a mother reading to her infant over the period from one month to 18 months and showed that far more than just reading is involved. The mother labeled and talked about the pictures, asked her non-verbal child questions about the book, then supplied the answer. In middle-class homes, storybook reading is an occasion for knowledge acquisition and for learning about a myriad of language conventions. Many parents use what has been called an expansionist strategy (Lancy, Draper, and Boyce, 1989). With somewhat older children, parents ask questions about the text that have a different structure from those asked about the illustrations (Many 1988). In another study (Altwerger, Diehl-Faxon, and Dockstader-Anderson, 1985), one "mother used prosodic features such as rising intonation followed by a pause to encourage the child to predict and join in . . . [she] was aware of her daughter's unfamiliarity with the word 'wink' and read it in a higher pitch with greater intensity thus calling attention to it" (p. 482). Heath (1982) and DeLoache (DeLoache & Mendoza 1985) have shown that the character of the bedtime story undergoes subtle changes as children get older. Mothers escalate their demands, but they seem cognizant of the children's "zone of proximal development"(ZPD) (Teale & Sulzby 1987; Vygotsky 1978). "I skipped some things because he doesn't know what they are yet. Then, as he learns more, I go on to something else. He doesn't really know what a kite is but he knows his brothers go to fly a kite, so I feel I can talk to him about that . . . . At least that's how I feel I'm teaching him" (DeLoache 1984: 15). Clearly, children are acquiring both a story schemata (Kintsch & Greene 1978) and a model of book reading

(Cochran-Smith 1986) during this process and, not surprisingly, by the age of three they "read" to themselves, their pets, and each other during make-believe play (Heath 1983, Teale 1984b) practicing the schemata before they can actually decode print.

Other social conventions not directly related to reading are also implicated in storybook reading. Language is broken down and treated as an object (Heath 1986a), and children are exposed to linguistic forms (termed information structures by Snow and Goldfield (1982, 1983)) that are implicated in school and in adult discourse in this community. "Picture-book reading may, in addition to its substantive contribution, be the basis for transfer to participation in the discourse structure of classroom lessons several years later" (Cazden 1992, 106). As we shall see, these efforts do pay off and account, in large measure (Adams 1990), for these childrens' success in school. However, it is interesting that mainstream parents do not view themselves as teaching their children to read or getting them ready for school in these storybook and "book-talk" encounters (Clark 1976; Cochran-Smith 1986; Svensson, this volume). They take these largely for granted. Rather, their primary goal seems to be to create "conversational partners," family members who will, when they are older, be able to hold their own in the heavily academic discourse that is characteristic of this society.

Growing up in a Storied Environment

While storybooks and someone who enjoys reading to children are clearly a central part of the support structure for emergent literacy, they are not by any means the only part (Bissex 1980). In mainstream homes, parents begin holding conversations with their infants. Throughout childhood, mothers, in particular, model more advanced communication structures than their children are capable of employing at the time but that may be within their ZPD. They also expand their children's simple two word utterances—"want ball"—into grammatically correct and conceptually sophisticated statements—"Tommy would like the red ball?" Children are asked "known answer" questions—"What does Tommy have on his head?" to stimulate the children's vocabulary development.

Families exploit a variety of "activity settings" (Wertsch 1985a) that are routinized and designed to assist with the business of enculturating children (Lancy, in prep.). Storybook reading and dinner-table conversations (Dickinson & Beals, this volume; Heath, 1986c) are two activity settings with ample scope to support emergent literacy. Cartrips are another activity setting where the parent may draw children's attention to signs and other print in the environment and engage them in conversations about the world passing by. Yet another example is provided by Hudson (Chapter Fifteen, this volume), in which a father uses the occasion of a football game to engage his son in a school-like lesson, as in "What's the story here? What's going on?"

Martini and Mistry (1993) demonstrate just how information rich and educational these parent-child exchanges can be. They note that preschool-age "children initiated 74% of their interactions with adults by offering or asking for new information (p. 182)," and "their parents acknowledged, accepted and responded to these initiations 77% of the time. The children knew they had an audience. Parents answered children's questions, commented on their statements, and asked questions of their own to encourage children to elaborate their reports" (p. 184). "The well-prepared children also talked a great deal about experiences they had had away from their parents . . . used complete sentences, explicit vocabulary and complex sentences . . . asked parents how to do things, what things were called, how things worked . . . [they] asked the observer if she was married, had babies, where she lived . . . what kind of car [her husband] drove (p183)." However, a contrasting pattern was found in families of children who were "less-prepared" for the linguistic and literacy environment of the public school. We will address these results below.

There appear to be two general outcomes of raising children in a "storied" environment. First, they learn an elaborated linguistic code, a way of speaking (and thinking) in which the immediate context is transcended. Children who have had this kind of stimulation, for example, use more metalinguistic verbs ("say," "talk," "listen") in their speech and this fluency is, in turn, predictive of success as a reader (Pellegrini & Galda 1991, this volume). Second, these children seem much more likely to engage in symbolic (fantasy, pretend, imaginative) play, which is implicated in emergent literacy, especially narrative competence (Pellegrini 1985) and vocabulary and story comprehension (Dickinson & Beals, this volume). Hall (1991) points out that the scripts children use in play closely resemble, structurally, the stories they will soon be asked to read in school (Mandler & Johnson 1977).

Pellegrini and Galda (this volume) find a stronger connection between symbolic play and writing, both empirically and, drawing on Clay (1975) and Vygotsky (1978), theoretically. Writing, at least initially—since it is largely pictographic—is seen as first-order symbolization, as is symbolic play. Reading is, from the beginning, second-order symbolization.

The following episode from Roskos and Neuman's (1993) extensive study of literacy-related elements in four-year old pre-schoolers' symbolic play illustrates both the influence of activity set-tings and the very obvious contribution that such play makes to the child's emergent literacy. Dana and Hilary are enacting a letter-writing and post-office script.

> *Dana*: (scribbling on paper) Now, this should be ready.
> *Hilary*: (writing name on paper) No! We hafta sign our names. Our real names.
> *Dana*: What is our real names?
> *Hilary*: (pointing to her name) See?
> *Dana*: (writing name on paper) Oh-h-h!
> (Both girls fold their papers carefully, put them in envelopes, and seal the envelopes . . . . For the next 22 minutes they repeat this sequence 7 times, taking turns "writing, reading, and receiving mail.") (pp19-20).

Where the Support for Emergent Literacy Is Less Certain

As we move out of the middle-class mainstream, the picture is less clear. We see both a "restricted" (Goody 1987) role for literacy in these communities and considerable variation among families within the same community (Chandler, Argyris, Barnes, Goodman & Snow 1986; Varenne & McDermott 1986).

Among the Amish, parents stress the importance of becoming literate and do a variety of things to promote early literacy, but the goals are different from the cultural mainstream. The family is annoyed if children bring work home from school, and they strongly discourage their children from continuing beyond the eighth grade. There is a wide variety of printed material in regular use; however, much of it is unique to the Amish, on the one hand, and on the other, many texts—

such as paperback novels—found in most homes are absent. The parents "attempt to carefully control the reading material that enters their home" (Fishman 1990, 31). Similar restrictions extend to writing at home and in school. Creative writing, for example, is nonexistent: "not only do community constraints limit the number of appropriate topics and forms an Amish writer may use, but original approaches to or applications of these topics and forms is explicitly discouraged" (p. 37). Similarly, in Roadville, a white working-class community:

> residents use writing only when they have to . . . . Few write let-
> ters . . . [and] the content and form of their letters are predictable. .
> . . Roadville family members . . . collect reading material . . . and
> . . . talk about how they are going to learn to do something by
> reading . . . but do-it-yourself projects and plans, old magazines,
> and brochures often simply accumulate in the garage, kitchen and
> beside the "reading chair" (Heath 1983, 231-32).

By contrast to Maintown,

> Roadville adults do not extend either the content or the habits of literacy
> events beyond book reading. They do not, upon seeing an item or
> event in the real world, remind children of a similar event in a book and
> launch a running commentary on similarities and differences. When a
> game is played or a chore done, adults do not use literate sources.
> Mothers cook without written recipes most of the time; if they use a
> recipe from a written source, they do so usually only after confirmation.
> . . by friends who have tried the recipe . . . . Adults do not talk about
> the steps and procedures of how to do things; if a father wants his
> preschooler to learn to hold a miniature bat or throw a ball, he says "Do
> it this way." He does not break up "this way" into such steps as "Put
> your fingers around here," . . . Over and over again, adults do a task and
> children observe and try it, being reinforced only by commands such as
> "Do it like this," "Watch that thumb.". . .They do not ask questions of
> the child, except questions which are directive or scolding in nature
> ("Did you bring the ball?" "Didn't you hear what I said?") (pp. 61-62).

Newly migrant Hispanic families also utilize literacy to a limited extent although some do read to their children. Many also tell stories specifically to enlighten and entertain children (Delgado-Gaitan 1990). Parent book reading outside the mainstream does not have an expansionist quality; parents merely read the book (Allexsaht-Snider 1991) or, at best, engage the child in picture-labeling (Miller,

Nemoianu & DeJong 1986). There is a tendency to wait for the child to initiate any literacy activity (Jacob 1984; Levin, Brenner, & McClellan 1993; Chapter Nine, this volume).

These parents apparently do see themselves as getting children ready for reading when they read to them. Those who fail to read to their children rationalize it by saying it is the teacher's job to teach reading (Lareau 1989). Those who do read with children stop doing so when the child starts school and, in contrast to parents who think reading should be for meaning and pleasure, parents who view reading as a skill, use a reductionist strategy when reading with children (Lancy, Draper, & Boyce 1989; Chapter Five this volume). They tend to punish the child for errors and to force him or her to rely exclusively on decoding rather than semantic or meaning-oriented strategies.

Talk between parents and children may be more limited in extent and variety. This is a typical finding: "Middle-SES mothers verbally engaged their children using more cognitively demanding language than low SES mothers who used language that basically directed and commanded the listener" (Roberts & Barnes 1993, 161). Réger (1990) finds that, even in a country as culturally and socially homogenous as Hungary, there are reliable differences across social class in mothers' speech to children. Lower SES mothers use shorter sentences and sentences of less variety, and rarely use other than the present tense. The connection that Bernstein (1971) identified over 20 years ago between speech patterns, social class, and children's development has held up in study after study.

In impoverished black communities such as Trackton (Heath 1983), children are not encouraged to ask questions and adults do not "scaffold" (see Vygotsky 1978) children's language acquisition by expanding holophrases, asking known answer questions, and simplifying speech directed to them. This same pattern has been observed widely in non-Western societies without print literacy (Duranti & Ochs 1986; Reder & Green 1983).

Earlier, I referred to a study by Martini and Mistry (1993) that compared home language and literacy experiences of Hawaiian children who were "well" or "less" prepared for school. Whereas well-prepared children were invited by their parents to exchange information, "the parents of less-prepared children ignored, refused, or actively rejected 66 percent of their children's initiations" (p. 185). These findings almost exactly parallel those of Norman-Jackson (1982) in an

East Coast African-American community and are strikingly consistent with the behavior of parents of "good" versus "poor" readers in Bergin , Lancy, and Draper's study (Figure 5.2, this volume). Also, as compared to their well-prepared peers, these children engaged in less symbolic play and less school or literacy play while they engaged in more physical play.

Where Support for Emergent Literacy is Almost Nonexistent

Scholars have also given us a glimpse of homes in which literacy is *extremely* limited:

> During our visits we saw no physical evidence of books, maga-zines, or newspapers. Ms. Pagliucca said she never read books and could not remember the names of any favorite childhood authors or books . . . . All the children in this family spent a great deal of time watching television. They had no special chores or other responsibilities around the house and participated in no organized after-school activities . . . . Mrs. Pagliucca did not seem to be interested in what Derek was doing in school, what kind of homework he brought home, or what he was reading. She knew Derek went to the bookmobile weekly with either his older brother or with friends, but she never asked to see his books or talked to him about what he was reading (Snow, Barnes et al 1991: 76).

Purcell-Gates (1991, this volume) describes how even environ-mental print is invisible for a nonliterate Appalachian migrant family in Cincinnati. When members of this family ask over the phone for directions they request visual cues that do not require reading signs. Since they are familiar with trademarks and logos from television ads, they are able to grocery shop without reading labels. There may be books in the home that parents have acquired at garage sales in the hope that children may read them, but they remain unread.

Communities where literacy is limited and where parents do not introduce children to books do tend to be poor, but are not associated with any particular ethnic group, nor are they exclusively comprised of single-parent households (Anderson & Stokes 1984; Teale 1986a). In these homes even literate parents who are positive about the value of reading do not read bedtime stories because they claim to find it boring, and their children would rather be doing other things

(Svensson, this volume). As Paula Levin and her colleagues (1993) note for the working-class Hawaiians they studied: "early literacy activities such as story reading and word recognition were recently accepted ideas for which parents had few models in their own experience. . . . When asked about the skills necessary for beginning school . . . [the] skills they mentioned . . . sound very much like traditional reading-readiness . . . emergent literacy skills were among the least well-defined" (p. 210). While these families had well-defined activity settings for socializing children into their culture—routines to teach helping, for example—they lacked the kind of activity settings found in mainstream homes like the bedtime story. "Children often choose their own bedtime, frequently falling asleep in front of the television" (p. 210).

As a sequel to her research in the three Piedmont communities, Heath has been investigating literacy in the lives of young Trackton females who find themselves living with their children in urban public-housing ghettos. If emergent literacy opportunities were somewhat limited in Trackton, she makes clear that they are even more limited here. "Young mothers, isolated in small apartments with their children, and often separated by the expense and trouble of cross town public transportation from family members, watch television, talk on the telephone, or carry out household and care giving chores with few opportunities to tease or challenge their youngsters verbally" (Heath 1989, 369). She asked Zinnia Mae, an unemployed mother of four, to tape-record her conversations over a two-year period:

> In only 13 instances within the [400] hours of taping did she initiate talk to one of the children that was not designed to give them a brief directive or query their actions or intentions. She once asked Donna to come sit beside her to see the puppet on television, twice asked one of the twins to give her a bite of cookie and talked about why she liked that particular kind of cookie . . . . On 9 occasions, she talked to the children as a result of introducing some written artifact to them . . . . Rarely involved in manipulative activities . . . and engaging in these without talk, . . . while they were in process, Zinnia Mae could provide few occasions . . . to co-construct tasks or talk for more than a fleeting minute or so (p. 510).

When Zinnia Mae went shopping, a neighbor looked after the children. They had no playmates and, whereas Zinnia Mae grew up in Trackton, a highly verbal and socially stimulating community composed of neighbors and extended family members, in the Atlanta slum her children call "home" no such community is available.

Even when children have access to playmates, the absence of literacy activities and literate talk in the home will be reflected in their play. Studies in Israel, the United Kingdom and the United States, all show that children's play activity varies as a function of social class. Symbolic play—of the sort that both reflects and contributes to emergent literacy—is far less common among poor children (Shefataya 1990). Indeed, Hispanic parents may actively discourage pretend reading and writing as being too immature (Goldenberg 1989).

We have traveled along a continuum. At one extreme we met families—anchored in broader cultural patterns—that provide a myriad of supports for their child's emergent literacy. At the other extreme, we found homes—again fully reflecting the values of their respective communities—which provide few to no such supports. In the next section we will consider the implications of such variation for children's acquisition of conventional literacy.

THE TRANSITION TO READING IN SCHOOL

A large part of the motivation to study the home as a literacy environment comes from research that links aspects of this environment to the classroom. We study "how families participate in reproducing their own literacy, and through this, the literacy of the whole society" (Varenne & McDermott 1986, 204). The mainstream preoccupation with providing a rich early literacy experience for children is not recent. As far back as 1800 in Sweden, books were published for parents advising them on the value of such experience. In this Lutheran country in which literacy was a precondition for church participation (indeed, one could not marry without first demonstrating literacy), teaching children to read was a family responsibility (Söderbergh 1990).

There is ample evidence of a connection between home and school literacy (Plessas & Oakes 1964). For example, "children who have been read to during their preschool years posses lexical and syntactic knowledge of sentence-level features typical of written narrative before they begin formal literacy instruction" (Purcell-Gates 1988: 129) and "there is a strong . . . relation . . . between children's knowledge of nursery rhymes and the development of their phonological skills . . . [which] children acquire . . . a long time before learning to read" (Maclean et al. 1987, 278).

Indeed some have found that storybook reading has an impact that goes well beyond emergent literacy (Hale & Windecker 1993):

> What is learned from books changes with development. At 2 1/2 years, the child's focus is vocabulary and syntax acquisition; therefore story-reading exposure predicts vocabulary and syntactic knowledge 6 months later . . . . At age 4 1/2 these . . . children were no longer learning labels from books; rather they were focusing on more complex linguistic and cognitive constructs . . . . These results suggest that story reading with parents is fueling the growth of knowledge at the "leading edge" of the child's development (Crain-Thoreson & Dale 1992, 428).

The Scollons (1981) provide one of the most compelling cross-cultural comparisons, utilizing their own culture to compare to that of the Native Americans of Fort Chipewayan. They show that, by the age of two, their daughter had acquired much of the culture of literacy short of actual reading, she was competent in using literacy conventions that were still not part of the repertoire of 10 year old Chipewayans with several years of formal schooling behind them.

Feitelson and Goldstein (1986) found that high-achieving children in Israeli schools inevitably came from homes with lots of children's books. Nearly 90 percent of the 50+ families in their "high" group had initiated a regular story time with the child before he or she was three, usually at bedtime. In most homes children were read to as often as they wanted and favorite books were read again and again. None of the low-achieving children had been read to before the age of three, and in 31 of the 51 "low" families the children were never read to. There weren't many picture books, and the few books present in the home tended to be on display in the parlor. The authors go on to document other profound cultural differences between the two sets of families, pointing to a lengthy history of a comfortable adaptation to literacy and schooling in the one case and not the other.

However, several studies show that limited storybook reading to children is not sufficient, by itself, to transmit these various conventions (Flood 1977; Lancy et al. 1989). On the other hand, school lessons in early reading are often structured in such a way that students can learn how to get "right answers," at least some of the time, without knowing how to read (Cole & Griffin 1986; Purcell-Gates 1991a).

Storybook reading aside, Heath's (1983) work shows how the different adult-child verbal interaction styles in Maintown and Trackton may contribute to differential success in "show and tell"(Simmons & Murphy 1986) or "sharing time [which] can be seen as a kind of *oral preparation for literacy*" (Michaels 1981, 423). Videotapes of sharing time reveal

> The discourse of the white children tended to be tightly organized around a single topic with a high degree of cohesion, and lexically explicit referential, temporal, and spatial relationships. There was a marked beginning, middle, and end, with no shifts in time or place. This style, which we refer to as "topic-centered," seemed to match the teacher's own style and expectations. With these children she was very successful at picking up on the child's topic and expanding on it through her questions and comments. With a shared sense of topic, teacher and child were often able to develop an account of an object or event that was more complex and lexically explicit than the spontaneous utterances the child initially produced without the teacher's help. The Black children, by contrast, were more likely to tell narratives consisting of a series of implicitly associated personal anecdotes, often involving shifts in time location, and key characters, with no explicit statement of an overall theme or point. This kind of discourse, which we refer to as "topic associating," is often difficult to follow for those who, like the teacher, expect the narrative to focus on a single event or object (Michaels & Cazden 1986, 136).

Children in Trackton are not encouraged to tell stories because adults do not see their narratives as opportunities to play the role of teacher, as Maintown parents do. On those occasions when adults seek information from children, they will permit the child to continue talking if the child is amusing. Hence, they are more likely to reward than to correct grammatical, logical, and pragmatic errors made by the child.

What happens to children whose emergent literacy experience has been less than ideal, who will, in all likelihood, have a difficult time learning to read?

> In every school some children find learning to read difficult, and such difficulties are, unfortunately, too often predictable. It is the children of poverty who are most likely to have literacy learning difficulties. These are the children who are most likely to experience retention in grade, transition-room placement, remedial or special education program participation, and permanent assignment to the "bottom track." Such experiences increase the likelihood that one will never become

truly literate, will leave school before graduation, will become a teen parent, and will be unemployed as an adult (Allington 1991, 237).

In short, while there are lots and lots of programs, few, if any, work very well. The gap between children who start school on the verge of conventional literacy and those who are still not sure about the functions of print will only widen as they progress through to high school (Snow, Barnes et al. 1991). However, research on children's emergent literacy offers a number of promising avenues for policy and program initiatives. We will examine several of these in Part Two.

NOTE

Portions of this chapter have been adapted from Lancy, D. F. (1994), Anthropological study of literacy and numeracy, a chapter in the *International encyclopedia of education*, 2nd edition. Used by permission of Pergamon Publishers.

2

Early Literacy From a Developmental Perspective

A.D. Pellegrini and Lee Galda

Exploring the ways in which young children become literate has been a major concern of early childhood educators for a number of years; after all, literacy accounts for two of the three Rs. However, only recently have students of child development turned their attention to the ways in which literacy is learned or develops in young children. In this chapter we will discuss children's development of literacy. From this developmental perspective we will discuss what we believe are appropriate educational practices to teach literacy. But first, let's talk about what we mean by literacy.

WHAT IS LITERACY?

This is not an easy question to answer. Literacy means very different things to different people. Wolf (1988), for instance, posits separate literacies, for text, visual arts, music, and the like. Literacy could also be defined as the ability to comprehend texts present in one's everyday environment, such as grocery store labels or a subway map. These literacy skills are found in individuals typically considered illiterate by most definitions of school-based literacy.

Let us now consider what we mean by school-based literacy. It typically refers to the comprehension and production of written texts that are used in school. These texts have been described by Olson (1979) as decontextualized to the extent that meaning is conveyed and comprehended primarily by and from the text, with minimal reliance on context. The simplicity is only superficial, however. The issue of the interrelation of reading and writing of school-based texts immediately comes into question. Are the same psychological processes at work as children learn to read *and* write?

Advocates of whole language (e.g., Goodman 1989) and emergent literacy (e.g., Teale & Sulzby 1986) make statements that reading and writing develop together and utilize the same mental processes involved in learning to use oral language. On the other hand, some researchers find that reading and writing among young children are minimally interrelated (e.g., Juel 1988; Pellegrini, Galda, Dressden, & Cox 1991). This issue is clouded to the extent that we do not have many good measures of reading and writing for the preschool child. By "good" we mean measures that are derived from a sound theory of literacy devlopment and that have reasonable psychometric qualities (i.e., they are reliable and valid). At a more basic level, there is also good theory suggesting that literacy is not a unitary construct (e.g., Vygotsky 1978).

The position that we take in this paper is that reading and writing in preschool and kindergarten children are independent. This position is based on two points. First, there is reasonably convincing theory that reading and writing develop initially as separate processes. Specifically, Vygotsky's (1978) discussion of early writing suggests that it, like drawing, begins as first order symbolization and only later becomes second order symbolization, like reading. Other related theories, such as context specific approaches to cognition, also posit that literacy is not a unitary construct (e.g., Laboratory of Comparative Human Cognition [LCHC] 1983).

The second point that leads us to consider reading and writing separate processes in young children is the empirical record. Researchers who have studied literacy development in preschool and early primary school children find only a minimal relationship between reading and writing (Juel 1988; Pellegrini et al. 1991). The relations become stronger as children develop during the primary school years. These results are consistent with Vygotsky's theory that suggests that writing starts off as first order symbolization and becomes second order symbolization as children treat written text as language, not graphic representation; reading is an example of second order symbolization.

That writing and reading may be independent in young children and become related with age is important for both child developmentalists and early childhood educators. In the next two sections of this paper we will outline the different developmental pathways of writing and reading in preschool and kindergarten children. Next, we will suggest ways in which this information can be used to design developmentally appropriate curricula for young children.

THE DEVELOPMENTAL ORIGINS OF READING AND WRITING

The argument that we will be advancing is a Vygotskian (1962) one: Children's cognitive processes originate in their interaction with a more competent other, typically an adult. Further, specific skills such as reading and writing originate in distinct and often separate contexts. Joint book reading between young children and their parents seems to be the context where children begin to learn the skills necessary for learning to read. Joint make-believe, or symbolic, play between parents and children seems to be an important precursor to the skills necessary in early writing.

An important locus for children's early symbolic competence—the ability to have one thing represent something else—may be in symbolic play with their mothers (Slade 1987); fathers tend to engage in rough-and-tumble play rather than symbolic play with their children (MacDonald & Parke 1984). The representational competence gained in symbolic play with mother seems to be then used in symbolic play with peers (Parke, MacDonald, Burks, Bhavnagri, Barth, & Beitel 1989). In our own work with preschool children we have found that preschool children's use of symbolic play transformations with peers is a reliable predictor of children's ability to write single words; however, symbolic play transformations do not predict early reading (Galda, Pellegrini, & Cox 1989; Pellegrini et al. 1991). Again, the argument here is that symbolic transformations have children using props or words to represent an object, role, or situation. Early writing in its various forms, such as drawing, scribbling, invented spelling, and conventional orthography, also has children using forms graphically, not linguistically. The written symbols represent the objects they refer to, *not* oral words. Because the symbolic play and early writing of young children has them using symbols to represent objects, not other symbols such as words, they are both examples of first order symbolization at this point in their development.

Reading for the preschool child is an example of second order symbolization to the extent that it involves treating written words in texts as representations of oral words. The developmental roots of this ability to treat written words as representations of their oral counterparts come from children and parents engaging in joint reading (Heath 1983; Snow 1983). An important aspect of the joint reading context for children's developing ability to treat language as a second order symbol system is their using language to talk about language; Olson (1983) refers to this form of language as *metalanguage*. A particularly important form of metalanguage in Olson's theory is linguistic verbs, or verbs denoting dimensions of linguistic processes, such as talk, write, read, and say, etc.

In our research we have found that mothers use linguistic verbs with their preschoolers as part of the reading process and they encourage children to use these verbs during joint reading episodes (Pellegrini, Perlmutter, Galda, & Brody 1990). Further, we found that children's use of these linguistic verbs while they are interacting with their peers is a good predictor of their ability to read (Pellegrini et al. 1991). In short, the results of our research and that of Parke and colleagues suggests that children learn important cognitive skills as they interact with their mothers. Children then seem to take these skills and practice them with their peers in playful interaction. These oral language skills and representational skills are then transferred to reading and writing, respectively. Like the work of Dickinson and Beals (this volume), our research suggests that literacy seems to have roots in oral language and symbolic play.

While joint book reading with a competent and caring adult and symbolic play appear to be directly implicated in the acquisition of reading and writing, respectively, it may be that there are other means to these ends. Biologists refer to this phenomenon as equifinality: There is more than one developmental pathway to a particular outcome. Let us consider a couple of alternate pathways to reading and writing.

Because many mothers must work outside the home or are otherwise unable to fulfill a round-the-clock care-taking role, young children are often "cognitive apprentices" to siblings or other older children. However, recent evidence suggests that older children, compared to parents or other adults, are less effective tutors (Rogoff 1991). Young children watch a great deal of television; here may be another possible pathway to literacy. There is a definite paucity of research on children who achieve conventional literacy without the benefit of home storybook reading so the search for alternate pathways has hardly begun.

Similarly, while we have suggested that symbolic play is an important pathway to representational competence, some children may gain this competence through constructive play, drawing, or music (Wolf 1988).

CURRICULAR IMPLICATIONS

In this section we will outline some general classroom implications for the research we have described above. An overarching concern here should be a developmental stance toward literacy. By this we mean that literacy develops in systematic ways in children and it takes very different forms at different points in this developmental process. The role of the teacher in this process should be to support and facilitate children's literacy as it appears at these distinct periods, not from the perspective of literacy as practiced by adults. In other words, we advocate literacy instruction for preschool children that facilitates their use of symbolic transformations and reflection on the linguistic processes. This is what literacy is for preschool children. It involves talking about language and gaining representational competence. These activities should be carried out in conjunction with exposure to print, through book reading and writing, as well as make-believe play among peers .

Let us begin with strategies teachers can use while reading books to children. There are numerous valuable outcomes that can be anticipated from reading books to children, such as children developing a love of books, learning the conventions of print, and learning the metalanguage of literacy (Galda & Cullinan, 1990). We will talk only about the last: learning the metalanguage of literacy.

We know that children learn best when they are encouraged to participate in the task at hand. Reading expository texts, such as alphabet and labeling books, are excellent vehicles for teaching metalanguage because they facilitate active participation by both child and adult in the reading process. When reading such texts teachers should ask questions that use and call for children to use linguistic terms, such as: What *letter* is this? The *ape* says "oooo!"

Such systematic exposure to linguistic terms is a necessary first step in learning these terms. The next level of instruction involves children practicing the use of these terms as they engage in dramatic play. Work by Roskos and Neumann (this volume) provides a number of excellent examples for the design of preschool classrooms that encourage dramatic play. We know that children are then able to generalize their knowledge of these terms back to reading texts. They seem to use their knowledge of the linguistic system to read.

Teachers can encourage the sort of representational competence that relates to early writing by encouraging children to engage in dramatic play. Two levels of representational competence can be encouraged: object transformations and ideational transformations (McLoyd 1980). The former are transformations based on objects, as where a child transforms a rolled-up towel into a doll. Ideational transformations involve ideas and simulations not objects, where children define a situation, such as "Let this be a doctor's office" or a role, "I'll be the doctor." The latter, obviously, involve more representational competence than the former. To move children towards more abstract transformations, teachers should begin by placing realistic props in play areas, such as miniature vehicles, dolls, and doctor kits. As children become facile with these props, less realistic props, such as blocks, Legos, and styrofoam shapes, should replace the realistic props. To provide a play theme, teachers could read books to children then provide opportunities for them to play with the themes.

Our work also suggests that children at three years of age and above use more advanced forms of play and language when there is minimal adult involvement in the play (Pellegrini 1983, 1984). By this age children are very capable of sustaining dramatic play. When adults intervene it seems they suppress children's exhibition of competence in both fantasy transformations and decontextualized language. For example, when adults are present children often depend on them to define the play theme and respond to adults' language; children's initiations are minimized.

CONCLUSION

In this chapter we have outlined ways in which children become literate. We have suggested that reading and writing travel separate developmental pathways before merging in the early elementary school years (see, e.g., Kamberelis & Perry, this volume). An important vehicle used by children in becoming literate is symbolic play. In symbolic play they develop the representational competence necessary for early writing and the metalanguage necessary for early reading. Further, as children become more facile at reflecting upon the language of play and peer interaction, they should be able to transfer that awareness to *both* reading and writing. Thus, reading and writing merge when they are both secondary symbol systems for the child.

NOTE

Work on this paper was partially supported by grants from the Mailman Foundation and the NCTE Research Foundation. The paper was written while the first author was an NIH Senior International Fellow at Sheffield University.

3

Not by Print Alone: Oral Language Supports for Early Literacy Development

David K. Dickinson and Diane E. Beals

Several decades worth of research have established that good things happen if you read to children during the preschool years: Children acquire important language skills, they learn to love books, and they do better in school (Heath 1982; Purcell-Gates 1988, in press; Taylor, 1983; Wells 1985a; Goldfield & Snow 1984). The value of reading to children is communicated to parents by newspapers, magazines, preschools, and pediatricians. The broad recognition of the value of reading to children flows, in part, from the fact that scientific data supports it. Acceptance also may result from the clearly comprehensible link between reading to children and children reading—it makes sense that reading books to children leads them to read books to themselves.

But are activities that involve the use of print (e.g., book reading by parents, reading cereal boxes, writing letters) the only kinds of experiences that support literacy development? We think not. We believe that teachers and parents support literacy development in a wide range of settings, some of which involve no print at all. The link between purely oral activities and literacy is not as intuitively obvious as the link between reading and literacy; therefore we first will describe the theoretical framework that motivates our work. We then will describe data showing the presence of a relationship between measures of children's language and literacy development in kindergarten and two kinds of experience during the preschool years: pretend play with peers in preschool and dinner table conversations with parents and siblings in the home.

THEORETICAL FRAMEWORK

Literacy is a complex phenomenon that draws upon a multitude of cognitive abilities. Learning to associate print with speech sounds is a major hurdle in early literacy development, but reading also demands a lot from children's oral language resources. In everyday conversations, children often do not need to rely strictly on words to communicate or interpret information, because gestures and intonation also provide considerable information. Also, people engaged in conversations often share considerable knowledge about the topic, reducing the amount of new information that must be communicated. In contrast, once children move beyond picture books, information in books is conveyed through words and syntax. Furthermore, the content may be new to the reader; hence he or she must acquire new knowledge using strictly linguistic sources. As children gain skill in communicating in ways that meet these demands that are associated with certain uses of literacy, they also begin to treat language in a new way— they begin to distance themselves from language and reflect on it. Instead of simply talking in order to attain some desired end, children begin to reflect on the activity of talking.

One view that has emphasized the connection between specific types of talk and later literacy outcomes is a controversial one presented by Basil Bernstein (1962, 1972), the British sociologist. While his view has pointed researchers and educators toward the study of social interaction at home, Bernstein has been heavily criticized for unjustly placing the blame of school failure on families from lower socioeconomic levels.

Bernstein believes that oral language shapes what and how a child learns, forming a basis for future learning. Studying families in Britain, Bernstein posited that some children are victims of *restricted codes*, styles of talk within their families that are specific to the current physical context. These codes are limited, condensed, and nonspecific. Restricted codes lack precision and specificity. Sentences are short and syntactically simple. On the other hand, another set of families, while using restricted codes in some situations, also use *elaborated codes*, in which the communication is not specific to the particular situation or context. Grammar is more differentiated and more precise, and thus allows for more complex thought.

According to Bernstein, early experience with codes is a powerful determining factor for later cognitive structures and modes of communication. The major result of exposure solely to restricted codes is a limitation of the scope and detail of the concepts or information available to the developing child. Children exposed exclusively to restricted codes have difficulty in school because "the different focusing of the experience through a restricted code creates a major problem of educability only where the school produces discontinuity between its symbolic orders and those of the child. Our schools are not made for these children; why should these children respond?" (1972, p. 173). These children, in his view, are not properly equipped to handle the demands of reading and writing in school.

Bernstein attributes differences in style of sociolinguistic interaction in the family to varying strengths in *boundary maintaining procedures*, which describe the hierarchical relationships within a family. In a *person-centered* family, talk is a major means of control over other family members, because of constant adjustment of behavior by family members to others' verbally elaborated motives and intentions. A person-centered family uses elaborated codes in order to change the behavior of the child; that is, the child learns behavior rules through elaborated discussions of a specific context, the rationale of a specific rule, and consequences of alternative actions. In the *status-oriented* or *positional* family, members respond to formal rules of behavior and status roles. The use of restricted codes is indicative of this kind of family structure. In order to teach the child appropriate behavior, parents simply state the rules and the appropriate roles that family members should fill. Status-oriented parents simply give commands and invoke rules, while person-oriented parents give explanations for commands and rules, allowing the child to broaden his or her understanding of social structures, behavioral consequences, and human motives.

Bernstein believed that social class was the source of such differences in oral language, with middle-class families employing elaborated codes and working-class families using restricted codes. However, it is not clear how social class would determine such family structures, nor is it clear how the differences in grammar that he found can be explained by family structures. This perspective presents a deficit view of low-income families and the development of children within these families. The terminology used to describe the findings is heavily value-laden; the term *restricted code* gives the reader a sense of pathology.

Despite the problems with his approach, there is some merit to the arguments of Bernstein. The interaction that takes place between adult and child can have clear consequences for the child's development. What needs to be done is to establish more direct connections between specific kinds of conversations between children and adults during their preschool years and later literacy abilities, instead of linking large, amorphous variables like social class to specific cognitive and linguistic outcomes.

There is mounting evidence of a relationship between children's emerging literacy abilities and the emergence of talk about one's own mental states, about words, and about the difference between the words one utters and the meanings one intends to communicate (Torrance & Olson 1985). For example, a longitudinal study that examined the talk of children when they were 3 1/2 years old found a relationship between the number of verbs they used that referred to language (e.g., tell, ask) and mental states (e.g., think, want) and early literacy development two years later (Pellegrini et al. 1991).

Children's ability to talk about language in a literate manner also can be seen in the way they define words. When asked for definitions, children can respond by mentioning characteristic actions (e.g., a dog—"it barks and bites") or functions (e.g., a spoon—"you eat with it"). Such definitions are called informal definitions and are characteristic of younger children (Snow 1990). Words also can be defined by using a copula ("is," "are"), placing the item being defined in a superordinate class, and providing additional distinguishing information. For example, a dog can be defined as follows: "It is (copula) a kind of animal (superordinate) that barks and bites (distinguishing information)." This type of definition is called a formal definition. Among children educated in Western schools, the frequency and quality of formal definitions provided during the elementary school years (beginning in kindergarten) is related to the child's literacy level (Dickinson & Snow 1987; Snow 1990; Snow, Cancino, De Temple, & Schley 1991).

Everyday conversations provide children with invaluable opportunities for acquiring basic language abilities. Unfortunately, having skill using his or her native language to converse does not necessarily mean that a child has developed the kind of language skills found to be associated with literacy—skill communicating information and the ability to reflect on and talk about language. Indeed, the two types of language skills have been found to be statistically unrelated; children can have strong conversational skills but weak monologue abilities.

Although conversational skills have social value, it is only the abilities to reflect on language and communicate novel information (with the assumption that the audience does not have this information) that are linked to literacy (Snow, Cancino, Gonzalez, & Shriberg 1989).

Informal conversations do not always provide settings in which children can develop literacy-related language skills, because there may be little need to use extended stretches of talk to communicate novel information. However, there are some conversational settings and topics that are likely to support these skills. We examine two such settings in this paper—pretending in preschools and narratives and explanations during mealtimes in the home. These provide an interesting contrast because they occur in two places, in preschool and in the home, and because the former occurs between children whereas the latter typically includes parents and other adults.

HOME-SCHOOL STUDY OF LANGUAGE AND LITERACY DEVELOPMENT

The data we will report comes from the Home-School Study of Language and Literacy Development. The goal of this project is to identify the types of language environments and contexts that support the development of literacy skills. We are following about 40 children and their families from the age of three through their preschool and early elementary school years. Subjects were recruited through preschools in the Boston area and are all eligible for Head Start. Approximately one-third of them are minority children and all speak English in the home. Each child has been visited at home and at school once a year in order to observe the child as he or she engages in different social and language environments. To date we have completed analysis of only the first of our two cohorts; therefore, we will report data from only about half of our sample.

During home visits mothers are asked to engage their child in several tasks (book reading, playing with toys, talking about a past event) and mothers are interviewed in order to gain a fuller portrait of the child's language environment. At the end of the home visit, a tape recorder is left behind for the mothers to record what they consider to be a typical mealtime. At school, children are observed in whatever activities are considered typical. We specifically attempt to observe a free choice time if that is a routine part of the classroom schedule.

Throughout the morning, children's talk is audiotaped, group times are videotaped, and teachers are interviewed.

When the children are five years old, they are given a battery of standardized tests and asked to perform a set of independent language tasks. These tasks serve as literacy outcome measures. The tasks are intended to assess a host of language and cognitive skills. Among these measures are the Peabody Picture Vocabulary Test (PPVT), a standardized test of receptive vocabulary. This test is commonly used and is known to be correlated with verbal intelligence tests and school achievement. Children also complete a collection of tasks assessing a child's early skill with print, such as reading everyday signs and labels, recognizing letters, matching letters and sounds, and writing their names (the Comprehensive Assessment Profile, or CAP). We also give a listening comprehension task, in which the experimenter reads the children's book *The Snowy Day*, by Ezra Jack Keats (1962) and asks a series of questions that tap the child's world knowledge and inferential ability. Also included is a definitions task, in which the child is asked to give definitions of 14 nouns. These definitions are rated on how formal they were (inclusion of a superordinate category with distinguishing information; e.g. "a thief is a person who steals").

Preschool Experiences: The Value of Talk with Peers

When we visited the preschools we wanted to learn as much as possible about the details of our children's daily experiences; therefore we audiotaped all of their talk throughout the morning using a small microphone that was attached to a small tape recorder they carried in a backpack. The content of children's talk was then coded and the amount of time they spent engaged in different kinds of talk was determined. The category of special interest is that of pretending. Talk was coded as "pretend" if the children were engaged in fantasy play that was accompanied by sustained talk (i.e., more than about five seconds). Silent pretending or pretend play accompanied by sound effects was not coded as pretend talk. When our children were three years old, of the time that we recorded their talk, they spent 6.3 percent of it engaged in pretending accompanied by talk. When they were four, 7.8 percent of their time was spent engaged in such pretending. Most of the pretend talk occurred between children.

As one would imagine, these pretend episodes included wonderful flights of imagination, such as that found in the following pretend episode between two three-year-olds.

Example 1

Selestra:	I'm going to church.
Jane:	I'm going to church and I'm gonna . . .
Selestra:	I'm going to church with my chair.
Jane:	I'm staying at home.
Selestra:	Hurry up Courtney I'm going to church now! Hurry up I can't wait for you! (She sings to herself briefly) I'm (unintelligible) to church.
Jane:	I, I'm not going to church, I'm staying at home.
Selestra:	Yes you have to go to church.
Wilma:	You have to go to church or you miss it and then everybody gonna give us some candy.
Jane:	Then we gonna pass out some money. Then (unintelligible) he gonna give us some money then (unintelligible).

Not only are these interactions charming, but they also are linked with the development of emerging language-related literacy skills. In this episode we see three girls creating a scene with words and acting within the constraints imposed by this setting invoked through language. As they play they move into an imaginary future, describe possible (albeit unlikely!) actions and assume roles. In order to maintain this activity they build increasingly more complex syntactic structures as they elaborate the simple declarative "I'm going to church," with the culmination being Wilma's sentence that combines the core "going to church" with two statements regarding the consequences resulting from not going to church.

This qualitative examination of pretend talk is supported by our statistical analyses. Analyses of our children's performance on our battery of literacy tests revealed strong correlations between the amount of time children engaged in pretend talk as three-year-olds and their test scores at age five. There were strong relationships (i.e., $p < .01$) between time spent pretending and performance on the vocabulary task ($r = .59$) and on the print skills task ($r = .54$), and a moderate relationship to story understanding ($r = .46$) and the definitions task ($r = .46$). There were no correlations between pretending as a four-year-old and our age-five outcome measures.

We cannot argue that pretending as a three-year-old caused the subsequent literacy skills to develop. What seems more likely is that children who were good pretenders were attracted to other verbal children. These children's strong language skills when they were three likely helped them get off to a quick start in the areas tapped by our tasks. While pretending time in preschool may not lead directly to acquisition of literacy-related skills by kindergarten, pretending is an activity that allows children the opportunity to use and develop important language skills that are linked to early literacy growth.

Home Experiences: Practice with Discourse at Mealtimes

The mealtime conversations are an especially interesting portion of our data from the homes because they were more naturalistic and contained more free-flowing exchanges than the other tasks. These conversations gave us a sense of the child's everyday language exposure. Mealtimes contained narratives around experiences of family members and explanations of events, actions, and emotions. We were especially interested in these stretches of talk because they provide excellent occasions for children to develop literacy-related language skills.

We recorded the length and frequency of each of the narratives and explanations in order to get a sense of the amount of extended discourse the child listens to and participates in with the rest of his or her family. These measures thus indicate the nature of the talk of the entire family and reflect the child's exposure to narrative and explanation. Example 2 contains a narrative in which two preschool-aged siblings, Elaine and Todd, participate in the telling.

Example 2

Elaine:	Darcy know what?
Elaine:	They made me look in Scott's yard.
Elaine:	Know what they saw under the table?
Darcy:	What?
Elaine:	A dead mouse.
Todd:	And we saw the blood!
Elaine:	And the heart.

Mother:	Okay okay we're eating.
Elaine:	No!
Elaine:	We only saw the heart.
Mother:	Yeah Elaine.
Darcy:	Oh.
Elaine:	I hated it.

Talk around narratives, which describe events that occurred in another place at another time, accounted for an average of 17.9 percent of all mealtime talk (ranging from 0 to 40.4 percent) when the target children were age three. Narrative talk made up 11.9 percent of the mealtime talk, on average (with a range from 0 to 30.1 percent), when the children were age four.

Explanations also were relatively frequent in mealtime conversations, accounting for an average of 17.3 percent of the talk (ranging from 0 to 28.5 percent) when target children were age three, and an average of 15.3 percent of the talk (ranging from 0 to 24.2 percent) when they were age four. Examples 3 and 4 contain typical explanations.

Example 3

Mother:	What did you do at school today Paul?
Paul:	Um uh I couldn't go to the computer.
Mother:	Why not?
Paul:	They were working on the lights.

Example 4

Father:	How many pieces of cheese did you have?
Mother:	Oh he had the whole quarter of a pound over the course of the day but...
Mother:	Come on.
Father:	It's no wonder why he's not hungry.
Mother:	He ate two pieces when we got back from the playground.

The proportions of narrative and explanatory talk during mealtimes were correlated with performance on a number of the age-five literacy tasks. The percentage of talk in mealtimes that was explanatory in nature when the target child was 4 years old was associated with performance on the PPVT ($r = .61$, $p < .001$). Discussions and descriptions of causes or intentions behind actions, events, or feelings may offer the child exposure to vocabulary that does not necessarily arise in day-to-day conversations about the here and now.

The proportion of mealtime talk that included narratives when the target child was four years old was associated with age-five literacy measures: vocabulary ($r = .55$, $p < .01$), listening comprehension ($r = .51$, $p < .02$), print skills ($r = .50$, $p < .03$), and the percentage of formal definitions given on the definitions task ($r = .44$, $p < .05$). Discussions of events, past or future, appear to be associated with a broad range of literacy activities. Again, as with explanatory talk, vocabulary development appears to be aided by narrative talk. The correlation between the amount of narrative talk and the definitions task indicates that the children who listen to and engage in narratives at mealtimes develop greater skill talking about language, suggesting that they may be getting early support for development of metalinguistic awareness. Children who are exposed to a high proportion of narrative talk at mealtimes also seem to be developing stronger story comprehension skills. Interestingly, narrative talk at mealtimes also is linked to print skills at age five, indicating, at a minimum, that families who support literacy-related oral language development also provide experiences that encourage growing understanding of print.

CONCLUSION

Exposure to and practice with print certainly aids a child in his or her literacy development, but experience with certain kinds of purely oral forms of language also help to lay the groundwork for future literacy growth. We have outlined a few examples of the kinds of talk that facilitate the ability to read and write.

Pretending is an ideal area in which children can develop literacy-related oral language skills (see Pellegrini & Galda, this volume). When they engage in talk as they pretend, children use language to create imaginary worlds. They then inhabit these worlds in ways that are in accord with how the worlds have been structured. The manner in which language is used when pretending has much in common with reading; therefore, it is not surprising that children's inclination to engage in pretend play is related to literacy. The fact that we found strong correlations between kindergarten measures and pretending at age three, but not at age four, makes clear the need to be cautious about inferring causation from this interesting correlation. The most likely explanation is that children who can sustain extended talk as they play when they are only three are especially skilled at using language in a sophisticated manner. This linguistic skill later is tapped as children encounter the challenges of literacy.

Explanatory talk at home offers children the opportunity to make connections between ideas, events, and actions. We have seen that, when children are four, the greater proportion of explanatory talk during family mealtimes appears to support vocabulary development. The amount of explanatory talk is a family measure, not a measure of the child's ability. Thus, this relationship suggests that family environment, not simply the child's linguistic sophistication, is a predictor of later literacy development.

Narrative talk within family mealtime conversations during the preschool years, another measure of the child's linguistic environment, also appears to be a strong predictor of literacy development. Conversations among family members about past and future events afforded children the opportunity to improve their vocabulary and to learn and practice the structure of event narratives. Such experiences could well be a precursor for reading, comprehending, telling, and writing one's own stories.

It is interesting to note that links between early experiences and kindergarten literacy appeared for child-constructed language environments (time spent pretending) when children were three, but that more adult-determined environments showed linkages when children were four (mealtime variables). These findings suggest that the younger children might not have been able to enter fully into the relatively complex adult-constructed dinner table language environments. In contrast, when pretending they controlled the complexity level and could fully exercise their emerging language abilities. Four-year-olds, on the other hand, appear to benefit from exposure to challenging adult-constructed discourse.

In conclusion, we encourage teachers of young children to see early literacy growth as multifaceted—as requiring growth in oral discourse skills as well as print-related abilities, and as occurring through interactions with peers as well as adults--and to see growth of print and language skills as occurring in the home as well as in preschools and schools. While they strive to enrich the literacy environments that children inhabit (see, e.g., Roskos & Neuman, this volume; Putnam, this volume), teachers should not lose sight of the vital importance of extended oral discourse. In addition to providing rich extended language experiences (e.g., during book reading, classroom mealtimes, and free moments during the day—Dickinson 1991), teachers need to provide children time and settings where they can use language with each other as part of sociodramatic play. Finally, teachers can help parents realize the important contributions made by home oral language experiences to young children's developing literacy abilities.

NOTE

This work was supported by grants from the Ford and Spencer Foundations to Catherine Snow and David Dickinson, and by a Head Start grant (#90-CD-0827) awarded to David Dickinson. We thank them for their support to this ongoing project.

4

Nonliterate Homes and Emergent Literacy

Victoria Purcell-Gates

All children born into a literate society learn many important concepts about written language between birth and the start of formal instruction. This precept lies at the core of the emergent literacy research paradigm, guiding and justifying the multitudinous inquiries into the nature of the process of learning to read and write. Researchers have documented the concepts about written language acquired by children of a literate society such as the United States: they learn what print signifies through experience with environmental print (Y. Goodman 1984; Harste, Woodward, & Burke 1984); they learn that print serves many different functions (Goodman & Goodman 1976; Taylor 1983; Clay 1979; Heath 1982); they learn that print takes different forms according to the function (Harste et al. 1984); they learn that print maps onto speech in fairly regularized ways (Dyson 1982; Ferreiro & Teberosky 1982); and, according to their experiences with these functions, they learn the specialized syntax and lexis of print within specified forms (Purcell-Gates 1988; Harste et al. 1984; Sulzby 1985).

Researchers are providing ever-growing support for the claim that success at learning to read and write in school depends a great deal on the possession of the above-listed basic concepts (Purcell-Gates & Dahl 1991). Literacy instruction can build on those concepts of written language held by children of varying classes and ethnic groups if the instruction meets the individual children's levels and experiences, according to many researchers. By "experiences" is meant the children's experiences with print, which, as the logic goes, is unavoidable in a literate society such as ours.

However, a recent research project reveals that this may not be entirely true. We are aware that certain subgroups of people in this country are classified as illiterate—they cannot read or write at basic functional levels. What we have not considered before is that, from an emergent literacy perspective, the children growing up in these homes may not experience the literate society that seems so pervasive to the rest of us. If this is so, the question becomes, what are the concepts of written language—so basic to success at learning to read and write in school—acquired by these children? Further, how can we facilitate literacy acquisition by children from these homes? Studying nonliterate families provides us the opportunity to examine from a different angle the relationships between basic concepts of written language and learning to read and write. This chapter provides an exploratory view of these issues emerging from a two-year ethnography of a nonliterate family.

THE FAMILY

Jenny and her husband, Big Donny, live in a large city in the Midwest. They and their two children, Donny and Timmy (ages seven and four respectively at the start of the study), are members of a minority group often referred to as "urban Appalachian." Urban Appalachians are either first-generation migrants or descendants of migrants to cities from the hills of Appalachia. While many urban Appalachians have assimilated and prospered in the urban life, a particular subgroup has not.

Members of this subgroup account for many of the very poor and uneducated members of those cities to which Appalachians have migrated. A recent study of urban, low-SES children learning to read and write in one of these cities documents that the overall scores of urban Appalachian children on a variety of tasks measuring emergent literacy concepts held at the beginning of formal instruction fell significantly below those held by children from the one other minority group in the low-SES sample (Purcell-Gates & Dahl 1991). These children knew very little about such concepts as intentionality, story structure, the language of books, alphabetic principles, writing as a convention, or concepts about print.

Jenny moved with her family to the city when she was three years old. However, as is true of many urban Appalachians, she still considers the hills of Kentucky as home, returning there on weekends and for extended visits as much as possible. The family regularly plans for the time when they will move back home—an event that depends on the elusive hope that enough money can be saved and a job found in the hills.

Neither Jenny, Big Donny, nor Donny could read or write beyond their names. Timmy could not read at all and only made random marks when given pencil and paper. Big Donny dropped out of school after repeating the seventh grade three times. He works sporadically as a roofer. Jenny also left school during the seventh grade. She works about one day a week at housecleaning and yard work. Some members of their own social community are literate and others are not. Big Donny evinces no interest in learning to read or write. However, Jenny is still trying to learn, mainly to help her children with their schoolwork. She is determined that her children learn to read. This brought her to the university-based literacy center I directed, to enroll Donny into the program. Her desire to sit alongside as he was instructed in the center prompted me to assume the double role of teacher/researcher in an attempt to gain insights into the role of a non literate home environment on children trying to learn to read and write.

Both Jenny and Donny were highly verbal, with inquisitive natures, visible alertness, and responsiveness to their world and those around them. Jenny impressed me and my colleagues who came to know her with her straightforward honesty and directness. Although always polite and sensitive to others, she never seemed to prevaricate or to call it other than how she saw it. Although to an outsider her life may seem burdensome and deprived, she was for the most part content and happy. Several times she expressed the opinion that rich people seemed to have too many problems and worries that stemmed from their wealth. All one needed, in her opinion, was enough money to pay the rent, buy food and clothing, and pay for inexpensive entertainment like riding four-wheelers through the woods back home.

Data Collection

Data for the case study were collected through various means over a period of two years. All instructional meetings were audiotaped and transcribed. These transcriptions were merged with other field notes written immediately after each meeting, along with artifacts such as writing attempts, examples of print brought to the center for me to read, and school work and reports. I also recorded all interviews and casual discussions with both Jenny and Donny. As time passed, and trust developed between us, I gained access to their home and was able to visit and explore their community. I also began accompanying Jenny and the kids on various errands around town, as a friend and a mediator with the literate world. I met other family members and personal friends. I observed Donny in school and interviewed his teachers. My observations were always recorded in field note form for analysis.

FORMAL LITERACY INSTRUCTION

School-Based Instruction

Donny's literacy instruction in school was traditional and skills-based. He attended one year of Head Start when he was five where he was exposed to the letters and sounds of the alphabet and some stories. First-grade instruction was from a basal system that featured an integrated language-arts program. The reading component consisted of weekly sight words, sound/symbol instruction, and simple stories incorporating the words and phonic patterns in the lessons. The writing component involved writing simple sentences and paragraphs, again incorporating the words learned in the reading lesson. Second grade instruction was a continuation of this program, with more complex stories and more advanced phonic generalizations to master.

Jenny had been attending adult classes for the previous four years. There she was given workbooks to work in, which focused either on reading half-page selections and answering comprehension questions or on language-arts skills such as pronouns, punctuation patterns, and spelling lists. She recalled very little of her reading instruction in grade school except the impression that she just "couldn't learn the words."

Literacy Center Instruction

Instruction in the Literacy Center is language-based, with teachers facilitating, on an individual basis, children's learning. A social-cognitive developmental view of literacy learning—from emergent behaviors onward—guide teachers' responses, and they engage the children in various reading and writing experiences, using trade books and other real-life print such as magazines, newspapers, journals, letters, and order forms.

From the beginning, it was apparent that Donny, who was repeating second grade, required immersion in an emergent literacy environment to allow for the formation of basic written language concepts. Jenny, on the other hand, was developmentally beyond this and, thus, her plan of "sitting alongside" was unworkable. We soon settled on journal writing and reading as the mode of instruction for her. I will go into this in more detail as I present some tentative findings of the study.

EMERGING PATTERNS

Almost No Knowledge of Functions

While Jenny's family lived and functioned within a highly literate society—one with print embedded in just about everything around them—they did not experience this world of print as other, literate, families do. Virtually no functions for written language existed within this home or as the family members transacted with the world outside. Thus, Donny and Timmy were children growing up in a world of speech and actions, places and objects, emotions and events, but not in a world of functional print.

Donny once constructed swiftly and skillfully a kite made of paper and string in the center. After admiring his work and acknowledging the interested glances from other students, I suggested that he make an instruction booklet that could become part of the center's collection so that other children could make kites if they wished. He stared at me dumbfounded. I repeated my suggestion, showing him several published how-to books in the center. "Why?" he demanded to know. Again, I repeated that if he produced such a book, other children could read it and know how to make a similar kite. "Why, I'll show 'em if'n they want to know!" he exclaimed.   "Well, you may not be here when they are here," I proceeded, drawing on the separation over time and space motive of written language. "Well," he persisted, "then you can show 'em." He did go on to dictate and then publish a simple kite-making book which, with my coaching, he shared with others and then observed that they could follow his directions to make their own kites. He remained convinced, however, for a long time, that "just telling" was much more efficient and likely to result in positive results.

The fact that Donny's world consisted of oral transactions and physical demonstrations rather that written information and communications was again revealed when I incorporated the concept of letter writing into the instruction. A few months after we began working together, I mentioned that I would be traveling to another country but that I would send him a postcard. Again, he was completely stumped. I asked him if he knew what a postcard or a letter in the mail was, and he said no. Jenny confirmed that no one sends them mail since no one in the house can read. I explained as best I could what a postcard was and urged them to watch for it. I duly sent two postcards from England to Donny and Jenny with simply worded messages on them. However, when I returned and asked about cards, neither Donny nor Jenny recalled receiving them. After persistent questioning and description of the pictures on the cards, Jenny did vaguely remember receiving such items in the mail. She never looked to see what was written on them, however, since "I never woulda' thought of it."

Even simple everyday tasks failed to incorporate the print around the family. Jenny did not read the print on grocery items, street signs, buildings, or doors. Print was not salient for this family. Other means of identification were used: colors, shapes, identifying trees and buildings. Sulzby (1990) claims that "all children in literate societies such as ours have exposure to the forms and functions of reading and writing long before schooling begins" (pg 1). However, living in a city, surrounded with print serving many different functions for many different people, this family did not experience it. In a sense, they did not live in the same city as the literate citizens did, and the children did not learn of the functional nature of print as the children of the literate families did. Phenomenologically, written language in all of its semiotic nature was almost invisible for this family.

School Behaviors Reflect Lack of Experiences

Donny's behaviors at school and in response to formal literacy instruction appeared to reflect his nonliterate experiences out of school. Despite having attended one year of Head Start and first grade, he still did not possess rudimentary reading or writing skills. He could read nothing besides his name consistently, and could read the word *the* occasionally when prompted to remember. Observations of his behaviors in school and in the Literacy Center revealed that he never looked at print. It was almost as if he didn't notice it. It was not interpreted as meaningful for his work at school.

As an illustrative example, one day his teacher was instructing the children on the completion of a worksheet on telephone manners. The sheet consisted of six sentences with blanks in them, to be filled in with single words. The list of words was located on the top half on the sheet. The teacher led the group through the sentences, soliciting orally the correct answer for each one, and writing that word on the chalkboard. The children were then to complete the worksheet on their own. Donny, who had not taken part in the discussion but had seemed to attend, appeared to know how to "do a worksheet," that is, he knew he was to fill in the blanks by copying a word from the list. His strategy for doing this, though, involved spatial cues rather than literate ones. He carefully measured each word with his index fingers on each hand, moved his fingers down to the blanks, fit the space marked with his fingers to the lines indicating the blanks, and made decisions about which word fit which blank according to the perceived match. Needless to say, none of the sentences made sense, but he felt that by completing the sheet by filling in the blanks, he had done the assignment.

At the Literacy Center, he actively avoided looking at print when it was pointed out to him for many months. One January day during the first year of the study, I asked him to take his turn reading from a Bill Martin book that he had just listened to on tape several times. He began by reciting the text from memory, mixing up some of the lines. I pointed to the print and said, "Look at the words; what do they say?" He immediately put his hands over the page and looked away, exclaiming "Oh no! No words for me! No words for me!"

Analysis of the data confirms that print was not linguistically significant in Donny's world. He did not recognize it as meaningful. Therefore, he did not perceive it against the background of life. When it was placed in the foreground for him by formal literacy instruction, the difficulty of dealing with a perceived nonmeaningful symbol system led him to actively avoid it. He was definitely stuck in a no-win situation in regard to literacy acquisition.

Literacy Tools Are Meaningless Without Functions

What to do to help children from low-literacy or nonliterate homes becomes the urgent question. Recently public attention and related policy has focused on the importance of the home and community in children's learning. One of the initial attempts at intervention for children from communities where few resources abide is to make literacy materials available. Providing books for homes and families is the most common solution. Other plans, coming from an emergent literacy perspective, include making writing materials, pencils, crayons, and markers available to children in their homes. Not included in these policy decisions, though, is a consideration of cultural issues and how these issues impact on the uses of literacy materials.

One of the themes emerging from this study is the relationship between community functions for written language and literacy materials. While it is true that a close correlation exists between low literacy and family income, it is simplistic to assume that lack of money is the sole cause of the paucity of books, paper, and pencils in the homes of many low-SES, low-literacy families.

One of the first instructional interventions I instituted with Donny and Jenny was to suggest making available paper, pencils, markers, and such to Donny so that he could begin to experiment with print in much the same way children in the emergent literacy studies had been documented as doing (Bissex 1980; Goodman 1986; Harste et al. 1984; Taylor 1983). While it took a while for this idea to become clear to Jenny, she did dutifully purchase the materials and made a space in Donny's room for them. She explained that she needed to keep them confined to his room to avoid their destruction by the many children who came trooping through the apartment on a daily basis. Although at first excited with his new possessions, Donny never used them in the ways I had hoped he would. Later home visits confirmed that the pencils had become guns or fishing poles and the paper fashioned into kites, hats, and so forth. In other words, the materials had been used to fulfill the social functions already present in the home rather than to introduce new functions. It became clear that until the community members perceived a need or function for reading and writing, making literacy materials available would contribute little to the acquisition of concepts or skills.

Functions Must Match Home Needs

Clearly, the instruction Jenny and Donny (and Big Donny) had received in their various schools had not contributed toward making written language functional for them.   Instruction in the Literacy Center, though, was based in functional reading and writing. Increasingly, it became apparent that the transfer to the home would occur only when real opportunities arose in the home, that matched those explored in the center.

As mentioned earlier, I began working with Jenny through journals.   One of her earlier complaints was that although she could read—with effort—most of the words in the workbooks from her adult classes (which she had completed), she could never remember them outside of that context.   At that point, I suggested that she write to me in a journal, the text of which I would type in standard spelling for her to read.   "Why, I ain't never read my own words before!" she exclaimed in wonderment.

We proceeded with this plan after I convinced her that I could read her writing even if she couldn't spell correctly.   Over time, her writings expanded and her word recognition ability increased dramatically as she read my transcriptions.   But although I suggested it, she never wrote in a journal at home.

However, in spring of the first year of the study an opportunity arose in Jenny's life to use writing.   Big Donny was arrested and jailed for selling marijuana, a relatively common cottage industry in Kentucky.   He was incarcerated for six months, and Jenny and the boys missed him terribly.   At that time, Jenny tried something she had never done before.   She wrote letters to him, "using that kind of writing we do here (at the center)."   This involved an incredible amount of effort on her part, with several attempts at drafts and worrying that the guard, who would have to read them to her husband, would not be able to read her spelling. However, her need to communicate with her husband over time and space drove her to persist.   She wrote and sent two letters over the six-month jail term even though she visited him weekly in person.   The instruction in the center had furnished her with the functional concept of communication through personal letters and with experience with the general act of writing to a reader. When the real-life opportunity for these concepts appeared, she could transfer them from the instructional context to her personal context. For the first time, a functional use of print became a part of the home/community in which Donny and Timmy were living.

Literacy began to emerge in the home in other ways during the course of the study. Toward the middle of the second year, Donny began replicating a center practice at home. Part of the instructional program at the Literacy Center is to read to the children from self-selected literature. Donny loved to be read to and always looked forward to snuggling close and interacting with me around the text as I read. In the second year, I received reports from Jenny, confirmed by Donny and Timmy, that he was reading to his little brother at home from books he had mastered. Timmy also loved being read to and was soon "reading" to his father, as he sat on his lap, from those books he had shared with Donny. Jenny reported that he would point to the words, as he had seen Donny do, as he pretend read to his father. Print was being used in the home to fill real interaction needs, and important concepts about written language were being learned by the children as they participated in these literacy events.

CONCLUSION

Sulzby and Teale (1991, 728) define an emergent literacy perspective as one that "ascribes legitimacy to the earliest literacy concepts and behaviors of children and to the varieties of social contexts in which children are becoming literate." This view may be true, perhaps, but the fact that the United States is viewed as a literate society does not mean that different groups within the society are literate in the same ways or to the same degree. Individuals are cultural beings (Ferdman 1990), and as such, they reflect socially, and culturally bound ways of representing reality and behaving. The United States is not homogenous. It is highly diverse and becoming more so every day. If we hope to extend access to literacy to all of our people, we must recognize and legitimize the culturally bound nature of literacy and literacy acquisition. We must continue in our efforts to understand how children construct knowledge of print from their own unique perspectives from within their own cultural communities.

It follows that as we work on literacy policy we must move from a mainstream perspective of literacy and incorporate cultural and social considerations in both our understanding of the issues and our proposed solutions. Much comparative ethnography remains to done before we can recommend effective suggestions for home and community educational efforts. Without this, we risk wasting a great deal of time and money on ineffective solutions to the literacy problems of many of our citizens.

5

Parents' Interactions with Beginning Readers

Christi Bergin, David F. Lancy, and Kelly D. Draper

INTRODUCTION

This chapter addresses the variation in parent's interactions with beginning readers within a white, working-class population and the aspects of that interaction that are associated with children's fluency and positive attitude toward reading. Many innovative early childhood intervention programs as well as school-initiated parent-involvement programs urge parents to read to and with their children. Policy in this area has been influenced by research that shows that children who learn to read easily and at an early age are read to at home (Durkin 1966; Teale 1987; Elardo, Bradley, & Caldwell 1975; Wachs, Uzgiris, & Hunt 1971; Walker & Kuerbitz 1979; Wells 1981a, 1985b). Home reading is also positively correlated with vocabulary and language development (Gordon & Guinagh 1974; Irwin 1960).

However, parents vary by social class in their contribution to reading acquisition. For example, the availability and function of reading and writing materials varies widely across families (Anderson, Teale, & Estrada 1980; Teale 1978; Teale, Estrada, & Anderson 1981) and regular storybook reading routines are not as prevalent in low income homes (Teale 1986). This variation is significant because the home literacy environment, in general, and the presence of storybook reading rituals, in particular, mediate the child's experience of and success with literacy instruction in school (Lancy, in press).

Because of the positive effects of reading on children, there has been a spate of new programs (e.g., Running Start, see Chapter Nine) designed to get parents to read to their children, particularly those at risk for reading problems. Thanks to the media it has become common knowledge among parents that children should be read to at home. A weak link in this process is that educators are not telling parents how to read to their children. Not all parents may be interested in or have the skill to read effectively to their child or serve as an effective coach for the child who is just beginning to read. Popular media ads encourage parents to "turn your child on to books," yet parents could have the opposite effect. What constitute supportive and nonsupportive home reading practices for beginning readers?

There is a dearth of research on parent-child reading in the early elementary years to provide an answer to this question. It is an important question because easy acquisition and enjoyment of reading in the early grades should facilitate subsequent academic development. The objective of this study is to begin to fill this research void. In this chapter we address both the variation in parent-child interaction during joint storybook reading, and specific interaction patterns associated with children's reading fluency and affect.

METHOD

This study is unusual with respect to both the age of the subjects and their fluency range. Children were in kindergarten or first grade. As each child reached the ability to begin to read books independently, as judged by the classroom teacher, a parent [1] was invited to come to the school to read with the child in a simulated home setting. Subjects ranged from early (reading independently in kindergarten) to late (still struggling near the end of first grade) readers. Thirty-two white, working-class parent-child pairs were videotaped for 30 to 40 minutes while reading to each other from a varied collection of picture books. The pairs freely choose which book to read and who would do the reading. All pairs included some parent-to-child reading and some child-to-parent reading.

Independent Variables

An elaborate coding scheme was developed to analyze both parent and child behaviors. To determine what limitations on the reliability of the data might be due to observer error, interobserver agreement was calculated based on the videotapes of four parent-child pairs. In all but one case, percentage of complete agreement was the statistic used, resulting in conservative estimates of agreement because this statistic is stringent and does not allow for close measures in categorical data.

The four independent variables under study were:

1. Parent's error correction tactics
2. Commentary on the books
3. Child's asking of questions about the book
4. Purpose for reading

Parents' error correction tactics are important at this age because children make many mistakes—the single most frequent kind of parent-child interaction was the correction of the child's reading errors—but the literature currently is mute on this issue. The next three variables were included because studies show that discussion of the book, asking open-ended questions, and stressing meaning facilitate literacy development in preschool-age children. It is logical to ask whether these same variables affect older children.

Dependent Variables

We studied two dependent variables, fluency and reading affect. Two factors were taken into account when children were placed into fluency groups: (1) number of words read per minute, and (2) age of the child.

Number of Words Read per Minute

At two different points in the observation session (beginning and middle) the number of words the child read in a three-minute period was tallied. The two observations were averaged to obtain a per-minute fluency rate for each child. Number of words read ranged, across this sample of children, from 9 to 153 words per minute. In addition, at the end of the session the observer rated the child as high, medium, or low in fluency so that the kind of book read (easy reader versus difficult narrative) could be taken into account. Both the count and rating data were used to rank the children's fluency from 1 (highest) to 32 (lowest).

Age and Fluency of the Child

Because the children were selected for study only when the teacher felt they had become independent readers, the age and time of year for testing varied for each child. We designated children as either early or late readers based on both their age and the time of year of observation. "Early" readers were in kindergarten or the first part of first grade and were five years, five months to six years, nine months old. "Late" readers were in the second half of first grade and were six years to seven years, six months old.

Age and fluency were combined, resulting in two groups: (1) good readers; children who were early and fluent (median age of six years, two months and median fluency ranking of eighth with the number of words per minute read ranging from 44 to 124) and (2) poor readers; children who were late and nonfluent (median age of six years, ten months and median ranking of twenty-fourth with words per minute read ranging from 17 to 53).   Both groups included 16 children.   The two observers had 100 percent agreement on fluency grouping.

Child Affect While Reading

The second dependent variable was the attitude of the child toward reading as seen in the display of affect during our observations. Affect group was constructed from a composite of the following five variables: (1) frustration, (2) task engagement, (3) discipline incidents, (4) subdued affect, and (5) weariness at the end of the session. These variables were derived from repeated viewing of the videotape; they are grounded in the data (Lancy, 1993). Furthermore, the variables were repeatedly reworked in order to get the best fit to the data. These variables are further elaborated in the appendix at the end of this chapter.

These five variables are associated with one another.[2]   The two variables most centrally related to the others were frustration and engagement level. If these two variables are analyzed without regard to the other variables, three prevailing patterns emerge. Seven children were low in frustration and high in engagement (i.e., enthusiastically working); eight were low in frustration and low to moderate in engagement (i.e., tuned out) and fifteen were high in frustration and low in engagement (i.e., having a miserable time). Note that almost half the children were having a miserable time.

Table 5.1
Characteristics of the Four Affect Groups

---

1. Negative group (*N*=8). Moderate to high in frustration and discipline. Moderate to low in engagement. Subdued in affect. Weary at the end of the session. These children were in the bottom third for four or more of the contributing five variables.

2. Moderately negative group (*N*=9). High in frustration. Moderate to high in discipline. Moderate to low in engagement. Weary at the end of the session. Their subdued affect rating varies across the spectrum. They were in the bottom third on more variables than in the top third.

3. Neutral group (*N*=7). Tired out. Moderate to low in frustration and engagement. Disciplined rarely or never. Some signs of subdued affect. Their scores on weariness varied. They were in the top third on more variables than in the bottom third.

4. Positive group (*N*=8). Upbeat and positive. Moderate to low in frustration. Moderate to high in engagement. Never disciplined. No signs of blunted affect. No weariness at the end of the session. They were in the top third in four of the five contributing variables.

The characteristics of each group are given in Table 5.1. The key difference between groups 1 and 2 is that, in group 2, negative affect is less marked than in group 1. The key difference between groups 2 and 3 is that group 3 is low in frustration. The key difference between groups 3 and 4 is that group 4 is high in engagement level and affect. The two observers had 100 percent agreement on affect grouping.

RESULTS

The child's reading affect and fluency are not strongly related. A comparison of extremes shows that of the six youngest and most fluent readers, none was in the negative group. Conversely, of the five oldest, least fluent readers, none was in the positive group. However, aside from these extremes, good and poor readers were found in all affect groups. Thus, the relationship with each independent variable —parent error correction tactics, text commentary, questioning, and purpose for reading—will be presented separately for the two dependent variables.

Parent's Error Correction Tactics

Little research has investigated the parent's response to child reading errors. Yet, in this study, it became clear that the single most frequent kind of interaction that occurred between parent and child was error correction. Reading was clearly a negotiated event. It follows that how the parent makes these corrections would affect the child's reading abilities and attitudes.

We tallied the number and type of corrections following each of the child's errors. We also included hesitations when the child made a clear signal for help (e.g., looking at the mother with eyebrows raised). Seven categories emerged, ranging from simply saying " n o " to telling the child the word while elaborating a general principle.[3] The categories are presented in Table 5.2.

Frequency and Range of Error Correction Tactics

Because of the prevalence of this kind of interaction and the lack of empirical information about it, a significant contribution of this study is simply the description of the range and frequency of parental correction tactics. The total number of error corrections, regardless of type, ranged from .40 to 6.65 per minute of the child's reading.

Parents varied enormously in their use of corrective strategies. For example, when a child hesitated over reading a word, some parents simply repeated (up to 29 times in one session) "sound it out," but without giving the child any clues, whereas other parents never gave this particular admonition. Similarly, some parents would quickly tell

Table 5.2
Categories of Parents' Correction Tactics

Correction Tactic	Example
1. Simply saying "No."	
2. Isolating the error, but not offering any other help.	"What's this word right here?" while pointing.
3. Asking the child to sound the word out without aid.	"Don't guess. Pronounce it."
4. Asking the child to sound the word out with aid.	"No, that's a 'b.' There's no 't'."
5. Giving a whole-word clue involving picture or text.	"What do ears do?" (for the word 'hear') or "Look at the picture."
6. Simply telling the child the word.	
7. Telling the child the word and elaborating on the relevant rule.	"No, that's not waterlemon, it's watermelon. Same letters, but see the order is different."

the child the word (91 times in one session) after only the slightest hesitation, whereas other parents never told the child the word.

The single most common error correction tactic was simply telling the child the word. It was the predominant tactic for the first attempt at correcting the child for 16 parents, and a common secondary tactic for other parents. That is, parents using a phonics-based reductionist strategy often began the correction episode by simply saying "no," pausing for a few seconds until the child made it clear she could not figure the word out, followed up with a "sound it out!" command, pausing for a few seconds until the child indicated he or she still could not figure the word out, at which point the parent told the child the word. Thus, it was often used in combination responses. The second most often used tactic was to ask the child to "sound it out," but giving the child aid in doing so. This was the predominant correction tactic of six parents. Simply saying "sound it out" with no aid was the predominant tactic of four parents.

The error correction tactics were grouped into those representing a decoding orientation (3 and 4, and their combinations) and those representing a semantic orientation (5, 6, and 7, and their combinations). Descriptive statistics for these are given in Table 5.3. Error corrections were calculated by absolute frequency per minute of child reading.

Table 5.3
Statistics for Parents' Correction Tactics

Type of Error Corrections	Minimum	Maximum	Mean	SD
Total # error corrections	.40	6.65	2.26	1.29
Decoding-ori-ented error corrections	.00	1.36	.41	.42
Semantic-ori-ented error corrections	.00	5.41	1.12	1.20

Relationship to Fluency Group

Which tactic parents used was associated with the child's fluency. Parents were readily classifiable into being predominantly semantically or decoding oriented in the use of correction tactics. The two observers had 88 percent agreement on error correction grouping. Children who were early, fluent readers had parents who were below the median in the use of decoding-oriented tactics (t=1.59, p=.06). Conversely, children who were late, nonfluent readers tended to have parents who were below the median in the use of semantic-oriented tactics (t=-1.17, p=.126).[4] See Figure 5.1 for a pictorial representation of these data. There was no association between the child's fluency and the number of error corrections (r=.01, p=.48). These results are not, therefore, simply a by-product of late, non-fluent children receiving more corrections. It is possible that early, fluent readers covered more text, and therefore had more chances to be corrected, but all children presented their parents with ample opportunity to correct them during the reading process.

Figure 5.1
Parent Error Correction Tactics By Child Fluency Group

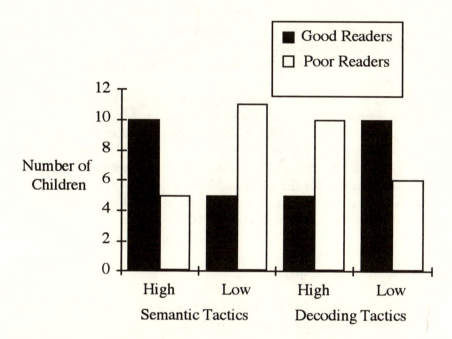

Note. Placement in "High" or "Low" categories is based on median splits on each error-correction variable.

Relationship to Affect Group

Which tactic parents used was also associated with the child's reading affect. Children in the most negative group had parents who were significantly higher in the use of decoding-oriented tactics than children in the other three groups ($F=4.96$, $p=.01$). The effect of using semantic-oriented tactics is not statistically significant ($F=2.1$, $p=.12$ for all four affect groups). However, when the positive and neutral affect groups are pooled, these parents used more semantic-oriented tactics than parents in the two negative groups pooled (t=2.35, p=.016). As with fluency, analysis of variance reveals that there is no relationship between total number of error corrections and affect group (F=1.9, p=.15).

The relationship between parent correction tactics and both the child's fluency and affect group were similar, although the relationship between parental error correction and child's affective response to reading was more pronounced than the relationship with child's fluency group. Thus, parents high in the use of decoding-oriented tactics have children who are poor readers and are particularly negative about reading. The use of semantic-oriented tactics shows the opposite trend, but the trend is not as statistically strong, presumably because the most common tactic used was a semantic one, resulting in less variance.

A striking observation was that the children whose parents used semantic-oriented tactics were able to maintain story flow. Children whose parents were decoding-oriented often labored over words to the point of losing the gist of the story. One child labored for a full minute over the word "was." This kind of disruption in the story flow was difficult for the child and boring for the researchers. It is easy to understand why such a correction approach would be associated with poor reading ability and affect.

Commentary on the Text

There are many studies in the literature indicating that discussion of the text during reading is effective. These studies focus on preschool children who are doing proto-reading at best. The dependent variable is typically not reading ability per se, but reading-related skills such as language acquisition and cognitive development. For example, Hayden and Fagan (1987) found that parents who contextualized books for their child had more print-aware preschoolers. (See also Goodsitt, Raitan, & Perlmutter 1988; Adams 1990.)

If this is an important dimension for the age group under study, it raises the possibility that joint storybook reading at home is more important than school-based reading for two reasons: (1) parents can more effectively personalize and contextualize reading because they read on a one-to-one basis and they have more shared experience with

Table 5.4
Categories of Parent & Child Commentary on the Text

Commentary Category	*Example*
1. Word-level Comprehension: Word Meaning	"A rut is a hole in the road."
2. Mechanics Instruction	"'!' means it's exciting."
3. Text-level Comprehension	
a. Text introduction (Book is previewed or reading is prepared in some way)	"Let's see if he went to the doctor."
b. Text Discussion	
i. Application to child's experience	"You didn't have to take a nap at your school."
ii. High mental demands	"Why isn't it hot under the house?"
iii. Medium mental demands	"Looks more like a hen than a kitten."
iv. Low mental demands	"What's that?" (a cop)
v. Emotive (Humor)	"Oh no!" or "This is funny!" as child smiles
vi. Emotive (Expressions about feelings.)	"I love baby animals, and my rabbit."

their child, and (2) teachers don't stress text-level comprehension. For example, Mason (1982) observed third and fourth grade classrooms. She divided reading activities into (1) word recognition, (2) word meaning, (3) text introduction, (4) reading, and (5) text discussion. Based on the literature she assumed a sequence of 3-4-5 would be the most effective teaching sequence. She laments that it was seldom used and that students spent very little time actually reading under a teacher's supervision; most of their time was spent on worksheets.

The present study addresses whether text discussion affects five through seven-year-olds who are beginning readers. Based on our review of the literature (see Goodsitt et al. 1988 and Pellegrini, Perlmutter, Galda, & Brody 1990) and experience observing joint storybook reading, we decided to tally nonreading, but on-task parent-child comments into the categories most likely to contribute to reading development. These categories are given in Table 5.4. We tallied the number of utterances for each child and parent for each book read.

Frequency and Range of Text Commentary

There was considerable variation in text discussion. The scores on total commentary (parent and child comments combined across nine categories) ranged from 0 to 58 (median = 19). Some dyads made no comment at all, while others made as many as 20 comments while reading one book. Given that all possible comments were tallied, including simply giggling, commentary was not frequent. Parents made more comments than children. The most frequent category of parents' comments was low and medium mental demands (e.g., "What's that?"). The least frequent category was text introduction, which only four parents ever did, and they did it only once during the observation. The most common category for children was expressing humor (e.g., "That's funny!"). The mean number of humor-related comments was 2.9 for the 30 to 40 minute session; the range was 0 to 15. All other categories of children's comments, besides low and medium mental demands, had a mean below 1 with over half of the children making no comment at all.

Of the 16 dyads below the median on total commentary, 15 were below the median on parent commentary and 13 were below the median on child commentary. Thus, the total commentary score represents a reading interaction pattern and cannot be explained by one member of the pair dominating the other (with four exceptions).

Correlation between the two observers for parents' commentary was $r=.80$; for children's commentary it was $r=.92$; and for total commentary it was $r=.83$.

Relationship to Fluency Group

The analysis of variance (ANOVA) suggested no relationship between amount of text commentary and the child's fluency group. MANOVAs run separately for child comments and parent comments similarly showed no relationship between amount of commentary and fluency.

Relationship to Affect Group

The amount of commentary by the child across all nine categories was related to reading affect (Hotelling's $T=2.34$, $p=.022$). The relationship is nonlinear: A priori contrasts show that groups 1, 2, and 3 are similar in amount of commentary, but the positive group is engaged in substantially more commentary. A similar but nonsignificant trend was found for parent commentary (Hotelling's $T=2.02$, $p=.144$).

Questioning

In addition to text commentary, we noted whether children questioned their parents during the reading episode. Whitehurst, Fako, Lonigan, Fischel, DeBaryshe, Valdez-Menchaca, and Caulfield (1988), Many (1988), and Goodsitt et al. (1988) found that the number of open-ended questions asked by mothers during reading was related to positive child development in toddlers. Is this a relevant dimension of interaction with beginning readers? Unlike preschoolers, children this age were the primary question-askers. In "Learning to Read without a Teacher," Torrey (1969) makes the point that children who are allowed to monitor and control their own reading education (via directed questions) do well. In addition, Whitehurst et al. (1988) argue that it is important that mothers effectively follow the child's cue. Does the parent capitalize on incidents where the child wants to discuss the text, or try to push on? Thus, it is probable that parent's responses to a child's questions would be associated with reading fluency and affect.

We tallied the number of child-initiated questions and categorized the parents' responses as either (1) encouraging, (2) simply answering (e.g., "uh huh"), or (3) discouraging (e.g., ignoring the child, or saying "Just read and find out"). The two observers had 100 percent agreement on this categorization.

Frequency and Range of Questioning

The group range for total number of questions asked during the observation session was 0 to 8, with 23 children asking two or fewer questions. This parallels the commentary results and indicates that there was very little discussion of the text during joint storybook reading. The children fell into three groups with roughly one-third (10) asking no questions at all; another one-third (12) had questions answered and elaborated on in an encouraging manner; the remaining one-third (10) had questions unanswered, or briefly answered and not in an encouraging manner. Only three children had one or more questions deliberately ignored. One parent ignored five questions from her child.

Relationship to Fluency Group

Both the highest and lowest fluency groups were as likely to ask (or not ask) questions. Chi square for number of questions asked by fluency level was 7.5 ($p=.48$). The group of children who asked no questions were evenly divided between early, fluent and late, nonfluent readers. On the other hand, how their parents responded to the questions was associated with fluency level (see Figure 5.2). For children who did ask questions, the majority (9 of 12) of those who had parents who encouraged questions were good readers and those whose parents discouraged questions were primarily (5 of 6) poor readers. All three of the children whose questions were ignored were among the very lowest in fluency. Conversely, only six children had three or more questions answered and elaborated on, and they were among the highest in fluency.

Relationship to Affect Group

There was no relationship between the number of questions asked and the child's affect group. There was also no significant relationship between the way questions were responded to and the child's affect group (Chi square=10.4, $p=.32$). Extreme comparisons revealed the same results in that the three children who had questions unanswered were in the moderately negative (*n*=2) and neutral (*n*=1) groups. The six children who had three or more questions elaborated on were distributed across all the affect groups.

Figure 5.2
Question Response by Fluency Groups

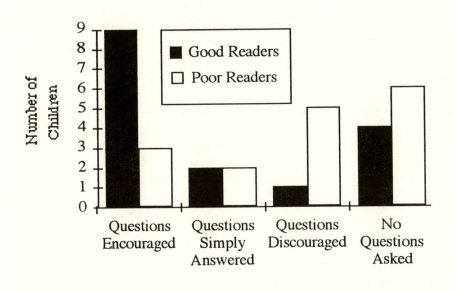

Purpose for Reading

Hayden and Fagan (1987) found that preschool children for whom reading is a meaning-getting process are more print aware and have higher proto-reading abilities. It is a logical assumption that similar effects would be seen for the age group under study. Indeed, in our initial analysis it was apparent that different goals for reading reflected the pairs' enjoyment of reading (Lancy et al. 1989).

In the present study we assessed purpose for reading in two ways. First, we categorized each child and each parent according to a subjective sense of their overall purpose for reading, as follows:

1. Meaning-getting process (understanding the story or plot, learning the content, etc.)
2. Having a good time (entertainment, the book is a vehicle for giggling, cuddling, etc.)

3. Learning skills (practicing sounds and words)
4. Just get through it (assigned duty, shows little interest in
    content, tries to finish quickly, parent says "come on" when the
    child initiates discussion)

The child's purpose for reading was not necessarily the same as the
parent's. For example, a parent may view the child's turn to read as a
time for practicing skills, whereas the child may view his or her turn to
read as a time for having fun. Second, we rated both the child's and
parent's overall reading style as either (1) monotone and robotic, (2)
normal, or (3) expressive and dramatic.

Frequency and Range of Purpose for Reading

The greatest variation in purpose occurs when the child is reading.
When the parent read, all but seven pairs read for fun. Parents viewed
child reading time as an opportunity for the child to have fun or as an
opportunity for the child to learn or display reading skills. Children
read to have fun or to just get through it. Neither group appeared to
read predominantly for meaning. The two observers agreed on 75
percent of the categorizations.

Each parent and child were given an overall rating of their reading
style. For children, this variable was not discriminating, because 28 of
the children read in a monotone/robotic style. For parents there was a
little more range. Four parents read in a monotone robotic style, 20
in a normal tone, and eight in an expressive, dramatic way. The two
observers agreed on 75 percent of these categorizations.

Relationship to Fluency Group

Purpose for reading is associated with children's reading fluency.
The contrast for parents' purpose for reading while the child reads is
given in Table 5.5. The Chi Square for this table is 8.29 ($p=.004$).
Thus, good readers have parents who appear to view the child's reading as a time for entertainment, rather than skill practice. A similar
finding was obtained for the child's purpose while the child reads
(Chi square=4.52, $p=.03$). Additionally, of the seven pairs who do
not read for fun when the parent is reading none of the children are
early, fluent readers.

Table 5.5
Fluency Grouping by Parents' Purpose for Child's Reading

Parent's Purpose for Child Reading	Good Readers	Poor Readers
Having a Good Time	11	2
Learning Skills	5	14

Table 5.6 brings together both the child and the parents' purpose for reading and reading style in a narrative format to show how these behaviors are associated with the child's fluency grouping. Descriptions of the pairs are given in each cell. The upper left to lower right diagonal shows the most dramatic contrast in purpose for reading. The upper left cell is predominantly high fluency readers and the lower right is predominantly low fluency readers.

Relationship to Affect Group

The parent's purpose while the child read was also related to the child's affect group; children who had parents who emphasized reading for fun were more positive about reading (Chi square=6.8, p=.08). The child's purpose while he or she read showed a similar, but non-significant trend (Chi square=2.6, p=.45).

The parent's style of reading was not associated with the child's reading affect. In fact, five of the eight parents who read in an expressive way had children in the negative or moderately negative group. While it is logical that the child's style of reading is related to the child's reading affect, there is not enough variation in the way the child reads to do an analysis. However, three of the four children who were not monotone readers were in the positive group.

Book Selection

Another interaction, also reflecting purpose for reading, is book selection. Some 30 books ranging from Golden Books to controlled

Table 5.6
Fluency Grouping Based on Purpose for Reading & Reading Style

Parent	Child	
	Have Fun	Just Get Through It
Have Fun	Purpose for both parent and child while child reads is to have fun. Same for when parent reads. They read in either an expressive/dramatic or normal tone. Good Readers N=10 Poor Readers N=1	Purpose for child when child reads is to get through the task. But for parent it is for meaning or fun, or parent is especially dramatic/expressive (i.e., parent does something fun.) Good Readers N=2 Poor Readers N=3
Practice Skills	Purpose for child while child reads is meaning or fun, but for parents it is to learn skills. Parent reads in a normal or monotone style (i.e., child has gist of fun reading but parent does not.) Good Readers N=1 Poor Readers N=3	Purpose for both while child reads is to learn skills or get through the task. Same for when the parents reads for seven dyads. Both read in a normal or monotone style. Good Readers N=3 Poor Readers N=9

(Dick and Jane style) readers to Caldecott award winners were spread casually over a coffee table. After observing each pair select each book we categorized reason for book choice as:

1. Familiar and liked
2. Seems interesting, funny, or appealing (e.g., "I want a funny one.")
3. Connoisseurship (e.g., familiar with the series or characters, likes the author)

4. Easy (e.g., "You can read all these words.")
5. Proximity (e.g., on the top of the stack)
6. No discussion
7. Unclear

In the instances where it was clear why the choice was made, children primarily choose a book because it was familiar and liked (18 instances) or because it seemed interesting or funny (9 instances). Other categories were expressed by children only four or fewer times. Parents, on the other hand, primarily choose a book because it was easy (12 instances); all other categories were expressed three or fewer times. Parents were more concerned with choosing books the child might have success with than the child was. No analysis with the dependent variables was done because of limited entries in most of the categories and most interactions being "unclear." It was interesting to us that so little discussion took place. There did not appear to be any tacit rules or communication of reasons for book choices. It appeared to be more random than a negotiated decision or an act of connoisseurship.

CONCLUSIONS

Educators encourage parents of high-risk children to read to them, but without a sense of how that advice is carried out by different parents. Because of the importance of this kind of interaction and the lack of empirical information about it for school-aged children, a significant contribution of this study is simply the description of the range and frequency of parent and child behaviors during joint storybook reading. This study provides a picture of the variation among beginning readers and their parents during storybook reading. The variation was striking even though the sample was from a relatively homogeneous working-class population.

One example of such striking variation was that although "expressing humor" was the most common kind of commentary made by children, some children never made such a comment, while one child made 15 such comments. Another example of wide variation is that one parent deliberately ignored five questions from her child, whereas another parent enthusiastically elaborated on eight questions asked by her child, while other children simply didn't ask any questions at all. A final example of variation in reading behavior was given in the section on error corrections: When a child hesitated over reading a word, one parent simply repeated "sound it out," without giving the child any clues 29 times in one session, whereas other parents never gave this particular admonition. Another parent quickly told the child the word at the slightest hesitation 91 times in one session, whereas other parents never told the child the word.

Clearly, this study indicates that how parents read with their children varies. It follows that some of this variation would have positive, and some negative, outcomes for the beginning reader. A second purpose of this study was to suggest which aspects of that variation are associated with fluency and positive affect while reading. This study suggests that pairs who view the child's reading as a source of fun, keep the story flowing without letting the child get bogged down in decoding (by using semantic-oriented rather than decoding-oriented correction tactics), encourage questions about the story, and express humor while reading have children who are more fluent and more positive about reading. To summarize our results: the way parents corrected reading errors and their apparent purpose for reading and reading style are associated with the child's reading fluency and affect; the way the parents responded to queries from the child was associated with fluency; and the number of comments children made while reading was related to their reading affect. It should be noted here that children primarily made humorous comments (e.g., "This is funny!"), with no significant number of comments made in any other comment category. The connection to positive reading affect is obvious. We might describe the profile of parent-child interaction for good readers as stressing function; they seem to operate from a motto of "reading is fun!" Conversely, parent-child interaction for poor readers stresses form; they seem to operate from a motto of "reading is work!" where storybook reading is a time for skill practice. This supports other studies in the literature that indicate a comprehension-based approach to parent-child reading is more effective than a skills-based approach.

Equally of interest are those variables that were not associated with reading fluency or affect. Overall, it appears that the quality of the interaction between parent, child, and book, but not the quantity, is associated with positive reading ability and affect in this population. That is, the number of error corrections and number of questions answered were not related to either reading fluency or affect, and the number of comments made while reading was not related to reading fluency. These findings are somewhat contrary to some of the published literature which indicates that mere quantity of interaction is predictive of reading abilities. We see two primary reasons for this apparent contradiction: (1) age, and (2) cultural background of the participants. First, the published literature focuses on preschoolers rather than school-aged subjects. DeLoache's (1984, DeLoache & Mendoza 1985) work suggests that the expansionist tactic is more characteristic of interaction with very young children. As the child grows older, attention shifts to the mechanics of reading and there is much less elaboration of and commentary on the text. A related point is that the books used in these sessions with fledgling readers were very familiar. It is possible that had we observed some of these pairs engaged in storybook reading several years earlier, we would have seen much more commentary and mutual questioning.

A second explanation relates to the cultural background of our participants (Chapter One, this volume). The literature that supports the view that storybook reading is an opportunity for a great deal of teaching and learning that goes well beyond reading has been conducted almost exclusively with upper middle-class families where the mothers were highly educated (e.g., Heath 1982; Many 1988; Ninio & Bruner 1978; Snow & Goldfield 1982, 1983; Taylor 1983). More limited research on parent-child literacy activity in working-class families (e.g., Heath 1983; Miller, Nemoianu, & DeJong 1986) suggests that joint storybook reading is limited in degree and complexity. Perhaps in our sample mere quantity of interaction is not predictive of reading fluency and affect because that interaction is not always enhancing, reflecting the relative poverty of some of these parents' repertoire of storybook reading tactics.

We should note that most of the children were struggling, uncomfortable, and sometimes negative about reading, reminding us what a difficult and arduous task learning to read is. Although more children were negative than positive about reading, there was tremendous variation in the affect displayed by children while struggling through a book. While one child would pout, push herself back into the couch, cross her arms, and communicate in body language "I hate this! I'm only doing it because you made me," another would eagerly grab a book, cuddle with her mother, and smile throughout the reading process.

It is also important to note that we witnessed what appeared to be well-meaning parents who actually may have damaged their children's attitude toward reading. For example, one of our late, nonfluent readers was accompanied to the session by both parents. They clearly valued reading for their daughter and mentioned in a follow-up interview that they had purchased flash cards and other reading readiness aids for her. As she read, slowly, painfully, they provided a steady stream of exhortations. But these were either of the "You can do it!" sort or were purely decoding-oriented, "When two vowels go walking . . . ." They even went so far as to prevent the child's attempts to "construct" meaning, telling her not to "cheat by looking at the pictures." When she didn't heed this advice, her father actually placed a piece of paper over the illustration. In other words, caring, enthusiastic parents who rely entirely on decoding (or reductionist, see Lancy et al. 1989) tactics may be doing their beginning reader more harm than good. These parents were trying hard to be good parents, they were conscientious, and they were not an isolated case.

Hannon (1987) discusses the mixed results that have been obtained in British research on reading in working-class families (see also Toomey & Sloan, this volume). Why are some, but not all, parent involvement schemes successful at raising reading scores in children? One possible answer, as our findings indicate, is that when it comes to storybook reading more is not better, unless it is more of a particular kind of interaction. Our study revealed tremendous variation in parent-child joint storybook reading with this age group, and that not all parents are effective coaches for their child. This underscores the urgent need for educators to convey more information to parents about how to be a good coach to the beginning reader, rather than just telling parents and children to read at home more.[5]

APPENDIX

Affect Variables

1. Frustration. At three points during the observation (beginning, middle, and end) we rated on a scale of 1 (low) to 6 (high) the child's display of frustration while reading. At each point of measurement the children were evenly distributed from low to high on the scale, with a mean of 3 and range of 1 to 6, indicating wide variation in frustration level. We then placed each child in one of five categories describing the pattern of frustration as the session progressed:

1. Frustration stays low
2. Frustration stays moderate
3. Frustration stays high
4. Frustration gets lower
5. Frustration gets higher

One might expect beginning readers to grow in frustration as the session wore on, but there was no such pattern, for the group as a whole. The majority of children (25 of 32) stayed in a stable pattern, as follows: Twelve children stayed low, eight stayed high, and five stayed moderate. Another five children became more and two became less frustrated.

2. Task Engagement. We repeated this procedure with task engagement, also using a rating scale of 1 (low) to 6 (high). The children were fairly evenly divided in degree of task engagement with a mean of 3 and range of 1 to 6, but slightly more children were at the lowest end of engagement at all three measurement times. Just as with frustration, the majority (26 of 32) of children were stable in engagement across the session: Thirteen children stayed low, five stayed high, and eight stayed moderate. Half of the remaining six children became more engaged, and half became less engaged.

3. Discipline Incidents. We tallied each incident of discipline and distraction that occurred during the reading session. Discipline was defined as verbal or nonverbal methods to get the child's attention back to reading when it had wandered. Examples ranged from "Come on. Let's finish" or "Concentrate. Don't fidget about so much" in gentle tones, to the mother swiftly slapping the child. Distraction was also measured and was defined as attempts to control nonreading behavior, such as "Quit picking your nose."

Across the group, number of discipline incidents ranged from 0 to 14. Fourteen children had none. For 12 children there were one or two incidents. The remaining children were disciplined from four to six times; one child had 14 incidents. Distraction incidents (one or two) occurred in only four sessions, and these children were above the mode in frequency of discipline. Thus, distraction and discipline incidents were summed to produce a single variable. Almost all in-stances (47 of 56) of discipline and distraction occurred in the first three books read. Therefore, the frequency of incidents cannot be simply explained by the growing weariness on the part of the child as the session progressed, but is more likely a reflection of parent-child interaction style.

4. Subdued Affect. We rated whether each child showed subdued affect using a coding scheme developed for family interaction re-search (Feldman, Wentzel, Weinberger, & Munson 1990). We rated whether the child's affect display appeared flat or showed a lack of emotional energy. Ratings ranged from 5 (neutral, blunted affect not seen) to 1 (highly subdued). To receive a 5 a child did not have to be percolating with energy, but rather have no sign of subdued affect. This rating was only slightly skewed, with subjects evenly distributed over 2, 3, 4, and 5.

5. Weariness. We categorized each child at the end of the session as to whether they were predominantly weary, neutral, or still enjoying reading. Most children (17) were rated as weary, six as enjoying the reading, and nine as neutral by the end of the session.

We categorized parent's weariness the same way. Parents demon-strated a similar pattern; 17 were weary, seven were still enjoying themselves, and eight were neutral by the end of the session. We did not use parent's weariness as a determinate of the child's affect group because we were interested in the child's attitude, not the parent's. The child's level of weariness did not necessarily predict the paren-t's—only 15 of the parents had the same rating as the child. However, parent's weariness category was related to fluency of the child.

NOTES

Earlier versions of this chapter were presented at the Emergent Literacy Conference at the University of Toledo in May 1991, at the joint SRCD/ ACYF/NCJW conference in Washington, D.C. in June 1991, and at the AERA conference in San Francisco in April 1992. Sarah Evans assisted with data cod-ing and analysis.

[1] We invited parents or "any person who reads to _____ at home" to come to school. We had one mother/father pair, a grandmother, a grandfather, one father and 28 mothers.

[2] Of the 16 children who appear to be most negative in reading affect, 15 of them are at or below the median in their scores on four of the five variables. Of the 16 children who appear to be most positive in reading affect, 12 are at or

above the median in four of the five variables. Discipline and weariness ratings were the least empirically related to the other variables, possibly because they were skewed with a strong floor effect. Weariness was related to frustration, in that children who stayed high in frustration were all weary by the end of the session, while children who remained low in frustration varied in weariness. Discipline was assumed to be related to level of engagement in the task because children occasionally used off-task behavior purposely to avoid reading. This is difficult to assess because of the floor effect of the discipline variable (i.e., most children had no discipline incidents), but a trend appears to confirm this assumption: two-thirds of the children who were low or became lower in engagement were sanctioned, whereas only one-fourth of the children who were high or became higher in engagement were disciplined.

3 Parental responses that involved a combination of these categories were coded in one of two ways. A *single* statement that crossed several categories was assigned to the category reflecting the provision of greater assistance to the child. For example, "No, not on a hill. They aren't on a hill. What are they on? (while pointing to a picture of a tree)" would not be coded as 1 or 2, but as 5. *Multiple* statements separated by waiting periods were tallied in a "combination" category. For example, one parent corrected a child by saying "No," waiting several seconds, then saying "W. What sound does W make?" waiting several seconds, then saying in exasperation "It's 'WAS.' Now go on." This interaction would not be adequately represented by a code of 1, 4 or 6, so it was coded as a combination response.

4 For analysis, we grouped the error correction tactics in two other ways: "helpful, supportive" (4, 5, 6, 7) vs. "unhelpful, nonsupportive" (1, 2, 3) and "active" (4, 5, 7) vs. "passive" (3, 6) tactics. Neither of these dimensions were related to the child's fluency level. Only six parents were predominantly "unhelpful" in their tactics, whereas parents divided evenly on the active/passive dimension.

5 A note on limitations: Support for our findings of a relationship between parent-child interaction styles and the child's fluency and enjoyment of reading would be strengthened with two design modifications. First, it would be helpful to sample across a wider class spectrum. Our sample did not include any families of the sort documented by Taylor (1983), where storybooks are central props in the drama of family life and joint storybook reading is the glue that bonds family members together. Nor did our sample include families where the printed word is virtually nonexistent (e.g., Purcell-Gates 1991a). By sampling more broadly we would significantly increase the variance available on the independent variables. It would also be helpful to conduct a longitudinal study of children from the age of four and a half to seven and a half, to capture changes in interaction patterns as a function of the child's age and changing status as nonreader, beginning reader, and independent reader. Also, quite obviously, we would be in a much stronger position to argue that something about the interaction patterns from four and a half to six years influence the child's interaction with academic reading instruction from six to seven and a half years.

6

Helping Parents Help Their Children: Early Language Stimulation in the Child's Home

Ann-Katrin Svensson

Many studies show that language development and the capacity to learn to read and write is related to stimulation in the home at an early age. This project—more fully reported elsewhere (Svensson 1993)—has developed a method to inform parents of the importance of language (and literacy) stimulation for their child's development. Twenty-five children were followed during a four year period beginning at two and a half years old and ending when the children were six and a half years old. Twice-yearly home visits were made to the families of these children. At every visit the parents received a booklet with information about language development and the children were provided with books and educational material.

This intervention study was based on the model of ecology of human development. Bronfenbrenner (1979) divides the environment into micro-, meso-, exo-, and macro-levels. The child's direct and indirect experiences in different environments are all important for development as a whole (Bronfenbrenner & Crouter 1983). Effects of intervention studies, such as the Head Start projects, have been models for the present study (Bronfenbrenner 1979; Berrueta-Clement, Schweinhart, Barnett, Epstein, & Weikart 1984; Bruner 1983; Lazar 1984; Lazar & Darlington 1982; Ramey & Campbell 1991; Sameroff & Fiese 1990; Schweinhart, Weikart, & Larner 1986; Schweinhart & Weikart 1983; Svensson 1989).

According to language stimulation research, there is a need for young children to interact with grown-ups in order to develop intellectual and linguistic competence (Björck-Åkesson 1992; Bruner 1983; Vygotsky 1981). Vygotsky (1981) emphasized the importance of parents helping the child to function in the "zone of proximal development" in whatever they are doing. In particular, studies have shown the importance and impact of reading to young children. Interaction between the child and the parent while reading books receives special emphasis (Bergin, Lancy, & Draper, this volume; Heath 1983; Ninio & Bruner 1978; Snow & Ninio 1986; Söderbergh 1986). Theories of Bernstein (1971), Wells (1985b, 1986), and Labov (1987) that focus on the way language and literature are used in different societies are also important in the present study.

Before presenting the results of the intervention study in this chapter, an overview of some aspects of Swedish childcare will be offered. Based on Bronfenbrenner's ecological model of development, it is important for the reader to get an understanding of the society in which the present study was administrated on the macro-level.

PATTERNS OF CHILDCARE AND EDUCATION IN SWEDEN

The macro-level can be described as including laws, regulations, governmental institutions, and attitudes within society. Sweden has approximately 8.6 million inhabitants. By American measures the population is homogeneous with a low mobility rate. For these reasons, it is possible to carry through longitudinal studies with little attrition.

Sweden has a very small lower income population and, consequently, the concept of children at risk has not been a focus in Sweden as much as in the United States. There are few Swedish studies in the area, however, there has been some longitudinal research published (Cederström 1990; Jonsson 1969; Sundelin Wahlsten 1991). Recent economic crises and growing unemployment (12 percent, per AMS statistics, February 1993) have led to an increasing awareness of children considered academically at risk. Also contributing to this emphasis has been an influx of refugees (SCB 1992).

It is common in Sweden for both parents to work. Approximately 85 percent of the mothers of children below the age of seven are gainfully employed. Of these mothers, 37 percent work full-time (SoS 1991, 28). However, it is most unusual for the mother to work before the baby is 18 months old. The social insurance system includes a parent insurance that guarantees one of the parents 90 percent of his or her wages during the child's first 12 months. During the next six months, this insurance allows one of the parents to stay at home (with a lower compensation), and after 18 months the parent can go back to his or her ordinary work. Swedish law also allows the parent to continue working at 75 percent of his normal time until the child is eight years old. At that time, the parent may start working full-time.

The exo-level (Bronfenbrenner 1979) is defined as the method different societies use to arrange for childcare when the parents work. In Sweden there are plenty of day-care centers and family day nurseries that are run by local authorities who obtain state grants covering half of the cost, with the balance of the cost being paid by fees and taxes. Childcare fees vary across the country. The childcare centers have high standards regarding staff education, the number of teachers in the group, and educational material available. Family day nurseries are most often staffed by nurses employed by the municipality, but there are also many women working privately. Another alternative that is found, but rarely, are grandparents or relatives taking care of the children.

The year before they start school, all children are offered three hours of preschool per day. If there are vacancies they can start at five or even as young as four. The local authorities are obliged to run the program without any cost to the parents. Nearly 100 percent of Swedish children go to preschool. The preschool also includes day-care programs for those children who need it. There are very few private preschools or other alternatives.

The meso-level is defined as the relation between the family and different other micro environments such as the preschool and school settings. Swedish children start school at seven. Recently, a new law established the child's right to enroll in school at age six. By 1997 all municipalities will be required to permit six year old children to start school if the parents desire. Consequently, there are a number of initiatives in the schools to develop programs for the six-year-old. Presently six and seven year old children start school together and then may choose their own reading and writing activities.

At this time, many cities offer the parents the option to place their six year old children in school; however, there is great resistance to this idea. The ninth biggest city, Jönköping, has about 122,000 inhabitants with about 2,500 children born each year. All parents of five-year-olds in this city were invited to enroll their children as soon as they turned six. Of approximately 2,500 eligible children, 19 were enrolled and 18 of these 19 children were immigrants. One of the reasons parents do not want their children to start school at six years is that they feel the child should have the opportunity to play one more year or that the child should not have to fit into schedules and demands at such a young age. Parents do not generally wish for their children to start learning to read before they start school because they do not want them to be stressed too early by academic demands. There is a great resistance against testing children, receiving marks in school, and comparing children's development and knowledge. In general, the parents do not want to speed up their child's development because this unconstrained period is considered critical.

Despite the late start in school, international comparisons show that Swedish children are doing well in reading (Elley 1992). Part of the reason for this phenomenon could be that activities in preschools are quite similar to activities in first grade in the compulsory schools in other countries (i.e., for five- and six-year-olds). However, the children are not *taught* to read and write. Another reason could be the fact that about 50 percent of the television programs are bought from abroad and subtitled, so the children practice reading while watching television. A few programs for preschool children are dubbed into the Swedish language as well. A recent study by Elley (1992) suggests a positive correlation between reading ability and watching TV for children between 7-14 years of age.

However, as in most countries, it is possible to go through school without becoming fully literate. One possible reason for this problem could be the absence of linguistic and/or intellectual stimulation in the home.

The description of Sweden on macro, exo, and meso- levels may be seen as a background to the micro-level on which the present study focuses. Because intervention studies are not common in Sweden, there were concerns when the present study started. We did not know how parents would react. Would they refuse to permit their child to be tested? Would they be insulted by our attempts to alter *their* behavior? Would they welcome us into their homes? As it turned out, all of these concerns proved unfounded—families were extremely cooperative.

THE LANGUAGE STIMULATION PROJECT

Parents and their children were the target group of this study. Due to ethical considerations it was not possible to select particular children who might be at risk for understimulation. Therefore, families were randomly chosen from the Child Care Health Center's registry, and then asked to participate. By this procedure, it was possible to reach a number of parents that did not know very much about the type of stimulation that children require for healthy development. Most of the families lived in a small town in the southern part of Sweden and all children were born within the same quarter of the year. A total of 50 children participated in the study. The families were randomly assigned to an experimental group ($N=24$, one family had twins) and a control group ($N=25$).

The home visits lasted one and a half to two hours, with most families receiving home visits twice a year. Some families needed more information, so they received visits three or four times a year. Also, booklets were given to the parents, which were graded to the present age of the target child (two, two and a half, three, etc.). These included information about the importance of reading to children, suggestions of books to select, nursery rhymes, songs, and various play activities.

Language development was discussed with the parents, and their role in stimulating the child's language from an early age was emphasized. To improve the child's phonological awareness, the parents received special training during the home visit and continuously received new language training programs by mail. These training programs were individualized according to the child's development and included rhymes and rhyming, segmentation of words into syllables, finding the initial/final sounds of words, studying the effect of adding or deleting initial/final sounds, segmentation of words into sounds, and synthesizing sounds into words.

The children received educational materials such as books, games, puzzles, and tapes with songs. During the home visits, parents discussed strategies used when reading with children such as the importance of explaining specific words or the entire story, and the importance of talking about the pictures. The parents were encouraged to involve the child in the text and to stimulate the child's use of language. Games were used to increase the child's interest in letters, to help stimulate them to talk about pictures, and to train memory and perception.

In between each of the visits, the parents received letters and postcards with information about stimulating the child's language development, with suggestions for books to purchase at book sales or for

Christmas presents.

Data Collection

The purpose of the study was to test whether it was possible to enhance parent involvement in children's language and literacy development. On the basis of this purpose the following questions can be specified: (1) Is it possible to influence parents to improve the stimulation for their children? and (2) What activities have the parents engaged in that may improve language and intellectual stimulation for the children?

During the four years of the project, parent-child activity was monitored at every home visit. Comparisons were made twice with a control group. Parent strategies were gathered via informal interviews at every home visit. Parents in both groups answered a questionnaire as the children were passing language tests at the ages of four and six. The questions concerned frequency of reading to the children, reading strategies, frequency of book loans from the library, frequency of explaining words and singing for the children, the children's frequency of television watching, and similar topics. We sought to measure change over time and differences between the groups to detect any impact our intervention might be having. Of course, we were also interested in whether enhanced language stimulation in the home had an effect on children's development.

The children were evaluated by a pre- and posttest, namely, Griffiths's Mental Development Scale, a general development test (Griffiths 1954, 1970) which is similar to the Bayley Scales of Infant Development (Bayley 1969). When the children were four and six years old the Eneskär language test was administrated (Eneskär 1978). Results

Initially, the similarities between the experimental and control families were more striking than the differences. That is, nearly all families were providing a range of language and literacy activities for their children, suggesting that parent responsibility for their children's literacy is deeply embedded in Swedish culture (Söderbergh 1990). For example, 80 percent of parents read to their child every day or almost every day. A similar percentage borrow children's books regularly from the public library. However, the stimulation program also introduced practices into the home literacy environment that may have been "foreign," not part of the general pattern for Swedish culture. And these introduced practices seemed to take hold. For example, virtually all experimental group parents began to read and recite nursery rhymes to their child by age four whereas this was done in only about half the control families. Similar differences were obtained for the purchase of children's cassette tapes.

The gap between the two groups seemed to widen over the four-year period. In the experimental group, fathers began to play a larger role, reading regularly to their child from age three on in 20 out of 24 families. More families in the experimental group enrolled their child in a book club. So, by age six, 14 children in the experimental group were conventionally literate, whereas, this was the case for only 4 of the control group children. These gains were hard won—it was difficult for many families to adopt these language stimulation ideas—as we will see in the case studies that follow.

Case Studies

Julia: two years, six months   Julia's father never reads to her due to his own reading and writing problems. Julia's mother stated that Julia has no interest in books and walks away before the mother finishes the first sentence. During the home visit the mother read very fast and in a monotonous tone to Julia for a short period of time.

3 years   The mother hardly ever reads to Julia, but when she reads Julia does not want to listen. The mother chose a 300-400 page book with fables and few pictures—suitable for six to seven year old children. When the home visitor discussed with the parents that this book might be too difficult for Julia, her mother seemed surprised. However, when the home visitor suggested to the mother some picture books with very little text, just like the books they had received through the program, Julia's mother complained that the story in these books is too thin and that she preferred books with more action.

3 years, six months   The mother reads once a week to Julia. During the visit the mother asked Julia to sit beside her when she started to read. She read monotonously and fast, making it difficult to understand what she was reading. Julia soon walked away.

4 years   The parents have not read to Julia during the summer months. The weather had been good and Julia had been outside all day. Julia suggested what to read for the most part, and her favorite book is a songbook. During the visit Julia received a book and the mother started to read fast and monotonously. Julia listened for a minute and then she walked away. The home visitor modeled appropriate reading practices by reading a book and inviting the child to fill in words. Julia seemed engaged and listened. The home visitor read two-thirds of the book before Julia showed a lack of interest.

4 years, three months   The parents do not read very often. Some possible reasons for this could have been the presence of a younger brother who disturbs reading sessions and also that Julia usually plays outdoors. The home visitor's suggestion that the mother should read a goodnight fairy tale was ignored. The mother reasoned that the children fall asleep at the same time and are always too tired to listen.

4 years, six months   The mother is finding it hard to set aside time to read or stimulate Julia's language. The younger brother occupied all her time. In addition, the mother started to work almost full-time.

4 years, eight months   During the last few months the mother has read several times a week to Julia.

5 years   At Julia's request, the mother is reading a goodnight book every evening.

To sum up, Julia's parents found it difficult to find a suitable level of interaction with her. The mother often did activities too difficult for Julia, exemplified by her choice of books. Not until Julia was almost five years old did the mother adapt the activities to Julia's developmental level. The mother received no support from the father in the interaction. It was noted that the father had very little contact with his children.

Fred: 2 years, six months   Fred is having difficulty concentrating and never sits still when it is time to read books. His mother reads once a week to Fred at the most. He is not interested in books and runs away when his mother starts to read. The father has a problem reading and writing and does not read to Fred at all. Fred owns five or six books and the family does not borrow books at the library.

3 years   Fred's mother feels that she reads to him more often than she had in the past. Every once in a while, his father reads to him. When Fred received a book, the mother started to read to him. Fred was calm and seemed to listen, but he constantly looked around the room. His mother read quickly, making it difficult to follow the story. The book invited the child to take an active part by making him try to find out what had disappeared from the pictures. The mother tried to engage Fred but his ability to concentrate was low.

3 years, six months   The parents read to Fred every evening. At times, they ask Fred questions or make associations to the text. During the visit, the home visitor read an easy book to him. He listened with attention and talked about the pictures.

4 years   The father recited from memory some lines from a long rhyming fairy tale and suggested that Fred fill in the rhymes. Fred was more interested in the new books and did not want to fill in the rhymes.

4 years, six months   The father learned to read and read books to Fred nearly every evening even though the parents had made an agreement about reading every other evening. In comparison, when Fred was two and a half years old the father never read a book to his son.

5 years   The mother did not want to read books during the daytime as she did not think it was suitable to do so, although the father read books in the evening. The father had also made recordings of himself reading the books, so that when he did not want to read or was not able to read, Fred could listen to the tape instead. The mother would laugh when the father stumbled and hesitated while reading.

In summary, Fred's parents learned quickly what Fred wanted and appreciated. It was not uncommon for Fred's parents to discuss the education of children, which could be one reason why they developed a positive interaction with Fred fairly early.

Jim: 3 years, six months   The father reads to the children in the evening. Because he works some nights, they read about three or four times per week. The father often reads cartoons to his children because he was not allowed to read cartoons as a child. The mother reads once a week to the children, but Jim often leaves while the mother is reading. The children often request cartoons to be read, but she will not read them because she does not like to read cartoons. After the children asked her to read cartoons several times and received a negative answer they lost interest.

4 years   The parents read to the children every evening. Jim likes to listen to short fairy tales and he stated that he and his brother would bring books to their mother while she was reading but she answers that she will read to them later. Jim and his brother wait for a while then remind her, but finally give up and walk away. The mother confirmed that this was the case.

5 years, six months   The parents are reading every evening. The father often changes the text and names and sometimes even reads two books at the same time just to see how crazy it will come out. The mother has found it to be great fun to read aloud to the children. She will only read books with chapters because she thinks Jim can read the picture books by himself. (Jim could read before he was five years old.) The father explains that he appreciates reading very much, especially documentary literature and fairy tales. He prefers reading long fairy tales and reads several books to the children every evening. The children usually choose one book each and the father chooses one book to read.

To sum up, Jim's parents gradually increased their reading to the children during the project period. They accomplished this in spite of the fact that the mother was not always in the mood to read and had strong opinions regarding appropriate books to read.

Jon: 2 years, six months Jon listens to books that are read to him almost every day but is not interested in reading himself. He only wants to turn the pages while being read to. His mother sometimes reads to him in the daytime and the father reads every evening. The mother does not explain words in the books because she thinks there is nothing to explain. The books are not adjusted to Jon's level of comprehension because his big brother may become bored and irritated. The books that were chosen to read were the kind his brother liked and very seldom does Jon decide what book will be read.

4 years, six months When the parents and children read they try to talk about something connected to the text, such as something the children have gone through or will take part in in the near future.

5 years, six months The mother tries to simplify more advanced books and explain more difficult things. Jon's mother has chosen more suitable books to read for Jon and has also changed her method of interaction with the children. She said that she had made these changes because of the information she received through the project.

Many parents have said that they now think of other ways to introduce books and games. The parents also have begun to show a changed attitude regarding what books are appropriate to read to their children and display new ways of talking about literature and discussing it with their children. One parent wrote the following when the children were six years old:

> I find it very difficult to buy other toys than educational ones. I prefer to buy Legos, games, books and drawing materials, but never plastic toys to pull up and sit and look at. (I think I would have done

this without the project.) The little brother also keeps up with some of the things even though he perhaps sometimes get jammed because his big brother takes all the time.

While the parents in the control group gave their children less stimulation between four and six years of age, many of the parents in the experimental group who had given their children little language stimulation at two and a half years old had increased the stimulation by age four and continued to stimulate them even more by the age of six. A comparison between the groups made it plain that the children in the experimental group had received considerably more language stimulation than the children in the control group. In summary, the parents' responses on both formal, structured and informal interviews indicates that it is possible, in Sweden, to influence them to increase their child's exposure to literacy activities. What impact did this have on their children?

First, we note that there were no differences between children in the two groups on the Griffiths test. To the extent that the project had an impact, it did so on emergent literacy development, not general cognitive development.

When the children were four and six years old, they received a language test designed to study articulation, vocabulary, and sentence construction. By the age of four the children in the experimental group had a larger vocabulary and better sentence construction, but the articulation was not better when compared to the control group. This could possibly be because three of the children had poor articulation and two had exceptionally poor articulation problems. However, these two children both had good vocabulary and sentence construction. At six years of age the children in the experimental group still had a bigger vocabulary and better sentence construction than the control group; however, there were no differences in articulation. Further, there were great differences in the children's ability to segment and synthesize, favoring the experimental group.

As mentioned above, many children had learned to read prior to starting school. By six and a half, 16 children in the experimental group were able to read, and three more children were very close to "breaking the code." However, some children learned to read without the parents noticing. Eva's mother discovered that she could read when there was a note in the kitchen that said "John is stupid" (John is Eva's little brother). The mother first thought Eva's older sister had written the note but after investigating the matter, it was determined that Eva had written the note. Mary's mother claims Mary cannot read. However, during a home visit, she received an ABC book in which everything was the wrong way round—"Tobacco" was written above a cheese shop. When Mary looked at the cheese shop she read "tobacco" and laughed. Her mother was surprised and asked Mary to read several words, which she proceeded to do. This element of surprise may well be related to the belief that parents hold that they are not teaching their children to read—this will happen once they start school.

Some Summary Comments

Comments by both parents and children about the project were almost universally positive, although it was also clear that our importuning sometimes added to what were already stressful lives. According to the parents, children often took the initiative in using the booklets (see also Chapter 9, this volume). They asked their parents to sing all the songs or read all the rhymes.

Some of the comments about the project follow:

"It has been pleasant during the time when you have visited us. It has also been interesting. My husband and I particularly think the small booklets have been fun and instructive. We have gotten so many easy and funny tips from the booklets concerning five finger rhymes, songs, etc."

"A few times I felt my integrity as a parent was challenged. But honestly, it can do good if you as a parent critically examine your relationship to the child and ask yourself if you can do something more to improve their development."

"When I am tired and have given what I might the project has felt like a burden—that I was obligated to read regularly and play regularly and stimulate."

"Very nice! We feel we are in a select company. In the beginning it was easy to do the activities but at the end (5-6 years old) we have felt a bit stressed just before you should come because we have not had time to do everything suggested in the booklets."

"Good! We got a push to stimulate our child a bit more, but most of the songs and plays they also do at the day care center."

"I was a little hesitant to do this because it might come in the first grade and cause the child to be bored in school. You should not know everything beforehand."

The answers we received indicated that the parents had been looking forward to the visits. They suggested that they needed a push to do this kind of activity more often and that they now realized how important these activities are. Furthermore, the answers indicate that they had found the project constructive, fun, and very interesting. Many parents have appreciated the tips through the booklets and others have appreciated the material for children. The answers indicated that the parents have thought about children's development just because of the project. Some said they had confirmed things they already knew but that they now understood better how important it is to put some extra time into these kinds of activities. A couple of parents said they had not been influenced at all and some parents said they had been a bit neglectful and indicated they sometimes had a bad conscience about it.

DISCUSSION

Changes were perceptible in the children's language development as well as in their micro environment, meaning that the parent's stimulation activities were affected. The intervention practices in the children's homes indicated that it was possible to influence language stimulation in the home as well as attitudes toward the children. The parents in the experimental group gave their children considerably more language stimulation than the parents in the control group. Almost all families in the experimental group read books every day, played regularly with nursery rhymes, did five-finger rhymes, and sang songs. Studies of individual children showed that it was possible to influence parents who did not stimulate the child very much at the age of two and a half years to increase the stimulation.

Our results indicate that, although most Swedish parents are already doing a great deal to stimulate their child's language and literacy—contributing to very high national literacy rates—some are not. But many, if not all, ofthese parents can be influenced to change. In a small country with a well established child health care system, there are great opportunities to inform most of the parents about the importance of stimulation of the children with relatively little effort.

7

A Microgenetic Study of Cognitive Reorganization During the Transition to Conventional Literacy

George Kamberelis and Michelle Perry

My eyes followed the black signs without skipping a single one, and I told myself a story aloud, being careful to utter all the syllables. I was taken by surprise—or saw to it that I was—a great fuss was made, and the family decided that it was time to teach me the alphabet. I was as zealous as a catechumen. I went so far as to give myself private lessons. I would climb up on the cot with Hector Malot's *No Family*, which I knew by heart, and, half reciting, half deciphering, I went through every page of it, one after the other. When the last page was turned, I knew how to read. I was wild with joy. (Sartre, 1964, 30)

Someone taught me to scribble out a versified reply [to my grandfather's poem letters]. I was urged to finish it, I was helped. When the two women sent off the letter, they laughed till the tears came at the thought of the recipient's astonishment. I received by return mail a poem to my glory; I replied with a poem. The habit was formed; the grandfather and his grandson were united by a new bond.... I wrote in imitation, for the sake of ceremony, in order to act like a grown-up; above all, I wrote because I was Charles Schweitzer's grandson. (Sartre 1964, 86-87)

As suggested by the juxtaposition of these two passages from Jean Paul Sartre's literacy narrative, *The Words*, learning to read and learning to write are by no means identical developmental processes. They differ in terms of linguistic knowledge, cognitive strategies, developmental timing, motivation, and function. And so to become conventionally literate—as both a reader and a writer—requires the integration of the different kinds of knowledge and strategies most crucial to both the comprehension and the production modes of written language.

Ostensibly, this integration seems a natural part of ontogenesis. However, it involves the development and coordination of many complex cognitive and metacognitive processes, some of which may actually impede the functioning of others at particular times in development. While a good deal of research has been done in the areas of both emergent literacy and early conventional literacy, much less research has explored the complex transitional period between the two. Specifically, very little work has addressed the issue of how children actually make the transition from emergent to conventional writing and reading. Even less research has focused on how children integrate the knowledge and strategies most central to becoming a conventional reader with those most central to becoming a conventional writer.

In the transitional period between emergent and conventional literacy, children integrate many constructs about reading and writing. This integrative process is complex, multileveled, dynamic, and recursive, and while engaged in it, children continually develop, test, and refine their theories about reading and writing (Ferreiro & Teberosky 1982). At any given time, children may hold different, even competing, knowledge and strategies about various aspects of reading, writing, and the relationships between the two. Moreover, it seems that during the transition to conventional literacy, children are faced with the task of integrating these many and partially conflicting understandings and strategies about reading and writing. In relation to this complex process, research in emergent literacy has suggested that the development of literacy in children does not proceed in a lockstep fashion and is not best characterized as having a smooth developmental trajectory (e.g., Clay 1979; Dyson 1986, 1988; Ferreiro & Teberosky 1982; Harste et al. 1984; Sulzby 1989; for a review, see Sulzby & Teale 1991). As children construct their literacy knowledge, they make many stops and starts, experience apparent regressions, and arrive at non-conventional constructions that seem peculiar and erroneous to literate adults. Eventually, however, they reorganize their literacy knowledge and strategies into systems that allow them to read and write in ways that we regard as conventional. The general goal of the study reported here is to illuminate this process of reorganization that leads to becoming conventionally literate.

The work reported in this chapter is based on a set of nine case studies of children who were followed longitudinally as they made the transition from emergent to conventional literacy. Fundamental to this transition is the integration of the relatively global lexical, semantic, and syntactic knowledge and strategies that have been shown to be so crucial to reading development and the more specific phonological and orthographic strategies that have been shown repeatedly to facilitate writing phonetic-based text and eventually spelling words conventionally. Among the global knowledge and strategies requisite for successful conventional reading are the concept of word (e.g., Morris, 1981), comprehension as meaning-construction (e.g. Pearson & Fielding, 1991), and structural knowledge of sentences and texts (e.g., Graesser, Golding, & Long 1991; Langer 1986). The specific knowledge and strategies crucial to spelling and writing development include the phonological and orthographic relations that underlie onset, rime, and letter-sound correspondences (e.g. Campbell 1985; Goswami 1988; Read 1986). Indeed, recent reviews by Adams (1990) and Goswami and Bryant (1990) have concluded with surprise that a disjunction exists between those strategies found to be central to reading and those central to spelling and writing.

The specific goal of the research reported in this chapter was to explore *markers* of cognitive change that occur as children became conventionally literate—that is, as they integrate more global lexical, semantic, and syntactic knowledge and strategies with more specific phonological ones. To accomplish this goal, we conducted microgenetic analyses of children's composing behaviors, metacognitive activity, and written products during the time that they moved through the transition from emergent to conventional literacy.

In relation to this goal, and following Luria (1984), R. A. Gundlach (personal communication, May 12, 1986), and Sulzby (1989), we defined *conventional literacy* as the integration of those strategies that are most useful for reading development with those that are most useful for writing development. Operationally, a child was considered to be conventionally literate if he or she produced a written text at least three clauses in length that both the child and a literate adult (with some knowledge of invented spelling) could read.

This operational definition of conventional literacy differs somewhat from other definitions of conventional literacy. Most other definitions rely either on reading tasks alone or on writing tasks alone, but not on writing-reading relationships. Moreover, most other definitions are often rooted in one or a combination of just a few of the many component skills within the complex activities of reading and writing. In connection with these points, because these definitions are derived from measures of conventional writing alone or conventional reading alone, they have little value with respect to understanding the integration of reading and writing. We argue that it is important to examine writing and reading in relation to one another and to define conventional literacy operationally as the ability to integrate these two cognitive-linguistic systems. This argument is rooted in the wealth of evidence (e.g., Ferreiro & Teberosky 1982; Sulzby, Barnhart, & Hieshima 1989) that demonstrates that, for quite a while before becoming conventionally literate, children have mastered many of the component skills for reading and writing. Thus, our operational definition is based on the hypothesis that the primary developmental task for children at this point in development is to polish and automate these component skills so that they can be integrated. With this integration, children will have reorganized their knowledge and thus obtained higher-level mental structures and functions. The specific result of this process is that children will be able to move fluidly and flexibly across reading and writing tasks.

Previous work by Kamberelis (1992; Kamberelis & Sulzby 1988) demonstrated a distinct developmental moment for many children wherein they produced narrative texts written in high-level invented spelling and conventional orthography but were unable to read back these texts when asked to do so. An example of this production-ahead-of-comprehension pattern is illustrated in Figure 7.1. This figure displays the child's actual handwritten personal narrative, his verbalizations while composing the text, and his unsuccessful attempts to read back his text upon request. Children who exhibited this production-ahead-of-comprehension pattern seemed to possess most or all of the components associated with conventional literacy but not to have integrated these components into a coherent whole. When watching these children write their stories, it appeared as if they put forth so much effort encoding microlevel structures (e.g., letter/sound relations on a word-by-word basis) that they lost sight of the need to integrate these microlevel structures with more macrolevel ones (e.g., words, phrases, syntax, story). While reading, the opposite seemed true. The children often seemed to focus almost exclusively on constructing meaning and to depend hardly at all on the more microlevel knowledge and strategies with which they had labored during writing. In general, the knowledge and strategies held by these children seemed neither well formed enough nor well integrated enough to work together fluidly and flexibly on both the difficult production tasks and

Figure 7.1
Text and Text Reading that Demonstrates the Production-Ahead-of-Comprehension Pattern

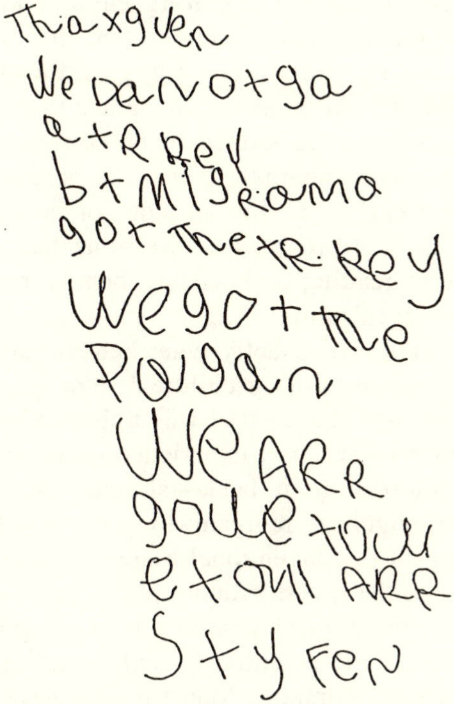

Child's Reading of His Story

We \d\ \d\ we did \d\ \ot\ we did, we went to our Grandma's. I got the, I got the third line, the second line, and the first line all wrong. We did \t\ oat oatmeal. We ate oatmeal instead of turkey. Grandma had the turkey in her fridge. Our Grandma said to eat our stuffing.

Adult's Reading of the Story

Thanksgiving. We did not get a turkey, but my grandma got the turkey. We got the pigeon. We are going to eat all our stuffing. (Words in the adult's reading corresponded to the words that the child uttered while composing the story.)

comprehension tasks they were asked to do. Importantly, and besides being a fascinating counter-intuitive phenomenon, the production-ahead-of-comprehension pattern turned out to be a good index of knowledge in transition. That is, children who displayed this pattern proved to be on the verge of integrating enough knowledge and strategies about both reading and writing so that they would soon be considered conventionally literate according to the definition presented above. In fact, all children who demonstrated this pattern in Kamberelis's (1992) study were judged to be conventionally literate soon thereafter (within two months). Thus, the production-ahead-of-comprehension pattern can be used as an index of imminent cognitive reorganization. As such, it provides a fortuitous benchmark for investigating changes in reading and writing behaviors and inferring changes in cognitive organization.

Careful documentation of exactly what behavioral and cognitive changes might be occurring during children's emergent reading and writing behaviors—through the point at which they exhibit this pattern and beyond this point to when they experience no trouble writing extended discourse and reading it back—should result in abundant knowledge about the cognitive reorganization that occurs during the transition from emergent to conventional literacy. Documenting such changes was the task of the investigation reported in this chapter.

As Siegler and Crowley (1991) point out, microgenetic accounts of developmental change are essential to understanding development in virtually all knowledge domains. Many studies have been done to see if particular kinds of knowledge or instruction are necessary for the achievement of conventional literacy—the most notable being phonemic awareness and whole word knowledge—but none have charted the many and various verbal-behavioral changes that occur as children make the transition to conventional literacy. Finally, close analysis of these verbal-behavioral changes is necessary if we are to make inferences about the cognitive changes that might accompany or even cause them, especially since these cognitive changes are likely to involve multiple and interacting components.

Based on these considerations, several specific research questions guided the present investigation of cognitive reorganization during the transition to conventional literacy. First, what changes in children's behavior occur as they make the transition to conventional literacy? Second, what might we infer about the cognitive changes that underlie these behavioral changes? Third, how do specific behaviors such as children's word recognition performances and their search behaviors during word recognition tasks change during the movement from emergent to conventional literacy? Fourth, what might be the functional import of these changes? Fifth, what changes in the amounts and kinds of metacognitive and metalinguistic comments accompany the achievement of conventional literacy? And, finally, how might these changes indicate changes in knowledge organization?

METHOD

Setting and Subjects

The study was conducted in a small city near Detroit. The population of the city is about 80 percent Caucasian and 20 percent non-Caucasian. The population of the school in which the study was conducted reflected the population at large. The classroom from which the children were selected was a whole-language classroom, for the most part. Most reading activities utilized trade books. The class had many "instructional conversations" (Tharp & Gallimore 1988) around the content and structures of these books. Children were engaged in both self-selected and assigned writing every day. The focus was almost always on composing extended discourse. Occasionally, pieces of writing would be reworked using the "writing process" approach advocated by Graves (1983) and Atwell (1987). In addition, children received about 10 minutes of phonics instruction in whole-group dialogic activities from September through December of the school year using the Phonovisual Phonics Incorporated materials and techniques. The teacher believed that without some working knowledge of phoneme-grapheme relations, children were at a disadvantage in trying to figure out English orthographic patterns. However, she also believed that such instruction should be short-lived and painless, involving lots of instructional discussions but no worksheets. Moreover, she always related the work done within the phonological awareness activities to the other reading and writing activities that occurred throughout the day.

Three boys and six girls participated in the study. Seven children were Caucasian and two were African-American. Six children were from working-class families and three were from professional families. At the beginning of the study, the children ranged in age from 5:11 (i.e., 5 years and 11 months) to 6:7, with a mean age of 6:4. Originally, there were 14 children in the study, but five children were excluded from the analysis for various reasons: two Asian children were excluded because they were only moderately proficient in English, which was their second language; one child was dropped because she was judged to be conventionally literate at the second data collection session; and two children were excluded because they had not yet achieved conventional literacy according to our operational definition by the end of the academic year.

Data Collection

To try to answer the research questions mentioned above, we conducted microgenetic case studies of these nine first-grade children. These studies began in late November of the school year and extended through May. No children were conventionally literate at the beginning of the study, but most were showing signs of becoming so soon. For example, these children could recognize no more than half of the preprimer words of the San Diego Word Recognition Inventory. They read below the frustration level in preprimer texts and they were beginning to use some phonetic-based spelling when asked to write individual words, but they hardly ever used phonetic-based text when asked to write extended discourse. We collected data from these children at approximately two-week intervals until several sessions after they were judged to be conventionally literate (according to the operational definition described earlier). All children were followed for between three and four months. All data-collection sessions were videotaped.

In all data-collection sessions, children were asked to write a story for the examiner. After the child had composed a story, he or she was asked to read the story to the examiner two times. In the first request, the examiner simply asked the child to read his or her story (e.g., the examiner would say, "That looks like a great story, read it to me so I can enjoy it"). In the second request, the examiner asked the child to read the story again and to point to it during the reading (e.g., the examiner would say "What a wonderful story; read it to me again, and this time point as you read"). If the child had pointed during the first reading, the request for pointing was omitted. The reason that we asked children to point was that we were also collecting data on the role of gesture in the integration of reading and writing strategies (Perry & Kamberelis 1993).

After children had read their stories twice, they were engaged in a word-recognition task, using the words in their own stories as task stimuli. The examiner asked each child to locate each word in his or her story. Each word was probed individually on two occasions in random order. This task was conducted to get a sense of children's ability to recognize individual words that they had written and also to examine their search behaviors. We expected that children might be able to locate individual words that they had written before they could read back their entire texts. This expectation was based on the considerable amount of evidence that children have mastered many component skills (e.g., locating individual words) before they organize them into more complex cognitive structures that are dependent upon the integration of reading and writing.

Coding

All written texts were coded for directionality (i.e., whether they were composed from left to right), orthographic representation, and evidence of perceptually distinct word boundaries. All readings were coded for reading level using a revised version of Sulzby's (1985) taxonomy. Judgments about when children were considered conventionally literate were made independently by two researchers. Interjudge agreement was 94 percent. All verbal transcripts of experimental sessions were coded for various kinds of metacognitive comments produced during the writing and reading tasks. In particular, comments were coded in terms of whether they focused on phonological and orthographic features or on more global linguistic features such as lexical choice, semantics, sentential and text-level syntax, pragmatic considerations, and genre.

RESULTS

All written texts were analyzed using descriptive and inferential statistics, where appropriate, for the different patterns of orthography (i.e., non-phonetic letter strings, syllabic invented spelling, intermediate invented spelling, full invented spelling, and conventional spelling) and for the presence of clear-cut word boundaries. All texts were also analyzed for differences across sessions in word recognition performance. Finally, all verbal transcripts were analyzed for changes in metacognitive commentary and metalinguistic awareness. Results of these analyses are presented in order, preceded by very brief summaries of theoretical positions and research findings relevant to the issues analyzed.

Orthography

Invented spellings seem to occur as a function of the many hypotheses children develop to translate speech sounds into graphemes, only one of which is visual. Many empirical studies and literature reviews (e.g., Adams 1990; Bradley & Bryant 1983; Bryant, Maclean, & Bradley 1990; Goswami & Bryant 1990; Lundberg, Frost, & Petersen 1988; Morais, Bertelson, Carey, & Alegria 1986; Yopp 1988) have concluded that a fair degree of phoneme-grapheme knowledge is necessary, and perhaps sufficient, for literacy acquisition. Other researchers (e.g., Read 1986; Graves 1983; Morris 1981; Chomsky 1981; Ferreiro & Teberosky 1982) have found that children continue to use various kinds of invented spelling patterns long after they can read and write fluently. Reconciling these perspectives, one might argue for some sort of critical mass of phoneme-grapheme knowledge that is necessary for the acquisition of literacy, but also suspect that a good deal of orthographic development would occur after this point. Figure 7.2 shows the mean percentages for the five orthographic patterns displayed by children in this study.

The percentages that are represented with a bold line are percentages of words in the children's texts in which all speech sounds were represented. In other words, this bold line represents the sum of percentages of the conventional spellings and the full invented spellings. This index of orthographic development is probably the most critical index in relation to the definition of conventional literacy mentioned earlier, in the sense that the more completely encoding is achieved, the more decoding will be facilitated (Newell & Simon 1972). When all speech sounds are represented, even if not conventionally, texts ought to be relatively easy for the children who produced them, and for adults, to read .

Figure 7.2
Orthographic Patterns Used by Children

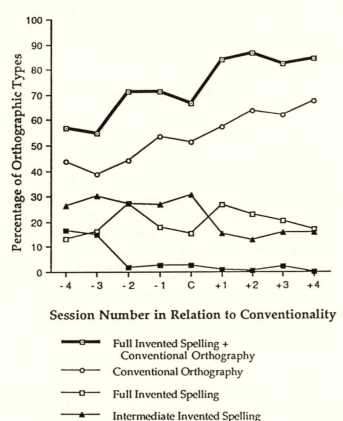

Session Number in Relation to Conventionality

—□—	Full Invented Spelling + Conventional Orthography
—○—	Conventional Orthography
—□—	Full Invented Spelling
—▲—	Intermediate Invented Spelling
—■—	Syllabic Invented Spelling

As Figure 7.2 shows, there was a steady, although not remarkable, growth in the quality of children's graphic representations of sounds before the achievement of conventional literacy. This increase was due almost entirely to an increase in conventionally spelled words (there was no substantial increase in any other type of orthographic representation). Moreover, careful analysis of the children's texts revealed that the specific types of words that children were spelling correctly with increased frequency were mostly one- or two-syllable, high-frequency words. This finding is important and will be discussed in greater detail when we consider children's developing concept of word.

We compared the mean percentages of conventional-plus-full invented spellings before versus after the achievement of conventional literacy and found that these percentages were significantly different from each other (t (8) = 4.06, $p < .004$). A careful look at Figure 7.2, however, reveals a positive but very shallow developmental slope prior to the achievement of conventional literacy, a jump just after the conventional point, and a complete leveling off thereafter. This suggests that it was more likely that conventional literacy facilitated the development of children's orthographic representation than the opposite (i.e., that orthographic development led to the achievement of conventional literacy). While the development of orthographic representation, in the sense of mastery or in the sense of a new-found skill, does not appear to be necessary for conventional literacy, it may still be true that some kind of critical mass of skill and knowledge about orthographic representation is requisite for decoding written messages. If this is the case, it would appear that approximately 70 percent of the speech sounds need to be represented graphically for children to systematically and reliably read back the texts that they compose.

Word Boundaries

Many researchers (e.g., Morris 1981; Spencer & Afflerbach 1988; Sulzby 1981) have suggested that clear-cut word boundaries are crucial to the achievement of conventional literacy. They argue, moreover, that children learn written words as structural or perceptual units before they learn them as semantic units.

Results of the extent to which children marked lexical units with clear-cut word boundaries in this study are shown in Figure 7.3. As this figure indicates, there was a systematic and substantial increase in the mean number of words in the children's texts marked by clear-cut boundaries before the achievement of conventional literacy. After that, relatively little development occurred. We compared the use of clear-cut word boundaries before versus after the achievement of conventional literacy and found a significant difference between these two phases of development (t (8)=4.30, $p < .003$). The steep increase in marking clear-cut word boundaries before conventional literacy, together with the marginal increase after that point, suggests that children's developing understanding of words as distinct linguistic units

Figure 7.3
Mean Percentages of Words Marked with Perceptually
Distinct Word Boundaries

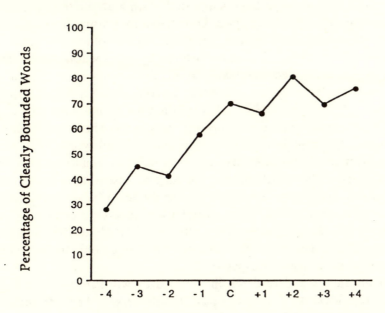

Session Number in Relation to Conventionality

may have been quite important to the achievement of conventional literacy as we have defined it. The importance of children's developing concept of word in the achievement of conventional literacy also was supported by the patterns of word recognition exhibited by the children over the course of the study. Accordingly, it is to the results from the word location task that we now turn.

Word Recognition and Location

For over a decade, literacy researchers have been engaged in a polarized and polarizing debate about the relative importance of word recognition or sight vocabulary in literacy development. A large number of theorists and researchers have argued that, in comparison to global lexical knowledge, knowledge about phonetic decoding/recoding is a much more important factor in learning how to read

(e.g., Ehri 1991; Gough & Tunmer 1986). Indeed, most basal reading programs have been organized in response to this position.
Moreover, recent theory and research based on the principles of parallel distributed processing have supported claims about the centrality
of phonological and orthographic knowledge in learning how to read
(e.g., Seidenberg & McClelland 1989). However, other theorists and
researchers have argued that children typically learn whole words first,
and, if they develop decoding skills at all, this occurs later, even after
they are actually reading extended discourse (e.g., Goodman &
Goodman 1979; Smith 1988). This position has found support in research on acquired dyslexia syndromes, which has shown that people
with certain types of brain lesions are able to read words that were
learned prior to the acquired dyslexia but have tremendous difficulty
reading non-words. Still other theorists and researchers have suggested the plausibility of a multiple access model of word recognition
wherein phonemes, morphemes, and lexical units are processed almost
simultaneously during reading (e.g., Juel 1991; Perfetti 1985; Sulzby
& Teale 1991). However, the precise relations among these related
processes remain largely unspecified.

In sum, theory and research in the area of word recognition have
evolved considerably during the past decade or so. The voluminous
and sometimes contradictory findings within the extant research literature on word recognition attest both to the importance of this component in learning how to read and to the complexity of word recognition as a psychological phenomenon. Indeed, following Lakatos
(1970), Stanonvich (1991) has argued that, despite partially
conflicting accounts of the cognitive processes involved in word
recognition, the "content-increasing" problem shift in theory and
research in this area signals its generative and progressive nature as a
scientific enterprise. Moreover, although many questions remain
unanswered with respect to describing and modeling the process(es)
of word recognition, virtually all theorists and researchers maintain
that word recognition is a foundation process (perhaps *the* foundation
process) of reading (Ehri 1991; Stanovich 1991).

The word recognition performance demonstrated by the children
in this study is shown in Figure 7.4. It is important to keep in mind
when viewing this figure that the word recognition task that we developed for this study was distinctly different from most word recognition
tasks. It required children to locate words in their own texts rather than
to read from graded word lists. The nature of this task is important

Figure 7.4
Mean Percentages of Words Recognized by Children in Their Self-Produced Texts

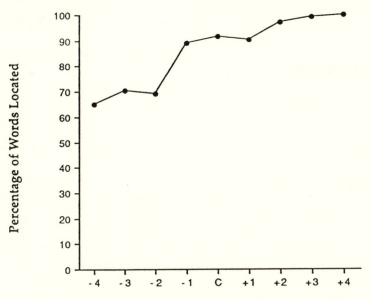

Session Number in Relation to Conventionality

because it is closely related to the integration of reading and writing on which our definition of conventional literacy pivots. The orthography and spacing of most of the texts that children had to use as stimuli were often far from conventional, especially early on in the study. Yet, as this figure demonstrates, the children exhibited a systematic and substantial increase in the mean number of words recognized and located before achieving conventional literacy. In fact, children had pretty much reached a ceiling in their performance before they were judged to be conventionally literate. We found a significant difference in word recognition performance before versus after the achievement of conventional literacy, (t (8)=4.98, p < .002.) It is clear from examining Figure 7.4 that this difference is accounted for largely by the relatively low initial performance at the beginning of our study and then a steep growth several sessions before achieving conventional literacy. As with the results from the analysis of word boundaries, this pattern seems to suggest that children's understanding

Figure 7.5
Word Recognition, Word Boundaries and Spelling

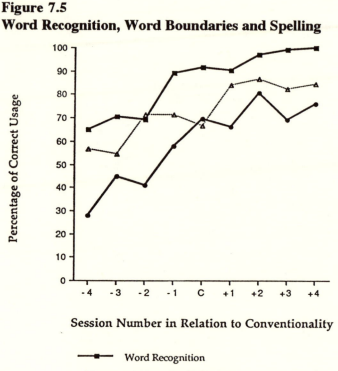

Session Number in Relation to Conventionality

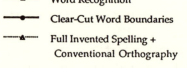

of word as a concept may be necessary for the achievement of conventional literacy as we have defined it. It is also noteworthy that before achieving conventional literacy, children's growth on this task and on the word boundary task far out stripped their growth in orthographic representation (see Figure 7.5). At the beginning of the study, for example, children recognized and located approximately 65 percent of the words in their texts; by the time they were judged to be conventionally literate, children's word recognition and location performance had increased to 91 percent, which represents an improvement of 26 percent. Similarly, in the beginning of the study, children were creating clear-cut word boundaries only about 27 percent of the time; this increased to approximately 70 percent by the time children were judged to be conventionally literate, which represents an improvement of 43 percent. Note that both of these measures of children's understanding of word as a critical unit in producing and comprehending text showed a pattern of large growth in the few sessions preceding the onset of conventional literacy.

In contrast, at the beginning of the study, children were representing all of the phonemes in the words that they wrote about 58 percent of the time. By the time they were judged to be conventionally literate, they were representing all of the phonemes in the words that they wrote about 67 percent of the time. This represents an improvement of only 9 percent. Note that a large increase in the skill of representing phonemes in text production only occurred after conventional literacy had been achieved. From these data, it appears quite possible that the achievement of conventional literacy is dependent on the concept of word as a critical unit of analysis.

These findings suggest that children's concept of word, as indexed by their word recognition performances and their increased tendency to mark words as distinct perceptual units, developed somewhat independently of their abilitiy to adequately encode all of the sounds in the lexical items in their texts. These findings also indicate that children's developing concept of word was not entirely dependent on their ability to separate lexical items perceptually with the use of spaces (or other indicators such as dashes). Indeed, even when words were marked by clear boundaries only 70 percent of the time, they were recognized and located by children 91 percent of the time.

In relation to this point, several aspects of the data suggest that children were developing perceptual and semantic components of the concept of word simultaneously, and that they were employing semantic and syntactic strategies in the development of this concept. First, as we have already mentioned, children's word recognition performance outstripped their abilities to create word boundaries and to represent phonemes orthographically, suggesting that children were using more than perceptual clues in the word location task. Otherwise, they could not have done as well as they did. What other clues might they have been using? Our data suggest that children were increasingly using several additional kinds of semantic and syntactic clues. The use of these clues was inferred from distinct changes in children's search behaviors during the word recognition task.

Children's search behaviors changed considerably during the course of the study. Early on in the study, most children searched randomly when asked to locate words in their texts. Despite these random searches and the fact that the children could not read their texts when asked to do so, they had surprising success. However, from approximately several weeks before they were judged to be conventionally literate and throughout the remainder of the study, children experienced much more success. This increased success was systematically related to several behavioral changes that we observed. For example, children began to read their texts (or sections of them) systematically until they found the words they were looking for. In connection with this point, they began to rely more heavily on lexical and syntactic markers in their searches. In particular, they began to use definite articles and prepositions as clues during searches for nouns. Also, they used nouns and noun phrases as clues in their searches for verbs. In addition to becoming much more systematic in their word search strategies, children began to locate multiple instances of words as they approached conventional literacy. Children's increased use of the syntactic and semantic features of their texts in their attempts to locate particular words appears to be important during the transition to conventional literacy, an issue we will treat in connection with metacognition and metalinguistic awareness.

As we noted earlier, the quality of children's orthography increased gradually in the course of the study. Yet, there was no marked increase in the quality of orthographic representation before the achievement of conventional literacy. Thus, it is unlikely that better orthographic representation played a major facilitative role in that achievement. However, it remains possible that a critical mass of phoneme-grapheme knowledge is necessary for the transition to conventional literacy to be accomplished. If this is true, a certain proportion of words with complete orthographic representation may simply have facilitated the use of more global word recognition strategies. In this way, letter-sound knowledge would not be sufficient for achieving conventional literacy as we have defined it; instead, a certain amount of letter-sound knowledge would facilitate the encoding and decoding of words at a level that is high enough to facilitate writing and reading a text. Support for this speculation includes the fact that most of the increase in children's development in orthographic representation was accounted for by high-frequency, single-syllable and two-syllable words that were spelled conventionally. This finding suggests that increased iconic knowledge of these kinds of words rather than increased knowledge of phoneme-grapheme relations may have accounted for ostensible growth in orthographic representation. Further evidence for the larger role played by a more sophisticated concept of word and concomitant global word recognition strategies was the tremendous development in the construction of clear-cut word boundaries and the dramatic increase in word recognition and location performance that occurred as children approached conventional literacy. Taken together, these findings suggest the importance of having a stable concept of word for the acquisition of conventional literacy.

These findings also suggest that this concept of word has both perceptual and semantic components. Moreover, it seems that word meanings and the grammatical relations among words are at least as critical for success in the word recognition tasks as more specific and concrete characteristics of the words themselves—characteristics such as spelling and spacing. In connection with this point, it is likely that the integration of reading and writing skills and strategies was more related to children's increased, albeit perhaps tacit, understanding of language as a system organized at a variety of levels—phonological, semantic, syntactic—than it was related specifically to understanding phonological and orthographic rules. Examining the various aspects of literacy that we have discussed so far in relation to one another supports the view that the major developmental task in finally achieving conventional literacy is the reorganization and integration of several already fairly well-learned skills and strategies. Before achieving conventional literacy, children demonstrated good encoding skills; they were creating clear-cut word boundaries in their texts and they exhibited excellent word recognition performance in an isolated word recognition task. However, they could not read their texts when asked to do so. The complex task of reading involves integrating all of the skills just mentioned (as well as comprehension strategies). Before being judged conventionally literate, children did not appear to have integrated these skills so that they could fluidly and flexibly draw on them as they attempted to read their own texts.

Metacognition and Metalinguistic Awareness

In addition to examining changes in text characteristics and word recognition performance during the transition to conventional literacy, we also coded and analyzed the spontaneous metacognitive and metalinguistic comments made by the children as they wrote and then read their texts. We thought that changes in the character of these comments would provide another window into understanding what might have been involved in the cognitive reorganization that seemed to allow for the integration of production and comprehension modalities of literacy. Thus, we examined spontaneous metacognitive and metalinguistic comments to gain access to the issues with which the children were grappling as they attempted to integrate and organize their developing knowledge and strategies.

Some researchers (e.g., Karmiloff-Smith 1985; Markman 1979) have found that increased metacognitive activity appears just before the acquisition of a new concept and seems to reflect the child's increasing knowledge of the concept. Other researchers (e.g., Case 1985; Schroeder, Driver, & Streufert 1967; Sternberg 1984) have found that increased metacognitive activity occurs just after the acquisition of a new concept. The explanation underlying this second finding has been that the cognitive demands of performance need to decrease before reflection on performance is possible.

Although none of the research we have reviewed has compared metacognitive and metalinguistic activity both before and after the acquisition of a new concept, one might expect that this activity should differ both in form and function depending on when it occurred. It does not seem necessary that we would have to choose between these two different theoretical accounts of the timing and functions of metacognition. In fact, it seems reasonable to suspect that metacognition, if investigated at different moments in development, might sometimes mark cognitive growth and thus be an epiphenomenon of cognitive change, sometimes actually facilitate cognitive change, and sometimes be a product of conceptual reorganization. However, we expect that the nature and focus of metacognitive activity would be different during different phases of development. To explore this possibility, it is necessary to account not only for the amount of metacognitive activity but also the content of that activity at particular times in ontogenesis.

In the present study, all transcripts of children's spontaneous talk during reading and writing activities were transcribed and segmented into clausal units. According to this segmenting procedure, any stretch of extended discourse containing a verb phrase was counted as a clause (Berman, Slobin, Bamberg, Dromi, Marchman, Neeman, Renner, & Sebastian, 1986). After children's texts were segmented by clause, all spontaneous metacognitive and metalinguistic comments

Figure 7.6
Clauses Containing Metalinguistic or Metacognitive Comments

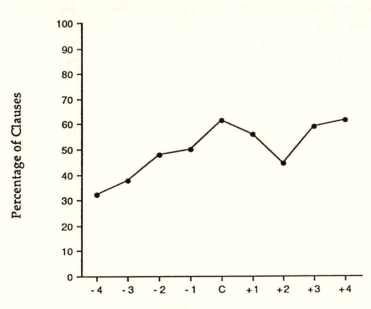

Session Number in Relation to Conventionality

were coded using a scheme developed from the data. This coding scheme appears in the appendix. Percentages of clauses containing each type of metacognitive or metalinguistic comment were computed in relation to the total number of clauses in the transcripts. The percentages of all types of metacognitive and metalinguistic comments uttered during each session are shown in Figure 7.6. As the figure indicates, metacognitive and metalinguistic activity increased systematically and substantially as children approached the achievement of conventional literacy and then leveled off. The finding of a systematic increase in metacognition and metalinguistic awareness before the achievement of conventional literacy suggests that these skills may play a facilitative role in development.

To try to determine this role, we analyzed the particular kinds of metacognitive comments uttered by children. Since we were particularly interested in the integration of the global lexical, semantic, and syntactic knowledge typically associated with successful reading with the more specific phonological and orthographic knowledge requisite for phonetic-based (especially conventional) writing, we examined the metacognitive and metalinguistic codes in terms of two comprehensive categories: (1) comments about sublexical linguistic units (e.g., letters, sounds, onsets, rimes, spelling) and (2) comments about superlexical linguistic units (e.g., lexical choice, semantics, sentential and textual syntax, pragmatics). Figure 7.7 shows the microgenetic developmental patterns of comments about sublexical and superlexical linguistic units.

Figure 7.7
Mean Percentages of Comments About Either Sublexical   or Superlexical Linguistic Units

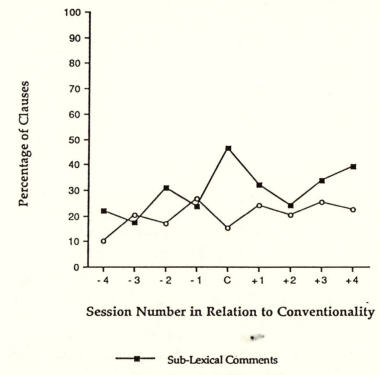

Session Number in Relation to Conventionality

———■——— Sub-Lexical Comments
———○——— Super-Lexical Comments

The general pattern of these results demonstrates that children were engaged in considerable and relatively equal amounts of metacognitive and metalinguistic inquiry that focused on both sublexical and superlexical linguistic units both before and after achieving conventional literacy. Moreover, and more interesting, children's engagement in talk about sublexical linguistic units reached a peak and their talk about superlexical linguistic units diminished considerably at just the time when they became conventionally literate. Even more interesting is the fact that 72 percent of all comments about sublexical linguistic units focused on onsets. Taken together, these findings suggest at least two things. First, it appears that an increased awareness of phonological and orthographic rules and relations was especially critical in the final integration of production and comprehension knowledge and strategies. If not exactly critical, it was certainly a salient focus of children's metacommentary. Yet, exactly how sublexical knowledge functioned for these children is difficult to say. One plausible hypothesis is the obvious one, namely that children need to develop sufficient working knowledge of both the encoding and decoding dimensions of phoneme-grapheme relations to integrate reading and writing knowledge and strategies. An alternative hypothesis—and one that fits somewhat better with many of the other findings in this study—is that children's intense focus on sublexical linguistic and metalinguistic knowledge was somehow related to their development of a more integrated and viable concept of word. Viewed from this hypothetical perch, sounding out and talking about onsets might have functioned much like using determiners to find nouns in the word location task, namely as cues in detecting words and perhaps in constructing meaning.

Second, and in relation to this suggestion, our results clearly demonstrated that children's knowledge about sublexical linguistic units developed in tandem with their knowledge about superlexical units. This suggests that both kinds of knowledge were necessary for the achievement of conventional literacy, as well as the possibility that both kinds of knowledge might have functioned to facilitate one another. In other words, although it is clear that children focused quite intensely on phonological and orthographic components of reading and writing just as they integrated reading and writing strategies, the cognitive developmental context in which this intense focus was embedded consisted of considerable knowledge about many levels of linguistic organization (e.g., phonological, orthographic, lexical, semantic, and syntactic) and the relationships among those levels. Indeed, when we examine all the evidence from this study together, it seems clear that many different kinds of linguistic knowledge operating in concert contributed to children's achievement of conventional literacy.

SUMMARY AND CONCLUSIONS

What preliminary conclusions may be drawn about cognitive re-organization during the transition to conventional literacy and about the possible mechanisms at work in the integration of reading (comprehension) and writing (production) knowledge and strategies? First, our data suggest a unique role for phonological and ortho-graphic knowledge in this transitional process. Phonological and or-thographic knowledge appear to be crucial at just the point when chil-dren are about to make the transition to conventional literacy, as was evidenced by the relatively large amount of metacognitive comments produced at this point in development. However, when viewed through a more wide-angled lens, the role of phonological and ortho-graphic knowledge appears less important to the integration of read-ing and writing knowledge and strategies when compared to other conceptual achievements. Recall that changes in orthographic repre-sentation within children's texts were few and gradual throughout the period before they were judged to be conventionally literate. We have raised the possibility that children may need to develop a certain amount—a critical mass—of knowledge about phonological and or-thographic rules and relations in order to integrate reading and writ-ing, but that the development of other kinds of linguistic knowledge are equally, or, potentially, more important.

We offer this interpretation even though children vocalized a con-siderable number of metalinguistic comments about letters, sounds, and spelling just when they were judged to be conventionally literate. Is this not a contradiction? On the basis of other findings in this study we think not, for several reasons. First, despite the flurry of children's comments about phonological and orthographic relations, there was virtually no temporally related improvement in the quality of their spellings. Moreover, what orthographic progress children did make was accounted for almost entirely by conventionally spelled, high-fre-quency, one- and two-syllable words. Additionally, 72 percent of children's comments about sublexical linguistic units focused on on-sets, suggesting that this focus operated in relation to children's de-veloping concept of word. Also note that, after integrating their reading and writing knowledge and strategies, children's orthography improved substantially, despite a concomitant diminishing of the vo-calization of metacognitive and metalinguistic utterances about these sub-lexical linguistic units.

Second, and related to the first observation, children's intense focus on sublexical linguistic units may have served a couple of different functions. It may have functioned to encode or decode onsets, rimes, or specific phonemes. Or, less obviously, it may have functioned to encode and/or index more global units such as particular words. Indeed, children's predominant focus on onsets suggests the increased plausibility of this latter interpretation. If this is so, children's metacognitive and metalinguistic activity may have been more related to their rapidly developing concept of word than their developing knowledge of phonological and orthographic relations. Although ostensibly it would appear to be the case, talking about letters and sounds does not guarantee that one is trying to work out phoneme-grapheme relations.

Third, children produced many metacognitive and metalinguistic utterances about various levels of linguistic organization both before and after achieving conventional literacy, suggesting that their short-lived intense focus on phoneme-grapheme relations was not independent of their developing knowledge about other levels of linguistic organization, specifically the concept of word, syntactic logic, and semantic relations. What contributions to the achievement of conventional literacy might the development of knowledge of these linguistic dimensions have made?

Several pieces of evidence discovered in this study suggest that children's developing concept of word played a critical role in children's achievement of conventional literacy defined as the integration of reading and writing knowledge and strategies. First, children's word recognition performance increased dramatically from the beginning of the study to the time they were judged to be conventionally literate (from 65 percent to 91 percent). Second, children's instantiation of clear-cut perceptual word boundaries also increased considerably during this time (from 27 percent to 70 percent). Third, children provided substantial evidence that their developing concept of word was not entirely dependent on their ability to separate lexical items perceptually. Even when words were marked by clear boundaries only 70 percent of the time, they were recognized and located by children 91 percent of the time. Additionally, children's word search behaviors indicated that they were relying increasingly on semantic and syntactic knowledge and strategies in locating and identifying particular words. Finally, most of children's metacommentary about sublexical linguistic units suggested that they were using onsets in the service of reading and writing whole words. Taken together, these findings suggest that children's developing concept of word was comprised of perceptual, phonological, semantic, and morphosyntactic components.

In relation to this point, findings from our inquiry into children's metacognitive and metalinguistic activity supported the idea that they were simultaneously working out their understanding of phonological, orthographic, lexical, semantic, and syntactic dimensions of written language production and comprehension. Moreover, taken together, the various findings of this study suggest that development along each of these dimensions did not operate independently of development along the other dimensions. Rather, increased knowledge about each level of linguistic organization appeared to scaffold the development of knowledge about the other levels. While it was clear from this study that increased knowledge about phonology, orthography, concept of word, semantic content, and syntactic structure all contributed to children's achievement of conventional literacy, it was much less clear that knowledge about any one of these linguistic domains should be privileged as most important. Having said this, however, we should reiterate that we did find abundant evidence for suggesting a central role played by children's developing concept of word in their achievement of conventional literacy. However, this evidence also implicated their developing knowledge of semantics, morphosyntax, and, perhaps, even phonology and orthography in children's increasingly sophisticated understanding of lexis.

To summarize, it appears that children have at least a tacit understanding of most of the levels of linguistic organization—phonology, orthography, lexis, semantics, and syntax—before becoming conventionally literate. Understanding and integrating these various levels of organization and coming to understand language as a system of relations among these levels appears to be a primary developmental task in the achievement of conventional literacy. This theoretical explanation fits well with Ehri's (1978) psycholinguistic model of beginning reading:

> It appears that initially the identities imposed on a new word are primarily syntactic and semantic rather than phonological, that these cues are amalgamated with only some graphic symbols in the word, and that only gradually the full printed form becomes associated with the abstract stored form stored in the lexicon. (p. 17)

In spite of Ehri's formulation, most research on the achievement of conventional literacy has continued to investigate the forms and functions of development within but not across each of these linguistic levels. Almost no research has been devoted to understanding the complex relationships among these levels or the ways in which development within particular levels might influence development within others. This tendency may be due, in part, to the fact that most research has focused on reading alone or writing alone but not on reading—writing relationships. Findings from this exploratory study suggest that research of this nature would be fruitful in our continuing attempts to understand the developmental moment in which children first move fluidly and flexibly across reading and writing tasks and thus, are considered to be conventionally literate.

IMPLICATIONS AND FUTURE DIRECTIONS

This study has several implications both for research and classroom practice. First, as Goswami and Bryant (1990) and A. D. Pellegrini (personal communication, May 20, 1991, Chapter Two, this volume) have suggested, and as the results of this study imply, while they are related activities, reading and writing appear to be largely distinct cognitive processes during early literacy development. The extent to which this is true needs to be examined in much greater detail.

Second, we paid little attention in this study to the instructional context and the possible role of instruction in children's achievement of conventional literacy. While there is some evidence that specific instruction about phonics, word recognition, reading comprehension, and the like played little if any direct role in the integration of reading and writing, careful studies should be conducted that pay more attention to the instructional context. Such studies should document not only the content of instruction but also the discourse patterns in which the content is embedded. The reason for this is that children's metadiscourse about the various levels of linguistic organization seemed quite important in their integration of reading and writing knowledge and strategies.

Third, while the spontaneous metadiscourse produced by children as they negotiated the reading and writing tasks of this study revealed much about the cognitive work in which they were engaged, future studies would benefit from collecting metacognitive and metalinguistic data somewhat more systematically. One way to do this would be to train children to conduct think-aloud protocols as they worked on the writing and reading tasks rather than relying simply on spontaneously uttered commentary.   Another way to collect metacognitive and metalinguistic data more systematically would be to conduct interviews in close conjunction with each reading and writing session that were designed to tap children's knowledge and strategies about different levels of linguistic organization.   Both of these techniques would increase the probability of yielding data that would contribute to a more systematic understanding of children's developing concepts about the levels of linguistic organization and the relationships among those concepts. It would provide a window into children's developing ability to operate on language as an object of knowledge. Viewed in relation to children's performance on reading and writing tasks, an understanding of children's developing linguistic and metalinguistic knowledge would be very useful in documenting the mechanisms at work as children make the transition to conventional literacy.

So far, we have discussed some of the implications of our findings for future research. These findings also have implications for classroom instruction. First, if the transitional period just before the achievement of conventional literacy is as dynamic a time of development and learning as this study suggests, it would be useful for teachers to have some understanding of the cognitive changes that children are undergoing during this period. Second, a better understanding of this dynamic developmental period would be useful to teachers in designing activities that might facilitate critical components of the transition process. It would also be useful in making decisions about how to time instructional activities to support particular components of literacy more appropriately. Finally, it might suggest principled ways in which to integrate these different instructional activities to make them mutually reinforcing.

In relation to the issue of timing, different instructional emphases may be more appropriate for different moments in development. For example, based on the patterns of children's metacognitive and metalinguistic activity in this study, instructional conversations about phonological and orthographic processes and relations might be most useful just as teachers suspect that children are about to integrate the more global knowledge and strategies that facilitate successful reading with the more specific phonological and orthographic ones associated with success in writing. In relation to integrating instructional activities more strategically, activities designed to facilitate children's developing concept of word might be integrated with activities designed to scaffold semantic and syntactic knowledge.

One of the primary findings of this study was the extent to which children's increased success on the word recognition task was related to their increased use of semantic and morphosyntactic clues. More generally, and as Siegler (1986, 1989) predicted, we found substantial evidence that the development of each isolated dimension of written language understanding that we investigated reflected contributions from the development of many other dimensions. This suggests that the achievement of conventional literacy was intimately related to children's developing ability to operate on written language as an object of study and analysis. Indeed, we found abundant evidence in our inquiry into children's metacognitive and metalinguistic commentary to suggest that they were trying to construct increasingly more adequate theories of language as a system of relationships among component processes. Wertsch (1985, 33-40) has referred to this process as the increased decontextualization of mediational means, and he has called attention to the fact that, for Vygotsky (1962, 1978), this process was conceived as the fundamental mechanism of cognitive development and self-regulation. In consideration of the importance of this process, it might be quite valuable to create language-arts activities that better scaffold children's attempts to analyze and reconstruct the components of their written language systems into increasingly more powerful ones (Lindfors 1987; Pappas & Brown 1987; Villaume 1988).

This study has provided an intensive, multileveled analysis of cognitive reorganization during the acquisition of conventional literacy, which was defined as the integration of reading and writing behaviors and the ability to move flexibly across reading and writing tasks. In becoming conventionally literate, the children in this study had to coordinate multiple types of interdependent knowledge and strategies. Discovering and demonstrating how various cognitive and linguistic processes operated in concert during this transitional period was possible, in part, because of the microgenetic method that we employed. Without following children closely and at frequent intervals, and without focusing on multiple levels of linguistic analysis simultaneously, the ways in which children's knowledge and strategies developed co-constitutively and were coordinated to facilitate conventional literacy might well have been missed.

In conclusion, we have begun to describe and explicate how knowledge and strategies at multiple levels of linguistic organization operate interdependently to facilitate the achievement of conventional literacy. However, further research is needed to understand more fully the complex processes of cognitive reorganization that occur as children become conventionally literate. Broadening and deepening our understanding of these processes, both in terms of what constitutes cognitive change and what influences that change, will help us to understand and to facilitate this important developmental achievement.

NOTE

This research was partially funded by grants to the second author from the Spencer Foundation and the University of Michigan. We thank these institutions and, also, John Ifcher, Taunya Beddingfield, Laura Ditchik for their assistance at various stages of this research.

APPENDIX

Coding Categories for Superlexical Metacognitive and Metalinguistic Comments

1. *Comments about Syntax, Semantics, or Text Grammar* The child commented specifically about task-relevant language (e.g., "I wrote it two times" or "I'm sure I wrote *fun* somewhere; now where is it?" or "I think that should say 'I ran to the car,' not 'I ran the car'").

2. *Planning of Syntax, Semantics, or Text Grammar* The child explicitly mentioned that he or she was considering how to deal with the text (e.g., "I am going to write the part about the slide before the part about Jason").

3. *Monitoring by Reading* The child read aloud to figure out where he or she was, or the child reread a section of text before composing a new section.

4. *Problem Recognition and/or Correction of Syntax, Semantics, or Text Grammar* The child realized that something about the structure or meaning of his or her text was misrepresented (e.g., "I *like*. . . I . . . I mean . . . I *have fun* there," or "Oops, that says 'I went to the mall Saturday.' It should say, 'I went shopping at the mall on Saturday'").

Coding Categories for Sublexical Metacognitive and Metalinguistic Comments

1. *Comments About Phonology and Orthography* As in the category "Comments about Syntax, Semantics, or Text Grammar," the child attended to the language of the text but in relation specifically to spelling or decoding (e.g., "I don't know how to spell Disney," or "I don't know what 'c' 'h' sounds like").

2. *Planning the Encoding or Decoding of Sounds and Syllables* The child explicitly mentioned that he or she was considering how to spell or decode parts of lexical units (e.g., "Does *fight* end with 't' or an 'e'").

3. *Monitoring by Sounding Out* The child uttered the sound components of words as he or she composed them or read them (e.g., "\Dis\ . . . \Dis\ . . . \Dis\ . . . \ney\ . . . \Disney\" or "\Ch\ . . . \Ch\ . . . this must be Chevy Chase").

4. *Problem Recognition and/or Correction of Encoding or Decoding* The child diagnosed and attempted to correct problems with spelling or deciphering words by focusing on their speech sounds (e.g., "House isn't spelled like that. It should be 'h' 'o' 'u' 's'" or "Then he, no, \th\ . . . \r\ . . . there he found. . .").

Part Two

The Design of Early Literacy Environments

8

Stimulating/Simulating Environments That Support Emergent Literacy

David F. Lancy, with Susan D. Talley

THE CHILDREN ARE DROWNING

Early last summer—as boating season approached—a close associate, in response to some query from me, mentioned that she had never learned to swim. Inevitably, I found this revelation—an otherwise normal person who cannot swim—deeply shocking. Why? I suppose because swimming seems so natural—like walking. Of course, it isn't *entirely* natural, since someone has to teach you to swim, but it always seemed so easy to learn. And isn't it also natural for a parent to feel obligated to insure that his or her child can swim—for safety's sake if no other? Second, perhaps I am shocked because I have always taken so much pleasure from water sports and being able to swim is a gateway to waterskiing, SCUBA, springboard diving, waterslides, kayaking, and so on. What a shame that, by not knowing how to swim, one is denied all these other pleasures. Third, there is the stigma attached to not knowing how to do something that "everyone else" knows how to do. And, last, I thought, "But this could have been *prevented*." Parents, other kin, swimming lessons, the YMCA, summer day camp—how could one miss *all* these opportunities society provides to help one learn to swim?

But I nearly missed becoming a swimmer myself. One of the earliest crises of my parents' new marriage arose because their home—which had originally been a summer cottage—lay on the banks of a river and my mother was absolutely terrified of the water. She had acquired this fear from her mother—who had apparently lost a close relative to drowning—and what she learned as a child about water was that one stayed as far away from it as possible. The crisis came to a head as soon as I could walk. So, as my mother cowered inside the house, torn by fear of my drowning and the greater fear of infecting me with her hydrophobia, my father taught me to swim in that muddy river. More, he taught me to love being in, on, and under the water, and I became so completely at home in it that my mother could actually take pleasure as I grew up in watching my aquatic antics.

Of course with literacy the stakes are much higher. It is harder to learn to read than to learn to swim and being illiterate is a far more serious handicap than being a nonswimmer. Nevertheless, meeting a second-grader who can't read (Purcell-Gates, this volume) should provoke the same kind of shocked disbelief that was provoked when an adult announced that she could not swim. The tragedy is that, unlike the failure to learn to swim, failure to learn to read is almost entirely predictable. That is, we can infer from only the briefest acquaintance with a six and half-year-old whether he or she is likely to sink or swim with reading. Such was the case with James (not his real name), a boy I discuss below.

As I observed him and his classmates over several months, I had a growing conviction that James was not going to become a reader. The state would offer him—free—at least 12 more years of schooling, summer school, special services, an Adult Basic Education (ABE) program, thousands of pages of exercises and hundreds of hours of instruction, and none of it would help. It would not help because, for James, school was a raging ocean and, in his entire previous history, water had been sipped from a glass, run out of a faucet, or sprayed from a shower-head. Nothing offered in the classroom helped him to do anything that he already enjoyed doing but needed to get better at. Fear of the unknown—of failure, boredom and confusion—were just a few of James's unpleasant feelings about school. So, not surprisingly, he withdrew; he was at school but not in school. A dropout at six and a half, James would never even get in the water.

In the United States we have had, for many years, compulsory schooling at least through eighth grade. This should mean that virtually every schooled individual is functionally literate—able to read and write at a level such that inadequate literacy is not the principal obstacle to his or her personal growth and economic well-being. Of course, this is patently not the case; otherwise I would not have written this and you would not be reading it.

Diane Slaughter (Slaughter-Defoe 1992) is justifiably critical of those of us working in emergent literacy on the grounds that "attention to [the] problem . . . of how to prepare low-income . . . children for successful acquisition of . . . literacy . . . is not coupled with a parallel commitment to human welfare and social justice" (p. 80). And, as Carole Edelsky (1991) has argued with such eloquence and conviction in *With Literacy and Justice for All,* literacy is not just about whether or not someone can read. If James were to confound my prediction and discover the potency of print to transform his life and those around him—especially his children's—it would be tantamount to a revolution. James is African-American and, like his forebears in the United States, he is locked into a repeating cycle of poverty, social marginality, fragmented and uncertain family life and, in all likelihood, early incarceration and/or death. Ultimately, then, the hidden agenda here is revolution. Sincere literacy workers—whether or not they are aware of it—have declared their solidarity with one of the most far-reaching movements of our time.

As we learned in Part One of this volume, the acquisition of reading and writing is profoundly social. Individuals become literate with the help of parents, siblings, classmates, teachers, and storybook authors. But by the same token, illiteracy is socially constructed. Would we say about an eight-year-old that had contracted tuberculosis that it was his or her own fault? Parents, teachers, legislators, corporate entities, and the public at large all must shoulder some measure of guilt for each case of illiteracy. The authors of chapters in Part Two explore various means of stimulating emergent literacy environments in the home—enhancing parents' and children's interactions with literacy materials and activities that are, for the most part, there already. Other authors describe how they have created simulations of common mainstream literacy activity settings in nursery school, after school, and regular classroom programs. Collectively this work demonstrates some of the ways our society can begin to shoulder its responsibilities vis-à-vis the Jameses among us. There are many encouraging signs of a willingness to do so. Policy makers and the public are now asking for guidance on how much of an investment will be necessary and on where best to make that investment. Hopefully, we will provide some answers.

DEFINITION OF THE PROBLEM

Stedman and Kaestle (1987) wrestle with the twin questions of what is the rate of illiteracy in the United States whether it is declining or rising. As they point out, much depends on how one defines illiteracy, but they contribute a very useful concept, that literacy has a both a vertical and a horizontal dimension. Vertical refers to level, as in "she reads on a tenth grade level" and horizontal refers to applications—how many different things one can do that implicate literacy. Their review suggests that, whereas there may be a large number of schooled individuals with low literacy levels (20-25 million), even low literacy may be perfectly adequate for survival. That is, they find that people can get by, even hold down steady employment, without any great facility with reading and writing. However, due to the loss of manufacturing employment and the changes in the nature of manufacturing, decent wages and upward mobility are no longer widely available to these people. Thus, illiteracy or low literacy is now symptomatic of a permanent underclass .

And this permanent underclass is probably growing. If, as we saw in Part One, parents who model and coach literacy behaviors in preschoolers serve as a kind of vaccination against reading failure, demographic trends (Coleman 1987) clearly show that fewer and fewer children are getting vaccinated. In the United States and, indeed, most of the world, the birth rate among members of the mainstream culture is rapidly declining. Well-educated parents are having fewer children and they are hiring surrogate parents—who may be less effective at creating emergent literacy environments—so they can continue to pursue their careers. Contrariwise, the birth rate among immature, poorly educated, and socially marginal women is growing rapidly. These mothers—unsupported by their children's fathers or other family members—are unable or unwilling to prepare their children for the rigors of learning to read and write. Can the schools redress this growing problem?

Juel (1988) followed the literacy development of 54 poor and mostly minority children from first through fourth grade. These children were not, however, in the maximum at-risk category. Most had parents who were employed (Juel does not indicate the proportion of two-parent homes), including many in the military. They attended a "good" school in a relatively affluent (Austin, Texas) community. The school was well equipped, one assumes, with the latest reading program and auxiliary materials. Texas has high standards for teacher certification and remedial/special education programs are well-funded. Nevertheless, Juel found that children who were identified as poor readers at the end of first grade fell steadily behind their peers. Moreover, they became poor writers and gradually withdrew their investment in literacy. For example, while good readers show a steady increase in recreational reading, among poor readers, recreational reading peaks in the third grade (well below the level of good readers) and then declines. It is not hard to imagine that poor readers first give up on literacy, then give up on school, and finally they give up on society itself. Given this protracted process of disengagement and resistance, is it any wonder that adult literacy programs have such a high failure rate?

Another significant aspect of Juel's (1988) report lies in her recommendations. She embraces one of the tenets of the emergent literacy paradigm by recommending that children need opportunities to read and/or listen to "lots of stories" (p. 446). She also rejects quick-fix skills approaches to the problem. "It seems intuitively obvious that it would be very hard to make up for years of lost experiences with words and concepts found in print with relatively short-term treatments" (p. 446). The initiatives she does recommend all involve intensive one-on-one work with the at-risk child and/or immersion in literature-rich experiences.

There has, in fact, been a virtual flood of such programs aimed at assisting young children to become literate. Many implicitly or explicitly embrace the tenets of emergent literacy as outlined in the first chapter. There seem to be four broad dimensions underlying these initiatives: locus, saturation, risk status, and funding structure.

Locus refers to the setting where the program gets implemented and includes the child's home, the preschool, an after school program, or the regular classroom. Obviously different loci implicate a different cast of characters—parents, volunteers, teachers—and different physical arrangements.

Saturation refers to the level of change in intensity and duration of the child's experience with reading and writing. Some programs, such as Running Start (see next chapter), may involve only minimal change in the child's literacy experience. Others, such as Reading Recovery (Chapter Seventeen, this volume), may plunge the child into a daily close personal encounter with print aided by a highly trained coach.

When we compare programs with regard to risk factors, we find some aimed at children who are at low to moderate risk of reading failure, such as the Sunrise Project (Lancy & Nattiv 1992), while others clearly target children who are likely to remain illiterate if there is no intervention, such as HELP (Chapter Fifteen, this volume).

The fourth prominent dimension concerns funding structure and this has several attributes—source, amount and duration. For example, Running Start is funded by the Chrysler Corporation, PACE by the State of Kentucky and private foundations, and the Boston University program (Chapter Eleven, this volume) by the U.S. Department of Education and several foundation grants.

STIMULATING THE HOME LITERACY ENVIRONMENT

As Heath (1983) and Anderson and Stokes (1984) show, most homes, no matter how poor, do incorporate some uses of print, and most parents are literate to some degree. Capitalizing on what is perceived as untapped potential, many organizations—including foundations (e.g., the Barbara Bush Foundation), churches, and private corporations have launched campaigns aimed at parents of young children. These campaigns have either narrow objectives—"read to your children"—or are broader in scope, encompassing the welfare and school readiness of the child. Public schools also have mounted parent involvement campaigns in response to the repeated finding that the level of parent involvement in children's schooling is predictive of their academic success (Epstein, 1987).

One such program, Running Start, was funded by the Chrysler Corporation and implemented in eight school districts. First-graders were rewarded for reading 21 books over a 10-week period. Their parents were encouraged to read to them and some written material was sent home to guide their efforts. Our limited evaluation (next chapter) suggests that programs of this sort do spark many children's interest in books. For a few, this heightened interest, in turn, motivates parents to read to them more often. But, for the most part, the program offers minimal saturation and works best for children who are only moderately at risk. Its principal virtue is its low cost. Although funded by Chrysler, most components of the program could be continued by the schools without outside funding.

The Partnership for Family Reading Program (Handel 1992) takes several steps beyond Running Start. Begun in Newark, New Jersey with funding from Metropolitan Life, the program has gradually expanded to 32 schools in the district. Workshops for parents and their children are held in the schools. Based on emergent literacy principles, parents are introduced to picture books and shown how to engage children with print. At each workshop a specific book is introduced and discussion ensues surrounding the parents' experiences with their children. Handel notes that for many parents the idea that children's literacy is rooted in experiences in the home is a foreign one. They assume that reading is synonymous with schooling. The program is very well integrated with the school's funding structure and other routines. Teachers and librarians act as directors for workshops held during regular school hours. Parents are welcomed with refreshments and attractive book displays. They may borrow books to read with their children at home.

Evaluation data are somewhat informal but if we compare it to Running Start, the Partnership program probably affected the same band of moderately at-risk children. For low-risk children, the additional effort put forth by parents did not make a measurable difference. Children who were at great risk of failing to read probably were not affected because their parents did not attend the workshops. So, although the costs of the program were higher than for Running Start, the saturation, at least for those families who participated heavily, was much greater. Active participants did acquire new strategies to use with their children, and they do use them.

Another approach has been taken in the United Kingdom, also with mixed success. In the Haringey Project (Tizard, Schofield, & Hewison 1982), parents were given training and encouraged to listen to their second-grader read from two to four times per week. As Toomey (1993a) points out, in his review of this project and of four replications, positive effects are illusive. In most cases, children who read regularly to their parents score no better on various measures of literacy growth than children who do not have this experience. At-risk children are at risk for the most part because of the absence of activity settings and strategies to promote their emergent literacy in the home. Working-class parents may require direct and extensive training before they can function as effective literacy coaches for their children.

Teale and Sulzby (1987) demonstrate how incredibly complex this can be. They show Joyce, a mother, constantly making adjustments in the support she gives her daughter Hannah so that the task of reading is always comfortably within Hannah's reach. They contrast Joyce's natural behavior with that of Charlene Thomas, a poor African-American woman who, despite some training (Heath, 1990; Heath & Branscombe, 1986), has mastered only a part of the jointly constructed picture-book reading activity.

Toomey and Sloan (this volume) report on a series of attempts to stimulate children's literacy activities in the homes of working-class Australians. They point out the trade-offs between costs and benefits. In one of their studies costs were high, primarily because it was necessary to employ an individual to visit homes and model reading with the children—which yielded positive results . Less expensive alternatives—where parents were to come to the school for training by regular staff—were, correspondingly, less successful. However, Toomey and Sloan note that these programs seem to have their greatest impact on children in working-class families of moderately low (e.g., not poverty) incomes where support of emergent literacy is low. In other words, and following Lareau (1989), where families already own the requisite cultural capital—they are themselves literate and have a store of parent-child routines to draw on—promotional campaigns (such as Jim Trelease's efforts) may be effective. Sending books home on a regular basis and exhorting parents to do more literacy work with their children may be all that is necessary to stimulate and activate preexisting routines. But what if such routines are lacking? According to Toomey (1993a), such parents may require systematic training in order to achieve noticeable results.

Pat Edwards (1989, 1991a; Edwards, Fear, & Harris, this volume) has been responsible for two widely acknowledged training programs for parents. As she points out, "although 'read to your child' is the most frequently requested parent-involvement activity in the schools, this directive cannot be effective until we shift from 'telling' to 'showing' non-mainstream parents how to read to their children" (1991a: 211). Edwards' first project (1989) undertaken with African-American mothers in a small town in Louisiana, was a qualified success. After extensive training and encouragement, many mothers began to read to their children on a regular basis. Not surprisingly, their low literacy level was a handicap as was their inability to "scaffold" for their children, tending to be overly critical of children's mis-cues (see also Bergin, Lancy, & Draper, this volume).

Edwards' Parents as Partners in Reading project (1991a)was un-dertaken with low income (18 African-American, 7 white) mothers in a midwestern city. The mother's own literacy level was not noted. The program, aimed almost exclusively at teaching mothers strategies to use in reading with children, was one of the most extensive and costly on record. There were a total of 23 two-hour long training sessions spread over eight months. Edwards mentions, however, that not all mothers attended all sessions. There were a number of features of the program that bear noting. First, as she had in her first program, Edwards used various community agencies including both ends of the spectrum—bars and churches—to assist in recruiting clients. As we shall see, children who are most at risk have parents who are the least accessible to the various parent involvement schemes. Edwards herself functioned as the trainer and, as the daughter of a preacher, is an ex-tremely effective and motivating speaker. She had broken down sto-rybook reading into distinct components (e.g., "picture labeling"), which she modeled or were modeled by actors in videotapes she had prepared. It is significant that, unlike many parent-involvement pro-grams, the instructional materials in Edwards' programs are *not* print based. This program, like those in New Jersey, actively enlisted partic-ipants as peer instructors. Training sessions gradually become more interactive as mothers modeled for their peers strategies they had used with their children. Finally, the Parents as Partners project also in-volved teachers in the design of the project and in developing the curriculum. No funding source was identified for this project.

Intergenerational Literacy [1]

One impetus for these parent-involvement initiatives has obviously been the elementary school. Teachers confronted with a wide range of preparedness recognize the critical role of parents and take steps to stimulate their involvement. But, more recently, there has been a sec-ond and very powerful force pushing the development of intergen-erational or family literacy programs. This is the Adult Basic Education (ABE) establishment.

There is a large and long-standing array of programs, supported by public and private funding, aimed at educating adults who dropped out of school and who now find their employment horizons to be narrow. Literacy is seen as the linchpin of their education as adults. Programs address, in the first instance, low literacy levels, moving on to treat other academic areas as literacy levels improve. Service providers began to bring children into this picture for several reasons. First, many of their clients are young mothers with no one to look after their children, so on-site day care was seen as a necessary component. Second, parenting skills classes—aimed at breaking the cycle of educational/economic failure—were already a central component in many ABE programs. Third, providers discovered (Quintero & Huerta-Macias 1990) that at least some of their clients were motivated to improve their own literacy in order to read with their children.

PACE (Heberele 1992) was one of the first intergenerational literacy (IGL) programs and is becoming widely disseminated. It began when an early-childhood educator (Jeanne Heberle) and an adult educator (Sharon Darling) happened to be in a car-pool together and began to compare notes. Their ideas were supported by a generous legislature which saw an opportunity to address a perennial problem in the state of Kentucky. Namely, that a high proportion of Kentuckians never finish school and their children are, equally, unsuccessful. "PACE seeks to raise parents' educational expectations for their children, and to develop positive relations between home and school" (Heberle 1992, 136).

Unlike programs we have seen so far where training may have occurred at school but where all the children's learning was to take place in the home, teaching and learning in PACE occurs at school and at home. Also, PACE integrates two forms of schooling—preschool and regular education—that are normally unconnected. Since the focus is intergenerational, the goal of meeting parents' needs for further education is as important as or more important than enhancing children's emergent literacy. Parents are brought to school on the same school buses as their children and are taught in separate but adjacent classrooms. Classes are held three full days a week. During the fourth day staff are present to do planning, record keeping, and home visits.

Although PACE is a family literacy program, the curriculum more closely resembles literacy education approaches that predate the emergent literacy paradigm shift (see Chapter One). Heberle estimates that the cost per adult client is about $1,666 per year. As compared to other populations (see the Chapter One section on "Where Support for Emergent Literacy is Almost Nonexistent"), the PACE client population does not represent extremes of poverty or family fragmentation. Most are white and speak English as their first language. Fewer than half receive Aid to Families with Dependent Children (AFDC) or come from single parent homes.

Nevertheless, client recruitment and retention is a formidable challenge for PACE staff, and may represent a significant portion of the budget. Community leaders are contacted, and provided with brochures, slide presentations, and videos. Many unemployed or underemployed adults seem not sufficiently motivated to take advantage of the program, either to improve their own or their children's chances. Even those with positive attitudes may find it hard to reorganize their lives to incorporate PACE classes and at-home activities. Husbands may not welcome new routines. As we saw in the first chapter, patterns of family life are profoundly cultural and, thus, resistant to change.

Despite these difficulties, PACE has had a measurable impact on those clients it has recruited and educated. Adults are earning their general equivalency diploma(GED), children appear to leave the program with enhanced readiness skills and, most importantly, parents develop much higher expectations for their children's education. The Kentucky legislature each year increases the PACE budget ($1.8 million to fund 33 sites in 1990). The program is being disseminated nationally and there is discussion in Kentucky and in Washington, D.C. of making participation in a PACE-like program mandatory for those seeking government assistance.

The Family Initiative for English Literacy (FIEL) is a program for limited English-proficient Mexican-Americans and their children. It advances beyond the PACE model in several areas (Quintero & Huerta-Macias, 1990). First, it draws much more heavily on the emergent literacy literature for its curriculum. For example, a wide variety of parent-child activities with language are introduced including songs, and a thematic approach (puppets, recipes, holidays) is used. FIEL classes—one hour per week for 24 weeks—for parents *and* children include a jointly constructed activity during the class period, followed by the parent and child writing a story about the activity that the child then reads to the parent (see Chapter Seven, this volume). Teachers use a guided assistance model (Holdaway 1979, Tharp and Gallimore 1988), giving direction to the pairs and as much assistance as necessary to maintain progress toward a goal. Guided assistance is a teaching strategy characteristic of mainstream parents but not commonly found in nonmainstream communities. The following episode is illustrative:

> Marilu begins to write. However, her mother grabs Marilu's pencil as she is writing, erases the letters she just wrote, and tells her to write them again . . . . The teacher . . . tactfully tells her . . . that it is not important at this point in Marilu's literacy development whether her writing is misspelled, not on the line, or that the letters are incorrectly shaped. She also tells Ms. Ramirez that her constant corrections will make Marilu dependent on her for approval for everything she does. The advice, however, has little effect on Ms. Ramirez. She continues to erase portions of Marilu's writing she doesn't like and at one point begins to dictate the spelling of a word. (Quintero & Huerta-Macias 1990, 310)

But Marilu and her mother make great strides together over the course of the program and, by the end, are reading and writing together daily.

FIEL grew out of an adult literacy program at El Paso Community College and has been funded by both the Texas and Federal Bilingual Education offices. Classes are bilingual and transitional, meaning that more and more English is introduced as students' proficiency grows. Specific evaluation data are not reported but for high-level participants gains seem evident. Like PACE, FIEL seems to have succeeded in changing parents' views of their instrumentality vis-á-vis their children's literacy: "This not reading is handed down. My mother couldn't read, and her mother couldn't read. Well, it's going to stop with me" (Quintero & Velarde 1990, 14). There is no indication of any plan, however, to replicate or extend FIEL to other sites.

Another early IGL program was the Family Literacy Center begun in 1985 by Ruth Nickse at Boston University. As she points out (Nickse 1992), funds were slim and little money was available to carry out a formal evaluation. Nevertheless, many important lessons were learned from that formative period. For example, as Svensson (this volume) also discovered, adults who do not read often or well do not necessarily enjoy reading the sorts of fantasy stories that children enjoy. There is then a narrow range of books that appeal to IGL parent and child clients. She also found that giving clients the "Reading Rainbow" tapes to view was not effective, because adults were conditioned to view films as entertainment, so they had a hard time extracting personally applicable information from the tapes. One obvious positive feature of the program was to use college work study students as low-cost tutors. Despite the lack of hard data on the effectiveness of the Family Literacy Center, its political impact was significant and gave rise to two major new federal initiatives in education—Even Start and Literacy Corps—which I shall discuss shortly.

Paratore (Chapter Eleven, this volume) developed a second IGL program at Boston University beginning in 1989. At various times these programs have received funding from federal, state, and foundation sources, but a principal funding source in recent years has been the university itself.

The particular low-income community served by Paratore's IGL project was noteworthy for the predominance of recent immigrants to the United States. This meant that, for the majority, English was their second language. But it also meant that as voluntary migrants (Ogbu 1988) they might have high aspirations for their children. However, 232 of the 367 clients served by the program between 1989 and 1992 reported that they rarely or never read aloud to their children. As noted for several IGL programs, recruitment of clients was difficult, especially in the initial stages. This was a relatively expensive program in that classes were held four days a week for two hours a day over about a 30-week period. Staff included a project director, two experienced teachers and three tutors. The center was located within walking distance of most clients' homes, so transportation was not an acute problem.

The instructional approach for both adults and children was closely aligned with the emergent literacy paradigm. Literacy instruction for the adults, for example, included such tactics as assisted reading and writing, paired rereading and cooperative learning—all rather uncommon ABE practices, which tend to use a skill and drill approach. Both one-on-one tutoring and small group instruction/discussion formats were used. As Paratore indicates, adults had ample opportunity to discuss their views and needs in an open and supportive atmosphere.

One advantage of the group discussion format is that idiosyncratic strategies may emerge that can be shared with the group as a whole. Ann Zupsic and I developed the Parent Partners for Literacy program at Riverside School in Toledo. Following Pat Edwards' (Chapter Eighteen, this volume) lead, we began by selecting parent literacy consultants. These were the parents of children whom the teachers selected as exceptional readers. Bringing this group together we first queried them about what they had done to enhance their children's literacy. All had read storybooks to their children, but there were some surprises too. One child—a boy—would not sit still to be read to but the parents noticed that he was fascinated by "Wheel of Fortune" on TV. So, the boy's father constructed a Wheel of Fortune, and as they played this game with him, he acquired a large sight vocabulary.

Not only is the Boston University program one of the most refined in terms of building on an existing base of research and practice, it is also one of the most carefully studied. Results are generally quite positive and are provided in Chapter Eleven, this volume. I want to highlight one somewhat incidental finding here that is germane to the issues raised below. When Paratore sought the cooperation of the children's teachers by asking them to monitor and support the children's literacy journal, only five of 16 asked gave their support. Of these, none "used the journal as the basis or the springboard for any other literacy task in the classroom."

As I mentioned, these early IGL programs encouraged the federal government to invest in this concept by making four-year Even Start grants available on a competitive basis beginning in 1989. The Toledo public school system was one of 76 original sites funded with the initial $14.5 to $15 million dollar outlay. Each year since 1989, 40 to 50 additional sites have been established. I served for two and a half years on the Toledo Even Start Advisory Committee. These remarks follow from that experience. Although the basic concepts behind Even Start were sound and although the core Even Start staff were incredibly dedicated, there were a number of problems, at least initially.

One problem was that the people who were awarded the grant knew virtually nothing about emergent literacy or family literacy. What they knew about was traditional Adult Basic Education. So the program received very uneven implementation. The ABE component and the on-site day care went easily into place. Implementing a program to encourage family literacy practices was far more difficult, although I did introduce them to Pat Edwards and they adopted her commercially marketed video series on parent/child reading strategies. This component came into focus gradually as the staff read about and attended workshops in family literacy. I am sure this has been true nationally—that policy implementation has run ahead of empirical support. Additionally, however, TES has been plagued by continual turnover of key personnel so the knowledge base on family literacy remains slim.

Another more serious problem was that the plan to recruit parents through elementary schools with the highest proportion of at-risk children in Toledo was a total flop. Sending literature home with children got no response. A door-to-door campaign did no better. Even Start had, apparently, targeted a population that was not eager to change its habits vis-à-vis literacy, schooling, and child rearing.

TES staff began to have greater recruiting success when they opened their doors to eligible clients from throughout the city and when they energized an "ABCDeria" of social support agencies in the community to help find clients. And, indeed, this has been one of their important findings—that the clients who are most persistent and who benefit the most are those who are the most "connected,"—who have well-established relationships with these various agencies including community centers, churches, and extended family, etc. The reverse is also true; young mothers with few regular ties outside the home are difficult to recruit and difficult to retain.

And as Park (1992, 164) notes, "given the length of stay in [IGL] programs it is difficult to imagine that solid cognitive gains can be made by adults let alone be transferred to children."

The picture that emerges from Toledo Even Start (Wilson & Aldridge, this volume), which is aimed at the most extreme at-risk group in the United States according to Ogbu (1988), looks like this. The majority of targeted parents will choose not to participate at all. A much smaller number will participate to some degree. But as Scott-Jones (1992) points out, their first concern will be for their own welfare. They will be more willing to invest time in their own education than in their children's. Thus, we find that, of the various program components, family literacy has received the lowest level of patronage. Nonetheless, TES has produced some real converts, mothers who have transformed the emergent literacy environment for their children.

The data are not all in. A national evaluation of Even Start is due out in 1993. What should be clear from the foregoing, however, is that in many homes there is virtually no emergent literacy environment to activate via parent intervention programs. We are starting from ground zero. We may find that the cost to transplant literacy activities into this rocky soil may be prohibitive. We must consider alternatives that do not require the active involvement of parents in their children's education.

SIMULATING THE HOME LITERACY ENVIRONMENT

Surrogate Parents

If parents are unable or unwilling to scaffold their children's language and literacy development, perhaps we can find substitutes and create a *simulation* of the mainstream home literacy environment. This was the reasoning behind the SUNRISE project (Lancy & Nattiv, 1992). Undertaken in a remote rural area in the northern Rockies, this program brought parent, grandparent, and teenage volunteers into kindergarten to read storybooks with pairs of children in a cozy reading corner of each classroom. Children were read to in rotation and each child received at least two twenty-minute sessions per week. The program represented a kind of transfer of cultural capital from mainstream adults to, in many cases, nonmainstream children. It relied on the assumption that volunteers would already be expert at co-constructing storybooks with children, and training was minimal.[2] Funded by a small state grant, the district easily absorbed the cost of the program and four years after the grant ran out the project has spread throughout the district, won a national award from the National Council of Teachers of English (NCTE), and earned the endorsement of all participants. The teachers' endorsement was particularly gratifying, as we had taken great pains to insure that the program would in no way interfere with their routines, and they were not responsible for managing the volunteers—this was done by clerical staff.

We were less successful with a second literacy volunteer program. As I mentioned, the Boston University Family Literacy Center also spawned the Literacy Corps (LC) program. LC was a federal initiative—modeled loosely on Peace Corps—designed to get undergraduates involved as tutors in various literacy programs. The University of Toledo program (codirected with Peter DeWitz), funded by a two-year, $25,000 per year grant privided to each LC program, took a different tack than most. Instead of assigning our tutors to work with adults, as was the norm with the 100+ LC programs nationally, we had them work with children in the primary grades. Also, in order to increase the likelihood of institutionalizing LC after the grant ran out, we drew mainly on undergraduate education majors who are obligated to spend at least one quarter in the field prior to formal admission to teacher education. They could meet this obligation by working through us.

The idea for the Literacy Corps is fundamentally sound. Again, it is an opportunity to transfer cultural capital—tutors tend to be middle class with strong literacy backgrounds, clients tend to be poor with limited exposure to books—at relatively low cost. In Toledo, the Literacy Corps cost one-tenth what Even Start cost and actually had the potential to influence more children and to a greater degree. The majority of tutors developed very close relationships as they worked with their tutees over a three to six-month period. But there were also problems, and these are informative.

We worked with one particular school district with which we had already established a good working relationship. They welcomed the opportunity to work with us but never took the necessary step of assigning a staff person the responsibility of coordinating LC activities at the building level. This lack of local coordination created continual headaches. As we were able to demonstrate that our tutors were making a difference in the lives of children, we felt the district would, eventually, have come around. Second, we had a surprisingly difficult time recruiting student volunteers. We had done a media blitz and got at most two or three volunteers per quarter from the student body at large (which numbers over 35,000). Hence, the majority of our 20 to 30 volunteers each quarter were education majors. We also, however, encountered some resistance from administrators in the College of Education who were loath to change their regulations and procedures to accommodate the LC program. Finally, we encountered difficulties with our client population. Although we repeatedly admonished teachers to refer children in kindergarden and first grades without any serious academic problems but who were considered merely slow or late readers, our tutors often had to cope with second- and third-graders with severe behavioral and/or reading problems. In effect many of our tutees were candidates for Reading Recovery (Chapter Seventeen, this volume) whose tutors are certified teachers with a year or more of intensive training in RR methods. I believe, however, that all of these problems were solvable and that we could have institutionalized LC at Toledo had we had four years to do so—as is the case with Even Start grants—rather than only two years.

Eileen Carr's project (Chapter Thirteen, this volume) involved, among other elements, the training of fifth-grade students to read storybooks to kindergartners from the same school. Like the SUNRISE program, volunteers read with pairs of children for twenty minutes a week. The volunteer selected a storybook, read it to the kindergartners, discussed the story and new vocabulary, then had each child retell the story. In addition, volunteers helped children develop print and phonemic awareness through simple exercises including rhyming and singing. After each session with the volunteer, kindergartners were encouraged to write about the story they had just heard.

Evidently, the project was a positive experience for both younger and older students. The fifth-grade volunteers offer some obvious advantages over outside volunteers. On the downside, however, is their loss of instructional time. Another noteworthy feature of this particular project was the integration of instructional focus across the classroom literacy program, and the activities of peer and parent tutors. This integration is absent from most of the initiatives to stimulate or simulate emergent literacy .

Taking a rather large leap of faith, let us now consider the possibility of robot-like *surrogate* parents. A crucial element in children's educational television (ETV) from day one has been reading readiness, print awareness, and so forth. Children, regardless of family income or ethnicity, watch a great deal of TV. Sometimes they watch ETV and, in many cases, this is beneficial. However, ETV has not quite lived up to its promise. Serendipitously, we may get another chance, however. As of July 1, 1993, all TVs larger than 13 inches must be equipped with circuitry to display closed captions. This means that even when children watch soap operas and reruns they will see text displayed. As Svensson notes (Chapter Six, this volume) in Sweden, unlike the United States, TV watching is positively correlated with early reading growth. This is explained by the fact that most children's TV is imported from other countries and dubbing is too expensive, so subtitling is extensive. Young Swedes must learn to read if they want to follow what is being said.[3]   In another development, classic children's storybooks (e.g., *The Tale of Peter Rabbit*) have begun to appear in CD-ROM format with accurate reproduction in color of the original pictures, with professional actors reading the stories. Most are interactive. Children can read it themselves and highlight—with a mouse—words they do not recognize, which the "surrogate parent" computer will supply them with. The PC parent is not very cuddly but it is infinitely patient and fully literate. Susan Talley and I will work with Bear River (Utah) Head Start during the 1993-1994 school year on a program that will provide heavy doses of CD-ROM story-book exposure to at-risk four-year-olds.

Compensatory Education

It is ironic, given our present understanding of the way children become literate, that compensatory education programs in general, and Head Start in particular, have been utterly lacking in activities and props normally associated with the emergent literacy environment. This is changing now, and very rapidly. All Head Start centers were to incorporate literacy activities by 1992. As Lubeck's (1984) classic study—a comparison of a Head Start center staffed by black females and a suburban Nursery School staffed by middle-class whites—shows, preschool programs tend to reproduce the literacy environments found in the surrounding community. Adult-child interaction in the respective schools closely matched what the literature says happens in the homes in these two communities (see Chapter One, this volume). Hence, the Head Start program was—at least as far as literacy was concerned—unlikely to serve a compensatory function.

Dickinson (1989) describes a truly compensatory Head Start program that seeks to create a simulation of the kind of emergent literacy environment found in mainstream homes. The curriculum is based on the model of Australian Don Holdaway (1979), an emergent literacy pioneer. Dickinson talks about the "before" and "after" in one of his project sites.

> Our initial interview and early observations made it clear that facilitation of language and literacy development were not high priorities. [The Head Start teacher] made no mention of literacy related skills or attitudes when asked to talk about important features of her program. She believed that the primary goal of Head Start is "socialization" of children, especially children from non-English speaking homes. By this she meant getting children acquainted with the routines of school and exposing them to other children from different cultural and linguistic backgrounds (p. 132). We saw very few teacher-directed activities, but what we did see again indicated little explicit attention to language . . . . Verbal interaction consisted only of minimal directions about how to cut (with scissors): "Look. Open, close, open, close . . . " we did not observe teachers engaging children in extended dialogue . . . Mealtimes were usually quiet (p. 134).

After the teachers were trained in various storybook reading and discussion tactics, "the amount of child talk and the relative balance between child and teacher talk was vastly different" (p. 143). "The children were extremely attentive when enlarged books were being read . . . . More books with more text were read (each session)" (p. 144).

While shared, big book reading was the centerpiece of the program, Dickinson (1989) noted many spillover effects in other areas of the curriculum. Teachers now exploited many more activities— singing, activity time, drawing, field trips—for their potential to promote children's language and literacy. And by the end of the year, one teacher remarked: "I have never worked with kids with the interest in books that these guys have" (p. 146).

However, the ripple effects were limited to those areas specifically emphasized by project staff. For example, "There was no change in teacher efforts to support development of children's oral language through informal conversation" (p. 147). This type of conversation was endemic in the nursery school that Lubeck (1984) observed, reinforcing, once again, the view that the emergent literacy support system comes as a package and is part of the cultural capital (Lareau 1989) that mainstream parents pass along to their children. We cannot assume that by inducing HS teachers who are themselves not part of the mainstream culture to adopt one or two elements that this will activate the entire package. Hence, replicating Dickinson's (1989) project, which involved extensive on-site coaching, may prove to be quite expensive.

Innovations in programs for at-risk students have tended to originate from Washington either directly or indirectly through the funding of grants. Several state legislatures have, however, taken steps to address what is perceived as a growing problem. We have already discussed Kentucky's PACE program. Missouri has invested heavily in parent training and Illinois has initiated preschool programs aimed at at-risk youths. School districts may bid for state funds on the basis of innovative proposals.

Early Start (McCormick, Kerr, Mason, & Gruendel 1992) was one of the programs that has been funded in the Springfield (IL) school district. By 1988, 240 four-year-olds were enrolled in 12 classes. The entire curriculum was scrutinized for opportunities to infuse language and literacy experiences. Teachers hold instructional conversations with the children, for example, and closely monitor and guide their activity while they are in the various "centers". In fact, the program description fits closely with what we would see in a typical nursery school but is very different from what one sees in a typical compensatory education program.

McCormick and her colleagues refer specifically to the incorporation of literacy activities in the dramatic play area. As we saw in Chapter One, children's symbolic play allows them to take on the role of a "literate person." In effect, literacy play provides children with a repertoire of real-world contexts for the literacy skills they will acquire and perfect in school. Kathy Roskos and Susan Neuman (Chapter Fourteen, this volume) have drawn on this important insight from emergent literacy research to fashion unique literacy play settings for preschools serving at-risk children. These play settings have included a kitchen, a Cozy Corner Library, and office. They take great care to include props in each setting that will stimulate children to behave as if they were literate. For example, the kitchen contained cookbooks, recipe cards, coupons, notepads, and pencils. These changes in design had a dramatic impact on children's play. In general, the amount of literacy-related play increased exponentially and play became quieter and more focused.

Nowhere is the contrast between the message that comes from basic research on emergent literacy and the reality of classroom practice greater than in the area of adult-child conversation. Children who are early readers have been conversational partners for their literate parents since birth. Many of these conversations follow a recognizable pattern that suggests that parents are using language quite deliberately to teach their children how to take in knowledge from the world. These are instructional conversations (IC) (Tharp & Gallimore 1988). The IC is a prominent feature of HELP, the Hilltop Emergent Literacy Program (Chapter Fifteen, this volume) based in an all-black housing project in Toledo. Children in HELP are exposed to the whole gamut of middle-class family enrichment experiences. They are taken to the zoo, the art museum, and the library. They make things in the kitchen, make greeting cards for relatives, and are read lots of stories. Most importantly, according to Lynne Hudson and her colleagues, all of these activities are accompanied by intense conversations between adults (undergraduate and teacher volunteers) and children (the ratio is about 1:3), so that children can verbalize and then internalize these myriad new experiences. Also, adults model an expanded linguistic code (see Chapter Three) that these children have not previously been exposed to and which is required in some situations in school.

HELP has been successful at enhancing children's academic success but its impact has been limited by what now appears to be a common problem—poor articulation with prevailing public school practice (see also Chapter Eleven). While the teaching philosophy of HELP may be in line with the latest thinking about children's emergent literacy, the public school that HELP students attend is not as up to date. As HELP staffers discovered when they observed their graduates in the regular classroom, their students were, indeed, much more able conversationalists and self-guided learners than their peers. However, the teachers rarely gave their students a chance to engage in discussion or other self-selected learning opportunities. Indeed, teachers seemed to resent the initiative and enthusiasm for learning that HELP graduates brought to their classrooms (Chryst, personal communication, 1992). We will return to the IC shortly.

Transforming the Public Schools

The reader may, at this point, be troubled by a nagging question. What about the public schools? Do we really need all these add-on programs? Perhaps not. With respect to current theories of literacy instruction in school, the perspective that meshes best with EL is whole-language, as even a casual perusal of a whole-language guide (Edelsky, Altwerger, & Flores 1991: K. Goodman, 1986) will show.

Although somewhat more controlled and structured than a typical whole-language classroom, Morrow's kindergarten curriculum (Morrow, O'Connor, & Smith 1990) is representative of the new thinking. Favorite children's storybooks form the foundation for a myriad of activities that expand upon the text. After reading *Bread and Jam for Francis*, for example, children prepared and ate bread and jam. There were discussions before and after the story reading; children retold stories that had been read; stories were reread frequently; children enacted stories using hand puppets; and books were sent home. The approach seemed to work well, and children in the story reading program progressed much further along the emergent literacy continuum than their peers who were in a traditional reading readiness curriculum. They seemed to be developing a robust story schema. On the other hand, the treated group did about as well as the control group on the reading readiness (e.g., letter identification) measures.

So what is the problem? Why hasn't there been a mass conversion to whole-language? For one thing, literacy programs are about like soap powder. The brand that works best will probably lose out to the brand that is more effectively packaged and marketed. To date, whole-language advocates have strenuously resisted anything approaching a packaged or canned version. Earlier, I referred to a program I started at Sunrise School. Saturating kindergarten classrooms with storybooks had a kind of catalytic effect. Gradually, the teachers began to introduce more authentic literacy activities into their classrooms, including, for the first time, student writing. Sunrise was looking more and more like a whole-language environment. But then a new principal took over the school and she was a "Writing to Read" (Martin 1986) disciple. So now a wholesale change in the early literacy curriculum at Sunrise is underway.

As distasteful as head-to-head comparisons are (Edelsky 1990) they may be politically necessary. This was Lynne Putnam's goal. In Chapter Sixteen, (this volume) she compares four philosophically distinct approaches, including both "Writing to Read" and a "literate environment" program, to early literacy instruction. It might be noted at this point that while there is a definite relationship between cost and effectiveness with respect to the parent-involvement and compensatory programs reviewed earlier—more is better—this may not be the case with in-school programs. That is, the whole-language approach, at least from a material/equipment standpoint, is actually far cheaper to implement than "Writing to Read" which requires, ideally, one computer for every four children and costly software, and also cheaper than a traditional reading readiness program, which requires a huge quantity of consumable worksheets. The principal cost associated with the literate environment curriculum is the two years of in-service training required.

One of the great values of Putnam's work here is that she provides process as well as outcome data. One gets a feel for what it is like to be a student in these very different classrooms. Putnam does find that the literate environment program is superior to the others, but she raises some troubling questions. It seems evident that implementing a whole-language curriculum is far more difficult than any one of the various packaged alternatives that "chop language into bits and pieces" (K. Goodman 1986, 40). A major challenge, then, is not just to get teachers to develop "brand loyalty," but to commit to the arduous task of learning to implement what is a very complex and comprehensive philosophy and not a set of neat prescriptions for classroom practice (Edelsky et al. 1991).

I attended a lecture/demonstration given by Jim Moffett in June 1993. Participants taught in schools serving white middle-class and working-class students. Every time Moffett called for questions or discussion there was a chorus of protests aimed at colleagues/ administrators/ students who would undoubtedly resist the changes in classroom routines he was advocating. The subtext of their comments again and again was "this is wonderful stuff but it won't work in my classroom/school/district." Parenthetically, I might note that the whole-language teacher described by Carr (Chapter Thirteen, this volume) was stabbed by a student half-way through the project—she survived but her career as an innovative inner-city teacher may be truncated. In short, whole-language seems bound to encounter the most resistance from the communities where it is most needed.

Goldenberg and Gallimore (1991) describe a process of transformation in one elementary school that took over four years to accomplish. Significantly, the transformation may never have occurred if there hadn't been "teacher turnover in the arrival of new . . . faculty .. [that] led to . . . a critical mass of . . . teachers and administrators . . . all of whom shared at least some commitment to changing the early literacy emphasis at Benson" (p. 7). It is also significant that Claude Goldenberg, as a teacher at Benson, served, like Putnam, as the mover and shaker to lead and shape the changes that were taking place.

Putnam also alerts us to the "catch-up" problem. Is one or two years of immersion in classrooms that simulate (and, indeed, improve upon) familial emergent literacy environments enough to close the gap? Can children who have encountered little more than environmental print and a restricted linguistic code (Chapter Four, this volume) make enough progress in preschool or kindergarten to erase what, political correctness aside, is clearly a deficit? Courtney Cazden (1992), one of the most respected scholars we have in this area, thinks not: "Classrooms cannot duplicate the conditions of . . . language immersion in the home " (p. 15). Alas, we have no longitudinal research that takes children who are at extreme risk of not becoming literate, immerses them in school-based emergent literacy environments, and then follows their subsequent progress, a` la Juel (1988).

What little evidence we have is not terribly encouraging. At the second Toledo Emergent Literacy Conference (most chapters in this volume came from the first conference), organized by Eileen Carr, Elizabeth Sulzby spoke about a project she had undertaken in an impoverished area of Detroit. She illustrated her talk with writing samples from a few focal children that showed their *development* from the beginning until the end of first grade. Yet, during the break, her audience of primary teachers could not stop talking about how far *behind* her focal students were and how unready they would be for the second grade curriculum. As Goldenberg and Gallmore (1991) point out, there is such a preoccupation with getting at-risk students to show some measurable progress that there is a tendency for teachers to be undemanding and to drastically slow down the pace of instruction—with potentially disastrous consequences for the students down the road.

Cazden (1992) believes that some students just will not catch up in even the most progressive classrooms and will require an "instructional detour" (p. 14) of the sort that Reading Recovery (RR) provides. Reading Recovery (Kelly, Klein & Pinnell, this volume) assumes that reading is a multipart system that, in most first-graders, will run with increasing smoothness and automaticity. For some children, however, the system is incomplete—a part or parts are missing or are not connected up properly. It is the job of the (very extensively trained) RR teacher to find out where the problems are, help the child to fix them, and get the system oiled, fueled, and up and running smoothly.

All this work takes place not via a laborious series of paper and pencil tests followed by an IEP prescription and a regular dose of worksheet "pills," but, rather, in the context of jointly constructed book reading, writing, and instructional conversations—about books, text, and language. Reading Recovery sessions—30 minutes daily for 12-16 weeks—are intense, structured, and focused. They represent an excellent instantiation of the Vygotskian principle of guided assistance (Tharp & Gallimore 1988) and reflect the best of what we have learned from research on emergent literacy. RR deviates from the whole-language philosophy in one important aspect, however: the setting and materials lack *authenticity*. As such, RR—invented by Marie Clay and far more compatible, philosophically, with whole-language instruction than traditional reading instruction—for this reason will most likely be spurned by schools that embrace whole-language. It is more likely to be adopted by districts that utilize a skills-based reading and reading readiness curricula—ironically. This is unfortunate because RR *is* expensive and skills programs—I'm guessing—produce far more RR clients than whole-language programs.

PUTTING IT ALL TOGETHER

Let us return to the question with which I opened the previous section. Do we really need all these costly add-on programs? The answer I believe, is yes, we do. Although I agree with Moffett's claim in the Foreword that fostering literacy should be cheap and easy when we exploit the natural avenues implied by the emergent literacy paradigm, he doesn't make enough of his own caveat: "If literacy plays a significant role in the culture . . ." The remarkable thing is that we have large segments of our population for whom literacy is *not* a significant part of their culture, certainly not the academic literacy of rhymes, storybooks, and book talk. So, unlike Moffett, I do not see a great deal of untapped potential in adults becoming unpaid emergent literacy facilitators for each other and for their own children.

As Snow and her colleagues (1991) have found, there needs to be a great deal of redundancy built into the system in order to insure that all children become literate. Obviously, parents must be the first line of defense. There is now a program which is aimed at spreading the gospel of storybook reading to mothers recovering in the hospital from the delivery of their infants (Sams 1992). We cannot do enough to get the message out to parents to read to children and to strive to make this a fun experience for them at all times. However, as Jeanne Paratore (personal communication, 1993) reminded me, some parent involvement programs are based not on the emergent literacy paradigm, but on the readiness paradigm (e.g. HIPPY—Arkansas State Department of Education 1991) and as such are likely to do children more harm than good (see also Chapter Five, this volume).

Some parents will not receive these weak signals (e.g. Running Start). More intense programs, ideally situated in institutional contexts that already hold parents and their children captive—ABE programs, Sunday schools, Head Start—will be required to stimulate the emergent literacy environment in these homes.

Teachers have to get the message, too. Preschool and kindergarten teachers seem more receptive than teachers at higher grade levels. The message to read to children and to encourage them to read voluntarily or to seek help with reading at home seems to penetrate more readily than other messages about emergent literacy. It seems more difficult to get parents or teachers to enable children's emergent writing, for example.

Media—TV, CD-ROM, even video games—have a critical role to play as well—not as "magic bullet" solutions to the problem (e.g., "Hooked on Phonics") but as adding yet another warp to make the literacy safety net a tighter, sturdier weave.

When all else fails, we need something like Reading Recovery, a last-chance effort to keep children from giving up on becoming literate, on school, on themselves.

And, most importantly, we need to bring all these disparate agencies and programs into greater harmony with one another. If we needed a drug czar to coordinate all the competing agencies and policies with respect to that national crisis, we could surely use a literacy czar for the same reason. It is disheartening to consider how many child literacy programs—many of considerable magnitude—are now extinct—Toledo's Even Start program, f.,i. (see Chapter Twelve). They did not become extinct because they did not work, but because the money ran out, the director took another job, the program made only a small dent in what was gradually perceived as a huge problem, there was a lack of community support (read bad PR), or whatever.

The last chapter in this volume allows us to look to the future with some optimism and direction. Pat Edwards—a veteran campaigner— and her colleagues have created a program that brings together parents, teachers, and enlightened school administrators with progressive emergent literacy-based curricula. Head Start and Reading Recovery are still not in the picture, but I suspect they soon will be. What the chapter does not adequately convey, however, is how incredibly difficult it is to accomplish such a program (Edwards, personal communication, 1992). Although all parties would appear to share the same goals, they, in fact, brought quite different agendae to the process. For example, as Goldenberg and Gallimore (1991) found out, teachers,initially, see parents as impediments to children's learning, and not assets.

Another problem noted by Edwards and others is that parents are more comfortable with the traditional reading curriculum. Parents do not welcome the sort of work represented by Figure 7.1. It is *sloppy* and full of *mistakes*! The dialogue between teachers and parents must be widened and extended, and Chapter Eighteen suggests a variety of ways to make this happen. Clearly the Kendon School can be looked on as a model for the future.

But, to return again to the bottom line, how much will all this cost? A great deal. Edwards' time is paid for by Michigan State University—not the school. State appropriations above and beyond the school's regular budget buys "released time" for Kendon's teachers to develop the curriculum and meet with parents. To replicate the Kendon experience would require increasing the budget of the typical elementary school by at least 25 percent.

How much would an advertising campaign to get parents to read to their children cost? How much has the antidrug campaign cost? How much does it cost to reach parents who are impervious to these media messages? PACE costs $1,600+ per family, Even Start 2-3 times that. Multiply this figure by half a million to do the job nationally. To extend a quality preschool experience to every child who is potentially at risk for illiteracy would require tripling Head Start's 3.33 billion dollar budget. There is considerable evidence that, to simulate the kind of emergent literacy experience that mainstream kids take for granted, Head Start teachers will need to be much better educated, better trained, and better paid than they are at present. What would it cost to convert all elementary school teachers to whole-language teachers? Using the National Writing Project as a comparable undertaking, expect about $100 million.

In short, we probably need to spend an amount similar to the total spent on public education by the federal and state governments combined, excluding local property tax-based contributions. But—and I know this will sound hackneyed but sometimes hard truths are just that—whatever this amount turns out to be it is *minuscule* compared to what we now spend on children who leave first grade not being able to read. From special education costs to summer school, to the cost of juvenile crime and detention, welfare, and life-long incarceration, it all adds up. Investing in children's literacy is about as close to a sure thing as there is around.

NOTES

[1] For a much more thorough treatment of this topic see Nickse (1990).

[2] Nickse (1990) reports on a program run by the Stride-Rite shoe company that brings senior citizens to read to toddlers in their on-site day-care center.

[3] Carolyn Chryst (Chapter Fifteen, this volume) questioned a mother of one HELP precocious reader who suggested that the child had learned to read by following the captions on MTV that she read to him.

9

Too Little, Too Late:
A Case Study of "Running Start"
David F. Lancy, with Ann Burke Zupsic

"You sell the pleasures of reading the way McDonald's sells hamburg-
ers: You advertise" (from a flyer announcing a talk by *Read-Aloud
Handbook* author Jim Trelease).

AN OVERVIEW OF RUNNING START

This chapter will report on the implementation of the Running Start
(RS) program in a transition classroom for at-risk six-year-olds. Our
purposes were twofold: to augment a program of research on the role
of parents in reading acquisition (Lancy et al. 1989; Bergin, Lancy,
and Draper, this volume), and to evaluate a corporate-sponsored and
highly touted national intervention program.

Running Start was announced in early 1989 as a $2.1 million
philanthropic initiative by the Chrysler Corporation. The funds were
donated to Reading is Fundamental, a Washington, D.C.-based non-
profit organization to develop and implement a family reading program. Toledo, Ohio was one of ten medium-sized U.S. cities—in
which Chrysler has a major interest—selected to participate. Each
district had to commit its entire first-grade population to the program
for a period of three years. Promotional materials packets were provided, and teachers could order trade (picture) books to augment
classroom libraries and to award to children. The promotional materials consisted for the most part of colorful stickers and posters.

In many respects the program resembles other corporate-sponsored reading programs like Pizza Hut's Book-It, in that children are

rewarded for the quantity of books they read, and there is inherent competition to see who will meet the challenge. This program differs in the exclusive focus on first grade and the explicit solicitation of parent participation. Students could meet the challenge if they had read (or were read to) 21 books between January 22 and March 30, 1991. In addition, at the end of the period, a Reading Rally was held where children, accompanied by their parents, received a book of their choice and could enter a drawing for various other prizes, such as a microwave oven. There was a speaker who addressed the need for parental involvement in reading with children and various displays.

Lee Iacocca (1989), then chairman of Chrysler, gave this rationale for Running Start:

> The concept is simple: Get books into the home and get the parents involved to make sure kids read, and read every day. If kids can read, and learn to love what they find between the covers of a book, the biggest education battle is won. But without reading skills, nothing that happens in school will matter much in the long run. And, of course, when kids fall behind in reading they fall behind in everything else and become prime dropout candidates.
>
> It's happening too often in this country, and if we don't turn it around fast we'll pay an enormous cost in the next century. We're already paying today in heavy welfare expenditures, crime costs and poor productivity from the American work force.
>
> I still have a hard time believing that in the United States of America, 20% of the adults are functionally illiterate. When I first heard that, I wanted to believe that those were old people who never had a chance to go to school. They're not. They're mostly young people who have been to school.
>
> A lot of them have even graduated. More than 600,000 of the kids who graduated from high school last year could barely read their diplomas. That's a travesty for those of us who paid for 12 years of useless schooling for those people, but it's a personal tragedy for them because they'll soon find out that their diplomas are worthless.
>
> We know how big the job is, and we know that passing out free books is just a start. I visited an inner-city school with all the social problems of every inner-city school. I found out that almost none of those kids had fathers in the house. And some of their mothers are still children themselves.
>
> We challenge the kids to get through 21 books. At first, somebody will have to read the books to them. By the end of the year, they should be reading some of the books themselves.
>
> When I think of those great little kids and wonder which ones will make it, I know that it will be the ones whose mothers are reading to

them every day. If mom doesn't read, the kids won't read. They'll pay a
stiff penalty some day, and so will the rest of us.

However, our interest in studying Running Start was piqued by a
healthy skepticism. While, on the one hand, we applaud the program's
focus on storybook reading as the foundation for reading acquisition
and fluency, the exhortatory quality of the message (much like "Just
say no to drugs") seemed rather fatuous. In the first chapter of this
volume, Lancy discussed the fact that patterns of parent-child interaction around literacy are mediated by cultural conventions and beliefs
that may be resistant to change. Research shows that children who are
at risk for failure do not read voluntarily and are not read to by their
parents or are read to by parents who may be using inappropriate
(e.g., reductionist) strategies. Ironically, Ruth Scott, Superintendent of
the Toledo public schools, reinforced this fear when she praised
Running Start as indicating that Chrysler "shares our enthusiasm for
teaching *sound reading skills* to our children" (cited in Wendorf & St.
Clair 1990, italics added).

Another cause for caution is the history of an earlier corporate-
sponsored reading incentive program—Pizza Hut's "Book It." Widely
disseminated, the program has received surprisingly little attention
from the reading/literacy establishment. There appear to be only two
unpublished studies (Adler et al. 1989; Erazmus 1987) of the Book-It
program and only Erazmus found that it had a positive impact on
reading scores and then only for students in the low reading group.

We had a clear sense that Running Start would be popular, but
would it work? Corporate intrusions in the classroom have not been
without controversy. Sheila Harty (1979) documented in *Hucksters in
the Classroom* that corporate support of education is often blatantly
self-serving. Examples from her monograph include a film distributed to schools by Samsonite entitled "Story of Luggage: From
Caveman to Spaceman," *Cooking with Dr. Pepper* and, our favorite,
Mr. (Planter's) *Peanut's Guide to Nutrition*,which advises students that:
"You can eat ice cream with your cereal if you still balance it into
your day's meal plans." On the other hand, the calls for corporate
support for public education continue unabated (see, e.g., *Fortune*,
vol. 121 [12] entire issue).

In this case, Chrysler's motives appear to be largely altruistic, and
the agency they chose to work with—Reading is Fundamental (RIF)—
has a stellar reputation. Further, the timing is right, in the sense that

after years of treating reading acquisition as a mechanical process that could only be effectuated in schools by meticulously trained teachers using highly specialized materials and techniques, there is a growing recognition that children learn to read from storybooks.   Crain-Thoreson and Dale's (1992) is only one of the more recent of a flood of studies showing direct links between story reading in the home and emergent literacy.   Other research (Anderson, Wilson & Fielding 1988; Cipieleweski & Stanovich 1992) extends this finding in showing that third- through fifth graders who read for recreation demonstrate greater reading growth—on various measures—than those who do not.

METHODS

A variety of data sources—each with distinct limitations, unfortunately—will be drawn on. We shared our plans with RIF and with the Toledo public schools' Office of Evaluation and they, in turn, agreed to share their unpublished reports with us. Hence, we had access to national summary statistics for the program regarding participation and completion rates.   In Toledo, the district evaluation specialist (Burke 1990, 1991) carried out teacher and parent satisfaction surveys and provided data on trends in reading achievement scores as well as on possible extended effects. The bulk of our findings, however, come from an in-depth study of the program in one transition class.

Ann Zupsic was the classroom teacher and project manager in this special class for children who had completed kindergarten but were deemed unready for first grade. The principle feature was small class size (12 at the time of this study), which permitted a great deal of individualized attention. The two girls and 10 boys came from a diversity of lower-middle-class and poverty backgrounds; four were White, two were Asian, and six of the children were African-American. At the time of the study the children ranged in age from six years, seven months to seven years, three months, with the median at 6 years, 9 months.

At the outset of the program, parents were informed about RS, given a handout ("Ten Tips for Reading at Home with Your First Grader," see Appendix) and their permission was sought to test and audiotape their child's story retelling. We began by administering Clay's (1979) Concepts About Print (CAP) test to each child. The story retelling was designed to complement and enrich the rather bare-bones tally of books read as a data source. Of course, story retelling is, itself, part of any emergent literacy-based curriculum.

Children could report that they had read a book at any time, and this fact would be duly recorded on the RS chart. However, a special effort was to be made on Mondays, Wednesdays, and Fridays to bring in a book that had been read at home. After the first couple of weeks it became evident that thetre children who had few or no books at home and whose mothers would not take them to the library, so Zupsic began to send books home. Students would then be called on, one at a time, to go to a reading corner to read/retell their story to the P.I. or one of the undergraduate assistants. These retellings were taped and later scored.

Just prior to the retelling, each child was asked the name of a book, its author, where it had come from (home, library, or class-room), and who had read it to them (mother, other, or self) and the program personnel noted whether the book was a storybook or a skill book. Looking at the book, the child would reconstruct the story. These retellings were then assigned to a low, medium or high category. A retelling in the low category was one in which the child basically named items in the pictures ("First there was a duck, and then a chicken, and then . . . "). At the medium level the child gave evidence of having a story schema and told a coherent story with plot lines and characters. However, at this level the story they told was far simpler than the actual text and, indeed, might have little relationship to it. In effect, these children used the pictures as the sole raw material for constructing the stories and some acted as if they were completely un-familiar with the text. At the high level the children basically retold, accurately, the story from the book, often embellishing the story with appropriate intonation and dialect and including telling details.

Beginning in week five, we began to ask children who were consis-tently in the high category to try and read the story after they had finished with their retelling. These readings were scored in a similar manner. Children who were able to sight read and/or decode about every fifth word were low; at the medium level they needed help with about every fifth word; and at the high level they read with accuracy.

At the end of the ten-week period, parents were asked to come to school for an interview to solicit their opinions regarding RS. Also using the "Ten Tips" (Appendix) they had received earlier as a guide,

Lancy interviewed them regarding parent/child literacy practices in the home.

RESULTS

Survey Results

In its first year RS was implemented in 15 school districts in 10 cities serving 24,000 first-graders. Sixty-nine percent of them completed the challenge of reading (or having read to them) 21 books. Surveys of parents and teachers showed opinions to be overwhelmingly positive (Wendorf & St. Clair 1990). Hubie Pitts, coordinator of RS in Toledo, gushed: "Running Start is a dream come true, for it has fostered in our youngsters a love of reading and the joy of learning" (cited in Wendorf & St. Clair 1990).

The only negative finding initially seemed to be that "some parents would not or could not participate, and a few clearly resented being asked to read with their child (they saw it as the teacher's job)" (Wendorf & Heland 1990:1).

Toledo public schools carried out their own, fairly extensive evaluation of RS. For example, standardized test (Metropolitan) scores were compared for the end of first grade in 1989—before RS, and in 1990—after RS, and showed significant improvement. Similar comparisons in other districts (Wendorf & St. Clair 1990) were less clearcut, however.

A nonsystematic sample of 100 parents were surveyed by phone, and, while opinions were overwhelmingly positive, the researcher felt that very poor parents may have been missed because they did not have phones or were not available when the surveyors called. "Over 80% felt the program increased their child's reading interest level and self-confidence toward reading. Respondents indicated reading from 0 to 140 books with their child" (Burke 1990, 6).

All participating teachers (99 percent of those eligible for the program) were contacted with a mail-out questionnaire, and 60 percent were returned. Results were also positive, 80 percent, for example, felt the program was an effective motivator. However, few "respondents felt the program was influential in promoting parental involvement or long term effect regarding reading . . . . It did not radically alter the pattern of parental involvement. That is to say, those parents who previously demonstrated interest in their child's education continued to do so. Conversely, the program did not involve parents who previously showed no interest" (Burke 1991, 3). Just over 12 percent of all parents of children in the program attended the Reading Rally, for example.

Another discouraging finding came through a sustained effects study. In 1990, the first year of RS, second-grade teachers were asked to sample, over a three-week period, the voluntary reading activity of their pupils. A similar survey was conducted a year later with teachers whose students had experienced RS the previous year. Rates did not change except for a slight *increase* in the number of children who reported they read no books at all. Interestingly, these data appear to be bimodal, with many students reading a lot of books and a substantial minority reading few or none. In any event, contrary to Pitts's rosy appraisal, these data do not suggest that RS had a lasting impact on a large number of early readers.

The Case Study

In Toledo, 75 percent of first-graders met the challenge of reading 21 books in year one, 84 percent met the goal in year two. Despite the added incentives—sending books home and thrice-weekly retellings to Lancy (which the children eagerly anticipated), none of Zupsic's students met the challenge. Since none could read at the beginning of the period, this was not too surprising. The most interesting finding was that involvement in the RS challenge seemed to parallel the children's literacy development. Broadly speaking, the children fell into three groups.

Two children, Joseph and Charles, made dramatic progress over the period, becoming avid, fluent readers. A third, Sarah, was clearly experiencing the transition to conventional literacy (Kamberelis & Perry chapter, this volume).

Joseph and Charles's fathers were in this country pursuing advanced degrees at the University of Toledo. From China and Malaysia, respectively, the boys spoke little English at the start of the year; hence their assignment to the transition class. By the time RS began, however, their command of spoken English was quite good, although heavily accented. Sarah was a petite, shy child whose lack of oral expressiveness was a factor in her placement. As she retold/read her books, she practically whispered.

These three children read/were read 14-17 books over the period. They moved quickly out of the low through the medium to the high retelling categories. Sarah lagged a bit behind the boys in reading after we asked them to read the books they had just retold. Charles was so keen to read, he refused to retell the stories. He told us that he did not watch TV before school—this was his reading time. The majority of the books these children were exposed to were storybooks and were drawn about equally from home and public library collections.

According to their parents, all three of these children were read to from birth; Joseph and Charles were first exposed to Chinese picture books and, in fact, Joseph was independently reading from these books in China. In all these homes the father modeled reading while the mother actually read with the children. All three mothers regularly took their children to the library before the onset of RS. None reported doing any writing—notes, stories—to or with the child. All three parents (the father in Charles's case) claimed that RS motivated their child to read and that the child pushed the parent to get more books and to read to them.

At the other extreme were three African-American children, LaToya, Darquon, and James, who made very little progress over the period. These children were the only ones whose "Concepts About Print" scores were exceptional. LaToya and James in particular performed as children a year younger would function. Each had five books read to them over the period.

In the cases of Darquon and James, they repeatedly claimed that there were no books at home, so Zupsic began to send books home with them. However, it wasn't clear that anyone actually read these books to them. LaToya kept bringing in the same book (*My "C" Book*), so books were sent home with her as well. James's and Darquon's retellings never moved out of the low category, although LaToya did register several highs by the end.

None demonstrated the acquisition of either a sight vocabulary or decoding skills. LaToya and Darquon but not James showed a growing awareness of print. Once Lancy helped them identify a word—during the few reading attempts—there was some likelihood that they would correctly identify it the next time they encountered it in the same book. Darquon and LaToya knew the letters and sounds.

Despite repeated attempts, including home visits, we never succeeded in contacting James'ss mother. LeToya's mother did grant us a fairly lengthy interview. She felt very good about the Running Start program but acknowledged her own limitations.   Not long out of her teens, she was single-parenting four children aged 9 weeks to ten years.   She prefered TV to reading but she did read romance novels occasionally.   She bought a set of alphabet books for LeToya—"she'll say, 'Momma, read this to me again' and I'll read it to her and sometimes I'll tell her 'not right now,' cause I'll be, you know, doin' something."   Similarly, Darquon's mother said, "He mainly reads to himself, when he gets stuck on a word, he gets kind of frustrated but I just tell him to 'just sound it out.'"

For the remainder of the children, all we can say is that the ten-week period did not afford us enough opportunity to assess their potential.   All of these children had acceptable CAP scores, and all showed growth in retelling.   They brought in from three to 11 books. With respect to the influence of home storybook reading, this group presents a mixed bag, as well.   Rory, a white child, would clearly be below grade level in reading if he were with his age-mates in second grade in the fall.   Yet his mother read to him from birth, limits his TV watching, regularly gives him books for gifts, takes him to the library once a week, writes notes to him, and has him listen to story tapes during the summer break.   Lancy had him read seven of the 11 books he brought in but all the readings were at a low level.   Terrel, an African-American child, seemed to clearly fit this same profile.

On the other hand, Paul, Irvin, Will, and Herbert all showed considerable development over the period and yet, in each case, the parent claimed not to have time to read to them or made comments such as, "When Will was little I read to him more than I do now, unfortunately."

CONCLUSION

Every single parent we talked to claimed that Running Start enhanced their child's interest in books and we have considerable evidence that this was the case.   Some children were clearly frustrated because they had no books at home and/or no one would read to them. Also, it seemed that the opportunity to retell their story to Lancy represented as great or greater incentive than the RS "challenge."   But the effects of RS are clearly mediated by parental attitudes and behavior and by the child's readiness to read.   In the case of Joseph, Charles, Rory, and Terrell, whose parents read to them regularly, RS seemed to make a difference only in the enthusiasm the children brought to this encounter but did not affect whether it happened.

In the case of James, LeToya, Darquon, Paul, and Irvin, their parents were unable or unwilling to capitalize on their enhanced enthusiasm for books. As Irvin's mother said, "He was really getting into it, you know. 'I gotta get this book read.' So he, he enjoyed it, but it's like, I had, I didn't have the time to really put into it, you know." As Iaccoca says, "Somebody will have to read the books to them." There's the rub, hence our pessimistic title: "Too little, too late."

Only with Sarah, Will, and Herbert was there the clear sense from the parent interviews that RS had a catalytic effect—that the children demanded greater involvement from their parents and achieved the desired result. In fact, in all three cases, there was a sense that the parents welcomed RS as complementing their attempts to motivate their children to want to learn to read.

Obviously these data are inadequate to reach any firm conclusions about Running Start, but we can see that the program's popularity is probably not due to any dramatic change in children's reading prognosis. It probably "works" for very few children, but that it works at all should be acknowledged.

One finding that surprised us was the fact that every single one of the parents we were able to talk to conceded the necessity of having children's books in the home and that they had some role to play in helping their child learn to read. This bodes well for parent-involvement programs that are more elaborate than Running Start—such as McCormick and Mason's (1986) Little Books or Paratore's (this volume) intergenerational literacy program.

APPENDIX

Ten Tips for Reading at Home With Your First Grader

Sharing books with your first grader helps him or her become a good reader. Besides, it's fun! Here are some suggestions for sharing books with your child, and making reading a natural part of your family life.

1. Set aside a regular time to read to your child each day. Even 10 minutes can make a big difference. Choose a time when there will be few interruptions from the television or telephone.

2. Keep books, magazines, and newspapers around your home so that your family will always have something to read.

3. Let your children choose the books they would like to read or have read to them. Don't worry if they want to hear some favorites again and again. Children learn from repetition.

4. Encourage your children to read aloud to you some of the time. For example, take turns reading a sentence, paragraph, or page. Don't feel they have to get every word right—even good readers skip or mispronounce words now and then.

5. Take your children to the library. Ask the children's librarian to help you find books they might like.

6. Let your children see you read. That will show them that you think reading is important, and that you enjoy it, too.

7. Write notes to your children. Pack them in a lunch box or tuck them in a coat pocket. The note might be a reminder of a special activity you will do together or might just say you hope your child has a nice day.

8. Share family stories with your children. Tell them how things were when you were growing up. Or pass along stories other members of the family have told you.

9. If you are going to a new place, read about it beforehand, or follow up with a trip to the library.

10. If you have a tape recorder, record yourself reading your children's favorite stories so that they can listen again and again. You may want to ring a bell or give some other signal when it's time to turn each page.

10

Discriminating Between the Disadvantaged: Adjusting to Family Differences

Derek Toomey and Judith Sloane

INTRODUCTION

This chapter will focus on differences between disadvantaged families in the literacy environments they provide for preschoolers, and on the ways in which schools differentiate between them in their home-school relations work. It will report results from an intervention program, the West Heidelberg Early Literacy Project that attempted to provide a book-lending program sensitive to differences in families' needs, and that operated via home visits. It will then report on a book lending program that operated in preschools, and appeared to raise children's emergent literacy and print knowledge.

Recently at an Australian conference on literacy, a paper (Williams 1990) was read reporting differences in the family literacy environments of children of differing socioeconomic status (SES). Mothers of preschoolers attending disadvantaged preschools (DPS) in lower/working-class areas were surveyed as were mothers with children in private preschools (PPS) in well-to-do areas. While socioeconomic differences were evident from the responses, in no way could they be said to indicate a poor level of home support in the DSP families in general.

The researcher went on to report that from the PPS group ten families were sampled in which the main breadwinner's occupation offered much opportunity for the exercise of authority and autonomy and in the DPS schools ten families in which the main breadwinner's occupation offered low opportunities for the exercise of authority and autonomy. This two-stage sampling method strongly polarized the samples. These families were then observed conducting book-reading sessions with their preschool children. The results showed the PPS families to have decidedly higher levels of parent-child interaction in discussion of the text. Also they more often asked "known answer" questions (see Chapter Five, this volume) of the kind frequently encountered in schools. The researcher emphasized the size of the differences according to socioeconomic background and experience of autonomy and authority in the work situation.

In drawing his sample to produce such strongly contrasting groups, Williams had a valid research intention. Following Bernstein (1971), he was interested in testing his theoretical claims that those with little experience of the exercise of autonomy and authority in the work situation would be inclined to re-create these authority patterns in the family situation, with authoritarian relations between parents and children, as opposed to more egalitarian relationships with fluid, reflexive patterns of social interaction that facilitate children's language and literacy development and an interactive pattern of parent-child storybook reading (see Chapter Three, this volume). For the purposes of scholarship it may be useful to study extreme contrasts between elite and disadvantaged groups so as to get an overall view of the class system. Studies such as those of Lareau (1989), Connell, Ashenden, Kessler, and Dowsett (1982) and Heath (1982,1983) have taken this approach.

Heath (1982) contrasted the language and literacy environments of young children from families of teachers, businessmen, and professionals in a sophisticated urban environment with those of children of mill workers in socially isolated, inward-looking, rural white and black communities. But it is quite mistaken to turn to such studies to attempt to understand the day-to-day life in disadvantaged communities and its significance for those who would attempt educational reform. For this approach tells one nothing about differences between families in disadvantaged localities. Such studies tend to treat the disadvantaged as a homogeneous group, whereas teachers have to deal with individual students and their families. Studies of this kind also tend to reinforce stereotypes about the disadvantaged as shown in the discussion reported above.

Variation Among Families Within the Same Socioeconomic Level

In Australia, research is beginning to show that the largest gap in student achievement occurs between children from a relatively small and exclusive sector of families of professional, well-educated parents and everyone else (Williams et al. 1993). An important reason for this is the great variation in family environments to be found at all socioeconomic levels. We shall cite evidence that there are many economically poor people who provide family environments that are supportive of their children's educational success and many well-to-do families that do not. Researchers who seek out positive family environments among the disadvantaged find them readily (e.g., Clark 1983; Bright, Hidalgo, San-Fong, Swap, and Perry 1993; Scott-Jones 1987; Goldman 1968). There is a large body of evidence that indicates that there are important differences within social classes or socioeconomic strata in these matters, and that between-class differences may be smaller than within-class differences. Evidence comes from studies using very different methodologies.

There is now a moderately large body of case studies of "spontaneous" readers who begin school already capable of independent reading, but who have received no formal instruction. Typically these children come from literacy-rich environments with a plentiful supply of children's books and other print material, paper, and pencils. The children are read to often and have their questions about print answered. They are library members, show a keen interest in reading, and regularly see adults reading and using print in other ways. Such early readers are found in families of low-income or poorly educated parents (Manning & Manning 1984; Clark 1976; Morris, Harris, and Averbach 1971). Observation studies of literacy-relevant events within the family also show substantial support for literacy development among low SES families (Teale 1986). The U.K. studies of Wells (1981) and of Tizard and Hughes (1984) both report that family environment differences in influences on children's literacy and language development are larger within social classes than between them. Elkins and Spreadbury (1991), in an Australian study of parent-child book reading at the preschool level, show that the amount of parental commentary on the text was predictive of the child's subsequent performance on literacy tasks in school at the first- and third-grade levels, but also showed a nonrelationship with socioeconomic status. Lancy,

Draper, and Boyce (1989), in a study of a working-class sample, showed substantial differences within the sample in the extent to which parents showed an open, interactive, fun-oriented pattern in parent-child book-reading sessions, labeled by the authors as an "expansionist" (as opposed to a "reductionist") pattern (see Chapter Five, this volume). The children of the expansionist parents read more fluently and began independent reading earlier. Ethnographic studies have also found support for children's emergent literacy in low-income families (e.g., Taylor & Dorsey-Gaines 1988; Miller, Nemoianu, & De Jong 1986).

There is a substantial body of correlational evidence that shows that differences in children's family environments is a better predictor of children's performance on tests of school readiness (including tests of literacy knowledge and competence) than is SES (e.g. White 1982; Iverson & Walberg 1982). A number of literature reviews establish the importance of within-class variations in the supportiveness for school success of children's family environments (e.g., Scott-Jones 1984; Hess & Holloway 1983; Toomey, 1989a). Jencks (1972) and Jencks and Bartlett (1979) provide similar evidence on the relative importance of class and family influences in affecting individuals' educational attainments and life chances.

Of particular importance is the fact that in Melbourne, the site of our research program, the catchment areas of disadvantaged schools tend to be heterogeneous, both socioeconomically and ethnically. Rates of geographic mobility are high, and settlement is of a low density pattern, such that local processes of social control are not well formed in a population that is highly privatized and home-centered (Parsler 1979; Toomey 1988). This situation lends itself to divisions within school populations.

Relevant here is previous work (Toomey 1983, 1986) done by the authors in mounting home-reading programs at the prep (Kindergarten) level in "disadvantaged schools." These are schools designated as such by the Australian federal government, which serve the most disadvantaged 10 percent of the school population. Like Sweden (Chapter Six, this volume), but unlike the United States, Australia provides nearly universal preschool education. In these programs, we found a distinction between the enthusiastic parents, who were relatively confident in dealing with the school, who provided a relatively supportive family environment for the child's school learning, and who readily became *au fait* with and implemented the literacy support practices approved by the school; and hard-to-reach parents, who were less confident in dealing with the school and in knowing how to help their children's education, but who were very interested in doing so. We found that teachers worked readily with the enthusiastic parents, who eagerly attended information sessions on how to help their children's literacy development through reading with them at home. These parents gave positive feedback to the teachers. No feedback came from the parents who did not readily visit the school; they were thus often perceived by the teachers as apathetic and not interested in their children's schooling. Our evaluation interviews showed the fallacy of this perception. Most of these parents were keen to help and very interested, but were often somewhat unsure in their helping role. Our most successful projects contacted the parents via home visits (Toomey, Keck, & Atkinson 1987).

A further project (Toomey 1983, 1986) in a disadvantaged school, intended to reach out to families of prep children, foundered because of those social processes that tend to identify the school as the sole legitimate site of education. An aide was employed to assist the home reading program for the prep families in one school, with a special responsibility to pay home visits to the families most needing support. She was a local woman, the school cleaner, who was perceived to be influential with the local parents, and her appointment reflected the interests of the school principal. As it turned out, she held very negative attitudes toward many of the local families whom she regarded as feckless and uninterested in their children's education. She preferred to work in the classroom assisting teachers with the distribution of home reading books and reading to individual children. In this she was encouraged by the classroom teachers. She opened a parents' room in the school, in which a small group of parents met regularly, and a number of them made a videotape about the prep program intended for the parents of the next year's prep children. Our evaluation found that she had made home visits only to parents who regularly came to the school, and that the parents most in need of assistance had received little help.

This study once again pointed to the processes in disadvantaged schools by which some families are included as part of the school community and others are excluded. As a result it was decided to study the effects of these processes deliberately. This study followed the fortunes of children in four disadvantaged schools from the prep year to second grade, with tests of the children's reading competence at both these levels and detailed interviews with the parents in the prep year. Teachers also made a number of ratings of how the parents supported their children's education, and they distinguished between parents having a high level of contact with the school and the rest. At the prep level the high-contact families were found to be distinctive. The children were more successful on tests of reading competence and the interviews revealed that the parents provided a family environment more strongly supportive of their children's literacy development (e.g., frequent reading to the child in the year before school, father reading to the child, parent praise for the child's reading, parental adjustment of reading support strategies to the needs of the child, interviewer's rating). These families also more frequently used reading support strategies of the kind recommended by the school, such as giving prompts while hearing reading. The teachers also gave these parents much more favorable ratings for the frequency and regularity of their reading with the child, the level of their interest in their child's education, and how active they were in their child's education. The high-contact families were not distinguished by SES, though they showed higher levels of fluency in English and were less likely to be from an ethnic minority.

The study showed that over time, the gap between the literacy competencies of the high-contact children and the rest increased, even with controls for the initial advantages of the high-contact children in terms of literacy competence and family environment support. The high-contact parents were more likely to have received advice from the school and to have found the advice helpful, and were more likely to report their satisfaction with information provided by the school on helping their child's reading and with the school curriculum. By opening up schools to parents we may well be enlarging the arena within which inequities of family background may affect children's educational opportunities even further, thus exacerbating the disadvantages of children most at risk.

A study by Tizard, Blatchford, Burke, Farquhar, and Plewis (1988) gives some support to these contentions. It showed that children's improvement in literacy competence in the early years of schooling in inner-city schools was not related to the frequency of parents reading with the children, but was related to the level of parents' contact with and gaining information from the school. Iverson, Brownlee, and Walberg (1981) in a study of "underachievers" in disadvantaged schools, most of whom were black, showed a positive correlation between parental contact with the school in the early grades and the children's growth in reading competence. An intervention study by Sullivan and La Beaune (1971) involving disadvantaged families in a summer reading program for children showed a significant gain in reading competence for the participant children and a decline for the children of families who were invited, but did not respond. Oyemade, Washington, and Gullo (1989), in a study of parent involvement in Head Start programs, showed that the more involved parents were of higher SES and tended to experience upward mobility as a result of their involvement.

It was against the background of these experiences and knowledge that we began the West Heidelberg Early Literacy Project.

THE WEST HEIDELBERG EARLY LITERACY PROJECT

In 1987 we began a home reading program for preschoolers in a disadvantaged locality (West Heidelberg). This was an exploratory program that delivered books to families by home visits with the intention of exploring parents' responses. We felt that home visits were necessary to reach out to those families most in need of help. Subsequently we set up a book lending program via preschools serving a larger area centering on West Heidelberg. The most depressed part of the locality was not represented in the preschool phase, nevertheless, the sample contained some very disadvantaged families. This kind of heterogeneity is quite typical of schools serving working-class and low-income families in metropolitan Melbourne, and will allow us subsequently to explore further this question of diversity.

The Home Visit Phase

West Heidelberg has a well-deserved public reputation as a poverty area. The housing is low-cost public housing. As with most Australian housing, the houses are single story and stand in their own grounds— in a pattern, typical of Australian cities, that tends to lack high-density settlement. Much of the housing is condemned, having been built as temporary accommodation for the athletes in the 1956 Olympic Games. In our sample some 51 percent of households were headed by female single parents. Levels of education were low by Australian standards: 42 percent of parents had left school before tenth grade (about age 16), 48 percent at tenth grade, and 10 percent above tenth grade. Fathers were in manual occupations or unemployed.

The target families were those with a child who was to enroll for the first time in school in January 1988 at two schools in the locality (in Australia the school year begins in January and ends in December). Families were identified through information from the schools, local preschools, and infant welfare clinics, by word of-mouth, and the through the local community health center in which the project was based. Families were recruited by an introductory letter followed up by a phone call and home visit. The home visitor took with her a large supply of attractive children's picture storybooks; the children were allowed to choose five and at the first visit she would read the child one of the books. Usually the enthusiastic response of the child was enough to quiet any doubts the parent might have had, and this proved to be a very effective pattern of recruitment. Families were visited once a week and remained in the program until they were judged to be self-operating—on average about six weeks. Of the 82 families targeted, 12 refused to participate and we failed to contact 10. We excluded two families as not needing the program and think that most of the refusals were of similar background.

We began the program in June 1987, and found it necessary to continue it after the children had begun school, in order to deal with all the families. The home visits were also designed to provide information on the families' responsiveness to the program and were carried out by Judith Sloane, an experienced researcher, teacher, and worker with families. Detailed interviews on the family literacy environment were conducted, which produced scores on a 25-item Family Literacy Environment Scale and on a 15-item scale indicating the child's interest in reading and writing. The interviews provided information on the child's literacy competence and the following performance tests were also used: knowledge of concepts about print, ability to read and write own name, and letter recognition and recognition of environmental print, with and without logo. After each visit comments on the families' participation in the program were recorded, along with any other relevant information. Visits were used to distribute books, model reading to the child, and give parents advice about encouraging their children's literacy development; fliers and pamphlets about this were also distributed. The main focus was on the child's enjoyment of books, and this was what drove the program. The children looked forward to the visits, and eagerly took part in the book exchange. Their enthusiasm helped to keep the adults involved, and much appreciation was expressed at the home visitor's modeling of reading with expression: "I used to read to her, and she didn't like it. But now I do it like you and it's fine."

The choice of books was important here. Books were chosen for their attractiveness to children in terms of their pictures, the strength and interest of their storyline, the elements of repetitiveness and phonologic attraction (e.g., rhymes, assonance, alliteration), not being crowded with print, brevity, and having rich, natural language. They were also nonracist and nonsexist. In many cases the children's and the parents' attention span for reading needed developing, and we chose many short books with rhyme and repetition. In particular we used a large number of books of nursery rhymes; each family received at least one of these and parents were encouraged to read and sing these with the children and to do the same with rhymes and songs learned by the child in preschool (see Chapter Six, this volume). An attempt was made to gradually build up attention span by varying the mixture of long and short books. Favorites were: Lynley Dodds's *Hairy McClairy from Donaldson's Dairy*, (Puffin Books) Jan Nicholls's *Meg and Mog* (Heinemann), and *Mickey Mouse's Book of Nursery Rhymes*. We encouraged children's writing and provided a regular supply of paper and pencils. We also gave to each of the families an alphabet frieze made by students in the nearby technical school. Pamphlets were given out encouraging parents to read often, to make it enjoyable, to discuss the text with the children and relate it to their experience, and to involve children in adult activities using print (e.g., cooking from recipes, writing birthday cards). Parents were also advised to watch Sesame Street and Play-School with their children.

The question of the child's attention to the story is a difficult one. Research suggests that in the early stages parent-child dyads will engage in simple labeling activity (e.g., Ninio and Bruner 1978). As de Loache (1984) indicates, a highly interactive style of doing this will help hold the child's attention. But with a story there is also a need to have the child pay attention to the progression of the story, which is essentially invisible (Harkness & Miller, 1982). Heath (1982) records that, at the age of about three, many children are encouraged to begin to engage in quiet, audience-like behavior, presumably in answer to the need to pay attention to the story. However, the received wisdom appears to be that discussion of the text is particularly facilitative of children's literacy development (Heath 1982; Elkins and Spreadbury 1991; Lancy, et al. 1989). In our project the senior researcher emphasized the importance of getting parents to discuss the text, but the home visitor pointed out that this was not always easy. Some parents expected passive, audience-like behavior on the part of the child. As she pointed out, the first priority was to get the parent reading to the child regularly in a manner that would encourage the child's enjoyment and interest in reading.

Moving the parent along to this goal—text discussion—required careful judgment, since parents (and children) differed so much. For families who have just begun reading to the child the need to build up attention might be more important than the need to discuss the text. Also, in some cases the energy for that attention was not always present, because it was taken up with dealing with more fundamental issues such as managing a busy household while having to cope with a sick relative or a violent husband.

Differences Between Families in Their Response to the Program

The following categorization was produced after a long process of analysis, discussion, and refinement. Some parents passed from one category to another as circumstances changed.

Supportive-sophisticated (12%). Parents were relatively sophisticated in the support strategies they used for the children's literacy and general educational development.

Frances had two children, the youngest of whom was involved in the project. She actively encouraged her children to form their own opinions on a variety of issues and claimed not to understand people who do not read to their children. She had always provided books for her children and all the family were library members. Although it had only been since the youngest was at preschool that he had been read to on a regular basis, any ideas that the project suggested were readily adopted. She was outspoken on educational and other issues. The preschool teacher treated her with "kid gloves." Frances was active in the school and was on the School Council. Both she and her husband were keen that their children should have the best opportunity, and they planned to give them a private secondary education. Now that the youngest was at school, Frances was attending night classes to get a better-paid job than the unskilled work she had before the children were born.

She treated me more as a friend and asked my opinion on a variety of issues. Her son invited me to his birthday party and I felt much at home there. My notes show that among other things, the following matters were discussed with Frances: borrowing books from the municipal library, reading nonfiction books as well as stories to the children, singing songs and saying rhymes with them, answering children's questions during story reading, memorizing texts as an early part of reading, using cursive script in writing words as requested by children, children decoding words, alphabet rhymes, letter recognition, counting from one to 10, and using reading to stimulate children's intellectual development.

Supportive-unsophisticated (69%). Parents were very interested in helping the children, but unsure about how to go about it, and needed guidance. This was the target group for our study.

Mary was a single mother living on a pension. She had two children, one at high school and one in prep that year. The family came into the project through contact with the community centre, with which they had considerable contact. Quite often we read books together in the park opposite their flat and a group of local kids would form to hear stories and to look at books.

Mary was quite keen to try the activities suggested when she saw that her daughter's reaction to books was so positive. Prior to being involved in the project she had not read much to her daughter, but she now found that stories are requested regularly and they enjoy books together. Mary often bought educational toys, such as plastic alphabet letters, a blackboard, and pencils.

She often had adult friends present when I visited and I took the opportunity to explain matters to them, as a way of reinforcing the main points about reading to children, such as the need for a regular time to read each night or day. I pointed out that instructional patterns had changed, that schools use books with more natural language, with rhyme, rhythm, and repetition rather than formal readers, that there is a tendency to immerse children in print, so that reading to children is important long after they begin school or begin independent reading, that books introduce a wide range of concepts beyond their immediate world, and that it is important to link books to the child's everyday experience (e.g., visits to Grandma, pets), and to point to text while reading aloud. Other points were the need for the adult to introduce and explain educational toys and that any writing or reading activity is good because it helps to motivate the child to learn while at school.

Supportive-independent minded (3%). Parents wanted to help their children, but were suspicious of professionals and educational institutions.

Lisa had three children all below school age. She lived apart from the children's father with whom she had intermittent contact. In the early stages I found it difficult to conduct an interview, as there were rarely fewer than four children present and they and the TV provided a formidable barrier to concentration.

Lisa asked to be in the project through her contact with the community centre. She had difficulty in creating a routine for sharing books with the children and often did not get around to reading the five books. Books that were discussion starters rather than actual stories were more popular with Lisa. She also preferred to read books with a small amount of text.

Lisa wanted to know what the actual school routines would be and she attended the induction meetings at the school. She told me of her extreme dissatisfaction with the number of new teachers her daughter had had since the beginning of the year. She said that if she could afford to buy a car she would drive her child and send her to the Catholic school.

I did all that I could to make the reading sessions enjoyable, reading to all the children in the family. I looked at the new books she purchased and encouraged her to choose short, simple books within the child's concentration span. I encouraged her to display and refer to the alphabet frieze and to discuss the books by referring to the pictures. I also encouraged her to elicit prediction from the child— "What do you think will happen?" I emphasized the value of pointing to the text to teach directionality, linking the text to the child's experience, having pencils and paper available, and modeling reading behavior herself.

Lisa was very independent minded and had a will to do all she could to help her children, but her parenting tended to be inconsistent.

Supportive-stressed (13%). Parents wanted to help their children but their energies were often taken up with other pressing matters, such as sickness in the family, low income, domestic violence, or drug dependency.

The initial approach to Sally's family was made through the preschool. Early on it was difficult to make contact and appointments were not kept, but this was usually followed up by an apologetic phone call. Sally listened to suggested activities but said as she had four other children and her husband was often away she did not have enough time to spend reading. An older sibling—a keen reader— sometimes read to the younger ones. This was one of the three project families who did not attend the induction activities at the school for prep children. During the visits I did most of the reading; Sally was usually busy elsewhere. I tried to involve her, but knowing her level of stress I did not press the point and instead tried to involve the older children. Sally was unreliable in making appointments and keeping to the program and the advice I gave was of a fairly simple nature, encouraging her to provide commentary on pictures and stressing the value of repetition. The books I left tended to have simple, undemanding texts and were short.

I later learned that Sally had left home and the children were cared for by their father and other relatives.

Non-coping (3%). Parents in this category seemed to be unable to cope with the tasks of parenting because of personal inadequacies rather than difficult circumstances.

One was a single parent with three children who was faced with a custody battle with the social welfare agency, which was threatening to take away one of her children. She probably enrolled in the program to help establish a reputation before the court of her parenting competence. She was well-intentioned and spoke in praise of the project, but never seemed to get any reading done with the target child. When visited, the mother was usually somewhere else and the child was next door with a neighbor. The visitor left books with him and attempted to involve the older child in reading to him. Subsequently the children experienced many changes of school.

It is clear from the above that there is a definite need to adjust the instruction to the needs of each family. It will be apparent from the above cases that how much instruction could be conveyed depended a great deal on the capacity, competence, and interest of the parent. Had the program been other than exploratory, we would have put much more time and resources into helping the supportive-stressed parents. In fact, one of the schools asked us to put in a special effort with visiting some children, which we did. All of these families fell into the supportive-stressed category.

The noncoping parents present a difficult problem. We felt that the project had not really helped and had merely succeeded in raising the level of guilt of the parents.

Program Outcomes

We will now present an assessment of the extent of implementation of the program during the period of home visits. This is based on the home visitor's observations and discussion with the parents, which naturally included questions about this, together with a follow-up evaluation interview. It was judged that all the parents in the supportive-sophisticated and the supportive-unsophisticated categories were reading regularly to their children. The two non-coping parents were not. Of the other two categories, about half of them were doing so, as far as we could tell. This indicates a success rate of about 86 percent. This also leaves out the refusals.

There is little doubt in our minds that this success rate is due to the regular supply of books delivered in such a convenient way. The larger of the two schools involved would not allow prep children to borrow books from the library and the books sent home by the classroom teachers appeared to be from a reading series, intended for the children to read to the parent. The second school provided a library of attractive books for parents to borrow and to read to their children. We were informed that only four of the parents in the program used this library. This is clear evidence of the need to reach out to parents and of the efficacy of a method of delivering books that bridges the home-school gap. Ideally children should take home books regularly from the classroom library, their choices being guided and known about by the teacher. The home visitor believed that most of the families who were reading regularly to their children would continue to do so, provided they received a regular supply of books.

We have also found that the kinds of books carried by supermarkets and newsagents tend to differ from those for sale in book shops. Parents in disadvantaged localities tend to have access to the former rather than the latter. The variety tends to be limited and often the language quality is not as rich. Obtaining short, predictable books with rich language from the supermarkets is more difficult.

Incidentally, the home visitor became a well-known figure in the locality and was greeted warmly by the children when she saw them in the neighborhood and the school. This created an identity for her that made access to the families easier, since many parents and children knew about her in advance. Her visits were usually welcomed and she often found that people asked her for advice on all manner of problems, such as custody issues, the school achievements of elder siblings of the target child, marital problems, choice of schools, when to begin school, and adult illiteracy. We are in little doubt that the project's success is largely due to the element of personal contact.

We will now examine differences among these families in the children's reading competence, the evaluation of them by the teachers, and their SES. Follow-up studies were carried out at the end of 1988 (the prep year) and 1989. The following information was obtained in 1988 on the children literacy competence as reflected in the Sloane-Tuer Early Literacy Profile, a teacher assessment schedule providing information on the child's self-concept of reading competence, mastery of print concepts and book handling, reading self-concept, and writing competence. In 1990 the children's school literacy scores were obtained from another teacher assessment schedule, the Griffin (1989) Literacy Profile.

We have arranged the categorization of families in a hierarchy, dividing the unsophisticated-supportive into upper and lower levels of support. Figure 10.1 shows the scores of the various categories on various measures of child literacy competence and interest, as well as a composite measure of SES (based on father's and mother's education and occupations). The results show a clear hierarchy in terms of children's literacy competence and interest (all but one statistically significant) but no significant relationship with SES. This gives strong confirmation to the general theme of this chapter.

No claim is made that the hierarchy of children's literacy competencies revealed in Figure 10.1 is the result of the program of book-lending, though it does make some sense to claim that it may result from the interaction between the book-lending and the use the family made of the books. We did attempt to test the effects of the book-lending with a quasi-experimental design and pre- and postesting (Toomey 1993b). The results did not show a significant pattern of effects on the children's literacy competencies and interests. However, this may be because of the weak experimental design in which membership of the project and comparison groups was confounded with attendance at particular schools. (Toomey, 1993b). It could also be that a mere six-week treatment was not sufficiently prolonged.

Figure 10.1
Differences Between Families in the 1987-1988 Study

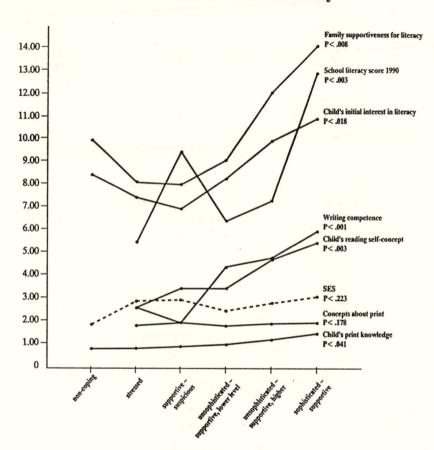

Although not a prime aim of the project, we have tried to improve the parents' confidence and competence in dealing with the school. This has had some influence on parents' participation in the school. For example, at one school the induction program for parents held toward the end of 1987 was attended by 20 parents, whereas normallyonly about five people would have been expected to attend, or so we were informed by the school's vice-principal who was in no doubt that this was a result of the program. The Parents Club also saw a considerable increase in attendance after the home visitor encouraged parents to attend, at the request of the school. A number of parents in the project are members of the School Council and, generally speaking, the parents have shown a greater readiness to be involved in the school, for example, in the infant-level motor program.

The Preschool Phase

The aim of the home visit phase had been to find whether our target population of parents would engage in regular book reading with their children and this had worked well. But a long-term aim was to develop a low-cost model that could be widely adopted. The home visit method of book delivery was costly, so we looked next to preschools as a means of delivering books to families. Unfortunately, the preschool serving the area of our home visit program could not be included, but four other preschools in the surrounding area did agree. One of the schools was chosen for its relatively high proportion of ethnic minority families, though ethnic concentration in this part of Melbourne is not high.

The research design was very simple. The intent was to ensure a regular supply of books and to see whether this had an effect on children's emergent literacy competencies, using a quasi-experimental design, with pre- and post testing of project and comparison children. In Melbourne, preschool teachers normally take two classes and this provided us with naturally occurring control and experimental groups, from which comparison families were randomly selected. Our choice of this approach had been encouraged by the success of a similar scheme by Mason and McCormick (1986) using "Little Books," though we deliberately chose children's picture storybooks having better quality paper and pictures and more developed language, as in the home visit phase.

We began the program in June 1989 and lent out three books twice a week for the children to take home for their parents to read to them; this continued until early December of that year. The program was wholly administered by the research team. The aim was to enthuse the children about reading, hoping that their enthusiasm would engage the parents, as in the home visit phase. We visited the preschools twice a week to lend out the books and on these visits spent two hours reading to the children. Whole class groups were read to using 'Big' books, as well as small groups and individuals. Books with repetition and rhyme were used, and children were encouraged to chant, chime in, and take part in oral cloze. It appeared that we were successful in our intention. The children, generally speaking, were excited about the books, took time to make their choices, and wanted to talk about them. We videotaped their pretending to read books, for the Sulzby Scale of Emergent Story Book Reading (Sulzby 1985), both before and after the program, and these videotapes showed much increase in the children's enjoyment of the reading activity. Of course, by this time the children were quite familiar with us, were older, and had also had the experience of their preschool teachers reading to them, so this development could not unquestionably be laid at the door of the project. For parents who could not read English, we supplied translations of the text and/or spoken voice versions on tape. These were parents for whom English was a second language, and we also used some books in community languages. Some 25 different ethnic groups were in the sample from northern, eastern, and southern Europe, the Mediterranean fringe, Asia, the Pacific, and South America. No one group was numerically large.

The aim was not to have a detailed program of instruction for parents, as our experience had taught us that information sessions in the school tend to attract those least in the need of help. We did hold two such instructional sessions, but these were attended by fewer than half the families. We also gave out pamphlets and fliers giving parents information about literacy development, and we also gave advice to parents in at-home interviews that were conducted at the beginning of the program for evaluation purposes. This advice emphasized the importance of making the experience enjoyable for the child, reading with expression, encouraging the child to talk about the book and ask questions, being physically close, asking questions, talking about the pictures, and relating the story to the child's own experience. Pamphlets with a similar emphasis were left behind at home visits.

Because our approach emphasized the importance of differences in family environments, we thought it important to gain information about this for the purposes of evaluating the effects of the program. One might expect family environment factors to have a different impact for different families. Accordingly, structured interviews were conducted with both the project and comparison families at the beginning of the 1989 program. We also gained information from the preschool teachers about the parents' ethnicity and spoken and written language fluency. From this information we compiled scales with acceptable statistical reliabilities that were intended to reflect the following: the socioeconomic status of the family (e.g., parents' education and occupations), the extent to which the family environment fostered the child's literacy development (e.g., book-reading activities with the child, discussion of the text, parents' reading behavior, availability of print), the child's interest in reading and writing (e.g., frequency of writing and reading behaviors, requests for being read to, buying of books, and library membership); the general supportiveness of the family environment for school success (e.g., patterns of TV use and rules about TV, interviewers' rating, and whether the family subscribed to "The Age" newspaper), the number of items indicating ethnic minority status (e.g, parents' and child's birth outside Australia, parents' language fluency), and parental illiteracy.

The same performance tests for the child's print knowledge were used with the project and comparison children, as in the home visit study, and these were added to by information from the parent interviews to make up a scale reflecting the child's initial print knowledge.

The most important test, which was used at both the beginning and end of the study, was the Sulzby Scale of Emergent Storybook Reading. This test requires the children to pretend to read a story with which they are familiar. We videotaped the reading and classified the child's performance on an eleven-category hierarchy from simple labeling activity through to independent reading. Important divisions within the hierarchy are between whether or nor a story was formed and whether the account was mainly oriented to the pictures or the print (the use of a monotonic recitation being a sign of the latter). Sulzby (1985) reports a series of studies with children of different ages from two to six that reveals a developmental progression in performance on the test. We regarded it as a useful indicator of children's emergent literacy development and used it as the sole outcome variable in the 1989 study.

The results of that study showed that the project children were significantly ahead of the comparison children in their performance on the Sulzby scale, controlling for the child's initial performance on the scale, initial print knowledge, and interest in reading and writing, as well as the array of family background and environment measures referred to above. Only 8.7 percent of the comparison group gave print-oriented or written language—like responses on the Sulzby post test, whereas 57.5 percent of the project group did so. If anything, the family background comparisons favored the control group (Toomey

& Sloane 1991), so this growth could be attributed to the project with some assurance.

The 1990 and 1991 Projects

Our next aim was to see whether the program could be run successfully by preschool teachers so in 1990 and 1991 the program was repeated. These were identical with the 1989 program with two important exceptions. First, the teachers in the preschools carried out the programs, targeting only one of their preschool classes, as in 1989. Second, we had realized that the Sulzby scale, although concerned with print-oriented responses, gives no account of the child's print knowledge. We were aware of the increasing number of research studies emphasizing the importance of the child becoming familiar with particular books and the fact that as the child became more familiar with the book, he or she was more likely to pay attention to the print. Accordingly in the last seven weeks of the program we introduced class sets of short books with repetitive patterns, accompanied by big book versions of the text. We asked the preschool teachers to pay particular attention to these texts with frequent readings in the class, accompanied by participation by the children. The children took these books home for use with their parents. We used seven sets of these books, which were cycled around in the last seven weeks of the program such that each preschool had experience with five of them.

We adapted the evaluation in line with this change. In 1990 we used the Sulzby scale as a pre- and posttest, and once again it showed a result in favor of the project, using the same experimental method of evaluation as in 1989, with the same controls for the child's competence and interest and the family background/environment variables. But we also conducted a posttest-only comparison with children from a nearby preschool serving a similar population, using both the Sulzby test and the performance tests of the children's initial print knowledge that had been used as a pretest. The results once again showed a significant advantage for the project group both for print knowledge and for emergent literacy development, as reflected by the Sulzby scale.

Table 10.1
Characteristics of Sample, 1990 and 1991 Preschool Studies

	1990	1992
Child's average age:	4 years 8.5mths S.D. 6.9 months	4 years 5.5mths S.D.4.3 months
Single female headed households:	16.3%	12.3%
Public housing:	28.9%	36.8%
House owning:	44.3%	46.2%
At least one parent has reading difficulties	9.2%	not available
At least one parent born outside Australia	34.2%	N.A.
Target child born outside Australia	3.1%	N.A.
Received tertiary education, fathers	23.8%	16.7%
Received tertiary education, mothers	15.8%	14.4%
Received 4 years or less of secondary education, fathers	52.6%	49.0%
Received 4 years or less of secondary education, mothers	47.3%	48.1%
Manual occupation or unemployed (fathers)	59.2%	60.9%
White collar occupation (fathers)	40.8%	28.1%

In 1991 the 1990 program was repeated identically, this time administering the tests of the child's print knowledge as pre- and posttests, using a nearby preschool as a comparison, and repeating the statistical controls used in 1989 and 1990. The results once again showed in favor of the project group. In summary, the evaluations have shown a consistent effect of the program on the children's print knowledge and emergent literacy development (measured by the Sulzby scale). They have also shown that a program managed by preschool teachers can be effective in enhancing children's emergent literacy.

The population dealt with in the preschool phase was heterogeneous. Accordingly, a reanalysis was conducted of the 1990 and 1991 data distinguishing families of high and low socioeconomic status within the sample, bearing in mind that those of high socioeconomic status were, generally speaking, of mid to marginal middle-class backgrounds (see Table 10.1). Sampling in more well-to-do suburbs would have drawn more families of upper-middle-class status.

The results showed for the 1990 study that the project had an effect on the children's performance on the Sulzby scale if they were from higher SES families, but not if they were of lower SES. For the 1991 study, using the child's print knowledge as the outcome variable, the reverse was true. An effect was shown on lower SES children's print knowledge but not at the higher SES level. These results are presented in detail in Toomey and Sloane (1993).

CONCLUSIONS

It seems clear that providing a regular supply of good children's picture storybooks, by means of loan, is a very useful strategy for enhancing emergent literacy in four to five year old children from disadvantaged localities. Doing this via preschools is a low-cost strategy. At this stage of children's development there is much overlap between the roles of parents and teachers (Katz 1982), and parents seem very willing to become involved in their children's literacy development (Hannon & James 1990). The large majority of working-class and low-income parents can read the relatively simple texts involved. The parents do not need to visit the school and can fit the reading activities into their daily routine. Our experience is that few books get damaged and we found the level of loss of books quite acceptable, bearing in mind that the lost books could well be contributing to some needy child's development. McCormick and Mason (1986) provide evidence of a similarly successful program (see also Swinson 1985). However, Robson and Whitely (1989) report no effects on the Infant Reading Test of a quasi-experimental program of book lending for children of the same age group; the program lasted a year but made available only two books per week. The test (posttest only) did not reflect the children's use of context to gain meaning nor their attitudes toward literacy. Two quasi-experimental programs of only six weeks duration (Robinson & Naumann 1993; Bus 1989) report nonsignificant effects. Also the home visit program reported above, which lasted about six weeks reported nonsignificant effects on children's emergent literacy, though this may have been due to a poor experimental design. Perhaps a six-week program is too short.

In the state of Victoria, some 90 percent of children attend preschool (Office of Pre-Schools and Child Care, 1992). Provision is especially generous in Melbourne, though poorer children's families may not be able to afford the modest fees involved. This means that delivering books via preschools could reach a considerable proportion of the target population. However, the variation in family environments pointed to above indicates a problem for this kind of intervention. The home visit program was highly successful in involving parents from the locality in question in reading to their children, but it had the advantage of the personal approach and the opportunity to adjust the program to the family's needs. Sending home books through preschools would lack these advantages and there can be little doubt that this method failed to reach some families. We were quite unsuccessful in trying to persuade busy preschool teachers to make home visits to parents who might have needed it. Hannon, Weinberger, and Nutbrown (1991) provide similar evidence of the superiority of a home visit over a center-based approach. Hirst (1990) also reports favorably on a book-lending program via home visits in a study using qualitative methodology. The work of Swift (1970) and of Edwards (1991a) also suggest the benefits of an individual approach with some families. So much of our own work has found the need to make special efforts to give help in some cases.

One possibility to deal with this problem is a peripatetic home visitor, who would visit homes referred by the preschool teacher. The home visitor's role would be to break the ice and bring about the parents' active participation in the lending program, and perhaps carry special resources for non-English reading or non-English speaking parents. The home visitor might also try to reach families not using preschools. In any case, it would be unwise to assume that programs of the kind proposed would be universally successful in enlisting disadvantaged parents in assisting their children's literacy development. It is unfortunate that there are some parents who will only become involved once their children have been to regular school and found to be struggling with reading (see Chapter Four, this volume). For such parents a program at the kindergarten level of the kind offered by Edwards (1991a) might be appropriate, or a Reading Recovery program with a parent involvement element, or one of the programs of parents hearing their child read aloud of the kind reported in Topping and Wolfendale (1985).

One very promising development is intergenerational literacy programs, which provide literacy and basic education to parents weak in literacy skills as well as parenting education, simultaneously with early education for their children parent and child time together and literacy education for the children, given by the parents (Nickse & Quezada 1993).

11

Parents and Children Sharing Literacy

Jeanne R. Paratore

In many ways, the field of family literacy is a complex and muddy arena. On the one hand, there is a steady stream of research and policy-oriented writing, which recommends that parents of at-risk children be trained in the literacy techniques practiced in mainstream homes (Anderson, Hiebert, Scott,& Wilkinson 1985; Clark, 1984; Teale, 1984a). On the other hand, writers such as Auerbach (1989) and Taylor and Dorsey-Gaines (1985) see this approach as founded on the discredited deficit model of child development in families that are culturally and linguistically distinct. Educators find themselves caught in the middle. Should the focus of family literacy be to teach families ways that they can "bring themselves into alignment with the standards of 'gate keeping institutions'" (Lareau, 1989:11) or to find ways to help schools recognize and acknowledge the learning environment created by non-mainstream families and "build effective communication linkages that enhance schooling opportunities for students and their families" (Delgado-Gaitan 1992, 513)? What are the outcomes and consequences of family literacy programs?

Answers to this question are elusive for several reasons. First, family or intergenerational literacy is broadly defined. Descriptions include programs that center around parent-child storybook reading projects (e.g., Bean, Southworth, Koebler, & Fotta 1990; Edwards 1989, 1991a); programs where parents and children each receive instruction, but where instruction is not explicitly designed to promote literacy interactions between the parent and child (Dolan 1992); and programs in which instruction is explicitly planned to increase the practice of shared literacy between parents and children, and by so doing, enhance the literacy knowledge of each participating family member (Ada 1988; Quintero & Velarde 1990).   But the type of program that emerges in a particular setting is dependent on the way family literacy is defined by those in charge. Auerbach (1989), for example, recommends defining literacy very broadly, and using the daily round of family activity—whatever this may entail—as the basis for enhancing the child's literacy experience.   She contrasts this approach with programs that would impose mainstream values and practices on families that are linguistically and culturally different.

Second, answers to the question posed are difficult to find because research related to the outcomes of intergenerational literacy programs, whatever their definition, is scant. A review of the existing literature reveals that investigations have focused generally on program definition and description (e.g., Ada 1988; Nuckolls 1991; Ranard 1989), or on the academic performance of either the adult (Nickse 1988) or the child (Bean, et al. 1990; Seaman, Popp, & Darling 1991). Although there is evidence that parents' views and understanding about literacy influence their literacy practices with children (e.g., Goldenberg, Reese, & Gallimore 1992), only a few studies (e.g., Ada 1988; Eldridge-Hunter 1992) have investigated the ways that intergenerational literacy programs influence parent-child literacy interactions in the home setting.   No study was found that explored the ways that intergenerational literacy programs influenced teachers' views, practices, or attitudes about families (but see Chapter Nine, this volume).

The study to be reported here was designed to add to the related literature by examining the influence of an intergenerational approach to literacy on the literacy learning of adults and on the practice of shared literacy at home.   It was based on the premise that an intergenerational approach to literacy would not only extend adults' own uses of literacy, but would also enhance the ways they support their children's school learning.   By so doing, it would increase the social resources nonmainstream parents have, thereby extending their own opportunities and providing greater access to successful schooling for their children. It differs from related studies in that the outcome studied was not academic achievement of children, but rather the influence of the project on adults themselves, and their resulting interactions with their children.

METHODOLOGY

Setting and Participants

The community in which this project was implemented is small, comprising approximately two square miles. It is considered a gateway for new immigrants. Families are ethnically diverse (47% Latino; 23% Caucasian; 20% Southeast Asian; 10% other) and generally economically deprived, with the average income below $10,000. The high school reports a dropout rate that exceeds 50 percent and the highest teen pregnancy rate in the state. During the first year of this study, the School Committee entered into a 10-year agreement with a private university to manage the school system. The project that served as the setting for this study was essentially the first major effort to emerge as a result of the school/university partnership.

Funded primarily by a grant from the U.S. Department of Education,[1] adult basic education classes in literacy were held in a community center located within walking distance of three of the four elementary schools, allowing parents to walk their children to school prior to coming to class. Free childcare was provided for preschool-aged children. During the three-year period of the study, there were 367 families enrolled in literacy classes for at least one instructional cycle, including 246 mothers, 73 fathers, 27 grandparents, 10 aunts, 8 uncles, 1 sibling, and 2 adults who were caretakers but did not have a defined relationship with children. Within the families, there were 816 children; 270 were kindergarten-aged or younger and 546 were school-aged. Ethnicity included 232 Latino, 102 Southeast Asian, 19 Caucasian, 13 African-American families, and 1 Arab family. Of the 367 adults, 351 spoke English as a second language. Families represented 28 different countries of origin and 13 different first languages. For second language learners, the range of English proficiency varied from limited to fair, and the range of literacy in the first language varied as well, from limited to high levels of proficiency. As one measure of parent-child literacy interactions, parents were asked on the enrollment form to describe how often they shared storybooks with their children. Two hundred thirty-two parents reported either rarely or never reading aloud to their children in their first language prior to participation in the study.

There were two criteria for parents' enrollment in the classes: a desire to improve their own literacy and a commitment to engage in shared literacy events with their children on a daily basis. The enrollment history of the project is interesting. During the first instructional cycle, only 16 families participated, despite space and funding for a total of 40. Over time and through intensive efforts to share information about the program through a broad community network, enrollment grew to 75 families during each instructional cycle with a waiting list of as many as 60 families.

The process of recruitment taught us two important lessons. First, the inclusion of the full range of community agencies was necessary to achieve widespread interest and participation. While elementary and secondary teachers were helpful in distributing program information, it was the community leaders who opened doors for us with parents. Project staff visited and called community agencies frequently during the early weeks of the project, bringing program information and attending meetings with staff and parents at various agencies. Of particular help in recruiting families were clergy, leaders of bilingual and cultural organizations, and health professionals. Announcements were made at church services and community center meetings. Community leaders reviewed written notices, suggested revisions, and helped in developing accurate translations for bilingual parents. They helped to distribute information by including notices in church bulletins, and posting information on community center walls and in neighborhood stores and centers. Many community leaders contacted parents directly to describe the project and ask if they would like to participate. After the first instructional cycle, our best recruiters were the parents who were participating. We found that classes grew as parents brought their friends and family members. In several cases, we enrolled the mother, father, grandmother, and/or grandfather from a single family.

Second, we learned that building a stable population takes time. It took several weeks and a great deal of networking to recruit the initial 16 families, and then several more weeks and several more meetings with community leaders to build beyond that initial enrollment.

Procedures

Parents attended literacy classes four days per week, two hours per day. During the first year, classes were organized within three instructional cycles of nine weeks, 12 weeks, and 13 weeks. After the first year, parents told us that nine weeks was too short. They did not think they had accomplished enough in so short a time, and the middle cycle was interrupted by the Christmas holidays.   During the second and third years, two instructional cycles of 15 weeks each were held each year. The longer cycle enabled parents to experience sufficient accomplishment and it fit well within the general academic semester cycle to which the university and the school system adhered.

The research on bilingual education, second language learning and multicultural education (Genesee 1985; Nieto 1992; Sleeter & Grant 1987; Weinstein 1984) led us to hypothesize that classes comprised of multicultural and multilingual learners would enrich the learning climate. Therefore, classes were deliberately formed to reflect the demographics of the community, with each class comprising approximately 70 percent Latino families, 20 percent Southeast Asian families, and 10 percent other ethnic groups.

In multiability, multilingual groups of 25 or fewer, instruction was planned to achieve three goals: (1) provide opportunities for adults to read and respond to literacy materials of personal interest; (2) provide a selection of books, strategies, and ideas for adults to share with their children in order to support their literacy learning; and (3) provide a forum through which adults could share their family literacy experiences with their friends and teachers, enabling us all to learn more about the uses of literacy in diverse families. Emphasis was placed on situating literacy experiences within the fabric of daily life. Parents were encouraged to join with their children in multiple literacy activities, including reading and writing oral histories, composing letters to friends and relatives as well as notes to family members, journal keeping, story writing, and publishing.   Parents were also taught how to help children with homework, types of questions they might ask the classroom teacher to find out about their children's progress, and how to ask questions of their children about the school day.

Classes were taught by a teaching team of five people, including two certified and experienced teachers of literacy and three tutors. The teachers were graduate students at the university. The tutors were undergraduate students who received financial aid through the college work study program. The tutoring assignment fulfilled their work requirement. In addition to tutoring a minimum of six hours each week, they attended a two-hour literacy tutoring seminar once a week throughout the academic year.   Each teaching team had at least one member who was fluent in Spanish and Vietnamese, the primary languages of many of the families in the project. Two teaching teams also had tutors who spoke Khmer.   This staffing framework allowed us to group learners flexibly to meet individual needs at different times during the instructional period, but maintain large multicultural and multilingual groups for discussion and response.

Of the two-hour class period, approximately half of it was devoted to reading and writing materials of adult interest and to developing specific skills to extend their own literacy abilities and half the time was spent becoming familiar with materials and strategies for supporting their children's literacy learning. These strategies were, of necessity, quite varied, as the children ranged in age from a few months to 18 years.

Instructional reading/writing strategies used with these adults have received support in the professional literature related to adult literacy education (Thistlethwaite 1983) and included assisted reading and writing, paired rereadings, cooperative learning, and metacognitive training.   Although experiences in each classroom and on each day varied, a typical instructional period looked like this.   At the beginning of each class, parents made an entry in a literacy log.   Here, they recorded a literacy event they had shared with their child the day before, and commented on their reactions to it.   Who initiated the event? Why? Did it connect to something else?   Did the child like it?   How did they know?   Did they like it?   Why or why not?   After writing, parents shared their log entries with a small group or with a partner. Often this included sharing and exchanging favorite children's storybooks.   Usually, a teacher or tutor joined the group to participate in this discussion.

Following the small group interaction, the class convened as a whole.   Sometimes questions raised in the small groups became the focus of a large group discussion.   For example, what should parents do if the child didn't seem to be interested in the book?   Is it good for the child to ask so many questions?   Should the parent ask the child questions?   How could they help their children write?   What could they do if they didn't understand their children's homework?   How could they talk to the child's teacher about a school problem?   At other times, the large group lessons grew out of a more formal plan designed to introduce parents to ways to support their children's literacy learning. For example, during the first week of classes, emphasis was placed on sharing storybooks with children. Teachers explained how storybooks could be shared with or without knowing the author's language, and demonstrated how parents could rely on picture book illustrations to tell stories. Throughout the week, teachers demonstrated how to interact with children with books, the kinds of questions that might be asked, and the ways children might be invited to participate. During the early days of the instructional cycle, teachers and tutors encouraged parents to consider the ways literacy was used routinely in their daily interactions with children. Literacy was broadly defined to include any interactions involving reading, writing, and language. These ideas were listed on charts and displayed in the classrooms for parents to comment on and discuss.   In later lessons, teachers, tutors, and parents discussed storytelling and talked about how they each share their memories and experiences with their children through their stories. That discussion led to an extended task in which parents wrote and published books for their children to read. Other lessons included discussions of television viewing, parent-child play, talking to children about school, and helping with homework.

Following this opening period, one of the teachers introduced a topic or an article that would be the focus of the day's lesson. Topics for reading and writing were deliberately chosen to stimulate a discussion of ethnicity and culture, as a way to discover and explore ethnic connections (Ferdman 1990). Reading selections came from many different sources, but all were considered to be materials that participants would encounter in their daily lives. Local and national newspaper articles, news magazines, school newsletters, short stories, and informational brochures were often used. Sometimes parents brought in articles that they wanted to have the class read and respond to.

Since there were many different first languages spoken by the parents, no attempt was made to provide text for in-class reading in different languages.[2] All written text was in English. Prior to reading, however, the class often formed into small groups of learners who shared the same language. Led by a teacher or tutor, each group discussed the topic first by introducing key concepts or vocabulary in the first language or by asking learners to connect settings, situations, or experiences in their reading to those in their countries of origin or their own cultures. This practice consistently led to a large group discussion of multiple perspectives on a particular idea or concept, which served as a bridge to the reading of the text in English.

After reading, parents again formed small groups to discuss and share their understanding in their first language, before reconvening as a large group to share their general impressions, questions, and comments. Then, some learners might form pairs to share a part that was particularly interesting to them; other learners might work individually or in a small group with a teacher or tutor to receive extra help on a particular reading or writing strategy.

Finally, learners ended their instructional period each day by making an entry in a personal journal to respond to the selection or the day's discussion. Parents chose whether to compose this entry in their first language or in English.

Throughout the instructional cycle, attention was given not only to the acquisition of literacy skills and strategies, but also to developing individual skill in exploring the relationship of literacy, itself, to the learners and their families. Parents were encouraged to reflect on the ways they used literacy to get things done, and to consider what they already knew about literacy, as well as what they wanted to learn.

At the end of each cycle, an award ceremony was held honoring participants with an individual certificate of completion and affording them an opportunity to share their accomplishments with their friends and family. At the award ceremony, some parents chose to read aloud their favorite piece and others chose to compose a group piece that described their thoughts about the project and their own literacy. At the most recent ceremony, some parents elected to create a display of the literacy artifacts that tie them to their own countries. Included were labeled photographs, envelopes from letters received and sometimes the letters themselves, articles about their countries, and objects accompanied by labels or longer explanations about the importance of the item in their country. Other parents chose to create a display of their children's uses of literacy at home. Posterboard exhibits were filled with children's stories, drawings, and letters. Old tape and torn corners suggested that items were taken down off home walls in order to create the display.

Data Sources

Several measures were employed to collect evidence of the impact of the program on parents' literacy acquisition and on the incidence of shared literacy events in the home setting. Measures included the following:

Reading Fluency

Within two weeks of entry to the project and again following 40 instructional hours, parents completed an assessment of their fluency in reading in English. The instructional cycle of 40 hours was selected on the basis of data that indicate that adults require between 50 and 100 instructional hours to make significant gains in reading (Mikulecky 1990). Since this project was designed to promote high attendance by being responsive to learners' instructional needs, by building a sense of community through daily use of collaborative learning strategies, and by calling learners each time they were absent to inquire about their health and to see if they needed any help or support, and since the emphasis on daily literacy interactions with their children was expected to provide relatively intensive and frequent practice at home, it was hypothesized that measurable gains would be made in a shorter time period. Parents chose an assessment passage in English from a representative sample of materials adults encounter on a daily basis. Included for selection were current newspaper articles of local and national interest, legal papers, short stories, nonfiction selections and children's picture books. The chosen selection was used for pre- and post project assessment. A running record (Clay 1979) of each adult's oral reading behaviors, performed following a silent reading of text, was completed. During pretesting, if the adult indicated that the task was too difficult to attempt, interventions were provided to decrease the level of difficulty. Interventions included previewing the passage before reading, by discussing the topic in the first language, a read-aloud by the examiner followed by discussion in the first language to familiarize the learner with the passage topic and ideas, and/or assistance with specific words or phrases during reading. No interventions were used during posttesting.

Data have been collected and analyzed on a sample of nine parents who were identified as having minimal literacy proficiency in both their first language and their second language. [3]   It was hypothesized that these lowest performing learners were likely to be the hardest to teach in the multilingual, multiability setting and thus would provide a valid measure of project effectiveness. Of the nine subjects in the sample, six were Latino; two were Asian and one was Portuguese. Years of schooling in their own countries ranged from four to 12 years, with an average of seven years.

Attendance

Daily attendance rates were recorded. The mean attendance rate for project participants for each cycle was compared to the average attendance rate for adults in basic education programs serving parents in a nonintergenerational model in the same community. These data are available for all 367 adults participating in the project.

Attrition

The number of participants who enrolled and completed at least one full instructional cycle was calculated and compared to national averages for program completion of adults in basic education pro-grams. These data are available for all 367 adults participating in the project.

Parent-Child Literacy

Self-report data on the incidence of parent-child literacy activities in the home setting were collected on a weekly basis. Data collected included: number of selections read to the child by the parent; num-ber of selections read to the parent by the child; number of times joint writing activities occurred; number of visits to the library; number of books borrowed or bought; number of times games were played in-volving words or reading; number of meetings held with the child's teacher; and number of times parents assisted the child in completing homework. Self-report data were analyzed and compared at the end of each instructional cycle, with a focus on the degree to which the incidence of literacy events suggested the existence of a routine or consistency in the utilization of literacy at home. Self-report data were collected from a sample of 10 families.

Making a Connection Between Home and School

Teachers of children whose families were participating in the project were asked to invite children to keep a journal of literacy events they shared with their parents. Teachers were asked to set aside time once a week when children could write about one literacy event that they shared with their parents and to provide time for the children to share their written entries with their classmates. No other specific directives were given. Sixteen teachers were invited to participate in this activity. Journals were collected from five children in five different classrooms.

RESULTS

Results are reported in relation to the impact of the program on parents' literacy learning and on the incidence of parent-child literacy events in the home setting.

Parents' Literacy Learning

The impact of the intergenerational approach on parents' literacy learning was evaluated on the basis of three behaviors: attendance on a daily basis, completion of at least one instructional cycle, and reading proficiency as measured by a running record. The average attendance rate was 74 percent. This contrasts with an average attendance rate of approximately 50 percent in adult education programs nationally (Sticht 1988-89), and an average attendance rate of 32 percent for adults in a traditional adult basic education program in the same community. It should be noted that in addition to the intergenerational versus nonintergenerational focus of the two programs, they also differed in grouping plans (multiability and multilingual in the focal program versus homogeneous and monolingual in the local program) and instructional strategies (strategy-based in the focal program versus skill-based in the local program).

With regard to retention, during the first year, 72 percent of all learners who remained in the program for at least two weeks completed at least one full 15-week cycle; during the second year, 93 percent of all learners who remained in the program for at least two weeks completed at least one full 15-week cycle. During the third year, 92 percent of all learners who remained in the program for two weeks completed at least one 15-week cycle. The average retention rate over the three-year study was 85 percent. Of those who discontinued, reasons for leaving the program included employment, relocation to a new community, serious illness, and pregnancy. In addition, 47 percent of all learners who completed one cycle enrolled in at least one more cycle. A review of attrition rates reported for other programs reveals approximately 50 percent as the most frequently reported statistic (Sticht 1988-89). Using the local adult basic education program as the comparison group, the attrition rate for the same academic years was 57 percent. In making these comparisons, however, it is important to note that the short-term length of each cycle (9-15 weeks) may differ from the instructional periods for which the comparison data are based.

To assess the impact of the program on reading performance, oral reading proficiency of nine adults was examined.

Figure 11.1
Change in Oral Reading Miscues for Each Subject

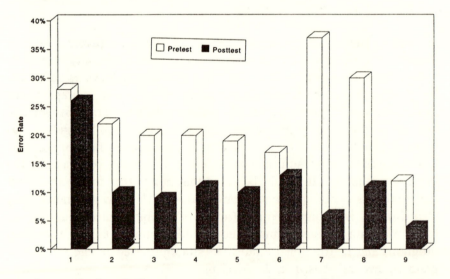

An analysis of the pre- and posttesting reading performances (Figure 11.1) reveals an average decrease in oral reading miscues of 13 percent after 40 instructional hours. Using Clay's (1979) criteria, six of the nine subjects shifted their performance on the tested passage from "difficult" to "learning." One learner shifted her performance from "difficult" to "easy." Since the pretest performance was accompanied by assistance from the examiner as appropriate and the post-testing performance was unassisted, the rate of growth was actually more substantial than the change in percentage indicates.

The Practice of Family Literacy

Analysis of family literacy behaviors is based on weekly self-reported data submitted by 10 families during one instructional cycle. None of the families in the sample reported that they had engaged in shared literacy activities with their children prior to enrollment in this project. The change in family literacy behaviors was measured by the number of literacy events reported during the first and last week of

Figure 11.2
Change in the Incidence of Shared Literacy Between Parents and Children

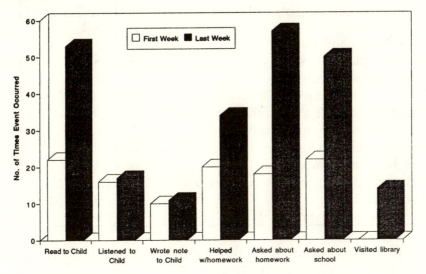

the instructional cycle. Data presented in Figure 11.2 suggest some significant changes. By the last week in the project, families reported reading to children three to four times each week, though writing still occurred infrequently. Increased emphasis was placed on asking about homework and on providing children help in completing it. In addition, most families had visited the library at least once during the last week of the instructional cycle, as compared to no visits by any of the families during the first week of the project.

In addition to assessing the general increase in the practice of literacy from the first to the last week, data were also analyzed to assess the influence of the project on the routine practice of family literacy. For this analysis, the average incidence of literacy events per family per week was computed during the last eight weeks of the instructional cycle.   The data indicate that families were engaged in shared storybook reading three to four times per week and interacted with school-aged children regarding homework and general school activities almost daily (4.17 times per week). However, writing occurred in the home setting relatively infrequently (1.05 times per week) and visits to the library occurred only about once each month (.38 times per week) for most of the families.

Table 11.1
Weekly Average of Parent/Child Activities for Marta

Weeks	1-5	6-10	11-15
Read to child	4.2	3.2	4.8
Listened to child read	4.2	2.0	2.8
Helped with homework	4.5	5.0	5.0
Asked about homework	5.0	4.2	5.0
Wrote note/message to child	0	0	0
Helped child write a letter/greeting card	0	0	0
Played a game w/ child involving words	1.2	1.2	.2
Viewed television together	2.6	.2	3.2
Discussed program viewed	1.6	.2	2.2
Asked child questions re school/ reading	1.0	5.0	5.0
Visited a library	0	0	1.4
Borrowed or bought a book	3.0	4.2	5.0

An examination of the weekly self-reports of one family reveals a typical family profile. As shown in Table 11.1, Marta, whose two children were ages five and seven at the time of her participation, read to and with her children several times each week, asked about or helped with homework daily, and frequently talked about school and reading. In addition, they frequently viewed television together and discussed the program they viewed, emphasizing visual and oral literacy as well as print literacy. However, Marta never reported writing a note or message to her children, and began to visit the library only in the eleventh week of the project, after her teachers had begun to place more emphasis on this literacy event.   Most striking about Marta's profile is its consistency across the weeks of participation.   She seemed to have developed a routine for sharing literacy with her children.   Marta was a participant in the project for two years and she later became a project tutor. Although she has since left the project to accept another job, she recently returned to report (gleefully) that she found $5.40 stashed in her seven year old daughter Viviana's backpack. It was her own money that she had saved to buy books from the school book club.

Making Connections Between Home and School

As noted above, in an attempt to connect family literacy to school experiences, classroom teachers who had children of parents participating in the project were invited to have children keep a journal similar to the one their parents were keeping.   Some teachers chose to create interactive dialogue journals, asking children questions and making comments about their literacy experiences (Figure 11.3). A teacher of a kindergarten child used the journal as a language experience lesson, taking the child's dictation and then having the child reread it (Figure 11.4). A third teacher simply had children write and share their entries with little or no interaction with the teacher (Figure 11. 5).

All teachers reported that children expressed great pride in sharing their entries and talking about their experiences with their parents. During sharing sessions, other children asked many questions, both about the literacy events themselves and about their parents' school experiences. No teacher indicated that she used the journal as the basis or the springboard for any other literacy task in the classroom. In one instance, use of the journal was discontinued when a parent reported that her child was being kept in during recess in order to   complete the task. Finally, the low participation rate among teachers (five of 16 initially targeted) suggests the work that must be done to build awareness of the need to build stronger home-school links.

Figure 11.3
Intergenerational Literacy Dialogue Journal Entry by a **Fourth-grade Student and His Teacher**

March 15/99 0

Yesterday my mother help me with my home wak. Whe did multiply dy three. Wlk had to check and do it. Fist we write on a piece of paper and cheek et. Then we put it on the math book. She all son help me with my spelling. We put on the paper and cheek it and if it is wrong aue eaer and do it on a other piece of paper. Then aue put the paper on the bok.

Your mom's help should really help your math and spelling marks to improve.

I am very happy to be able to participate in the Intergenerational Literacy Project with you and your mom.

DISCUSSION

Discussions about families and schooling often turn to the issue of parents' motivation and interest in their children's learning. Often, when the school population under study is one that is linguistically orculturally different, educators make an assumption that children reside in families where there are lower educational aspirations. Recent work, however, has disputed that assumption. Delgado-Gaitan (1992), for example, found that parents with very few years of formal schooling were eager to help their children with homework assign-

Figure 11.4
Intergenerational Literacy Journal Entry Dictated to the Teacher
by a Kindergarten Child

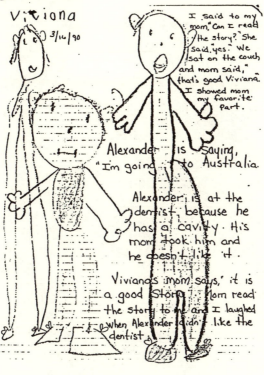

I said to my mom "Can I read the Story?" She said, "yes. We sat on the couch and mom said, "that's good Viviana."
I showed mom my favorite part.

ments, but did not understand how to help. Further, when they found discrepancies in teachers' reports of their children's progress, they were unaware of alternatives available to them, such as contacting the teacher or someone else with whom they could consult to solve their children's problems. Delgado-Gaitan concluded that although poverty and limited education affect child rearing, "the problem is more generally one of missing out on the resources and access to advantages otherwise available to middle-class families" (p.497). Similarly, in a discussion of her study of parent involvement among low-and middle-income families, Lareau (1989) found that parents in the low-income community either did not have or did not know how to access the resources necessary to comply with teachers' requests for assistance.

Figure 11.5
Literacy Journal Entry by a First-grade Child

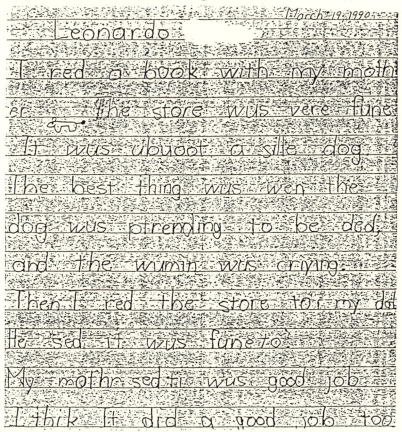

Results from the present study suggest that projects that incorporate an intergenerational approach to literacy may help in several ways to address the problems that Delgado-Gaitan and Lareau report. One issue, as Lareau points out, is the lack of cultural capital that non-mainstream parents possess. One way to increase such capital is to become more familiar with the ways of gate-keeping institutions, and this can be accomplished through adult education classes. Although research suggests adults often have low attendance rates in adult education classes, the participants in this project had very high attendance rates. We attributed these high rates to several factors. First, while helping their children was a shared goal among all participants, they also came to the project with personal goals. Interviews and discussions with parents convinced us that while the intergenerational focus may be a hook, it alone will not keep parents coming. Their time is valuable and their personal goals are important. They must experience some personal, academic, or social growth as a result of participation. Second, classes were collaboratively planned and implemented. Adults began each day with their own experiences from the day before, experiences that were linked to their children; they had a say in what they would read and write and consequently, topics were of importance in their daily lives. I believe this process was important in communicating a sense of mutual respect. Third, adults interacted throughout each class, building a sense of community and camaraderie. Within large and small groups and in pairs, they were given time to share their own thoughts and test their ideas. We encouraged adults to use their first language to express their thoughts, and we created a teaching team that could respond to them in their languages. Fourth, we demonstrated concern and respect for learners by calling them when they were absent to offer support and assistance. There was a fine line here. Some parents found this practice to be intrusive. We learned to be somewhat selective in implementing the policy. The consistency of attendance rates across learners and across instructional cycles in the project reported here indicates that an intergenerational approach combined with effective practices in the teaching of literacy supports high and long-term attendance in literacy classes, providing adults the time that is necessary to improve their own literacy and, in at least some ways, their own cultural capital. In addition, self-reported data indicate a steady and systematic practice of shared literacy in the home setting. Such events provide the parents frequent opportunities for practice in natural and meaningful settings, promoting more rapid growth in literacy.

In looking more closely at the self-reported data, several findings are important. The relatively rapid acquisition of a range of shared literacy behaviors is consistent with data reported by Fitzgerald, Spiegel and Cunningham (1991), as well as that reported by Delgado-Gaitan (1992), that indicate that both high- and low-literacy parents are positive about home literacy practices and need not be persuaded of their importance; rather, these researchers suggested that low-literacy parents need to be shown how they might serve as role models. In the present study, where shared literacy was broadly defined to incorporate storybook reading, parent-child play, shared television viewing, and discussion and talk about school and homework, opportunities for demonstration, modeling, discussion, and sharing led to the regular and frequent practice of family literacy within a relatively brief period of time. Yet others have found that not all parents are willing or able to participate in their child's literacy learning (e.g., Bergin, Lancy, and Draper, this volume). What factors make the difference? While one can only speculate, there are several possibilities. Bergin, Lancy, and Draper focused exclusively on shared storybook reading. While this is clearly a valuable shared literacy event, it represents only one of many. In the study described here, several other literacy events were shared, demonstrated, and encouraged, providing parents choices that may have accommodated both the range of literacy proficiencies and their own family routines.

In addition, at those times when storybooks were the focus of discussion and interaction, parents were strongly encouraged to use the illustrations to compose their own story if they could not read the words. Many wordless picture books were provided early in each instructional cycle to encourage parents who saw themselves as poor readers to participate in storybook reading. Much time and effort were placed on building an awareness among parents that whatever their literacy proficiency, they possessed the requisite knowledge and skill to share storybooks and other literacy events with children.

In the literature that supports the importance of reading aloud to children, it is unclear whether the simple act of sharing a storybook or the specific interactions that occur during the sharing make the difference in children's successful acquisition of school-based literacy. It may be that family literacy educators will need to be a bit more global in conceptualizing the ways parents and other family members can engage in storybook reading, providing parents options that range from a word-for-word reading to a story telling.

The finding that storybook reading emerged as a frequent behavior while shared writing did not is also consistent with the finding of Fitzgerald et al. (1991) that parents tended to characterize early literacy development mainly with regard to reading and to the exclusion of writing. Despite a fair amount of emphasis on shared writing (e.g., examples of the kinds of notes parents and children might compose to each other, discussions of parent-child dialogue journals, the recording of family histories), few families reported that shared writing occurred regularly. Third, the finding that parents visited the local library only once per month reveals what may well be a flaw in the project's design. Since parents routinely borrowed books from the lending library available through their literacy classes, it may be that they did not have a need to obtain additional reading materials. However, since using the local library is one way to establish a resource for life-long support of literacy, the need to develop and promote a library habit is an important one that the design of the project did not, apparently, promote effectively.

Finally, the intergenerational literacy journals kept by children provide some important insights about interaction between parents and children and between families and schools. First, comments from parents, children, and teachers indicate that children take great pride in their parents' schooling. Second, entries suggest that children feel a strong sense of support from their parents as they read and write together. Third, there is a good balance in entries on both school-based and family-based literacy events, indicating that families are not allowing school-like activities to replace or substitute for existing home practices.

With regard to families and schools, however, the low rate of participation among classroom teachers who were willing to allocate time for children to keep and share their journals raises questions about how schools can more effectively recognize and acknowledge the learning environment that parents work hard to create at home. There was a decidedly low rate of interest among classroom teachers in this particular activity. Despite several opportunities to plan and discuss the project, and a biweekly visit by a research assistant to answer questions and collect copies of journal entries, few teachers participated in either planning or implementation. Is the integration of such a task likely to be successful only in classrooms where teachers are already keeping journals? If journals are not already a part of the classroom curriculum, are there other ways for teachers to affirm and reinforce the practice of family literacy? Would teachers have more willingly participated in an oral family sharing time? Questions such as these need to be explored with teachers to discover ways that family literacy can find its place in the classroom community.

Despite the indicators of success of this project, there were parents who inquired about it, demonstrating at least initial interest, who did not choose to stay. Are there lessons to be learned from the 7 percent who left before completing an instructional cycle? Would a different instructional framework have worked for them—one that required a smaller time commitment, one that was perhaps home- rather than community-based, or one that was individual rather than group-based? Questions such as these need systematic and careful exploration if family literacy initiatives are to have wide-reaching effects.

CONCLUSION

At the end of this three-year project, I find myself asking many questions about the directions of family literacy.   I am encouraged by the positive findings regarding the influence that an intergenerational approach may have on what parents know about literacy and literacy learning in schools. However, I am constantly "tugged at" by those who suggest that programs such as these intrude in families' lives, impose school-like literacy in home settings, and ignore the life circumstances of individuals in diverse families. Are we not too focused on what families should do, rather than on what they are already doing, to support their children's learning? In addition, I wonder if work such as this is contributing to a tendency to look outside of school, rather than within, to explain children's academic success or failure? Finally, I ask whether we are being careful to place equal emphasis on programs that teach parents about schools and schooling and programs that teach educators about families and homes.

As we continue to explore family literacy it is important to learn more about the range of perspectives that exist. Are there ways that family literacy educators can acknowledge and be responsive to each of these perspectives? The increasing diversity in America's schools and communities convinces me that we must try.

NOTES

[1] In addition to the grant from the U.S. Department of Education, the project received support from the Commonwealth of Massachusetts Bureau of Adult Education, Xerox Corporation, and the Ratchevsky Foundation. Following the completion of the initial three-year funding period, the project secured support from the Barbara Bush Foundation, Commonwealth of Massachusetts Bureau of Adult Education, and Boston University. Beginning with the fifth year of implementation, a major portion of program funding was been included as part of the school department's budget.

[2] The exception to this was in the children's books that parents borrowed to share at home. The lending library included many books in Spanish, and some in Vietnamese. It was difficult to find picture books in Vietnamese and Khmer. Parents were encouraged to read or share picture and wordless picture books in their first language.

[3] Subjects selected for study were those whose pretest performance on the running record exceeded an error rate of 10 percent. Using Clay's (1979) criteria, this error rate indicated that the selection was within the "difficult" or "frustration" range, even with intervention and support from the examiner. Interventions included as many as three read-alouds prior to the subject's rereading.   Given the level of support and the demonstrated degree of difficulty, it was concluded that these learners could be considered to have entered the project with low print literacy in English.

12

The Even Start Initiative
Ruth A. Wilson and Jackie Aldridge

THE EVEN START MODEL

Overview of the Model

Intergenerational literacy is an emerging practice in the field of adult education. A major advantage of this approach is the "opportunity to combine agendas of mutual importance: adult basic skills improvement and literacy development in children" (Nickse 1990, ix). One federal initiative mandating such a combining of agendas is the Even Start program.

Even Start is a literacy program authorized by the Elementary and Secondary Education Act of 1965 as amended by the Hawkins-Stafford Elementary and Secondary Improvement Amendments of 1988. Clearly stated by the law is the need for integrating services and providing a unified program. As outlined in P.L. 100-297, the intent of Even Start is to "improve the educational opportunities of the Nation's children and adults by integrating early childhood education and adult education for parents into a unified program . . . that build[s] on existing community resources to create a new range of services" (P.L. 100-297, Sec. 1051). Families eligible to participate in Even Start are those families (1) with educationally disadvantaged adults (i.e. those without high school diplomas or GED) who reside in an elementary school attendance area designated for participation in the basic Chapter 1 program and (2) who have young children, ages one to seven.

Congressman William F. Goodling from Pennsylvania led the efforts toward enacting the Even Start legislation. Goodling was familiar with work done at the National Center for Family Literacy in Louisville, Kentucky (see discussion of PACE in Chapter Eight) and incorporated components of that model in the Even Start concept.

Since the problem of illiteracy is entrenched in the home, that is where the solution needs to focus. Program developers working from this approach view parents and children as a learning unit and plan shared literacy experiences designed to benefit both children and parents. Choosing and exploring books together at the public library is one example of a shared literacy experience. A family systems and family involvement approach to intervention is strongly supported by the professional literature (Bailey, 1987; McGonigel & Garland 1988). While little research has been done on family and intergenerational literacy programs, *per se*, research from the early intervention and early childhood education literature suggests that the impact of educational programming "may be more profound and lasting if the whole family. . . is involved" (Nickse 1990, 3).

Funding for the first Even Start projects was made available in fiscal year (FY) 1989. At that time, 76 grants, totaling $14.5 million, were funded. Over 96 percent of the grants were awarded to projects in Chapter 1 elementary school attendance areas and are being implemented out of the Chapter 1 offices of those local school districts. At least one of the Chapter 1 area projects, however, is housed in the Family Life program of the local school district. This is the Toledo Even Start (TES) project, discussed in greater detail in the second part of this chapter. Three of the initial Even Start grants were made to state departments of education serving migrant populations. The grants were distributed across small rural and large urban school districts in 44 states and the District of Columbia. During the second year of funding (FY 1990) 46 new awards were granted, bringing the total to 122 Even Start projects. As of the 1992-93 academic year, funding for Even Start projects is managed through state departments of education and total allocations are over $90 million.

Even Start Services

Basic Even Start services can be grouped into three distinct areas: (1) core services, (2) support services, and (3) special one-time events.

The core services are outlined in the Even Start legislation and consist of the following:

- Adult basic education
- Parent-child activities
- Parent education/child development services
- Early childhood education services

Adult basic education.

Adult basic education activities represent the regularly scheduled core services for adults. These services include ABE (Adult Basic Education), ESL (English as a Second Language), and GED (General Educational Development)—all designed to improve basic educational skills, particularly literacy skills in adults. While a number of the Even Start projects offer all or several of these adult basic education activities directly through the Even Start program, other projects refer project participants to ABE services already being provided through other community programs.

Parent-child activities

Parent-child activities consist of regularly scheduled core services for adults and children together. Many Even Start projects conduct these parent-child activities in the home; other projects offer these activities in the center with a number of families participating at one time. Parent-child activities often focus on language development and literacy and may include a variety of instructional games, as well as having parents and children reading together.

Parent education/child development services

One of the major goals of the Even Start program is to help parents become full partners in the education of their children. Toward this end, a regularly scheduled core service for adults provides parent education and child development instruction. This parent education component is "designed to enhance parent-child relationships and help parents understand and support their children's growth and development" (St. Pierre, Swartz, Nickse, & Gamse 1991, 11).

Early childhood education services

The Even Start early childhood education services are designed for children, ages one through seven, and are often offered in a group setting. The purpose of the early childhood education component is to "enhance development and prepare children for success in school" (St. Pierre, Swartz, Nickse, & Gamse 1991, 14). Early childhood education services may be offered in a typical nursery school or daycare program and often include a screening component to identify young children with special needs.

Many of the activities offered during the early childhood education component of the Even Start program center around books and reading. Stories are read, picture books displayed, experience stories written, and literacy-related materials added to the learning centers in the early childhood classroom. Literacy-related materials might include a phone book by the phone in the children's pretend play area, a recipe book in the kitchen area, and a note pad and pencil in a desk or office area.

Support services

In addition to the four core services outlined above, Even Start projects typically provide an array of support services. Support services are designed to enable Even Start participants to more readily access the core services. Support services in many of the Even Start projects include all or some of the following: transportation assistance, childcare, meals, nutrition assistance, health care, special care for family members who are disabled, and referrals to other community services, such as employment assistance, protection for battered women, screening/treatment for chemical dependency, mental health/ family counseling, and child protective services.

Special events

In this category fall such activities as information fairs, highlighting a variety of community agencies and services; book exchanges, whereby participants swap books and other reading materials; and periodic presentations or demonstrations on topics of interest to participating families.

Even Start activities may take place in the family's home or at a center (e.g., a school, community service building, or library). At times, families may receive some of their Even Start services in the home and other Even Start services in a centralized location. What makes Even Start different from many other literacy programs is the emphasis on the family and a unified approach to providing services, whether these services are offered in or outside of the home setting.

THE TOLEDO EVEN START PROJECT

According to figures from the National Center for Family Literacy, there are about 50,000 adults in Toledo, Ohio who are non-readers. This obviously means that there are many young children in homes with nonreading parents. These children are at risk for academic success. Poverty adds to the at-risk status of many of these children. According to a 1991 report developed by the Children's Defense Fund, there are 5,626 Head Start-eligible children in Lucas County, the majority of whom live in Toledo. Children eligible for Head Start are those whose family income is below the poverty level.

In response to the concern about nonreading parents and their at-risk young children, Toledo Public Schools applied for and obtained an Even Start grant during the first year of Even Start funding (1989-1990). The TES project was the only Even Start program in Ohio at that time. Its first year award was approximately $250,000. By the third year, the federal award had increased to over $300,000.

Federal regulations require a local match that differs from year to year: at least 10 percent of the total project cost during the first year, 20 percent the second year, 30 percent the third year, and 40 percent in the fourth and any subsequent years. Local match for the TES project includes salary contributions for a portion of administrators' and teachers' time devoted to the project, a portion of the fringe benefit costs for project personnel, classroom, and office space, and access to a basic skill computer curriculum and management system.

Of the total budget (federal portion), approximately 31 percent is allocated to personnel, 14 percent to fringe benefits for personnel, 10 percent for acquisition of childcare services, 2 percent for evaluation services, 2 percent for access to the computer curriculum and management system, and 2 percent for instructional and office supplies. Also supported through the federal portion of the budget are expenses related to transportation for staff and participants, phone usage, staff development activities, and publicity. Allocations for each of these latter areas is for less than 1 percent of the total budget. Materials purchased through the grant include computer equipment, early childhood education materials, parent education books and videos, literacy/life skills materials for adults, and children's books. The children's books are used as family literacy incentives, with approximately $20 worth of books allocated for each family. These books are given to the families enrolled in the core services of Even Start as a way to promote family literacy activities in the home.

An interagency advisory committee was formed and invited to assist in the planning and development of the TES program. The committee has been meeting quarterly and has been involved in establishing a local evaluation plan, a coordinated referral system, and community awareness procedures. The advisory committee also reviewed and made recommendations on different aspects of the educational program including assessment, curriculum for children and adults, community linkages, and recruitment and retention of participants.

Staff directly involved with providing services to the TES participants include a project coordinator, an adult literacy teacher, two parent educators, an early childhood education teacher, a paraprofessional, and a recruiter/assessor. The role of the recruiter/assessor is to contact potential Even Start participants, share information about Even Start with them, and determine their eligibility to participate in the program. The recruiter/assessor plays a major role in collecting background information on the families and providing information about Even Start to interested families and the general public. The professional background of the recruiter/assessor is in the area of social work.

According to the original plan, the recruiter/assessor would be doing frequent home visits for the purpose of recruiting families and then later working with them on their Family Education Plan (FEP). The parent educator was also scheduled to do some home visits. However, home visits never became a regular part of the program. Also, while many of the initial staff have remained with the project over time, staff turnover has been a constant. For example, the first coordinator left to take another position within the school system (moving from a part-time to a full-time position) and her replacement became ill and had to take a disability leave.

Public Awareness and Recruitment

Initial estimates of the number of families to be served by the TES program were set at 80 percent (or 468) of the 585 eligible parents and children living in the TES catchment area—the area identified as including the "most in need" families in terms of family resources. Recruiting clients has been extremely difficult—a common problem for IGL programs. To date—three and a half years after the project began—TES has worked with only 250 families, and many of these participated to only a limited degree. On the other hand, those clients who have become heavily involved in TES have kept the staff working very hard.

The TES program utilizes several strategies for identifying and recruiting eligible families. Many referrals are received from an extensive network of over 60 community-based agencies and programs that serve at-risk families with young children. Whenever possible, personal contacts are made with all families referred. TES, in turn, refers its clients to other agencies, when appropriate. During the screening and assessment of Even Start families, it often becomes evident that some families may be experiencing food and housing problems; others may be dealing with a family member with serious medical or emotional problems. When community agency referral needs are included on a family's FEP, an Even Start staff member initiates the referral and provides the support and assistance necessary to ensure that the referred family or individual gets linked to the appropriate resources. It is obvious that a strong interagency network is critical to the success of the TES project.

Recruitment efforts also include staff presentations to interested groups, print and electronic media exposure, and, occasionally, home visits to eligible families. A major part of each public presentation is devoted to eligibility criteria and referral procedures. The presentations usually conclude with the opportunity for members of the audience to receive referral packets which may then be given to interested families. Within the first two years of the project, TES staff had made approximately 137 presentations to area organizations or individuals. TES also disseminates information about the program through a variety of community publications, with special attention to publications servicing the target recruitment areas.

Even Start information is also disseminated to the community through a program brochure and a slide/tape presentation. Area community agencies are encouraged by the TES staff to incorporate both the brochure and slide/tape presentation in staff training as well as client education sessions. Additionally, the TES program was highlighted on local television and radio newscasts on several occasions. Program staff report area print and electronic media coverage to be invaluable to the recruitment process.

Toledo Even Start Clients

Client Margaret Garcia said she heard a discussion about TES on TV and decided right then to try the program out. She now reports, "Since I started with the Even Start program I read a lot. I enjoy books better and I read to my kids." She says she reads about six books a week to them, whereas before the Even Start experience, "it wasn't that way." Margaret has two sons and says that she now takes them to the library at least twice a month. In addition to enjoying books at the library, they also enjoy movies there.

In the initial phases of the TES project, recruitment efforts focused on families residing in only two of the Chapter 1 school attendance areas. These two schools, King and Lincoln, are located in the inner-city section of Toledo and are considered to be in the neighborhoods of the families that are most in need . Since very few of the targeted families chose to respond, recruitment efforts were soon expanded to include the other 35 Chapter 1 schools in the city of Toledo.

Most of the clients fall within the federal description of "most-in-need." Of the families participating in the TES project during the 1990-1991 year, 63 percent were single parent families, 74 percent relied on government assistance as their primary source of financial support, 85 percent were unemployed, 79 percent of the adults did not have a high school diploma, and 57 percent of the children did not have any other type of early childhood education. These percentages were similar for other years of the project as well.

Kim Griffin's story is typical of many of the Even Start parents. Kim is 28 years old, white, and the single parent of four daughters. Kim's daughters are aged six, seven, eight, and nine. Kim attended school until eighth grade and then dropped out. Kim depends on Aid to Families with Dependent Children (AFDC) as a source of income. She rents a three-bedroom home and has been unemployed for several years. Andrea, the eight-year-old, has a speech impairment and attends speech classes during the summer. Kim heard about Even Start when the recruiter/assessor disseminated information in one of the catchment area schools.

Cheryl Harvey is another typical Even Start participant. She is African-American, 33 years old, and the single parent of two girls. Her daughters are aged three and nine. Tiffany, the three-year-old, attends Even Start with her mother. Cheryl heard about Even Start through a Head Start teacher.

Sharon Turner also heard about Even Start from a Head Start teacher. She reports:

> I had registered Tina for Head Start and her birthday came two days too late for her to be in Head Start, so her teacher—the lady who was going to be her teacher over there—she told me about Even Start; so I called and got an appointment and came here.

When asked if she was surprised that Even Start would be for both her and her daughter, Sharon said that it was a surprise to her, but that she was really excited to get into the program and that she was glad she did. She indicates that she learned a lot from Even Start, especially about reading and parenting:

> It helped out a whole lot with my reading and reading to Tina. She enjoys me reading to her—the laughter and the excitement she gets out of me reading to her now—because before the program with me reading to her I would just pick up the book and just read to her. Now we really get into the book, the excitement, and we do things from the book. If there's jumping or bouncing a ball or whatever, we get into it—do some of the things that the book is doing . . . . It's more alive, you know; she really gets into it and loves it.

During the fourth year of the project, interviews with some of the participants indicated that they were interested in taking a more active role in recruiting other families. One individual, in discussing why present participants or graduates of the program would be effective recruiters, commented, "We know how valuable it [Even Start] is." Another participant, Wilma Willis, indicates that she has been recruiting others to the program ever since she started. Limited success in recruiting families during the first phase of the program seems to be due, in part, to the lack of success stories of individuals to share with their friends, neighbors, and acquaintances. Once a group of individuals had participated in the program, word of mouth and information about success stories proved to be the most effective recruitment strategy. Cheryl, a client with a good education but in a dead-end job, said:

> Adult literacy has helped me to refresh my memory in reading and in math. We do many assignments. Some are on job information and writing letters. I enjoy it because I'm picking up things that I had forgotten about.

Corliss Baker, a participant who felt she had benefited from TES, talked about how she first got involved:

> Well, I think her name was Peggy Wilson called and gave me some information on it—Even Start. She was asking me did I feel like I'd be interested in this. I said "Sure," plus it's only a couple of hours a day, and since I wasn't doing anything at home, I said I think I'll enjoy this. The class has helped me understand and comprehend more. We discuss how I can help Wendy in reading. . . . My daughter and I go to the library now and we didn't before. I am also more motivated to get my GED than before.

Before families are fully enrolled in the TES program they go through a screening process to confirm eligibility and to obtain more specific background information about the family. The adult applicants also complete a series of tests focusing on literacy and basic skills. The primary test used for determining adult literacy level is the Comprehensive Adult Student Assessment (CASA). Test results, along with the information on the enrollment form, are then used in preparation and implementation of an individualized Family Education Plan (FEP). In the process of developing the FEP goals, parents are asked to discuss their hopes or plans regarding education, their family or parenting needs, and job-related goals. One participant, Theresa Mills shared the following:

> Well, when I was younger, my mother worked and my father worked and nobody really read to me or showed me that reading is a way of learning things with your self-esteem and other things in life. And I

quit school in tenth grade and I just stayed home and didn't do too much. I got part-time jobs and I wasn't very happy at all. I got married and was married seven years and was divorced and found myself with no diploma and I needed a job. I have two children, a five-year-old and a six-year-old . . . . I got into Even Start to work on my GED and help me with my reading and to help me with my children to teach them that reading is good in life so that they wouldn't . . . make mistakes that I made in life—that they'll finish school and they won't be afraid to learn.

Another participant, Margaret Garcia, indicated that her main goal was to get her GED. Margaret attended high school in Mexico. She later married an Iranian, and their two sons were born in Iran. After getting a divorce she moved to Toledo to be near other family members. She has 12 brothers and sisters and she lived with one brother until a few months ago when she moved to an apartment in South Toledo. She and her sons receive a $302 AFDC check monthly—the father pays no child support.

Margaret says that Even Start has helped her with her academic skills and in reading to her children. "I learned vocabulary, better English, and math. Since I started the program, I read a lot. I enjoy books better and I read to my kids."

Parent-Child Interaction

The "Family Life Parent/Child Interaction Observational Checklist" is used to get an initial assessment of the parent's style and skill in interacting with his or her young child. Throughout the parent education component of the TES program, parents are given instruction on how to relate to their children in positive, nurturing ways. Periodically, follow-up assessments are done using the same checklist as well as a "Parent/Child Reading Observation" form. The items on the observation form all focus on parent behaviors during a parent/child reading session. Included are items relating to the parent's sensitivity and responsiveness to the child's level of interest and need to be actively involved in the process (see also Chapter Five).

Materials from the *Parents as Partners in Reading* program, developed by Patricia Edwards (1989, 1991a), are used extensively in the adult literacy component of the TES project. This program includes videotapes of parents reading to their children. As recommended by Dr. Edwards—she gave a workshop for TES staff during the first year—parent-child interactions are periodically videotaped. The parent and parent educator then critique the videotaped interactions together to determine strengths and needs relating to parent-child interaction. The Parent/Child Reading Observation form is used to guide the observations and discussion and not for grading or evaluating the parents' performance. Parents often report on changes in their own behaviors in reading to their children. Cheryl says that Even Start has helped her become a better "reading parent:"

> Before coming to this program, there was no excitement when I read to Tiffany. I have learned to make reading enjoyable for her. She laughs and has fun while I'm reading and she loves it.

Families participating in the TES program attend half-day sessions, at least two days per week, Monday-Thursday, 9:00 a.m.-11:30 a.m. or 12:30 p.m.-3:00 p.m. Parents' time during each session allows for instruction in adult literacy, parent education, and parent-child interaction. Parents usually spend more time in adult literacy than in the other components of the program. The children participate in the early childhood education program while their parents are in class. There are no Even Start classes on Fridays. Staff use this day to assess new enrollees, develop new FEPs, review and revise existing FEPs, and attend staff meetings and in-service sessions.

A typical day begins with the parents accompanying their children to the early childhood classroom. There they spend about 45 minutes interacting with their children in learning centers set up around the room. They may also use this time to look at books with their children. The early childhood teacher uses a part of this time (approximately 10-15 minutes) to lead a large group activity, which may consist of music and movement, a simple game, or show and tell. Parents are invited and encouraged to participate in (not just watch) this activity.

Emphasized throughout the parent/child sessions are behavioral expectations, language development, and family management issues such as discipline, family communication strategies, emotional and physical nurturing, nutrition, safety, and personal hygiene. After participating in the program for several months, one participant, Elaine, noted that "for the first time in my life, I can juggle the children, husband, and housework very well. I think that is one thing you have to make a habit of, in order to keep it up." And about her most exciting accomplishment, Elaine writes,

> I have raised two beautiful, well mannered—mostly—and extremely smart little boys. I have been their main caregiver from birth, so whenever I am confronted by how intelligent these little people are, I am amazed by how much they have, in fact, learned all they know from me.

Gloria Carter, another Even Start participant, also talked about ways in which the program helped her with her self-esteem and parenting skills.

> I always had a low esteem about myself, always thought I never was doing a lot, you know. . . . But now since I've been to Even Start, it has really given me a better outlook on life. And also it has helped me how to deal with the children now coming up. . . . So now I have my grandchildren and my children when they want to talk about their problems, I hear them, you know. It's not like in older days—you're not allowed to talk because that would be acting disrespectful; but now I learned, let's talk about it.

The parent education class lasts 30-35 minutes. Parents have given mixed reviews as to the value of these classes, some indicating that child management had never been a problem for them. Corliss, however, got help:

> The class has helped me understand and comprehend more. We discuss how I can help Wendy in reading. I can also relate to my older children better. . . . My household seems more stable than it was.

Corliss is a 46-year-old widow with three children: Wendy, her six-year-old who participates in Even Start with her, and two older sons, aged 16 and 18. Corliss dropped out of school before ninth grade and has never been employed. Her older son works at a restaurant part-time. Her family receives a $413 AFDC check monthly.

Sharon Turner also says that the parenting component has been especially helpful. Sharon is a single parent with two daughters. Her daughter, Tina, is three years old and participates in Even Start with her. Her other daughter, Ann, is 11. Sharon says that through the parenting classes she has learned to deal with her children's behavior "without spanking or hollering." She adds, "I've learned that these children have feelings just like we do so we have to treat them the same way that we want to be treated. So that has helped me out a lot, a whole lot."

Stimulating Environments for Emergent Literacy

Other activities provided by Even Start to encourage joint participation of parents and children are family outings to such places as the public library and the Toledo Museum of Art. These are preceded by lessons that prepare the family for the educational and/or cultural experience as well as such follow-up activities as family discussions, related art projects, and reading activities. Even Start also encourages families to spend some "fun time" together on the school system's computer network. This computer network offers not only basic skills instruction for adults, but also a variety of reading and reading readiness programs that can be enjoyed by both parents and children.

The TES program also developed take-home activity packets, with a variety of materials and suggestions for parent-child activities. The purpose of these packets is to assist parents in transferring from the classroom to the home those parenting concepts and skills presented during the parent education component of Even Start and to encourage positive parent-child interactions in the home. Parents are given specific instructions and suggestions on how to use the take-home activity kits with their young children. Included in these discussions are ideas on when and how to appropriately introduce the materials and activities in the home setting. Time is also provided during parent education classes to discuss successes and difficulties experienced by the parents in using the take-home kits and applying the parenting goals presented during class.

Adult Literacy

Parents devote one hour per day to adult basic education and adult literacy. For some parents, this is not enough time. Wilma Willis shared some ideas about the adult literacy component of Even Start:

Even Start is what you make of it. You must let the staff know what you are weak and strong in. Adult literacy can help you with this. I could not comprehend well when I first came here. In class, we worked on comprehension and I am doing better now. I still have problems, but it will take more time. We also do math and learn to punctuate.

Wilma is a 38 year old African-American single parent. She has a son, Marvin (age 7), and a daughter, Marsha (age 8). Wilma heard about Even Start at Marvin's school. Growing up in the South, she dropped out of school in the eleventh grade, got married, and then, shortly afterwards, separated. Employed at a factory for many years, she moved to Toledo after being laid off. Supported by her weekly unemployment check, she is enrolled in a GED class and volunteers in the Toledo public school system's Chapter 1 program.

The adult literacy component of the TES program focuses on reading comprehension, basic skills, and life skills. Parents with low reading skills are provided with a tutor who works one-on-one with them. Other parents receive instruction in a small group setting. All parents receive some programmed literacy instruction on computers. Lessons are individualized and include instruction in basic skills, such as vocabulary, math, and language mechanics. Math lessons include multiplication, division, fractions, and word problems. Reading comprehension lessons include distinguishing between facts and opinions and recognizing main ideas. Life skills lessons include balancing a checkbook, reading maps, and interpreting classified ads.

The adult literacy teacher plans for fun as well as hard work. Kim Griffin, one of the participating parents, describes the adult literacy program as follows:

> We learn different ways of filling applications out, getting jobs, things you could put on applications. How much fun it is. How crazy we act, like we used to when we were kids. . . . I've been learning a whole of different things I really didn't understand or know—really know about. How to get along with people you don't like. . . . I enjoy my-self. . . . A lot of different things they done taught me that I really did-n't know—looking up things in phone books, because see I don't know how to spell that good, and they teach you how to look up stuff in the dictionary and stuff, where I haven't opened up a dictionary in a long, long time. But I learned. I went and got me one. Got me a dictionary to look up certain words. . . She had us look up certain things on what

doctors are about—optometrists. She told you all about phone books and dictionaries and stuff.

Those Who Cannot Participate

While Even Start met the needs of some families, it was not a panacea for all.   The following five parents expressed interest in Even Start, but for various reasons, did not pursue the program fully.

Alvin Wilson, a 40 year old African-American male, enrolled in Even Start in May 1990. Alvin was married and had a five year old son, Dale. He had dropped out of school in tenth grade and had been in special education classes. Alvin is unemployed and receives a $225 General Relief check monthly.   When interviewed in August 1991, Alvin indicated that he had stopped attending Even Start sessions due to personal illness and hospitalization.

Twenty year old Mitzi Coleman enrolled in Even Start in May 1990. Mitzi is a white single parent.   Mitzi and her three year old daughter, Jenny, attended the program until June 1990. Mitzi attended high school until eleventh grade. She dropped out when she became pregnant. Mitzi and her daughter receive $274 monthly from AFDC. They live in an apartment in South Toledo.   In an interview in August 1991, Mitzi explained that she had stopped attending Even Start because of a second pregnancy. She indicated that she would like to return after things were situated with the new baby.

Barbara Fisher is a 38 year old African-American mother of three. Barbara and her five year old son, Michael, enrolled in Even Start in December 1990.   Barbara dropped out of an Arkansas school in eleventh grade. Barbara's family lives in North Toledo. They receive a $487 check monthly.   Although Barbara expressed a strong interest in Even Start initially, she excused herself from several sessions. When interviewed in August 1991, Barbara described her family situation as "overwhelming."

Barbara's older daughter, 15, has been suspended from school several times during the 1990-91 school year. Michael was having behavior problems in kindergarten. Barbara expressed the difficulty of dealing with family crises and pursuing her goal of getting a GED.

Rana Bakla's experiences with Even Start were unique. Rana was the only participant who was East Indian.   She graduated from a South American high school.   She is 33 years old and married to a carpenter.   Their monthly family income is $800.   The family owns their North Toledo home.

Rana enrolled in Even Start in August 1990 and attended for three months.   Rana was having a difficult pregnancy and dropped out of the program when she was six months pregnant.   When interviewed in August 1991, Rana commended Even Start for providing cultural and literacy experiences for her family.   She also stated that her six year old daughter, Rashi, is doing well in kindergarten.

Twenty-seven year old Carlita Morales enrolled in Even Start in May 1990.   Carlita is Hispanic and married.   Carlita and her two year old daughter, Rita, attended the program until July 1990.   Carlita graduated from high school in Mexico.   Carlita's husband is employed by a utilities company in Michigan and earns approximately $800 monthly.   The family receives food stamps and lives in an apartment in South Toledo.   In an interview in August 1991, Carlita explained that she had stopped attending Even Start because of a second pregnancy.   She indicated that she had problems caring for her new baby.

OUTREACH

Two kindergarten teachers at King School worked with the Even Start staff in providing once-a-week parent-child interaction sessions for children ages 5-7 and their parents.   Parent education and adult literacy were also offered as part of this off-site initiative.   There were approximately 20 participants at King School during the third and fourth years of the project.   These participants were recruited from an active parent group at the school.   Even Start staff noted how this particular group of parents became a cohesive social support to each other, encouraging each other in attendance, praising each other for accomplishments, and planning family outings together.

Two additional outreach projects were started during the third year.   One such project is housed at Washington School and represents collaborative programming with Toledo Head Start.   All three components (parent-child interaction, adult education, and early childhood education) of the Even Start program are available at the Washington School location.   By the fourth year, there were approximately 30 participants.

Another outreach project was started at Sherman School where, again, all three components of the Even Start program are available on site. Even Start collaborates closely with Chapter 1 in offering the program at this site. Parents come to the Chapter 1 extended day kindergarten class each Wednesday to make games and get ideas to help their children. Parents were scheduled to come either in the morning or the afternoon, but it ended up that they came and went as was convenient for them. This appears to be successful as far as getting parents involved but requires a great deal of flexibility and preparation of materials by the teacher.

During the fourth year of the TES project, linkages were established with the Toledo public school system's Graduation, Occupation, and Living Skills (GOALS) program. GOALS is a six-week parenting and self-esteem program for young pregnant and single mothers. Participants in the program receive Even Start services during the six-week period. After completing GOALS, they have the option of continuing with Even Start. Approximately 20 Even Start families have come from the GOALS classes. Expansion efforts during Even Start's fourth year also included the establishment of linkages with the JOBS/LEAP programs of the Lucas County Department of Human Services (LCDHS). The goal of the JOBS/LEAP program is to provide educational and employment opportunities for its participants. LCDHS caseworkers make referrals to Even Start on a regular basis. Approximately 30 percent of Even Start participants are enrolled in JOBS/LEAP.

DISCUSSION

In addition to numerous personal testimonials, survey data suggest that the TES program has been making positive changes in people's lives. A one-year follow-up study of kindergarten children who participated in Even Start some time during their preschool years indicated that none of these children was eligible for the Chapter 1 extended day kindergarten program (Wilson 1992). The TES program has also had modest success in retaining clients over time—a critical factor in the success of ABE programs.

IGL programs advance on the traditional ABE model by attempting to "break the cycle" of illiteracy. And, as Nickse (1990) states, "Prevention of low literacy is less expensive, economically and psychologically, than costly remediation" (p. 10). Even Start works from the premise that, if illiteracy begins in the home, parents can and must play a major role in reducing their children's risk of school failure. Efforts to prevent low literacy must reach beyond the educational realm.   The public schools, alone, cannot solve the problem. Anything other than a multiagency, unified approach will prove to be inadequate. Of utmost importance is the understanding that poverty is a major factor in low literacy. Educators, legislators, and, indeed, the whole of society need to recognize that "low literacy is often an economic problem as well as an educational challenge" (Nickse 1990, 10).

13

It Takes a Whole Village to Raise a Child: Supplementing Instruction for "At-Risk" Kindergarten Students

Eileen M. Carr

According to the Carnegie Foundation (1991), as many as 35 percent of all entering kindergarten pupils may be ill prepared, particularly with regard to their readiness for literacy instruction. The major cause of this lack of readiness is a limited exposure to the kinds of language experiences that are precursors to reading and writing.

This chapter describes a program implemented in an urban elementary school kindergarten class that lasted for fourteen weeks. It had three components that were designed to be interdependent and mutually interactive: encouragement of increased exposure to reading and its uses in the home; an innovative approach on the part of the classroom teacher, who sought to emphasize accelerated literacy development; and the use of cross-age and peer tutors to facilitate such development.

This program sought to redress the mismatch experienced by these pupils between what they had experienced (or failed to experience) at home and what is necessary for them to know if they are to succeed in school. At all economic levels, families differ in the amount and type of literacy activities that they share with their children, but such exposure is least frequent among poorer families (Teale 1986; Heath, 1983). The schools, however, tend—despite the differing extent to which children are likely to have been exposed to literacy before entering kindergarten—to be directed primarily toward middle-class experiences and expectations. A child cannot be expected to identify letters and sounds in words if the child does not understand the concept of a word. Yet, this is what we have traditionally expected of children, including low SES children, as they begin school.

In addition to basic expectations about a child's readiness for literacy instruction as he or she enters kindergarten, our educational system has typically relied on prepackaged programs designed for children who have acquired the fundamentals of literacy knowledge, such as an understanding of the functions and conventions of print. Such scripted programs provide, in effect, lock step instruction regardless of prior experience and knowledge. Letter/sound associations are learned in isolation, apart from the meaningful context of a story. Writing usually is not included in such programs, because most are based on the perception that children cannot write until they can read.

This program, by contrast, is rooted in the theory of emergent literacy (see Chapter One, this volume). Its three primary components—parental involvement in the development of literacy skills at home, a print-rich classroom environment, and cross-age tutoring by older pupils and peer tutoring—have all been supported by recent research. In effect, we are recruiting all of the child's social resources in aiding him or her to become literate, which reflects the African adage that "It takes a whole village to raise a child."

Our "whole village" approach was implemented in a kindergarten class in a middle-sized (population 350,000) urban area in the Midwest. The students in the kindergarten program were racially mixed (74% Black; 22% Caucasian; 4% Hispanic), with the majority of the students living in two nearby housing projects. Most of the students came from single-parent homes receiving public assistance. A profile of the class at the beginning of the school year showed that the children had not had rich EL experiences and had not yet developed an awareness of the functions, conventions, and form of print.

In order to determine the effectiveness of the different components of the intervention program (home involvement, enriched classroom learning, and tutoring), the progress of students in this class—the accelerated group, were compared to the two other kindergarten classes. One comparison class—the enriched group, was taught by the program teacher and received the same classroom instruction as the accelerated group and also participated in the home intervention portion of the program. The enriched group did not, however, work with fifth-grade tutors or receive the follow-up practice in writing a response to the story with the help of peer tutors. These two classes were also compared to the traditional group, which did not use a meaning-based, integrated approach to learning, nor participate in the tutorial or home reading activities. The purpose of this design was to examine the influence of different classroom instruction and support activities on specific aspects of children's literacy development.

In some respects, the traditional classroom instruction was similar to the accelerated and enriched classrooms. In the traditional group the teacher's instruction in oral language development and interactions with storybook reading were similar to the other classrooms, because she read and discussed many stories with the class. The teacher also used the same packaged letter identification program as the other two classes (see also Chapter Sixteen, this volume). However, she did not use big books to provide phoneme awareness training in context. As a result, children in the traditional group did not always make the connection between letter/associations and reading. The students rarely participated in individual storytelling or writing of any kind. The traditional teacher believed that children could not write until they learned to read and spell words.

HOME INTERVENTION

In an effort to encourage the parents to undertake literacy activities with their children, materials were sent home with their children and the program was highlighted during parent-teacher conferences. In addition, follow-up materials were sent home periodically. As a result of these efforts, most parents (or other family members) read regularly with the children. A lesser number worked with the other activities that were a part of the program's content, which included phoneme awareness exercises and concepts about print development. A small number of parents showed little interest, despite the efforts of the program's participants, in working with their children. On the whole, however, parental and familial involvement in the home were considerably greater than had been customary before the children had entered school and participated in the program.

Parents were asked to read storybooks to the children and were given a folder with activities to reinforce classroom learning. We wanted to enable the parents and children to learn to enjoy reading and literature, and to make reading a regular activity within the home. From a more abstract pedagogical standpoint, we wanted to enable the children, through repeated exposure to stories, storybooks, and reading, to develop an understanding of important story elements. Students were given a different storybook each week. Their parents were asked to read to them as often as possible during that time. After reading, the parents were instructed to have the child retell the story to them.

Parents were given the opportunity to view a videotape of educators reading to several children in kindergarten classes. As the readers (who were both men and women) read the books, an overvoice on the tape described what was occurring as the adult and child read and discussed the story. On the tape, I explained the procedures and reasons for predicting, developing vocabulary, asking questions, and relating story events to the child's previous knowledge. Unfortunately, few parents availed themselves of the opportunity to view the tape. Otherwise, parents did not receive formal training about how to interact with their children during reading. It was hoped and anticipated that as books were made available natural parent-child interactions would develop as the books were read, questions were answered, and the children undertook to retell the stories after they had been read. Given the findings of Lancy and his colleagues (Chapter Five), this was, perhaps, naive.

Each week, as the books were returned, each child retold the story again to a research assistant who noted how complete the retelling was and provided a selection of books for the following week (see also Chapter Nine). Because students received a new book only after they had returned the previous one, the number of books read by each child varied. On average, the children were each exposed to ten books during the fourteen-week period of the study.

The activity folder gave an explanation and directions for practicing some "rules of reading" and phoneme awareness. In addition, parents were encouraged to point to words when reading so that children could learn directionality and the concept of word. Initially, the folder only contained one activity. More suggestions were added as the children practiced in the classroom. Dyads were also encouraged to practice rhyming words selected from familiar nursery rhymes that were read in the classroom. There was space for the children to draw their interpretations of the rhyme or other readings. As time passed, the children developed materials that were uniquely their own.

The appendix at the end of this chapter contains an excerpt from the activity folders. It presents an activity to help children develop phoneme awareness.

CLASSROOM INSTRUCTION

The second part of the intervention program focused on the different kinds of classroom experiences teachers and schools can provide for the children. The kindergarten teacher was selected to participate in the program because her philosophy of instruction and teaching practices included an integrated approach to teaching that was responsive to the needs of each child and promoted accelerated learning for students.

This teacher's approach to learning was based on the needs of the children. To meet those needs, the teacher developed a print-rich environment to emphasize reading and writing in meaningful contexts. Each day several storybooks were read to the class and were readily available for perusing during school hours. Big books were used to reinforce this knowledge and learn about concepts of print and phoneme awareness, including letter/sound associations in a meaningful context. The teacher also used a prepared program ("Letter People") to teach letter/sound association to provide direct instruction in this skill.

Children wrote daily and also participated in group and individual writing. These exercises included such materials as thank you letters and language experience stories. Frequently, writing was in response to a text read or a class activity. Students would write about a favorite part of a story or what they saw on a field trip. Writing was often displayed in the hall for others to see and read. Children progressed through writing stages from drawing to invented spelling as they increased their overall literacy competence. Overall, the approach taken resembles the successful program developed by Karin Dahl (Dahl & Freepon 1991).

TUTORING

To provide additional support for the children to develop a firm literacy foundation, two types of tutoring programs were initiated in the classroom: cross-age and peer tutoring.

The cross-age tutoring involved fifth-grade students who were above-average readers who volunteered to participate in the program. The cross-age tutors worked with two groups of kindergarten students once a week for approximately twenty minutes per group. During these sessions, half of the pupils read with the tutors and the other half worked with the teacher on other activities. The groups then reversed tasks.

The tutors were trained by a researcher who explained how young children become literate and modeled the literacy procedures that the tutors were expected to use in each session. The fifth-grade tutors were informed each week about which literacy—print and phoneme awareness—activities to review to ensure that their tutoring work would support and extend classroom instruction. Each week tutors also selected a storybook from an assortment provided by the researcher and read it to a pair of kindergarten pupils. They discussed the story and the unknown vocabulary words with their pupils, who, in turn, retold the story to them. Initially, after each tutoring session, the kindergartners were encouraged to write about their favorite part of the story and explain what they wrote to the researcher, who transcribed their retellings.

This support system was developed particularly to meet the needs of students whose parents did not participate consistently or regularly in the literacy activities at home. In other words, the fifth-grade tutors emulated the behaviors we had asked of parents.

As the students' literacy knowledge developed, the researchers introduced the concept of peer tutoring to the class to support phoneme awareness acquisition and writing development. At this point the role of the researcher was diminished and that of the peer tutors increased. Groups of students at different levels of writing development worked together to support and learn from one another. Because some of the children had already developed knowledge of phoneme awareness, they were encouraged to write their responses using invented spelling.

Classmates acted as peer tutors and frequently helped each other spell a word or write a sentence as this transcript shows:

C-1: How you spell milk?
C-2: What sounds you hear?
C-2: Mmm   Mmm   Mmm   milk
C-1: Mmm   Mmm   Mmm
       How you spell it?
C-2: What letter says Mmm Mmm?
C-1: Mmm Mmm munchy mouth
       How you make it?
C-2: Look up there (alphabet chart)

Peers helped each other apply their knowledge of phoneme awareness to their writing through invented spelling. The peer tutors would slowly repeat the desired word for the other student to hear. The peer tutor would encourage the classmate to listen for the sounds in the word and write them. If children forgot which letters made the sounds, they were told the letter and encouraged to look at an alphabet displayed on the wall to guide their formation of the letters. This pattern of interaction became more common as children developed knowledge of phoneme awareness and confidence in their knowledge.

RESULTS

All pupils participating in the program were individually pre- and posttested through an array of tasks that have been shown to be related to reading and writing in school. The measures included: (1) Concepts About Print (Clay 1979), which identified the child's understanding of the function of print, directionality, concept of letters and words, and letter and word identification; (2) understanding of story structure as measured by story retelling; (3) the Peabody Picture Vocabulary Test for assessing vocabulary; (4) phoneme awareness was examined using procedures to test students' knowledge of rhyming, alliteration, and phoneme segmentation (Yopp 1988); and (5) writing development was evaluated in accordance with prior research (Purcell-Gates 1991b; Sulzby & Teale 1985), and my own coding system.

The results demonstrate that the intervention program had a strong impact on specific types of literacy growth. Findings also indicate that school tutoring and home literacy programs were beneficial to children when they reinforced specific literacy activities that had been introduced in school and that required accelerated practice to ensure that students would incorporate them into their daily academic activities. Children in this program benefited when extra support for specific activities was provided in writing and phoneme awareness development. The effects of the individual components of the program (home intervention, classroom instruction, and tutoring) will be discussed concurrently as the growth in specific areas is discussed.

The test results indicated that the teachers' beliefs in what constituted appropriate developmental literacy activities greatly affect students' learning. Likewise, the amount of practice students receive to reinforce their literacy knowledge also has a favorable effect on the development of that knowledge.

One instructor was a meaning-centered whole language teacher, while the other teacher can be described as a traditional classroom teacher who focused on isolated skills instruction. The teachers shared, however, some beliefs about literacy growth; these similarities were reflected in comparable test results when instruction had been similar.

Both teachers read a wide range of storybooks to the students. Such extensive exposure to print through storybook reading in all classrooms explains the lack of significant differences among the students in story retelling and knowledge of the concepts of print. It appears that the instruction in all classrooms was sufficient for students to acquire these concepts. The additional exposure to storybook reading and retelling with tutors and home reading was, in this instance, unnecessary to develop these abilities.

There was also no significant difference among classrooms on letter and word recognition. These results are likewise attributable to the similarity of instruction between the two classroom teachers. Both teachers concurred in the importance of direct instruction for letter identification and both used the "Letter People" program.

With regard to vocabulary development, the traditional classroom was better on general vocabulary knowledge than the two treatment classes. This improvement can be traced to the type of vocabulary learning that occurred in the traditionally taught class, where the teacher focused on functional vocabulary using pictures and artifacts from daily life, rather than vocabulary derived from the readings.

The two experimental groups showed some differences in vocabulary development. The class with the tutors showed gains in comparison to the intervention class without the tutors. The cross-age tutors discussed unfamiliar words from the readings with the pupils. This suggests that tutoring may be beneficial for children if it focuses on a specific skill that needs additional practice.

The different instructional focus of the teachers and the extra support did, however, make a significant difference in the areas of phoneme awareness and writing. The importance of exposure to literacy activities was apparent in the results of the phoneme awareness test. The accelerated group and enriched group were superior to the traditional class on this measure.

Phoneme awareness, not considered a priority for the traditional teacher, was important to the accelerated group teacher and was one focus of her accelerated learning practice. The findings indicate that classroom instruction and the extra home support encouraged by the use of the activity folders (Appendix) helped increase the experimental students' knowledge of phoneme awareness.

The result of this lack of training in phoneme awareness and writing experience can be seen in Timothy's simple drawing of a fish in Figure 13.1.

Figure 13.1
Story Retelling

Traditional Class

Timothy

A fish

Whole Language Class

Katie

C AMY VO

The magic fish

Whole Lang/Tutors Class

Marcel

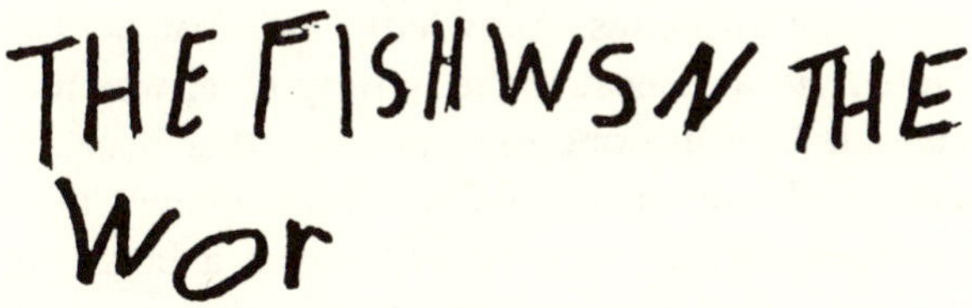

THE FISH WS N THE Wor

The fish was in the water

Timothy, who had little training in phoneme awareness and writing, did not change his writing level throughout the kindergarten year. His work can be compared with Katie's and Marcel's writing, which progressed throughout the year to reflect attainment of different stages of phoneme awareness and confidence in the ability to write.

In contrast to the accelerated group, in which seven students successfully applied their knowledge of phoneme awareness in their writing, only one student in the enriched group used any level of phoneme awareness when writing. Students in the traditional group remained at approximately the same level of development as they had exhibited at the beginning of the project. Because the teacher of the traditional group believed the students were incapable of writing, the class never engaged in writing activities. These students likewise had not attained a level of phoneme awareness that might have encouraged them to write and spell words.

This can also be seen when comparing the work of Katie (from the enriched group) with the writing of Marcel, a student in the accelerated group. As evidenced by the random, unconnected letters in Figure 13.1, Katie was unable to apply her phoneme awareness knowledge in her writing. Marcel, on the other hand, used her phoneme awareness knowledge in the simple sentence seen in Figure 13.1. The differences between the Accelerated Group and the Enriched Group can be attributed to the additional writing practice of the Accelerated Group that followed each storybook reading by the fifth-grade tutors and by the encouragement the students received from their peer tutors to apply their phoneme awareness knowledge as they wrote.

Indeed, the support received by the pupils in the accelerated group to use their phoneme awareness knowledge appears to have been the critical factor in their development. In the enriched group, which did not have peer tutors, the teacher encouraged the students to write. The students in that group were, however, unable to apply their phoneme awareness knowledge as capably as the students in the accelerated group. Because the writing level was more developed in the accelerated group, one can conclude that peer tutors may be an effective means of supporting literacy development in the classroom.

One way to reap benefits from a home and tutoring intervention program is to ask participants to focus on a specific skill as a supplement to school instruction while continuing the general reading activities such as storybook reading that occur in many intervention programs. Specific skills may vary according to each child's needs. But specifically designed activities performed by a parent or tutor can provide the necessary practice to attain the goals. If one compares the work of Carlos and Ciera it is easy to identify their individual needs, to which a parent or tutor could respond. In Figure 13.2, Carlos gives a detailed rendition of *The Three Billy Goats Gruff*, reflecting his highly developed understanding of story structure. His writing level is not,

Figure 13.2
Writing Post-test

Carlos

Story Retelling:

Once upon a time there was three Billy goats. One Billy goat said, "Let's go up to the mountainside to nibble the tender grass." When they was going across the bridge there was a big ugly troll. The first Billy Goat said, "Don't eat me. Wait for the other Billy goat." The second Billy goat came across the bridge and said, "lets go across the bridge and eat the tender grass." The big ugly troll said, "Who's that clip cloping across my bridge?" "It's me, the last Billy goat Gruff." "You're the one I want to eat." "You can't eat me because I'll run and hit you with my big strong horns and you'll look like Swiss cheese." He knocked him off the bridge into the river. he was dead and them they all went across the bridge to eat the tender grass.

Writing:

L O D R O S

Ciera

Story Retelling:

The mouse was asking for cookies and milk.

Writing:

T H E M S W S

A S K E   F R

K K E
  /

however, equally advanced, as there is no application of phoneme awareness in his writing. A parent or tutor could help Carlos develop and use phoneme awareness in his literacy activities. A good source for such materials would be his home and tutoring folder. Ciera's work, on the other hand, displays the opposite need. She has a high level of phoneme awareness that she applies successfully in her writing. Unlike Carlos, her story retellings lack detail. Thus, a parent or tutor could encourage her to improve this ability through wide reading and discussion of story concepts.

Results of this three-pronged intervention program indicate that it is important to continue to study interactions between the home and school community in order to develop effective programs to support the literacy growth of young children. Future research should focus on the use of peer and cross-age tutors and home intervention programs that provide individual support for literacy development as a supplement to classroom instruction. Only through the combined support of each child's own "village"—his or her home, school, and community—can we have hope that at-risk students may be able to have the opportunity to become high achievers.

APPENDIX

Please reread the rhyme several times and have your child identify the rhyming words (words that sound alike). Some of the rhyming words are the same words repeated (Mack, Mack). Others are words that have similar ending sounds but different beginning sounds (Mack, Black). Your children may want to join in the rhyme with you as you read. Initially, rhyming may be difficult for your child to understand. We will practice it in class many times during the year.

Please review the rhyme and activities with your child each day that the folder is home. This enjoyable reading time will help your child associate reading with fun as they learn and practice important reading and writing skills.

Miss Mary Mack, Mack, Mack
All dressed in black, black, black
With silver buttons, buttons, buttons
All down her back, back, back
She asked her mother, mother, mother
For fifteen cents, cents, cents
To see the elephants, elephants, elephants
Jump over the fence, fence, fence
They jumped so high, high, high
They reached the sky, sky, sky
And never came down, down, down
Till the Fourth of July, ly, ly

14

Play Settings as Literacy Environments: Their Effects on Children's Literacy Behaviors

Kathy Roskos and Susan Neuman

When you write, you just hafta make lines (demonstrates). . . lines is very easy. We don't need no help to make lines. Claire (almost 4 years old).

From Pestalozzi to the present there has been an abiding belief in the importance of the physical environment as an agent in young children's learning (e.g., Atwell 1987; Graves 1983; Morrow & Weinstein 1986). Despite the longevity and tenacity of this belief, however, there is only a limited body of knowledge regarding how the architectural forms and structural features of classrooms and settings may be constructed to enhance learning (see Weinstein's integrative review, 1979). Even rarer is research that addresses how literacy environments might be designed to enhance young children's opportunities to actively engage in reading and writing.

This dearth of information is not for lack of theory. That people influence and are influenced by their environment is the cornerstone of an interactionist view of human development (e.g., Piaget 1962). And ecological psychologists have for some time examined the interdependent relationship between individuals and their environments (e.g., Barker 1968; Bronfenbrenner 1979; Lewin 1935). Roger Barker and his associates, for example, extensively studied children's behaviors in a variety of settings in the Midwest—at recess, at basketball games, and such (e.g. Barker & Wright 1955).

More specific to learning in early childhood, ecologists have explored those features of architecture and settings that may enhance the value of play in children's development. Their research suggests that variables of materials and setting exert a strong pull on the nature and quality of children's learning through play. Rosenthal (1973), for instance, was interested in children's attention spans and considered what attracted and held children at a play setting. Block play proved to be a setting with high attraction (visited by many children) but only moderate holding power (keeping them there). Art and role play, on the other hand, had strong appeal and high holding power. Subsequent analyses suggested at least two reasons why these settings "held" children to a greater degree than others: the role play offered a variety of actions and the art activity provided concrete "point outs" of progress—factors which may determine children's responses to play settings, not to mention the development of their attention spans.

That the environment or physical aspects of the play setting may shape or "press" toward different forms of behavior has important implications for literacy learning in early childhood, as well. Through carefully designed indoor play environments, we may be able to enhance and extend literacy opportunities for young children and subsequently encourage developmentally appropriate literacy activities and learning. This was the main theme of a seven-month research project we undertook to examine the influence of a literacy-enriched play environment on children's literacy behaviors in play.

Our endeavor was not without precedent. Earlier observational studies had documented the natural occurrence of young children's literacy behaviors while engaged in play—"run ups," as Bruner (1984) referred to them (Isenberg & Jacob 1985; Jacob 1984; Roskos 1987). However, extension of this descriptive work appeared to be hampered by a paucity of literacy objects (paper, pencils, books, magazines, environmental print) in childcare settings that fostered children's spontaneous interactions with print in play contexts. Clearly, play with print was not popular in childcare settings.

Consequently, to examine how literacy-related play might influence literacy behaviors, several studies attempted to enrich play centers in childcare environments with literacy materials (Christie & Enz 1991; Morrow 1990; Neuman & Roskos 1990; Vukelich 1989). Play centers became flower shops, banks, veterinary offices, post offices, and the like. But, while demonstrating more literacy-related play, these studies did not clarify the utility of these literacy play settings and their associated objects as entities of influence or meaning to young children. In short, we still did not know if playing with relevant objects in these settings built up "stores of represented meanings" which children could use in other literacy contexts. Furthermore, relatively little had been done to examine how literacy-based play settings might impact play itself.

With the above theoretical and research history in mind, then, we set out to examine the press of the play environment in relation to literacy learning a bit further. We began by designing an indoor play environment that included literacy-based play settings representing prototypical contexts of literacy use for young children. We viewed these as pivots that may assist children in developing literacy networks (roles and routines) and behaviors (language, skills, and strategies) which might be used in other contexts. We also saw them as settings that might produce more sustained and elaborated play sequences of which literacy was an integral part.

Following our design efforts, we sought to determine the effects of these literacy-based play settings on children's literacy behaviors, specifically the frequency of their literacy demonstrations, the duration and complexity of their literacy-related play, and their use of literacy objects. However, our intent here is not to examine the details of this investigation (Neuman & Roskos 1992). Rather, we wish to discuss the design specifics of the two play environments central to it and then to briefly summarize their differences vis-à-vis children's literacy behaviors. After providing some necessary background, we will treat each play environment as a case study, placing description in the foreground and keeping quantitative analysis in the background. In this way we hope to make our point: that young children's functional engagement with reading and writing in carefully designed literacy-based play settings serves their natural curiosity about written language in ways that empower them.

BACKGROUND OF THE STUDY

We were fortunate to have developed a fine working relationship with the director and staff of a rather large urban childcare program that offered a wide array of services. We were most interested in the program's day-care centers housed in two buildings located in close proximity to each other. They served families from diverse ethnic backgrounds (62% Caucasian; 31% Black; 5% Southeast Asian and 2% Hispanic) and were similar in many ways: philosophical orientation ("learning by doing"), teacher-child ratio, day-to-day administration, daily schedule, curriculum, and organization of physical space.

Given these conditions and after consulting with the director and day-care staff, we selected one of the day-care environments for literacy enrichment design purposes (Site B), leaving the other as it was (Site A). There were 46 children (24 boys; 22 girls) in Site B, targeted for change, and they were slightly younger ($X=3.68$) than the 45 children (25 boys; 20 girls) in Site A, slated to remain the same ($X=4.17$).

Before making the physical design changes to transform Site B into a literacy-enriched play environment, we established a baseline of the frequency of children's literacy behaviors during free play and their uses of literacy-related objects in four play settings common to both environments: housekeeping, book corner, small manipulatives, and arts and crafts. Taking a wide angle view of children's literacy behaviors, we defined them as instances of handling (physical exploration of literacy objects), reading (attributing meaning to printed marks) and writing (using printed marks to communicate). Observers tallied these for each child during four different 15-minute segments of spontaneous play. In addition, 30-minute segments of the children's play were videotaped in each of the four play areas four different times.

Having obtained a sense of the children's naturally occurring literacy in their play environments, we then undertook the redesign of Site B, which we more fully describe below, contrasting it with Site A, which remained essentially the same physically. Following the changes in Site B, videotaped samples of the children's free play were gathered weekly, for total of 18 hours of videotaped play per site. During this time the teachers and aides were encouraged to do as they normally did during free play. Generally this meant setting the stage for play and monitoring it, with little direct intervention by the teachers into the play flow.

In the final two weeks of the study, we repeated the same systematic observations and videotaping procedures that were used to establish the baseline of literacy activity in play. Our data, then, consisted of a fairly substantial quantity of observations of children's play (120 minutes per child) and videotapes of their free play (44 hours) before and following the physical design changes in Site B. Using these data we conducted several analyses which, as we mentioned previously, can be found elsewhere. Their results will be summarized following the site descriptions, to which we next turn our attention.

Description of Site A

Site A was located on the bottom floor of a massive stone church that housed a variety of human services, including the main office of the childcare program. The front of this building faced a busy urban street and the back faced an expansive park with trees, shrubbery, and garden-like pathways. A basic floor plan of Site A is depicted in Figure 14.1 to provide a general sense of the shape, architecture, and structural features of the site's play environment.

As can be noted in Figure 14.1, the Site A Day-care environment has an unusual shape. This is due to the fact that it is located below ground level, buttressed by church walls on two sides and banks of earth on the other two. The outdoor play area cuts into a small grassy mound of earth, providing a protected yet highly textured and interesting place to play. The much smaller window area directly across from the outdoor play area faces a concrete wall, thus allowing for light, but not a pleasant view. Because of this layout, the indoor play environment had rather poor lighting, affecting especially the play settings along the back wall. On cloudy days, these were quite dimly lit.

The placement of the play settings were placed around the perimeter of the space creating a large open area in the middle of the room. Based on ecological play research, this open arrangement presses for certain behaviors over others, that is, it encouraged noisy, active, motor-dominant play behaviors over quieter, sustained, language-dominant play behaviors (Day & Sheehan 1974). Another feature is the predominance of block play settings in this play environment—there are four in all, and they are centrally located in the physical space. According to ecological psychologists, such an arrangement sends a powerful message about what counts as play in this environment (see Gump 1989). And indeed block play accounted for much of what these children did as play activity, along with the high noise level that often accompanies it. Hence, even a brief survey of the basic architecture, structure, and placement of play settings provides us with some sense of the general tenor of free play in Site A.

Our more immediate interest is the nature of the play settings targeted in the study: arts and crafts, the book corner, housekeeping, and the small manipulatives area. What were these like in this environment and how conducive to the activation of children's literacy behaviors

Figure 14.1
Regular Preschool Environment—SITE A

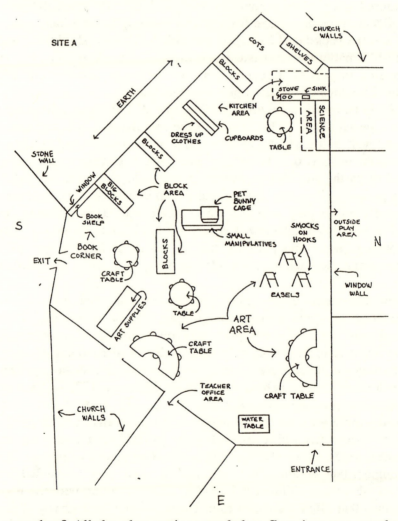

were they? All the play settings tended to flow into one another with no clear demarcation where one began and another ended. What distinguished one from another were the props located within each and these, alone, served as signals of what to do in that setting. No print or pictures were used to identify the nature of play settings.

The arts and crafts play setting sprawled along the east wall, with the easels located somewhat distant from it, closer to the windows to make use of the light. Although there were ample art supplies, these were not organized in any discernible way nor labeled as to type of paper or location of crayons, paints, and so forth. Most often arts and craft items were placed on the tables in the immediate area and used under the direct supervision of an adult. Demonstrations of literacy behavior by children in this setting were extremely rare, with adults assuming responsibility for signing children's names on drawings and projects.

The book corner was sandwiched between arts and crafts and the big block in the only other window-lit area of the environment. It included a bean bag chair, several small chairs, and a bookshelf. Generally there were about a dozen books in the area, some on the shelf, others lying about on the floor. There was an ABC chart mounted low on the side of the shelf that contained the blocks for the block play setting. Because of its close proximity to the block play area, the book corner tended to be a noisy place often subject to disruption, making it difficult for children to attend to books for any sustained amount of time.

Housekeeping seemed to occupy the entire southwest corner of the indoor play environment; however, it more often became an extension of block play rather than a place for domestic play. Since it was the most dimly lit area of the environment and also contained equipment and a shelf for teaching supplies, it was not visited frequently by the children. It contained the common fare of housekeeping play settings: small-scale furniture (stove, etc.), dress-up clothes, plastic fruit, pots and pans, tableware, dolls, and doll cribs. There were no literacy-related items, such as grocery packages. Most often, housekeeping items were transported to the block area or into the middle of the room and played with there.

The small manipulatives play setting was located in the "thick" of things, near the large blocks and toward the center of the room. On a nearby shelf, various types of manipulatives (such as Legos) were stored in baskets. These were not labeled in any way. Used more often as an extension of art activities or a part of large block play, children did not "stay put" in this setting. No instance of literacy behavior was observed here during the study.

In sum, this indoor play environment contained ample space and the playthings common to early childhood: blocks, small toys, items for domestic play, art and craft supplies, and some books. However, other than books, it included few literacy objects directly accessible to children and no play settings that capitalized on the literacy activities and routines that flow through real life (e.g., restaurants, banks, offices, stores). In fact there was little use of print in any environmental way, such as to locate space or label items. Overall, the play settings seemed to favor block play and engagement with art and craft materials under adult supervision. Over the seven-month period of the study, relatively few literacy-related play episodes spontaneously occurred during free play (15 in total), with these being of short duration on the average (about 66 seconds) and containing few literacy demonstrations (an average of 2 per episode). Table 14.1 inventories the objects-literacy and non-literacy- in the two sites prior to our attempts at literacy enrichment.

Table 14.1
Non/Literacy Objects in Play Areas Before Intervention

BEFORE				
	Site A		Site B	
PLAY AREA	non-literacy	literacy	non-literacy	literacy
housekeeping	kitchen setup, pots, pans, plastic fruit, tableware	none	same	same
book corner	bean bag chair, small chairs	8 bks. (est.) wall poster	same	same
manipulative	legos, lock-blocks, beads	none	same	same
arts/crafts	easel, paints, brushes, paper, aprons	none	same	same
office	N/A	N/A	N/A	N/A

Description of Site B

Site B was located in a modern office building that also housed medical facilities, an art store, and a coffee shop. It, too, faced a busy street, but did not have access to a park, being surrounded by other office buildings. The day-care program occupied the majority of space on the ground floor of the building, opening onto a patio-like outdoor play area. At the outset of the study its indoor play environment was similar in design to that of Site A, with play settings located around the perimeter of the space, a large open area in the middle, a seeming preference for block play, few literacy objects, and little use of print environmentally.

To redesign this environment into one more literacy-rich, we established three design principles along the lines of segments research (Fernie 1985; Gump 1975),which encourages the implementation of environmental design theory by focusing on the segment as the unit of change. A segment is comparable to a learning center in a classroom.

For our purposes, we viewed a segment as a play setting and its related objects; therefore, the three principles addressed the creation of literacy-based playsettings (see Neuman & Roskos 1992, for an extended discussion). Briefly, we refer to the three principles as follows: (1) the principle of definition, that is, clearly demarcating play settings from one another; (2) the principle of adaptation, that is, reworking typical settings to resemble real-life literacy contexts; and (3) the principle of familiarity, that is, inserting a network of prototypical literacy objects into known settings.

Guided by these principles, we designed (with the able assistance of the childcare staff) a literacy-enriched indoor play environment, the basic floor plan of which is provided in Figure 14.2.

As we did previously with respect to Site A, we need to point out some fundamental architectural and structural features, here, which go a long way in influencing how children behave at play. The space in Site B is more "broken up," especially the spaces designated for dramatic play and small muscle activities. To accomplish this, semi-fixed features and print were used.

For example, through the strategic placement of artificial trees, plants, low shelves, and classroom furniture, we were able to create small, intimate play areas, which have been found to encourage more interactive and sustained play (Neill 1982). In addition, space became more sharply defined through the use of environmental print, including directional signs, labels on bins of objects, posted inventories of setting contents, and hanging mobiles that identified specific sites.

Coincident with defining the play settings in space was an equally strong interest in their placement. Recognizing that different settings "press" for different kinds of behaviors (e.g., blocks as opposed to books), we located like settings near one another (Barker 1968). Quieter areas (e.g., thebook area) were located away from noisier ones (e.g., blocks). This respect for the patterns of behavior elicited by specific settings appears to reduce play conflicts and to foster the emergence of play themes (Proshansky & Wolfe 1975).

Figure 14.2
Literacy Enriched Play Environment—SITE B

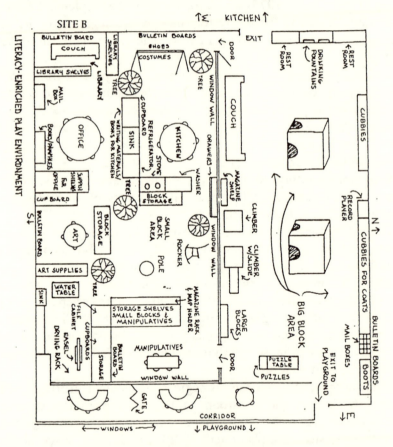

Following these larger-scale changes, we then created three play settings that reflected real-life literacy situations for the children in the day-care program (as reported by their parents and caregivers), including: a kitchen play setting, the cozy corner library, and a generic office. Existing play centers (housekeeping, the book corner, and the paper table in the art area) could also be readily reworked to capitalize on print contexts already known to the children. Table 14.2 details the literacy and other "props" used to create the enhanced play areas. Contrast with "before" in Table 14.1.

Table 14.2
Non /Literacy Objects in Play Areas After Intervention

AFTER				
	Site A		Site B	
PLAY AREA	non-literacy	literacy	non-literacy	literacy
housekeeping (kitchen)	same	same	same+...tree, phone	bks (10 est) phone bk,cookbks (5 est.) recipe cards, recipe boxes, small plaques, stationery, coupons, store ads & fliers, play money, grocery pakg., message board, calendars, notepads, pens, pencils, markers, decals
book corner (library)	same	same	sofa, area rug, rocker, book rack, tree, telephone, table.	return cards, library stamps, 70 bks. (est), marks, magazines, pens, pencils, markers, paper, signs, calendars, telephone bk., wall posters, file folders, stick.
manipulative	same	same	same+ buttons	labeled bins, magazines, maps, paper, pencils
arts/crafts	same	same	same	inventory, art posters, pencils, labeled supplies
office	N/A	N/A	table, chairs, telephone, computer, keyboard, file racks, in/out trays, clipbds., plastic clips, small bins, tree	calendars, appt.bk., message pads, signs, books, (10 est.) pamphlets, magazines, file folders, index cards, business cards, forms, ledger sheets, paper, pencils, pens, markers, small notebks., stencils

How were these props utilized to create authentic literacy settings and how did the children employ both these settings and their contents to their literacy and play advantage?

In the library in the far southwest corner, every attempt was made to give it the feel of a library, with many books, magazines, pamphlets, and comfortable places to sit and read (e.g., child-sized rockers and bean bag chairs). On the walls were posters related to children's literature and authors. On the floor were labeled baskets for storing written material as well as small stuffed animals. The library included library rules drawn up by the children, including one three-year-old's contribution, "Don't never spit on books." Overall it was a quiet, pleasant place where the children frequently 'talk-read' their way through books. Over the course of the study, most of the literacy-related play episodes occurred here (a total of 25), consisting primarily of book handling and reading behaviors.

Diagonally across from the library was the somewhat more boisterous kitchen play setting.[1] The setting contained numerous cookbooks, recipe cards, coupons, and grocery packages in the cupboards. The most popular items were the notepads and pencils which were used to make endless indecipherable lists. On the window wall of the kitchen nutritional information was posted along with language experience charts detailing cooking done by the class (e.g., recipes). Somewhat like kitchen settings in real life, print flowed through the kitchen on its way to other places. For example, 'homework' would be brought into the kitchen, tossed about (once it was put in the refrigerator) and then taken to some other area to do. A total of nine literacy-related episodes occurred in the kitchen, some of these being the most complex and longest of those observed during the investigation. For instance, one episode created by two boys centered around a cookbook as a "magic genie book" and lasted for nearly 18 minutes.

Directly across from the kitchen and adjacent to the library was the office, a setting that provided diverse opportunities for literacy in play, such as writing letters, signing checks, doing homework, and writing plans. In it were a myriad of recycled office supplies: pencils, pens, and markers; forms and file folders; assorted paper and envelopes; stamps and stampers; stickers and sticker holders; telephones and telephone books; a mailbox, and so on. All supplies were easily accessible to the children, a sufficient but not an overly abundant amount being placed out at the start of each day. The children's writing dotted this area—messages, notes, pictures, labels, and jottings.

A total of 19 literacy-related episodes occurred in the office, including a broad range of handling,reading and writing behaviors.

Although the children ranged the total play environment when engaged in literacy-related play, the bulk of their literacy demonstrations were concentrated in these three play settings. Overall, the ambiance and tone of the play environment in Site B was in stark contrast to those of Site A, being in general more subdued, interactive, intellectually challenging, and attention-holding. Specific to literacy, the children in this site devised numerous literacy-related play episodes (a total of 53) of substantial duration ($X=5$ minutes), with an average of seven literacy behaviors per episode. Furthermore, they increasingly incorporated the behaviors and language of literacy into their play scenarios, referring to and using literacy objects for distinct play purposes.

THE EFFECTS ON CHILDREN'S LITERACY BEHAVIOR

With these descriptive blueprints of the two play environments in mind, what, then, were their effects on children's literacy behaviors? And what might such effects mean for early childhood learning environments?

A detailed account of the effects of the play environments is presented in Neuman and Roskos (in press). Briefly, the deliberate redesign and enrichment of Site B significantly influenced the literacy behaviors of the children enrolled there. They engaged in substantially more literacy behaviors (handling, reading, writing), and their literacy-related play became increasingly longer in duration and more complex, consisting of "strings" of interrelated literacy behaviors or "contingent sequences" (Sylva, Roy, & Painter 1980). In sum, the children at Site B demonstrated and practiced literacy behaviors to a significantly greater degree (quantitatively and qualitatively) than the students at Site A.

Site B children used literacy objects in more imaginative ways than the Site B children, creating new uses for them as tools to further their play, such as changing a book into a "magic genie book." Unlike most commercial toys, which tend to encourage handling over invention, the prototypical literacy objects sparked literacy-oriented transformations—a play interaction of considerable developmental worth (Fein 1984). As Sutton-Smith (1984) has remarked, "Some toys make little difference and some make a lot of difference," promoting larger response repertoires that may be adapted to other contexts (p. 218). It appears that within well-designed literacy-enriched play environments, literacy objects can become toys that do "make a difference" with respect to literacy experiences.

Additionally, the children at Site B used the language of literacy in conjunction with sections to negotiate meaning in their play, whereas the children at Site A relied primarily on action alone. Put simply, Site B children used literacy talk as well as objects to accomplish literacy ends within the context of their play, while Site A children did not. Given the value of language in thinking, such interchanges involving the lexicon of literacy may provide a form of scaffolding which assists children's comprehension of the act of literacy (Wood, Bruner & Ross 1976).

As for what all this may mean for early childhood literacy learning environments, we offer our interpretation in the form of a comment accompanied by a word of caution. Clearly, literacy-enriched play environments are of value. They allow children to practice literacy behaviors and language in ways that make sense to them. In so doing, such environments may facilitate children's creation of stores of meaning, which may be transferable to new (and often more formal) literacy situations. Thus, they may provide a "leg-up" in literacy development.

However, literacy rich play environments do not just happen. Simply "littering" the places where children play with print will not do. Play environments that become literacy learning environments must be carefully planned by informed adults—adults who use information about learning, about physical design, and about language to create stimulating places where children can play with literacy on their own terms.

NOTE

[1] The kitchen setup included kitchen furniture and appliances, e.g. a wooden stove. The trees added to the play environment at the intervention site were artificial. Sofas of various sizes were also added as part of ongoing equipment purchasing by the day care program at the site. All books added were children's literature selections.

15

"Goin' to Grandma's House": Using Instructional Conversation to Promote Literacy and Reduce Resistance in Minority Children

Lynne M. Hudson, Carolyn F. Chryst, and Dianna Reamsnyder

INTRODUCTION

In an ethnographic study of elementary school classrooms, Gumperz (1981) contrasted the responses of middle-class and poor African-American children to teachers' instructions. He observed that most middle-class children settled down to work quickly and quietly, while poor African-American children were likely to appear uninterested in the task, wander about the room, and make comments such as "I don't want to do this," or "I can't do this," or "I don't know" (see also Branscombe 1991; Dyson 1992). According to Gumperz, these comments were all made with similar intonational contours that included a high pitch, sustained tone, and an elongation of the final vowel. What is most notable about this example, however, is not the linguistic features of the responses themselves, but the ways in which adult listeners interpret the responses. In our own experience, many white, middle-class teachers accept such responses literally as signaling lack of ability, lack of motivation, or both. However, when Gumperz played back audiotapes of the children's responses to African-American listeners, none of them entertained the possibility that these children really lacked ability or motivation to perform. Instead, they glossed the children's remarks as an indirect request for company; they were, in essence, saying "Help me; I don't like to work alone."

These divergent interpretations of intent illustrate how the cultural gap between minority students and their predominantly white, middle-class teachers creates a context for cultural bias in evaluations of children's ability and potential for academic success. What is critical about the difference between these two interpretations is that they lead to quite different responses from teachers. The former interpretation, "I can't/don't want to do this," suggests an antimotivational syndrome and a teacher-student value conflict that invites separation. This interpretation is likely to decrease teacher expectations for pupil performance and increase the physical, social, emotional, and cognitive distance between teachers and students. With low expectations for pupil performance, teachers are more likely to emphasize repetition of low-level tasks and isolated drill and practice, often in the form of seatwork. Students from whom little is expected are rarely asked to read extended texts, ask questions, analyze, think critically, or form their own opinions (Oakes 1985). Findings from a variety of studies converge to support the power of this self-fulfilling prophecy.

Self-fulfilling prophecies need not be negative, however. When teachers interpret statements such as "I can't do this" and "I don't want to do this" as invitations to work together, the potential is created for reducing the physical, social, emotional, and cognitive distance between teachers and students. Close and sustained collaboration with culturally different students enables teachers to understand and appreciate what these students do know, as well as what they still need to learn. Teachers who engage children in extended discourse and witness them reasoning in complicated ways about real-life problems are less likely to accept lack of ability as an explanation for poor performance on standardized tests, reading worksheets, or other traditional school tasks.

We believe classroom culture can be changed to accommodate these children. In particular, we examine a form of social interaction that promotes literacy by encouraging teachers and students to use language in purposeful activities involving reading, writing, speaking, and thinking.

THE INSTRUCTIONAL CONVERSATION

Tharp and Gallimore (1988) have called this form of social interaction the *instructional conversation* (IC) and define it as discourse in which teachers and students weave spoken and written language together with prior knowledge and experience to create new understanding. In their most generic sense, ICs are informative chats that accompany actions involving children and any more knowledgeable other. In some families, they occur between parents and children as they engage in a wide range of joint activities—setting the table, shopping for groceries, planting flowers, playing with Legos, reading a book, or attending special events (see Chapter One, this volume).

The richness of IC is well illustrated by an interaction between a father and his nine year old son, who were seated in front of one of the authors at a university football game. Before the game began, the announcer introduced a number of seniors who would be playing their last game. The boy's question about why it was their last game elicited a discussion in which the father explained what being a senior meant. He talked about how this was a happy and a sad time for these players—happy because they would be graduating and getting a job, perhaps even getting married and beginning to raise a family, but sad because they wouldn't be playing football anymore, and football had been an important part of their lives all through high school and college. Somewhat later when the boy asked why a coach was yelling at the defensive linemen seated on a bench below, the father explained that the coach was trying to get his players to try harder. The father went on to say that the coach might have accomplished his purpose better by explaining to the players exactly what they needed to do when they got back on the field. The father asked his son what worked best for the boy when his behavior needed changing—yelling or explaining. Throughout the game the father provided explanations of positions, downs, penalties, and plays, most of which were prompted by questions from his son, and all of which were artfully woven into the boy's current understanding of and interest in the event he was experiencing.

The father in this example illustrates clearly what researchers have come to recognize as a middle-class American cultural pattern. The father treats his son as a conversational partner, acknowledging, valuing, and encouraging his questions. He even allows him to direct topic selection, in this sense treating the boy as a conversational peer. At the same time, however, the father realizes his own status as the more knowledgeable other and takes responsibility for adapting the situation to the boy by simplifying his own language, by recalling relevant shared knowledge and experience, by negotiating meanings, and by cooperating with his son to build new knowledge (Rogoff 1990).

Vygotsky (cited in Tharp & Gallimore 1988) called the understandings that develop through such interactions *everyday concepts*. Two key characteristics of such concepts are (1) that they are learned primarily through speech, and (2) that they are learned "upward" from sensory experience to generalization. He contrasts everyday concepts with *schooled concepts*, which are learned (1) primarily through written symbols, and (2) "downward" from generalization to specific example. Examples of schooled concepts are terms like vaccine, immunity, and bacteria, which fifth-graders might encounter as key words in their science textbooks.

An ever-present danger in acquiring schooled concepts such as vaccine and immunity is that written symbols and generalizations, if they lack concrete referents, carry little meaning. Just because Katie, a fifth-grader, can define vaccine as "a substance composed of living or dead bacteria which when introduced into the body helps build immunity to disease," we should not infer that she can also define bacteria and immunity or explain how the former produced the latter. Furthermore, while Katie might refer to the scar on her arm as a vaccination and even know that it kept her from contracting a serious disease, she might not *spontaneously* relate this personal experience to the terms she is learning in school.

Katie is more likely to construct such a relationship in the context of a guided discussion with a responsive teacher, one who understands that meaningful learning requires making connections between new information and the child's existing knowledge and experience. Such a teacher might call attention to Katie's vaccination scar, asking what it is and how and why it got there. She might write both the familiar word (vaccination) and the unfamiliar word (vaccine) on the chalkboard and invite children to speculate about their common root. She might also ask Katie to explain terms she used in defining vaccine. In the absence of such a dialogue, Katie may memorize the glossary definition without understanding and be unable to recognize or recall it in a testing situation. She may convince herself and her teacher that she is more knowledgeable than she really is. The point here is that unless schooled concepts are related to the learner's experienced world through everyday concepts arising from practical activity, they will lack concrete referents.

The unique function of the instructional conversation is to provide a context in which connections between concrete and abstract ways of knowing can be formed, a context in which the discrete bits of knowledge children acquire can be organized and integrated into a meaningful whole. It is this capacity to relate new information, whether from written, oral, or visual text, to existing information, to evaluate its usefulness, and to use it to solve problems, that is the hallmark of the literate person (Langer 1987).

INSTRUCTIONAL CONVERSATION IN THE CLASSROOM

Making connections between everyday and school-learned concepts is more difficult in the classroom than it is in parent-child interactions for a variety of reasons. Parent-child conversations occur within a context of shared experiences built up over many years. Teachers cannot know their pupils in the same way that parents do, and this lack of shared knowledge has implications for the quality of their interaction. Parents are also less constrained than teachers. They can more easily allow their instructional conversations to be guided by the particular and often shifting interests of their children. Teachers, however, must contend with 25 or more children simultaneously, as well as with a prescribed curriculum. It is the pressure created by these contextual variables that led Tharp and Gallimore (1988) to characterize the instructional conversation as a paradoxical concept. Instruction implies planning and authority, while conversation implies responsiveness and equality. The task of teaching, they contend, is to resolve this paradox, that is, to create opportunities to be responsive to the varying interests, abilities, and background knowledge of pupils while, at the same time, ensuring that *a priori* goals are achieved.

Figure 15.1 is a transcript of a teacher in the act of resolving this paradox. The teacher is engaging her second-grade pupils in an instructional conversation about concepts for which they have little experiential knowledge. The excerpt comes from a social studies unit about the earth (Hyder & Brown 1982). While the children had sensory experiences for land and water, most other concepts were unfamiliar—land formations such as islands, peninsulas, and continents; the fifty United States; directions; globes; and ways of expressing one's love of country. The teacher succeeds in resolving the paradox, we believe, because she is able to further her instructional objective— helping pupils learn to extract meaning from expository text—by making use of the children's comments or, to apply the weaving metaphor, by weaving their ideas into the fabric of her lesson.

While this instructional conversation consists of question and answer sequences, it should not be equated with the standard recitation script so prevalent in American classrooms. The recitation script relies

Figure 15.1
An Instructional Conversation in a Second Grade
Classroom

The teacher (T) began by orienting children to a picture in their social studies book and asking:

T: What is in this picture? (a snowy river bank with two animals watering). What kind of animal?

C1:   (yells out) *A horse!*

C2   (yells out) *A deer!*

T: What time of year is it?

C1:   *Christmas.*

C2   *Winter!*

T: (moving to the picture on the next page of people from many lands) How are the people different? (pulling down a very colorful map of North America)

The children all react with delight at the sight of the map, and the teacher's questions is forgotten.

C2:   (from his desk, talking to no one in particular, points to and names areas on the map that he knows) *California, Ohio, Florida, Mexico, ...* Then he raises his hand, waiting to be called on. *What I want to know is what states winter is in?*

C3:   *It's muggy in Florida.*

T: (Using hand to illustrate and starting from Canada, she points out areas that will have winter soon and those which rarely get cold. She tells the class that there are exceptions, and relates an anecdote about her trip to Florida last year when it was very cold. Then, returning to the earlier question, she refocuses the children's attention on the textbook picture of people from many lands and asks) What makes people different?

C4:   *Some can be from China?*

C2:   *Can we guess where people are from?*

C5:   *This one is from Texas!*

T: How do you know? What lets you know he might be from Texas?

C5:   *He's wearing a hat.*

T: Why is he wearing a hat?

C2:   *It's sunny.*

C6:   *Africans* (referring to persons in tribal dress pictured in the textbook)

C5:   *Dang, I was going to say that. Africans. That's what I was going to say.*

T: I'll leave the map down. When you finish your work, you can come look at it.

C2:   (looking at the map) *I'm going to ask my parents to take me to the end of the world! Yeah, the end of the world.*

T: (pointing to the next picture in the book) What kind of land is this?

C5:   (hand is waving vigorously)

C2:   *Uhm, I know, I know, uhm. . . .*

T: Were you thinking plains?

C2:   *Yeah, that's it. Plains.*

T: What are flat lands good for?

C5:   *Walking.*

T: Anthony says for walking. That's right, but what else could we use flat lands for? (long pause with no response) Why are these big machines in the picture?

C3:   *For growing food.*

T: That's right, grains grow very well on flat land.

C5:   *Are grains food?*

T: (Nods head and then moves on.) Jessica, name another type of land.

C7:   *Hills.*

T: (Nods. Another child reads last paragraph. Then it is time to change rooms.)

---

more heavily on known-answer questions and direct recall. The questions in instructional conversations are more likely to be responsive to students' interests and ideas (illustrated here when the teacher responds to a child's answer by asking, "How do you know?"); are more likely to assist students in developing more complete or elaborated ideas (e.g., when the teacher cues children to attend to relevant stimuli by asking, "Why are these big machines in the picture?"); and encourage divergent responses (e.g., when the teacher asks, "What makes people different?").

An obvious strength of this IC is that its primary objective, helping children extract meaning from text, directly promotes literacy. The teacher accomplishes this objective by querying the children, most of whom have limited reading skill, about the pictures in their book—the animals, the people, and the farming scene. She shows that thinking is valued by acknowledging and extending the children's ideas (e.g., her elaborated response to C2's question about which states have wintry weather). She provides peer models for less able children by encouraging the more thoughtful children to verbalize their thinking processes (e.g., asking C5 what led him to think that the man wearing a hat was from Texas). She encourages them to continue the dialogue by accepting their ideas (e.g., animals in the first picture might be horses or deer and flat lands are good for walking). Rather than telling the children why flat lands are useful, she assists them in formulating an answer (by asking what big machines are used for).

It is sometimes difficult to capture the strengths of an IC because the particular example cannot encompass the whole tapestry, which includes past experiences as well as anticipated ones. In this IC, for example, the teacher's use of the map foreshadows later aspects of the unit, which will deal more explicitly with maps as symbolic representations. Other benefits that accrue from this IC are more obvious from a careful reading of the text. One is that the teacher gains information about the children's prior knowledge that will help her to assist later performance. She learns that C2 recognizes several states from the map. His question "What I want to know is what states winter is in?" tells the teacher that he is able to link previously mentioned topics (winter and maps) in logical ways to create extended discourse. This question, coupled with his later question asking if the children could guess where people in the textbook picture are from, tells the teacher that C2 has the capacity to be a true conversational partner, capable of initiating topics as well as responding to teacher-initiated topics.

The only other child in this excerpt who appears to have skills similar to C2's is C5. His ability to make logical inferences is evident in his conclusion about the textbook picture of the man in the ten gallon hat (i.e., he was from Texas). His critical thinking skills are evident in the last few lines of the transcript. He realizes that the teacher's conclusion that grains grow well on flat land does not follow clearly from C3's remark that big machines are used to grow food *unless* grains are food. His question ("Are grains food?") signals not only that he detects this missing step in her reasoning, but also that he is attending to meaning and monitoring his own comprehension carefully.   It also signals that he, and probably many other children in the class, are missing background knowledge that the teacher may have assumed they had. Why didn't the teacher "seize the moment" to explore and extend the children's knowledge base? Did the opportunity go unnoticed? Was the teacher constrained by the clock? This is not clear from the transcript.

What is clear from the transcript is that this instructional conversation generated a great deal of student interest and mental activity. Children were given opportunities to think critically, to make inferences, to draw conclusions, to support their arguments, and to actively create meaning through dialogue with text, each other, and their teacher. This instructional conversation gave children practice in using a variety of strategies to derive meaning from text, including silent reading, oral reading, looking at pictures, looking for relations between pictures and words, relating text to prior experience, and asking questions.

Having highlighted some of the strengths of instructional conversations generally and this IC in particular, we must regretfully acknowledge that research shows that ICs are rare occurrences in U.S. classrooms regardless of grade level and content area. John Goodlad (1984) concluded from his comprehensive study of 38 geographically and socioeconomically diverse U.S. schools that open-ended discussion that encourages students to reason (or even to offer personal opinion) occupied less than 1 percent of instructional time. Our own data are consistent with this finding. This IC was the only instance found in a data set consisting of more than 21 hours of observation in three second-grade classrooms. Our purpose in observing these classrooms was to determine whether or not an after school literacy program that some of these second-graders had attended since kindergarten was having any effect on their performance in school.

THE HILLTOP EMERGENT LITERACY PROGRAM

The Hilltop Emergent Literacy Program (HELP) is housed in the community room of a subsidized apartment complex near the campus of the University of Toledo. Almost all the residents of the 90-unit complex are African-American. HELP began in 1988 as a research and development project sponsored by the College of Education and Allied Professions. Salaries of the director and graduate assistants are paid by the college while student interns meet program requirements by volunteering at HELP. Staff also includes two certified teachers from the local elementary school whose time is donated. At most sessions the staff/student ratio is 1:3.

The research goals of the program include adding to our understanding of why the transition to school is difficult for many poor and minority children and determining if the pattern of declining achievement often exhibited in this group can be stemmed by increasing academic learning time and by using more culturally sensitive instructional methods. An important teaching goal of the program is to provide preservice teachers, most of whom are white and middle class, with a supportive introduction to the demands and rewards of teaching in an urban setting and opportunities for guided participation in working with children who are culturally different from themselves.

While HELP was conceived initially as an emergent literacy project aimed at primary grade children, the interest of older children and their parents prompted the staff to allow older elementary children to attend during the first year and, in subsequent years, to plan programming geared to the needs and interests of older children. At the present time, the program is open to all Kindergarten through eighth-grade children who live at Hilltop, and the active roster includes about 50 children—16 kindergarten and first-graders who come two afternoons each week between 3:30 and 5:30 p.m.; 10 second- and third-graders who come on opposite afternoons; and 25 third- through eighth-graders who come two evenings each week between 5:30 and 8:00 p.m. The program is voluntary and attendance rates vary, but at least 70 percent of the children attend more than 80 percent of the time. Attendance rates would be even higher if children had more control over their lives. Some mothers use the program as a disciplinary tool; when children misbehave, they are not allowed to come to the program. Other mothers often choose to visit relatives or shop during program hours; they take their children with them rather than interrupt their outing to return home to pick up their children. Other parents pick children up early to go shopping or run errands. When this happens children are typically distressed because their activities are interrupted, and tears are common.

The HELP curriculum is eclectic. The evening study night program includes homework assistance, sustained silent reading, and hands-on math, science, and creative arts activities. Frequent study night activities include baking, writing, creating and enacting dramatic events, visiting the public library, and attending special events at the university. The afternoon program for second- and third-graders focuses on homework assistance, hands-on math problem solving, and reading. The specific reading goals stressed at this level include learning to extract meaning from expository texts dealing with thematic topics such as life in the sea, and developing an understanding and appreciation for longer and more complex story structure. For example, in keeping with the ocean theme, third graders researched sea animals and produced both written reports and a collaborative mobile depicting all the animals they had studied. In addition, they listened to the teachers read exemplary texts such as *Island of the Blue Dolphins*, which is beyond their independent reading level but well within their listening comprehension level.

On the afternoons when primary grade children attend, the curriculum includes math experiences with manipulatives such as pattern blocks, dinosaur counters, and base ten blocks; *Sing, Spell, Read and Write* (Dickson 1972), a phonics-based language arts program that uses music to teach reading; and many reading and writing activities typically found in whole-language classrooms. Aside from story time, which is usually done in a large group, children spend most of their time in self-selected activities assisted by an intern or in small instructional groups led by an experienced teacher and one or more interns.

Instructional conversation is very much a part of these small group activities. For example, after reading *The Underwater Alphabet Book* during large group time, the teacher placed children in small groups to work on their own underwater alphabet book. Children drew letters of the alphabet from a fishbowl and created imaginary underwater animals that began with the letters they had drawn. As children shared their ideas during the prewriting phase, the teacher assisted them in accessing relevant prior knowledge. She asked Dominique, who had drawn the letter "P" and decided to create a pearfish, what a pearfish might look like. Accepting Dominique's response that its head would be shaped like a pear, the teacher encouraged children to bring shared knowledge about fins and tails to bear on the present task by asking the group what else Dominique's fish would need. Another child who had drawn the letter "R" created a rubyfish, which she drew in the shape of a gemstone and colored an iridescent red. As this child and others around her colored their alphabet book pages, the group had lively discussions about favorite colors, about objects in the plant and animal world that displayed these colors, and about a host of other interesting topics that emerged spontaneously from their work. Conversations such as these make visible the children's prior knowledge and enable the teacher to expand their knowledge base within a meaningful context.

It is important to make explicit what is implicit in the examples of program activities described above. Namely, there is considerable continuity and consistency across age levels in both thematic content and in the cognitive and social processes used to implement the curriculum. Students and teachers at all grade levels are exploring ocean life at the same time, albeit in different ways. This creates opportunities for interesting conversations outside the program, as peers and siblings share with each other and with their families what they are learning. The processes used to implement the curriculum are consistent across age levels as well. All students are encouraged to take personal responsibility for their own learning, to make good choices about how to use their time, to work effectively both alone and in collaboration with peers, to engage in meaningful dialogue about activities of interest to themselves and others, to think critically, and to solve problems effectively. Students vary, of course, in the degree to which they can carry out these functions unassisted. In addition to variability across children, there is also a fair amount of intraindividual variability across time, which is probably attributable to the inconsistencies and stresses in the daily lives of many of the children who attend the program. Despite this variability, the consistencies built into the program function to create a distinct culture. We have become a community of learners with shared expectations about what it means to learn and know.

EFFECTS OF HELP ON SCHOOL PERFORMANCE

The positive effects of participation in HELP on outcome measures such as standardized achievement test scores and report card
grades have been reported elsewhere (Bergin, Hudson, Chryst, &
Resetar 1992). While we found these results gratifying, we were not
satisfied. We wanted to know how the things we had stressed at HELP
were being played out in the children's school. To identify HELP
program variables that might be contributing to the achievement differences assessed in school, we needed to do a school observation
study. We hypothesized that the after school-program's emphasis on
collaborative activity, instructional conversation, and student choice
would produce more self-regulated learners who could work well with
others, think critically, reflect upon their own understandings, and
communicate these understandings clearly to others. To test these
hypotheses, we observed in the classrooms of second-graders who had
been in HELP since the fall of their kindergarten year. In addition to
observing the HELP children, we also observed the matched controls
with whom HELP participants had been paired as kindergartners.[1] In
the fall of the children's second-grade year, one of the HELP teachers,
a graduate student in educational psychology, spent more than 21
hours across a six-week period in September and October conducting
a case study of HELP children in the three second-grade classrooms.
As part of the ongoing program of research, she functioned as a participant observer, taking field notes, collecting artifacts, interviewing
children and teachers, and assisting the teacher when asked. She entered the setting intending to focus on process variables, comparing
HELP children and their controls on self-regulated learning, peer
collaboration, critical thinking, and self-expression. However, this
proved to be problematic because the classroom environment provided few opportunities for the behaviors of interest to emerge.

The research goals were subsequently altered to include an examination of differences in individual seatwork and recitation performance, because these were the predominant instructional modes that
were observed. A comparison of the seatwork assignments of children
who participated in HELP and their matched controls indicated that
HELP children were more likely to understand and follow directions,
to complete assignments first, and to use complex sentence structure
on open-ended language tasks (e.g., using spelling words in sen-

tences).   A comparison of the recitation performance of the two groups revealed no significant differences.

Recitation and seatwork were not, of course, the most likely places to find confirmation of our hypotheses.   The predicted differences were more likely to be revealed in the context of instructional conversations.   Unfortunately, only one (see Figure 15.1) instance of instructional conversation was observed.   While it would be inappropriate to draw firm conclusions on the basis of a single IC, an analysis of this transcript is at least consistent with our hypotheses.   In this IC, seven children contributed to the conversation.   Two of these children had been enrolled since kindergarten in HELP.   These two children, C2 and C5, were the only children to initiate topics or engage in extended discourse, thereby distinguishing themselves as true conversational partners.   Moreover, despite being in an environment that does not encourage pupil questions, these two boys asked three very appropriate questions during the 15-minute lesson.   While this may not seem cause for celebration, it is certainly better than the average of fewer than two questions per 30 minutes cited by Sarason (1983, p. 97).

The contributions of students C2 and C5 to the IC are different in significant ways from the contributions of their peers, and illustrate how their ways of being in the world have been positively influenced by participation in HELP.   In a classroom where the attention of pupils is constantly focused on filling in blanks or responding to known-answer questions with expected responses, these two boys alone clearly focus on meaning.   C2 refines his classmate's response that it is Christmastime by supplying a more general, and more situationally appropriate, word (winter).   C5's question "Are grains food?" reveals not only that he has learned to monitor his own comprehension, but also that it matters to him that things make sense.

Throughout this dialogue, C2 and C5 insist upon their rights to use language to make meaning and share it with others.   Unlike other children in the class, these boys use language not only to respond to the world but to transform it.   By responding to the teacher's rather vaguely worded question ("What makes people different?") with a question of his own ("Can we guess where people are from?"), C2 modifies the teacher's task, making it both more relevant to his own interests and more intellectually challenging.   C5, his collaborator in this transformation, picks up this challenge without missing a beat, chiming in immediately that one person in the picture is from Texas.

C2 and C5 have learned to use language to inquire, to solve problems, to collaborate, and to persuade. Why are such uses of language so important? According to Wirth, "The right to converse—to hold dialogue with texts and each other in reaching for understanding about the world and ourselves—is the distinctive characteristic of being human" (Wirth 1992, 22). Wirth credits Gadamer (1986) for his own understanding of the importance of language, noting that "language is the medium in which we live. Therefore, the way we use it and learn it affects who we are and who we may become, and what our society is and what it can become" (1992, p. 22). C2 and C5 have already learned to use oral language in the ways that educational and economic researchers agree will be critical to success in the global economy of the next century (Reich 1991).

ENHANCING OPPORTUNITIES FOR INSTRUCTIONAL CONVERSATION IN SCHOOLS

If instructional conversations are so valuable in promoting meaningful discourse, learning and critical thinking, why are they so rare? Discussions with classroom teachers have implicated a variety of interrelated factors. One thing teachers tell us is that instructional conversation doesn't feel like teaching—it's just chatting. Many teachers, then, do not recognize the benefits of instructional conversation. Furthermore, they do not know how to do it. Because ICs are rare in school, teachers have had few models or opportunities to develop expertise in their use. A second thing teachers tell us is that they don't have time to do instructional conversation. ICs are perceived to be less efficient than direct instruction, and efficiency is a high priority in an educational system that is increasingly complex, comprehensive, and constrained by state and locally mandated performance objectives and testing programs. A third thing that some teachers tell us, especially elementary teachers who must function as generalists, is that they do not know their content well enough to do instructional conversation. ICs do require considerable teacher expertise and flexibility. Teachers must attend simultaneously to the text, to student comments, and to their own behavior. Repeated "in-flight" adjustments are necessary to be responsive to students and, at the same time, move toward a specified instructional objective (Tharp & Gallimore 1988).

How do we respond to such teacher concerns? One way is to stress that there is nothing as efficient as a good chat. Prescriptive teaching requires an understanding of the learner's entry level knowledge and cognitive skills. Such understanding is a natural product of instructional conversations because ICs make children's thinking and conceptual knowledge *visible*. Another way to respond to teacher concerns is to stress that teachers do not have to know a content area in great depth in order to engage in instructional conversation, especially in the elementary grades. They need only be open to learning with and from their students. Reluctant teachers may also be encouraged to risk trying instructional conversation if they are made aware of its affective benefits. The intersubjectivity created through IC does more than establish a shared frame of reference; it establishes a mutual bond as well. It fulfills a basic human need to know and be known.

Having identified factors that teachers acknowledge inhibit them from engaging in instructional conversation, we should add that we have identified additional reasons why teachers find it difficult to relate schooled concepts to children's practical experience. First, many teachers may not know—or even want to know—a lot about the lived experiences of their pupils. The cultural gap between public school pupils and the teaching force is widening at an alarming rate. The majority of teachers are white, middle-class, and female. Well-intentioned though they may be, they often know very little about the lived experiences of poor and minority pupils. When they do have such information, teachers may see no way to make use of children's experiences in furthering classroom goals and objectives. Also, some teachers view a child's real world as a Pandora's box—better left unopened. On the surface this seems uncaring and even cruel, and it is undoubtedly experienced by many children as rejection. But our experience with teachers who adopt this stance is that it often serves a self-protective function, as a coping mechanism that prevents them from being horrified, even overwhelmed, by what they might find.

A related reason it is difficult for teachers to use instructional conversation to assist children in making schooled concepts meaningful is that the everyday concepts of many children are not especially useful for making sense of schooled concepts. Such children are often identified as educationally at risk. Children considered to be educationally at risk do not lack a rich body of everyday concepts; rather, what places them at risk is a lack of fit between their everyday concepts and the school curriculum. In other words, many of their everyday concepts are not helpful in making school learning meaningful because they do not overlap sufficiently with the concepts to be learned in school. Consider the following example. All children in our urban school district are expected to learn to read the word "map" in first grade and to use maps in second grade. For Chad, who has vacationed regularly with parents and has had encounters with maps, the word "map" has a referent. It elicits a visual image of a concrete object and an association with a personal experience, planning a trip to Disneyland. Bobby, on the other hand, has never seen a map or ventured outside his neighborhood. There is little in his knowledge base that can serve as a building block for developing an understanding of maps. For him, the word map elicits no visual image. It has no meaning. At best it might be understood as a "short a" word that rhymes with cap, but only if he knows his short vowels and has a good ear.

What do teachers do when the lived experiences of pupils are not easily or appropriately related to the curriculum? The answer, we think, is for teachers to *create* shared experiences with their pupils through joint activity and conversation. These shared experiences can then become the basis for making schooled concepts meaningful. For example, pupils with no direct experience with liquid measurement might discover the value of standard units and learn to use them by making pancakes. Children from families where most adults are unemployed may begin to envision what the future holds for them as a result of opportunities to interview classroom visitors engaged in interesting occupations. All children, but especially children from less advantaged backgrounds, need to be in classrooms filled with lively discussion about interesting activities in which they are collaboratively engaged with peers and a more knowledgeable other. This is precisely what an instructional conversation is.

A value-added feature of creating such shared meanings is that they can function not only to enhance meaningful learning, but also to reduce cultural mismatch and the sense of alienation that cause pupils to drop out of school and teachers to leave the profession. The instructional conversation is a form of guided participation, a collaboration of experts and novices in activities arranged and structured by the experts to function as bridges for novices. The basis for guided participation is intersubjectivity, a shared focus and purpose between novices and their more skilled partners. A key product of such teacher-pupil collaboration is a sense of community (Rogoff 1990). A community of learners stays together because pupils and teachers feel a commitment to one another and to their human pursuit of making meaning.

HELP has demonstrated that classrooms can and should be such communities. This commitment is evident in the voices of the children, teachers, and interns who have participated in the program. An undergraduate intern, who was enrolled in two different field placements simultaneously, summarized her experiences by writing:

> I hope eventually to teach in secondary, but I know I will have long forgotten the students in my junior high placement before I forget Kim, Max, Jackie, Robert, Brandon, and the others [HELP participants]. *Observing* [emphasis added] at the junior high made me realize everything I must brace myself for when I start teaching. HELP showed me what I can look forward to.

A public school teacher who volunteered to work at HELP wrote:

> As a result of HELP, I have developed an attachment to the children, who have taught me as much, if not more, than I have taught them. I feel a commitment to make a difference in their lives. HELP has provided me with many other learning experiences. Contacts with University faculty enable me to be current with teaching methods and research and gain insight on developing children and their progress. HELP has also given me a chance to practice teaching within a team rather than in isolation in my own classroom and the privilege of sharing my ideas and experiences with interns.

This teacher states explicitly the value she places on the kind of communication and system of support present at HELP. The value that the program has for children is less explicit—but perhaps more poignantly—conveyed in the words of one of the HELP children, who likened attending the program to "goin' to Grandma's house." Our readers can use their own expanded literacy skills to ponder, unpack, and interpret this child's capsule summary of what being part of such a community means to her.

CONCLUSIONS

It has been argued that gifted and talented education is simply better education and should be available to all children. While many of the gifted educators agree, they also believe that the absence of challenging, open-ended activities and variety is more harmful to gifted children than to so-called normal children. By the same logic, we believe that IC is beneficial for all children, but the absence of IC is particularly detrimental to poor minority children.

School is much more likely to make sense to middle-class children because schools teach the beliefs, values, attitudes and skills that reflect the dominant culture of which they are already a part. These children are likely to understand school success as the means by which they will find and take their rightful place in adult society. School is less likely to make sense to poor minority children. They enter school with a different set of culturally learned behaviors, behaviors that are frequently neither understood nor valued by professional educators, the majority of whom are from the dominant culture. When the mismatch produces learning problems, these children are likely to be tracked into instructional programs emphasizing repetition of isolated skill and drill exercises that rely heavily upon worksheets that are to be completed independently. Relegated to low-level tasks with little relevance to their lives and forced to work in social isolation, these children are likely to become disengaged and alienated from school life. This alienation is exacerbated by the failure of teachers to help children make school more meaningful, and by a perceived lack of opportunities for academically talented minorities. This perception is derived from the historical practice of denying minorities access to high-status positions in the dominant culture (Ogbu 1993). Not surprisingly, many of these alienated students begin to actively resist adopting the behaviors associated with school success and eventually to develop an oppositional identity that defines such behaviors as "acting white." When a critical mass of such students exists within a school, academically motivated minority students feel caught between two worlds and forced to choose between affiliating with their minority peers and moving into a dominant culture where neither social acceptance nor success is certain.

Few would disagree with the conclusion that public schools have not done an acceptable job of preparing poor and minority youth to develop their talents and find their niches in the adult world. If we continue with our present practices, economists predict that about 30 percent of us will become richer in the next century while 70 percent of us will become poorer. Minorities, of course, will make up a disproportionate percentage of those who become poorer. If we are to interrupt this trend, one key goal of educational policy will need to be implementing procedures to reorient peer group pressures toward the work required to achieve high levels of literacy (Labov 1987). That is, we must find ways to encourage poor minority students "to take on the language and behaviors which lead to literacy and full participation in the mainstream culture" (Smith-Burke 1989, 8).

It is clear from our work at HELP that the use of instructional conversation is one way to encourage poor minority students to accomplish this goal without having to forfeit their own cultural identity. Through their repeated interactions at the program, children from Hilltop have discovered that learning can be exciting and rewarding and that their white teachers can be trusted. At the same time, their white teachers have learned that poor minority children are bright, interested, and interesting, and that these children have much to teach their teachers. This kind of mutual understanding and appreciation is a key component of any strategy for eradicating the inequities in the present system.

NOTES

HELP has been generously supported by the General Mills Foundation.

[1] A few of the control subjects were added later. This was necessary because several control subjects were retained after kindergarden or first grade and were no longer part of this second grade cohort. This, in and of itself, speaks to the success of HELP.

16

Three Different Early Literacy Programs and Their Effect on Inner-City Kindergartners' Emerging Sense of Story

Lynne Putnam

"Now can we dramatize it?" a student asked eagerly. For the past half hour on this April morning, Ms. Hager's kindergartners had been listening to a reading of *The Hungry Fox and the Foxy Duck* (Leverich 1978). This was the third time they had heard the story read aloud, and as always, their teacher elicited lively discussion. Before reading, they thought about a time when they had tried to trick someone else, thus linking their own life experience to the experience of the story's central character. During the reading they stopped to analyze why the duck acted as he did, to predict what would happen next, and to discuss the meaning of important words (such as "wise," "pond," "peaceful," "hut," and "cranky"). After reading, they talked about their favorite scenes, then thought about the problem in the story and how it was solved.

Now it was time to dramatize. All 21 children participated enthusiastically, choosing for themselves the roles they wished to play. "I want ducks to stay in the pond, which is the carpet," directed Ms. Hager. "I want foxes to go away out of the pond." Those choosing to play the part of the bull would have to stand to one side until their scene at the end of the story.

> Okay ducks, let's get up and swim now. Wise little
> ducks swimming in the pond. It's peaceful and quiet.
> The sun is shining up there. There you are sunning
> yourselves. Then one morning, what happened?. . . .
> Okay, stop and let the fox talk.

The bits of story narration that Ms. Hager provided as a frame for the dramatization were interwoven with stage prompts, questions about what happened next in the story, and cues for characters to produce dialogue. For the next seven minutes, she collaborated with her kindergartners to reconstruct the story they had just heard read aloud—not as outsiders *telling* it, but as insiders *living* it.

Reminders of *The Hungry Fox and the Foxy Duck* threaded their way throughout the school day. During Choice Time, students could opt to make "foxy ducks" out of construction paper and write about them. During Math, partners added or subtracted sets of paper cut-out ducks in response to teacher-created number stories.

That afternoon, the class listened to and discussed a nonfiction Let's-Read-and-Find-Out science book about ducks. During the reading they dramatized preening behavior, dipping their beaks into the oil gland located near their tail and smearing the oil over their feathers to waterproof them. They also searched for food, tipping their heads into the water and flipping their tails up in the air (a passerby would have thought the class was preparing to do headstands). Afterwards, they returned to their desks to illustrate and write about what they had learned.

The next morning, as classmates got together to read and write stories of their own choosing, *The Hungry Fox and the Foxy Duck* was much sought after. Key vocabulary, phrasings, and character dialogue from the book echoed in the youngsters' pretend readings, a legacy of their repeated opportunities to hear, discuss, and dramatize the story with classmates.

BACKGROUND TO THE STUDY

Ms. Hager's class was one of four full-day kindergartens participating in a study that asked how philosophically different approaches to early literacy instruction would affect inner-city kindergartners' developing sense of story.

From the earliest grades on, an overriding concern that shapes many curriculum decisions in schools serving low-income, minority group students is the development of children's basic literacy skills. Yet the connection between the orientation of early literacy programs and children's development in areas beyond phonics and decoding has been insufficiently documented.

One important contributor to story comprehension, for example, is knowledge of the structural frames that give shape to stories (Stein & Glenn 1979; Mandler & Johnson 1977; Thorndyke 1977; Bower 1976). Story grammars, as these frames are called, constitute "the macrostructures which underlie the organization of narrative text" (Gordon & Braun 1982, 262); embedded within are "the ideas, events, and personal motivations that comprise the flow of narratives" (Pearson & Fielding 1991, 821). While story grammar knowledge appears to increase with age (Whaley 1981), instruction that calls attention to story structure has been shown to improve elementary school children's reading comprehension (Short & Ryan 1984; Whaley 1982), as well as their ability to predict, recall, and compose stories (Gordon & Braun 1982).

Since listening to stories read aloud is the primary means for developing young children's concept of story, and since story reading appears to be a less common occurrence in working-class families than in middle-class families (Teale 1986; Anderson & Stokes 1984; Heath 1983), it seems likely that youngsters from lower socioeconomic status homes enter school at a disadvantage with respect to story grammar knowledge. If that is the case, then it becomes important to examine the extent to which they can benefit from various preschool and kindergarten programs with different approaches to the read-aloud event and other literacy-related experiences.

The study reported in this chapter examined three distinct curricular approaches, representing the three most common philosophical orientations to kindergarten literacy at that time in Washington, D.C. schools.

a. Two of the kindergartens used a Literate Environment Program, developed by the author in earlier research (Putnam 1983). Consistent with an emergent literacy/whole-language perspective, this approach emphasized the read-aloud experience, along with plentiful opportunities for youngsters to experiment with reading and writing in their own ways.

b. A third kindergarten used IBM's *Writing to Read* program, designed to develop youngsters' early reading skills and to move them toward conventional-looking writing. As used in District of Columbia schools at the time of the study, the core program was complemented by classroom routines that strongly emphasized phonics skills.

c. A fourth kindergarten used a combination of commercial materials with teacher-led and workbook activities reflecting a traditional concept of reading readiness, with its key assumption that children need to develop certain subskills (especially letter name and sound knowledge)before they can be successful in learning to read.

Four veteran teachers were chosen to participate in the study. All were African-American, possessed excellent interaction skills with children, and were committed to developing their students' academic and literacy foundation through the respective programs they used. The two Literate Environment teachers were selected from among a group the author had trained over a two-year period, while the other two teachers were selected on the basis of recommendations from early childhood supervisors in the school district. The high level of expertise across teachers was intended to maximize the likelihood that observed classroom differences would reflect program variations rather than variations in quality of teaching.

The 66 kindergartners who remained in the final study sample were African-American and attended schools serving a mixture of financially impoverished and blue-collar neighborhoods. Over half the student population in the represented schools qualified for free lunch (55% in the reading readiness approach school, 56% in one of the Literate Environment schools, 70% in the *Writing to Read* school, and 90% in the second Literate Environment school).

The study's major limitation resulted from an unforeseen, uneven distribution of subjects across classrooms, which occurred when a number of children from the two Literate Environment classes moved during the year, and when several others for whom English was a second language were dropped from the study sample. As a result, only 14 of Ms. Hager's 21 children and only eight students from the other Literate Environment kindergarten (which operated in a small, open-space area and was thus assigned only 16 children to begin with) remained in the final sample. In contrast, 21 out of 23 children in the *Writing to Read* sample, and 23 out of 24 in the traditional reading readiness approach sample, remained.

Data collection was designed with two purposes in mind: to develop a portrait of program differences and to measure students' developing story grammar knowledge.

To document what teachers and children said and did in each program, particularly during read-aloud events, each kindergarten was observed for two full days, once in late fall and again in spring. In addition, all story reading events were audiotaped for one week in February.

To document program effects, all children in the study were audiotaped at the beginning and end of the school year as they "read"
Emily McCully's wordless picture book, *Picnic* (1984). Readings
were then transcribed and scored to reflect the extent to which children had included and correctly identified important story elements.

PORTRAITS: A DAY IN THE LIFE OF EACH PROGRAM

Over 600 single-spaced pages of notes resulted from classroom
observations and transcribed story reading events, yielding information about how time was spent in each of the three observed programs,
what kinds of literacy events were valued, and how literature was presented—the kinds of texts that were selected, how children were invited to interact with that text, how many and what kinds of questions
teachers asked, and the extent to which book language was highlighted.

While these notes provide the basis for some quantitative comparisons, a narrative description of daily classroom life is much more
likely to convey a picture of what each program looked like. Thus,
the following set of portraits is presented, based on the final set of
classroom observations that were conducted late in the school year.

The *Writing to Read* Kindergarten on a Day in Early May

Some of the children arrived early and looked at books or chatted
with each other until the teacher arrived. The opening routine began
with the Pledge and the singing of a patriotic song. The alphabet
song followed, after which two children were called on to share the
stories they had written with the class.

At that point the day's agenda surfaced. "We're going to review
charts all day long," announced the teacher, reminding the children
that it was the end of the year, and they would be expected to know
these things when they reached first grade. They began by singing a
rhyming words song, naming both short and long vowels, identifying
color words the teacher spelled, defining the term "classification," and
reading items from a classification chart. Attention then shifted to a
picture of a mother serving food to a child. The day before, the class
had discussed what was happening in the picture, and their answers

had been recorded on chart paper under the categories: "Who?" "What kind?" "How?" "When?" "Where?" and "Why?" Today they read the items on the chart.

The story reading for the day, which lasted 14 minutes was chosen because Mother's Day was around the corner. "I'll read *Are You My Mother?*" the teacher announced, "and then in the Writing to Read lab, we'll write about our mothers."

As the class moved to another area of the rug for story reading, one of the children asked to read a favorite (easy-to-read) story to the class. His wish was granted, and everyone listened as he decoded fluently and with expression. "I love the way he said his beginning and ending sounds," the teacher commented with enthusiasm.

She then went on to read the simple and predictable *Are You My Mother?* (Eastman 1960), stopping to ask 17 questions—such as "What do you think the kitten said?" "Where was his mother?" "Did he have a mother?" "Do you think a plane could be his mother?" "What is a plane?"—which the children generally answered with one or two words. After reading, in keeping with an emphasis on classification skills, the teacher turned everyone's attention to a poster chart entitled "Who Is My Mother?" which pictured sets of young and mature animals. "All right, let's look at the chart," she directed. We want to name the mothers of these little animals up here." She then proceeded to ask what you call the mother of a puppy, cub, duckling, calf, piglet, kitten, foal, chick, and kid.

A 15-minute spelling dictation followed. Students were asked to write 10 words related to the "mother" theme: "love," "Mom," "kiss," "happy," "hug," "kind," "sweet," "like," "nice," and "good."

The top reading group (Rabbits) then worked with the teacher for 20 minutes, proceeding smoothly through a round-robin reading of two stories in a beginning basal reader, stopping to answer a few questions from the teacher after each one. Meanwhile, the Frogs and Turtles (lowest group) were directed to color worksheets the class would complete that afternoon; in reality, they were more interested in eavesdropping on the top group's reading session.

It was time to attend the IBM lab. As children lined up to leave the classroom, the teacher assigned partners to work together at specific learning stations. During the 38 minutes they actually spent in the lab, students took turns interacting with computers that introduced "cycle words" that contained common spelling patterns (like m*a*n and sn*ake*). Other learning station activities included writing stories that incorporated those cycle words, typing story drafts, listening to story records while looking at the book, reading illustrated word cards, or spelling words to match pictures in a work journal. In her exchanges with the children, the teacher focused primarily on their reading, spelling, and punctuation. Virtually no mention was made of the content or message children were trying to communicate in their stories.

When everyone returned from lunch, some of the children began to look at books, until the teacher reminded them, "We have to work on our chickens. Everyone's going to sit and color. Put up all the books. You have work to finish." For 32 minutes, the class colored the chicks that were pictured on their worksheet, then wrote an "ick" word inside each chick, then cut and pasted the chicks and "ick" words onto a strip of construction paper. This was followed by a 21-minute math lesson on halves, after which the class joined two other kindergartens to watch a cartoon about a family's trip to a farm.

A Mid-April Day in the Traditional Reading Readiness Kindergarten

The day began with 25 minutes of singing songs, reciting poems, discussing the date and weather, taking attendance, and chorally reading the day's plan, which was written on the board. A 10-minute phonics activity followed, in which students printed three words beginning with "g" in their alphabet books.

In keeping with the upcoming Easter holiday, the teacher read *Jennie's Hat*, by Ezra Jack Keats (1966), stopping to let children examine the pictures and briefly answer a few questions. After the 19-minute reading and discussion, she handed out paper and told the class, "I want you to make Jennie a hat, a very special hat . . . so use your what?" "Imagination," answered one of the children.

For 14 minutes the class quietly created their illustrations of Jennie's hat, printing only their names on their papers, which were collected and taped to the board for everyone to see.

A formal reading readiness lesson followed, designed to develop children's story comprehension and decoding skills. The teacher taped a picture to the wall and proceeded to ask the class a series of questions about who and what was in the picture. Answers were recorded on chart paper next to the picture: "little boy," "grandmother," "rolling pin," "apples," "table," "gift," and so forth. With much prompting the teacher then elicited "a little story about what we see" from the class. This, too, was recorded:

One day grandmother was making an apple pie.

Benny said to grandmother, "I have a surprise."

The teacher read the story, phrase by phrase, and the children echoed her. Several youngsters were called on, one at a time, to come to the board and circle all the words in the story that contained "g"—their "magic letter for today." All this took 32 minutes. An additional 10 minutes were provided for everyone to draw what they imagined was inside the box the boy was giving his grandmother.

The final 12 minutes of the morning were devoted to a math worksheet, which required children to join sets together and write number sentences.

Work-Play time followed the afternoon rest period, during which children were given 41 minutes to paint, play in the housekeeping area, use building blocks or Playdough, color shapes and letters with stencils, or work at a computer matching shapes and numbers.

A special event followed: the school's principal visited the classroom to act as a judge of the children's drawings of Jennie's hat. After careful consideration and explanation of her choices, she awarded two prizes, one for the prettiest and one for the most creative drawing. Disappointed looks flashed across the faces of all the children who did not win.

For the next 22 minutes, children copied an Easter message from the board onto Easter cards to take home to parents. The message read:

> Mr. Bunny comes
> to say
> Have a happy
> Easter Day!

The children who finished first gathered on the rug to recite a poem they knew, and to begin learning the lines of a new poem.

The focus then switched to science. For the next eight minutes, the teacher asked questions designed to review terms and facts about the life cycle stages of butterflies and frogs. No text was associated with this discussion.

When the class was asked to review what they had done that day, answers included "played at the computer," "played with numbers," "finished all my work," "cleaned up my desk," "took a nap," "went to lunch," and "had Work-Play time." The teacher said she was disappointed no one mentioned drawing Jennie's hat, or having the principal come in to judge the drawings.

Teacher and children sang a song called "Little Bird," while pretending to be birds flying around the room. Then a group of smiling children donned their coats and exited while reciting their "Good-Bye Poem."

A Literate Environment Kindergarten on a Day in Early May

Collaborative reading and writing time began as soon as the first kindergartner entered their small, open-space classroom. For the first 45 minutes of the morning, children clustered together on the rug as they pretend-read favorite storybooks with friends, or sat together at tables, talking and drawing pictures in preparation for writing stories. A purposeful hum filled the room. From one corner rose a troll's warning —"I'm coming up there to gobble you up!"—while several feet away Peter Rabbit's mother was warning her children, "Now run along, my dears, but don't get into mischief." Topics generated by the writers ranged from "The two Teenage Mutant Ninja Turtles was driving cars" to "Spring was blooming, growing plants." Most of the writers represented their stories with random strings of letters, although some were able to invent spellings, including Donel who wrote: "I RUN aWY FRoM hom BE COS No FOOD HOm BE COS MY BROt eat IT."

After a nine-minute opening routine, which included a choral reading of the daily plan, it was time for the main event of the day: a 55-minute reading and dramatization of *The Tale of Peter Rabbit* (Potter 1902). Although the story had been read, discussed, and dramatized on six previous occasions during the year, Ms. Thompson continued to elicit a good deal of response before, during, and after reading. Far from boring the children, this repetition seemed to stimulate greater interest in the tale and to increase comprehension.

Before reading, Ms. Thompson asked, "How many of you have ever been disobedient? Tell me about it." Everyone listened as classmates told their tales. During the reading they stopped frequently to clarify what it means to "get into mischief," to be "dreadfully frightened," or to "implore" someone to "exert" himself. Other word meanings were dramatized: the class became Peter "wriggling" out of his jacket when he was caught in the gooseberry net, "trembling" when he was lost, going "lippity, lippity" through Mr. McGregor's garden, "scuttering" under the bushes and then "peeping" over the wheelbarrow. After the reading, students related their favorite parts of the story, then discussed the central problem ("He was bein' disobedient," as one child put it) and how it was solved. Of course, a dramatization of the story followed, with most of the class choosing to play the role of Peter as he squeezed under the gate into Mr. McGregor's garden, stuffed himself on vegetables, was chased by the angry farmer, and finally managed to escape. Supplying narration and stage prompts, Ms. Thompson made sure to weave in as much of the book's sophisticated language as possible.

For the remainder of the day, most activities contained some link to *The Tale of Peter Rabbit*.

During Choice Time, children could opt to draw and write about Peter Rabbit, or play with toy dinosaurs, pegboards, puzzles and other manipulatives. In addition, the McLiterate's stand was open, with its golden arches (fashioned after McDonald's), a lunch menu, and play cash register. "Rules for McLiterate's Restaurant" were listed on chart paper next to the booth:

1. *Write down* food order.
2. Put food in bag.
3. Take customer's money.

In the 10 minutes prior to lunch, Ms. Thompson showed her kindergartners a series of illustrations she had made of some key actions and objects from *Peter Rabbit*, and asked them to guess what words were represented from the story. The class then sounded out the words and invented spellings, which the teacher wrote on a small slate. "Squeezed" was spelled "sqezd," "parsley" became "prsle," and so on.

After lunch, the children gathered on the rug with books chosen from their richly stocked classroom library. For 12 minutes they engaged in sustained silent reading (SSR), while their teacher, sitting in a nearby chair, remained deeply absorbed in her own book.

Afterwards, Ms. Thompson introduced a half-hour math activity by reading the following letter from their imaginary math mentor: "Dear Intelligent Children, I enjoyed the story *The Tale of Peter Rabbit*. ["How does she know that?" Ms. Thompson asked, smiling.]

Will you join the rabbit sets to make the new set? How many in all? Don't let me trick you. Love, Astra." Packets of cut-out rabbits were handed to the children, which they manipulated to reflect different "number sentences."

The afternoon's nonfiction reading, lasting 34 minutes, focused on the real-life habits of rabbits and hares. Before reading, the class discussed what they already knew about rabbits, as well as what they would like to know. Ms. Thompson recorded their comments and questions on chart paper, and the class read them. Following this introduction, Ms. Thompson began reading from the text, stopping after each sentence or two to discuss meaning. For example, after reading that "great numbers of rabbits have been used for medical experiments," she asked the children whether they remembered the experiments they had done in class. Toward the end of the reading, they stopped briefly for a mini-drama of what they had learned: the class became "gentle rabbits" who were caught in a "trap" and later "roasted"; the teacher then pretended to take their fur and spin it into yarn. After reading, they revisited the questions posed before reading, to determine how many had been answered by the text.

Before leaving, everyone checked out books from the classroom library to take home and read with parents.

PROGRAM DIFFERENCES

One can sense from the preceding portraits just how different the three programs in this study were one from another, an impression which is corroborated by looking at some of the quantitative data on instructional differences (see Table 16.1). While some similarities are apparent between the IBM *Writing to Read* program and the traditional reading readiness approach program, even more apparent are the sharp differences both have with the Literate Environment program.

One of the most striking differences is the balance between time allotted for reading aloud, and time allotted for formal skills instruction. In the Literate Environment classrooms, read-aloud events clearly took center stage. The reading of nonfiction as well as fiction consumed slightly more than one-quarter of the class day, compared to only 5 to 7 percent of the day for phonics-related lessons. Just the

Table 16.1 Instructional Differences Among the Three Programs

PROGRAMS	Literate Environment Program		Write To Read Program	Traditional "Reading Readiness" Program
	Teacher 1 (N=14)	Teacher 2 (N=8)	(N=21)	(N=23)
Sample Sizes	Teacher 1 (N=14)	Teacher 2 (N=8)	(N=21)	(N=23)
Average Time for Reading Aloud and Responding to Text	75 min. (28% of 270 min. day) F=43 min. NF=31 min	82 min. (27% of 300 min. day) F=42 min. NF=40 min.	22 min. (7% of 317 min. day)	23 min. (7% of 318 min. day)
Average Formal Instruction Time (Literacy-related)	18 min. (7% of day)	14 min. (5% of day)	115 min. (36% of day)	79 min. (25% of day)
Average Time to Look at Books/Pretend Read	31 min. (11% of day)	54 min. (18% of day)	21 min. (7% of day)	8 min. (3% of day)
Average Number of Text Words Read Per Day	1366 words F=971 NF=395	1125 words F=758 NF=367	1120 words F=1120 NF=0	847 words F=847 NF=0
Daily Average of Primary Questions Asked about Fiction	49	59	36	14
Most Frequently Asked Categories of Story Questions	Vocab. (14%) Predict (12%) Recall (10%)	Vocab. (25%) "Why" (25%)	Skills (29%) Yes/No (16%) Recall (13%)	Recall (14%) Cloze (13%) Vocab. (10%)
Dramatizations of Text	Yes - usually	Yes - always	No	No
Other Responding Activities	Choice Time art activity (fiction) Write/draw in journal + worksheet (nonfiction)	Choice Time art activity (fiction) Write/draw in journal (nonfiction)	"Skills" Worksheet	Drawing/painting pictures related to storyreading about 3 times a week.

Note: Data base consists of two full days' observation, plus transcriptions for all read-aloud events during another five days in each classroom. F=Fiction; NF=Nonfiction; T-L=Text-Life questions.

reverse was observed in the traditional kindergarten, where one-quarter (25 percent) of the class day was devoted to reading readiness lessons, versus 7 percent for story readings and accompanying (artistic) responses. The IBM *Writing to Read* class also spent only 7 percent of class time for story readings, but was even more skills focused, with over one-third (36 percent) of the instructional day consumed by phonics worksheets, spelling dictations, small group reading lessons, and *Writing to Read* activities in the computer lab.

The Literate Environment teachers approached story reading sessions differently from the other two teachers. Although they read just one story a day like the others, unlike the others they often chose a story that had been read on previous occasions to the class. This fondness for repeat readings meant that over the course of the school year, the Literate Environment youngsters were actually exposed to a smaller repertoire of storybooks than were youngsters in the other two programs.

However, they spent far more time responding to each story, for the Literate Environment teachers made reading aloud a more active and interactive event—marked by lengthier discussion in response to more teacher questions, frequent dramatizations (which did not occur in the other two programs), and optional participation in related art and writing activities during the choice times that followed story readings.

Of the other two programs, only the reading readiness approach offered kindergartners an opportunity to respond to stories in some manner other than answering teacher questions: approximately three times a week, students were invited to draw pictures (but not write) about something related to the day's story.

Story Questions Reflect Different Emphases

The greater number of questions asked by the two Literate Environment teachers reflected their belief that discussion facilitates both children's enjoyment and comprehension of a story. It should be noted that while both teachers operated from the same philosophy and employed the same strategies, they were not carbon copies of one another. Teacher 2 tended to ask more questions and spend a little more time dramatizing than Teacher 1; as a result, she read fewer text words per session.

There were also some differences with respect to the kinds of questions each teacher emphasized, although a consistent pattern was evident overall. Both clearly favored questions which focused students on story structure and meaning. The majority of their questions (59% and 70% respectively) consisted of the following: questions that clarified word meanings and elicited relevant world knowledge, questions that examined characters' feelings and why they acted as they did, text-life questions that linked the children's own feelings and experiences to those of the story characters, questions that invited predictions about what would happen next in the story, and questions which focused on a story's central problem and solution.

In contrast, these types of questions accounted for only 21 percent of all questions posed by the IBM *Writing to Read* teacher, and 37 percent of all questions posed by the traditional approach teacher. Both these teachers gave more emphasis to factual recall questions, rhetorical questions requiring a simple yes or no response from the children, and invitations to predict the next word in the text, or to join in on saying certain lines of a text.

While the IBM *Writing to Read* teacher gave the least emphasis to meaning-oriented questions, she gave the greatest emphasis to questions that focused on skills, such as sequencing and categorizing, that were unrelated to story content. Almost three out of every 10 questions she asked (29%) fell into this category. For example, she led into a reading of *I Can Do It Myself* (Little & Greenfield 1978), by reminding the children that "this morning we talked about opposites. . . . When I finish this story, I'm going to ask you some opposites. Some of the words will come from right out of the story, and some of them will be words that we already know." While reading the story, she stopped six times to ask what the opposite was of a word that had just been read. As a follow-up to the story, she showed 18 flashcards illustrating actions for which the children were to supply the opposite word, then ushered the class into a cut-and-paste activity where students matched pictures of opposites. The overall effect was to divert children away from thinking about the story and its characters, to focusing on the skill of the day.

In contrast, the traditional approach teacher asked this type of skills question only 8 percent of the time, and the Literate Environment teachers not at all.

Measuring Kindergartners' Sense of Story

What effect did exposure to such different programs have on youngsters' developing sense of story?

To measure student progress, kindergartners in the study were asked at the beginning and end of the school year to look through Emily McCully's wordless picture book, *Picnic* (1984), and to make up a story to go with the pictures. They were then audiotaped as they pretend-read their story to a stuffed animal and a researcher.

As this delightfully illustrated picture book begins, a mouse family is depicted climbing into a pick-up truck with their picnic paraphernalia. No sooner have they set off down a bumpy country road than the problem occurs: the truck hits a rock, and as it bounces high in the air, the youngest child, who is sitting at the open tailgate, is thrown out of the truck with his stuffed toy mouse. The family rides off, unaware of the mishap.

The wordless story is made more complicated by a series of scene shifts: from the family setting up their picnic things and playing games, back to the lost child crying, then searching for food; from the family being called to eat, to the lost child picking and eating berries. Next comes the pivotal "realization" scene, in which it dawns on the parents, as the children line up to eat, that someone is missing. After tearfully searching the area to no avail, they pack up their picnic gear and head back to the truck. Meanwhile, the lost youngster is shown lying in the grass, seemingly relaxed and full, several uneaten berries lying next to him.

Driving back over the road to home, the mouse family searches for the lost child. They find him standing in the middle of the road, and soon everyone is hugging and leaping for joy. The reunited child goes back to retrieve his toy mouse, which was left behind in all the excitement, and the family finds another picnic spot by the side of the road, where they can resume their interrupted meal.

The way in which young children read these illustrations is revealing, for they must draw on their underlying concept of story. As Sulzby's (1985) research indicates, young children's emergent reading behaviors remain stable "across storybooks," and, therefore, reflect a "generalized" understanding that is "indeed conceptual and not just a stimulus-response pattern to a particular book" (p. 479).

To measure this level of conceptual understanding, transcribed *Picnic* readings were scored with a series of half-points, indicating the extent to which youngsters had included and correctly interpreted key events and their causes, the central problem and its resolution, character relationships, feelings, actions and motivation, scene shifts, setting and other important story elements. Inter-rater reliability for the scoring system was established at .83, with differences quickly resolved through discussion. (Details of the scoring system are included in the Appendix.)

Differences Between Higher Scoring and Lower Scoring Readings

Since a perfect score of 13 signals a very sophisticated reading, (and even my graduate students miss a point here and there), it is not too surprising that none of the inner-city kindergartners in this study reached that upper limit. Scores for the study group ranged from 0 to 9. Within that range, however, wide differences occurred with respect to story construction and comprehension.

Current research generally corroborates Thorndike's 1917 view that for successful comprehension to occur, "the reader must weigh many elements, select the right elements, combine these in the right relationships and give each the appropriate amount of weight" (McCormick 1992, 75). Essentially, that is the process required to interpret *Picnic* illustrations and construct a valid storyline.

Those children who produced the lowest scoring, least proficient readings seemed to have difficulty perceiving the relative importance of elements and how they were connected. Their disjointed storylines revealed a tendency to treat each page as a separate entity, rather than as part of an ongoing storyline. Irrelevant and minor details (such as a bug crawling across the path), often grabbed their attention over central actions. Character motivation and causal connections were omitted or misinterpreted.

In contrast, children who produced higher scoring readings perceived more connections. They seemed to approach *Picnic* with the expectation that the pictures would tell a story. Thus, they were better able to maintain focus on the central thread of events, and to interpret different scenes and actions within the context of that storyline.

Consider, for example, how differently high and low scorers in this study read the two-page spread where the lost mouse is shown holding his toy mouse upside down, while looking at bushes laden with berries (drawn in such a fashion that they resemble flowers). Typical of lower scoring stories were the most literal of descriptions: "he looked at a flower an' his doll-baby was upside down." In contrast, children who produced higher scoring stories were typically able to disengage from a purely physical description, place the scene in context, and infer character intent: e.g., "The little one was so sad; he went to look for some food," or "Then she was hungry, so she said she gonna have her own picnic by herself with her little mouse toy."

These contrasts mirror the developmental progression Sulzby (1985) detected in her landmark study, when she concluded that emergent readers move "from treating individual pages of storybooks as if they are discrete units to treating the book as the unit, using speech that builds a story across the book's pages" (p. 478).

Greater Gains for Literate Environment Kindergartners

The fact that the mean score for the entire study group at the beginning of their kindergarten year was only 2.5 points (out of a possible 13 points) suggests that most of the children had not been read to extensively enough during their preschool years to have internalized a detailed knowledge of story structure.

Given this starting point, the central question was whether philosophically different approaches to early literacy instruction would generate different degrees of story concept development during the kindergarten year.

With both Literate Environment classes pooled together in one group, an overall analysis of covariance for posttest *Picnic* story schema scores, adjusted for pretest scores, established significance under the .01 level ($F=6.41$, $p=.003$). A further analysis of pairwise differences (see Table 16.2) showed a statistically significant advantage for the Literate Environment youngsters ($p=.002$ when compared with the IBM *Writing to Read* class, and $p=.02$ when compared with the reading readiness class). Overall, the Literate Environment kindergartners gained an average 2.7 points during the school year, compared to 1.3 points for the traditional class and 1.1 points for the IBM *Writing to Read* class.

Table 16.2
Analysis of Pairwise Differences for Story Schema Scores

Pair-Wise Grouping	Adjusted Post-Mean	F	F Prob.
Literate Enivronment	5.0	10.9	.002 **
IBM *Writing to Read*	3.3		
Literate Environment	5.2	6.4	.02 *
"Reading Readiness"	4.0		
"Reading Readiness"	4.0	.8	.36
IBM *Writing to Read*	3.6		

$$* \ p<.05 \qquad **p<.01$$

While the greater progress of the Literate Environment kinder-gartners was clearly significant, the size of the gain seems relatively small when compared to the possible total. This suggests that, like any complex cognitive activity, a mature sense of story develops gradually, over time. While a rich literature-centered program can speed up young children's progress, the amount of exposure that can be logged during one academic year is not sufficient to move relatively inexperienced kindergartners to an expert level.

Literate Environment Kindergartners Better at Drawing Inferences

A secondary question raised by the study was whether any pattern existed with respect to the kind of story elements youngsters from different programs picked up during the year. When an item analysis was conducted to answer that question, an interesting finding surfaced: the Literate Environment kindergartners, it seemed, made greater gains on story elements requiring higher levels of inferential thinking.

Of particular note were the children's interpretation of two scenes. One, the "realization" scene, qualifies as the turning point of the story, for it is here the family finally catches on that one of the children is missing. In the beginning-of-year reading, only one Literate Environment student, one IBM *Writing to Read* student, and three students from the traditional reading readiness class correctly interpreted this scene. By year's end, however, an additional 27 percent of the

Literate Environment kindergartners had caught on—compared to an increase of 9 percent in the traditional approach class, and 0 percent in the IBM *Writing to Read* class.

The second scene implies a subtle causal connection: on the left-hand page family members are pictured hanging out of the truck, scanning the countryside as they retrace their route to look for the lost child, while on the right-hand page the lost child is pictured moving through the grass, leaving his toy mouse behind. In the beginning-of-year reading, only one child in the IBM class and one in the traditional approach class were able to infer that the child was moving through the grass because he heard the sound of the truck. By the end-of-year reading, however, nearly a quarter of the Literate Environment group (23 percent) were able to draw that inference, compared to an increase of 9 percent in the reading readiness approach class, and 0 percent in the *Writing to Read* class.

This is an important finding, given the significant role inferential thinking plays in reading comprehension (Anderson 1978; Rumelhart 1980), and given the fact that poor readers have difficulty drawing inferences (Bransford, Stein, Nye, & Perfetto 1982; Davey & Macready 1985; Holmes 1987; Wilson 1979).

ACCOUNTING FOR THE DIFFERENCE

What aspects of the Literate Environment program might account for its students' greater improvement on end-of-year *Picnic* readings?

Scanning the program differences captured in Table 16.1, one might conclude that the Literate Environment kindergartners made a little more than twice the progress made by youngsters in the other two programs, because their teachers spent almost twice as much time reading fiction to them. (It seems unlikely that exposure to nonfiction would have prepared children to make sense of *Picnic*.) It is important to remember, however, the way in which that extra time was spent. It was *not* spent listening to more text words, from more storybooks. Indeed, based on transcripts of read-aloud interactions during seven days, it appears that the IBM *Writing to Read* kindergartners, who made the least amount of gain on the *Picnic* task, actually heard the most words read aloud from storybooks during the year. No, the extra time Literate Environment kindergartners spent with fiction was used to *process* the words they heard, and it is that processing which appears to have made the difference.

Although the design of this study does not permit firm conclusions regarding the relative contribution made by individual program components to youngsters' growing sense of story, findings from other research provide solid clues.

Indications from a variety of studies are that it is not simply the fact of being read to that counts, but how that experience is mediated by adults (Bergin, Lancy, & Draper this volume; Flood 1977; Ninio 1980; Teale 1981; Heath 1982). Of particular importance, it seems, is the degree to which children are encouraged to be active participants in responding to story readings. Asking youngsters to retell stories after hearing them read, for example, has been shown to promote story comprehension, recall of major story elements, oral language complexity, and improved quality of dictated original stories (Zimiles & Kuhns 1976; Morrow 1985; Morrow 1986; Gambrell & Koskinen 1991). Dramatizations have also surfaced as an effective means of promoting story comprehension in young children (Pellegrini & Galda 1982, this volume). After reviewing eight studies focusing on the effects of story dramatizations, Christie (1987) concluded that when low-income children were read stories and then provided with opportunities to reenact them, this promoted both "comprehension of the specific stories that were enacted and of stories in general," especially for kindergartners and first-graders (p. 42).

As for helpful ways of discussing stories, Pearson & Fielding (1991) concluded, after an extensive review of comprehension instruction research, that "comprehension, particularly inferential comprehension, is improved when relationships are drawn between students' background knowledge and experience and the content included in reading selections" (p. 847).

Taken collectively, these research findings suggest that the Literate Environment program features that most supported youngsters' growing sense of story included story dramatizations, daily opportunities for children to reconstruct storylines while pretend reading, and elaborated story reading discussions that emphasized linkages between the children's lives and story characters' experiences. Each of these ways of responding to literature placed children in the position of actively constructing meaning, while maintaining focus on the whole—that is, the interconnected sweep of events and episodes across an entire story.

In contrast, the lion's share of literacy-related time in the other two programs, especially the IBM *Writing to Read* program, was devoted to the study of isolated segments of language (especially alphabet letters and spelling patterns) that were disembedded from a connected story.   Unfortunately, this has been the traditional approach in American schools, which, historically, have "been driven by a model of literacy that focuses on discrete skills and bits of information instead of big ideas and deeper understandings" (Langer 1989, 2).

This study provides yet another indication that our schools need to change instructional paradigms. It is through emphasizing a search for meaning that we can best nurture the roots of reading comprehension and mature literacy in our youngest and least experienced students.

Further Questions

Like most research, even as this study answers some questions, it raises others.

How effective, for example, would the Literate Environment program remain if implemented by teachers less expert and less well trained than the ones in this study?

How would youngsters who have been read to extensively in their preschool years compare to youngsters in this study in terms of their story schema development? How great an advantage would they have at the beginning of kindergarten, and what kind of progress would they make if exposed to the same early literacy programs observed in this study?

While the Literate Environment program provided its students with a kind of literacy head start, one year is not enough. The larger question is how far inner-city youngsters could progress if exposed to a consistently well-implemented whole-language environment throughout their elementary years. Given such an opportunity, how long would it take them to "catch up" with children who started out further ahead? These are crucial questions if we are interested in educational equity, questions worthy of our best efforts.

APPENDIX

Scoring *Picnic* Readings

SETTING THE STAGE: first few pages (1.0 point)
    1/2 point—noting mice are getting ready to go on a picnic
        (no credit if picnic is mentioned after problem occurs)
    1/2 point—attributing some kind of motive for, or thought given to,
        or wish to go on a picnic (e.g., "One evening they *decided*
        to go on a picnic.")

CHARACTER RELATIONSHIPS: throughout text (0.5 point)
    1/2 point—recognizing family relationship among characters
        (indicated by "mother" *and* "father," etc. —*anywhere* in
        story; misidentification of some of the characters means no
        credit)

IDENTIFYING THE PROBLEM: pp. 2-5 (1.5 points)
    1/2 point—noting that mouse falls from truck
    1/2 point—noting cause (they went over a rock, or bump)
    1/2 point—noting that the others left, or that no one noticed one of
        the mice fell out (saying "truck left" is not enough)

IDENTIFYING THE SETTING: pp. 6-9 or anywhere (.5 point)
    1/2 point—correctly naming their location (a "farm," "meadow,"
        "park," or "the country" would be accepted; "grass," "a
        spot," or "picnic place" would be too imprecise to count)

SUMMARIZING FAMILY ACTION: p. 10 or pp. 14-15 (.5 point)
    1/2 point—summary statement of what they were doing—e.g.,
        playing games, playing, having fun, exercising (no credit
        for "doing their stuff;" no credit for just listing separate
        activities, like "playing baseball")

SCENE SHIFT: pp. 11-13 (1.5 points)
    1/2 point—noting affect of lost mouse—he is sad or scared—
        or noting *why* he is crying.
    1/2 point—clearly identifying lone mouse as the one who fell from
        the truck, or the "lost mouse," indicating linguistically that he
        is separated from the rest of the family.

1/2 point—noting he is looking for food ("looking at flowers" does
    not count)

SUMMARIZING ACTION: pp. 14-15 (.5 point)
    1/2 point—indicating it is time for the family to eat; mother is
        calling them to eat, etc. (inventory of separate actions
        does not count)

SCENE SHIFT COMPARISON: pp. 16-17 (.5 point)
    1/2 point—identifying mouse's action as eating or about to eat
        (accept eating "berries" or "fruit" or "flowers," but not "candy")

THE PROBLEM IS REALIZED: pp. 18-19 (1.0 point)
    1 point—family realizes someone is missing (full point or nothing)

THE SEARCH: p. 20-21   (1.0 point)
    1/2 point—summary statement: family is looking for missing child
    1/2 point—noting they are upset or *why* they are crying
        (just noting they are "crying" not sufficient for credit)

WHY THEY LEAVE: p. 22 (.5 point)
    1/2 point—noting *why* they leave: to find lost mouse.

SCENE SHIFT / CHARACTER AFFECT: p. 23 (.5 point)
    1/2 point—indicating lost mouse is resting, relaxed, not worrying;
        ate too much and has a stomachache; or feeling sad and
        missing/ thinking about family (no credit for "sleeping"
        or "laying down")

THE SEARCH: pp. 24-25 (1.0 point)
    1/2 point—noting family is looking for lost mouse as they drive
    1/2 point—noting why lost mouse is moving: he hears sounds; he is
        looking for his family, etc.

THE REUNION: pp. 26-28 (1.0 point)
    1/2 point—indicating they find him: also "There he is," "He's safe,"
        etc. ("They *see* him" is not enough to score, but "They
        saw him and got him" would count)
    1/2 point—indicating group affect: *they* are happy, glad to have
        him ("hugging" is insufficient; indicating just one member of

the group is happy is insufficient) back, celebrating, etc. "They say, 'Yeah'" is accepted.

SOLVING MINOR PROBLEM: p. 29 (.5 point)
   1/2 point—he forgot his toy mouse and goes back to find it. (Credit given for acknowledging either forgetting or retrieving toy.)

HAPPY RESOLUTION: p. 30 (1.0 point)
   1/2 point—recognizing they have a picnic
   1/2 point—providing a reason (because they were hungry, because they were all there, etc.)

17

Reading Recovery: Teaching Through Conversation

Patricia R. Kelly, Adria F. Klein, and Gay Su Pinnell

INTRODUCTION

Six-year-old Kim and an adult partner, Ann, are getting ready to read *Spider, Spider* (Cowley 1987), but first, they look at some of the pictures in the book. Below, we describe a bit of the conversation:

> *Ann*: Oh, look at the caterpillar. He's going to get caught in the spider's web.
>
> *Kim*: Caterpillar. Why did he get caught?
>
> *Ann*: Because the web is sticky and the spider uses it to catch other bugs.
>
> *Kim*: Will I get caught if I touch a spider's web?
>
> *Ann*: No. It's sticky, but you're much stronger than the caterpillar. You can pull your hand out of the web. I wonder who's going to get caught in this spider's web.
>
> *Kim*: I don't like spiders. I'm glad I won't get caught.
>
> *Ann*: No, you can get away. But little bugs can't. They get caught by the spider's web.

We have been eavesdropping on the conversation between Kim and Ann as they look together at a book that is new to the child. In this social exchange Ann and Kim are sharing information and ideas prompted by this piece of literature. They examine the pictures, specific words, and phrases and the overall theme of the book in a natural dialogue.

This interchange could have taken place in a variety of situations that involve adults, children, and conversation about books. In fact, the dialogue took place during Kim's Reading Recovery(RR) lesson, and the book was selected by Ann, her teacher, as a text that would support and extend her repertoire of reading strategies. The conversation above occurred before Kim attempted to read this new book. Through the conversation, Ann wanted to set the scene so that Kim would know what to expect in the new book and also would have in mind some of the language that she would need to produce when cued by the print.

The teacher-child conversation is an example of how experts, through oral language, can help novices take on more complex tasks (see Cazden 1986, 1988; Green 1983; Green & Wallat 1987; Wood et al. 1976). Young learners having difficulty with school-based learning are especially in need of rich, supportive conversations with adults (Clay & Cazden 1990). RR, an early intervention program for young children having difficulty in reading, is designed around opportunities for teachers and children to talk together while the child is actively engaged in reading and writing. Conversation thus forms the basis for instruction in RR lessons.

In this chapter we will briefly describe RR and will examine in depth a RR lesson, presenting examples of conversational exchanges between a teacher and child. Additionally, we will explain how learning is supported through conversation within RR and explore ways that teachers can become more aware of the power of their moment-to-moment interchanges with students.

READING RECOVERY LESSON

Reading Recovery, developed by New Zealander Marie Clay, provides early help for children having difficulty learning to read. Designed for the lowest achieving first-graders, this short-term intervention has had remarkable success in helping even those having the most difficulty become good readers (Clay 1979; Lyons, Pinnell, & DeFord 1993). Children are provided daily, 30-minute lessons with a teacher who has completed a year-long course. Lessons are individually constructed for each child based on the teacher's daily analysis of his or her emerging understandings about reading and writing. Progress in learning to read is usually accelerated and when a child can read independently within an average range, his or her program is discontinued. The child is now able to profit from ongoing classroom literacy activities and will progress without further external support. Evidence from research on the program indicates that most children provided RR lessons reach and maintain average levels of achievement and also exhibit the kinds of effective strategies seen in good readers (Her Majesty's Chief Inspector of Schools 1993). For additional information about RR see Clay (1979) or DeFord, Lyons, and Pinnell (1991).

Lessons in the RR program follow a routine framework of activities. Prior to the beginning of lessons, ten 30-minute sessions are spent in an interactional period called "roaming around the known." During this time, the teacher and child explore what is known by the child and establish a low-risk partnership for supported reading and writing. The lesson activities are listed and briefly defined here; they will be explained more fully as we present the conversational examples in the next section. RR lessons include:

1. Familiar reading: The child reads several previously read books. An individual collection of short, highly patterned books which are selected during roaming, are continuously expanded, and form the basis for these rereadings.

2. Running record: While the child reads a book that was newly introduced the previous day, the teacher records reading behavior using a notation system developed by Clay (1985).

3. Writing: Together, the teacher and child write a short message or story. First, the child is helped to compose the message, and then it is written word by word with the tasks shared between the two. Next, the child's message is quickly written on a sentence strip by the teacher and cut up into phrases or words. The child then reconstructs the sentence and reads it.

4. Reading a new book: The teacher introduces the child to a book especially selected with the reader's characteristics and strengths in mind. Then, the child reads the book for the first time, reading independently for the most part, but with teacher support when needed. This book will be read again on the following day during the running record portion of the lesson, and then becomes part of the selections for familiar reading.

This lesson framework is routinized and the familiar structure itself is supportive of the child's learning. (For more information see Pinnell, Fried, & Estice 1990.) By being constant and familiar, a trusting partnership is quickly established. Yet the individuality of each child's program—constructed during the coversational ex-change—means that no two lessons are alike for a given child and no two children's programs are the same.

LOOKING AT A LESSON

For each component of the lesson framework we will present an example of conversation that supports the child's learning. The ex-amples are from lesson 24, which means that the child has had five hours in roaming around the known and 12 hours of individual lessons over about seven weeks. This means that the child is about halfway through a typical program of 12-16 weeks. Kim is reading at the first-grade primer level. When she began RR, Kim could write her name and the words "a" and "I" and she knew some letter/sound rela-tionships (score of 4 on a dictation task) but she could not read even simple and repetitive texts or locate any known words. The examples in this portion of the chapter are drawn from a single lesson in Kim's program; it is important to note that behaviors and interactions change during the course of a child's program. The teacher is always encour-aging the child's independence, which would be more apparent in later lessons as the child takes on more and more responsibility. Kim has participated in RR for only a few weeks but is making good progress toward the development of what Clay (1991) calls a "self-extending system," one that fuels its own learning and enables the child to keep on increasing skill through reading and writing.

While the child is rereading books that are easy and familiar, teachers support fluency and problem solving "on the run" by brief comments and conversations that help the child attend to productive examples. A teacher might ask a question like, "Did that make sense?" or, "Are you right?" The idea is to help children think about their reading, self-monitoring, checking on themselves, and searching for information such as meaning or visual detail. In the example below, Kim is reading her second book of the lesson, *Two Little Dogs* (Melser 1990). This short story is about two dogs who escape from their yard and explore their neighborhood, running after various animals. They encounter a big dog and decide not to run after him. The text on page nine says, "'That's bad,' they said. 'We won't run after him.'"

Kim: (Reading) "That's bad, they said."

Ann: Nice work, and I like the way you picked up speed.

Kim: (Reading) "We not. We not?"

Ann: Good, you noticed that looked like "not." (Kim's voice indicated her awareness of an error that did not make sense or fit with her knowledge of syntax. The teacher was quick to notice Kim's self-monitoring.)

Kim: We would?

Ann: Does that make sense? Would the little dogs run after the big dog?

Kim: We wouldn't?

Ann: That's good thinking! "Wouldn't" would make sense. It's "won't."

Kim: We won't run after him.

In this exchange, Kim tests several language structures and uses meaning to eliminate incorrect choices. Ann supported her efforts by asking her to think about the meaning of the story. This modeling helps Kim to extend her predictions and eventually will help her to begin asking those questions herself. Kim spontaneously reread the text to help herself hear and confirm her reading. Ann praised her productive attempts.

Ann: Good, run your finger under "won't."

Kim: (Looking closely at the word and running her finger under it while saying it) "Won't."

Ann: Do you see that "t" at the end?

Kim: (Nods.)

Ann: Good work.

Kim: (Reading) We won't run after him.

Each rereading of the line by the student evidenced increased expression, supporting the idea that meaning was being kept central even when attention was momentarily focused at the word level.

Ann: Oh, why did you get louder on "him?"

Kim: Cause the letters are bigger and that means loud.

Ann: Yes, loud. Keep going.

In this third rereading of the line, Kim emphasized the words "won't" and "him." The word "him" was printed in larger type.

This excerpt was from one of several books that were read during the lesson. This level of interaction is not likely to occur on every book; some books may be read completely independently without teacher comment. For example, during the next familiar book read by Kim, the teacher commented only at the end as they talked about the story. The goal is to bring to the child's attention selected examples, those that help him or her build understandings and a repertoire of strategies that will support the independent extension of knowledge. In support of interactions that accompany the reading, Clay says, "the teacher has role which is to be a party to the interaction of reader and text supporting and discussing as the need arises" (Clay 1991, 196).

Figure 17.1
Running Record of Kim's Reading of *Go Back to Sleep*

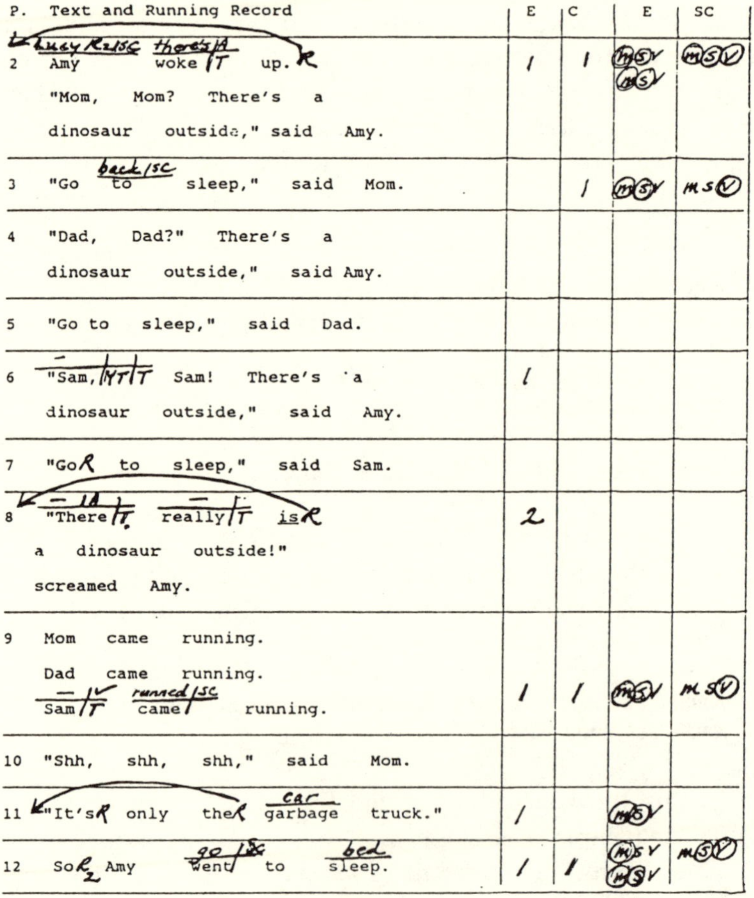

P.	Text and Running Record	E	C	E	SC
2	~~Lucy Russ theres A~~ Amy woke /T up. R	1	1	(m)(s)v (m)(s)v	(m)(s)(v)
	"Mom, Mom? There's a				
	dinosaur outside," said Amy.				
3	"Go ~~to~~ back/sc sleep," said Mom.		1	(m)(s)v	m s(v)
4	"Dad, Dad?" There's a				
	dinosaur outside," said Amy.				
5	"Go to sleep," said Dad.				
6	"Sam, /YT/T Sam! There's ·a	1			
	dinosaur outside," said Amy.				
7	"Go R to sleep," said Sam.				
8	"There /T_ really/T is R	2			
	a dinosaur outside!"				
	screamed Amy.				
9	Mom came running.				
	Dad came running.				
	Sam /T came/ runned/sc running.	1	1	(m)(s)v	m s(v)
10	"Shh, shh, shh," said Mom.				
11	"It's R only the/ garbage car truck."	1		(m)(s)v	
12	So R Amy went/ go/sc to sleep. bed	1	1	(m)(s)v (m)(s)v	m(s)(v)

During the running record portion of the lesson, the teacher assumes the role of an observer. The idea is for the child to move independently through the text, using the resources available. The teacher may supply a word at a point of difficulty or encourage an additional attempt when necessary. But if the book has been well selected for the child and carefully and supportively introduced during the previous lesson, there should be a minimum of difficulty and few interventions. Conversations occur after the reading and they are based on particular behaviors the teacher has observed in the child's reading. The teacher may praise the child for problem-solving work or return to a difficult part of the text and help the child to discover problem-solving techniques.

In the preceeding example (Figure 17,1)[1], Ann's running record is of Kim's reading *Go Back to Sleep* (King 1989b). Before the reading, Kim anticipated the events of the story, saying, "Oooh, *Go Back to Sleep*, there is a dinosaur!" Kim read the book with accuracy of above 90% and several times she self-corrected.

A section of Ann's running record is included below, indicating Kim's behavior on page twelve. Text (p. 12) : So Amy went to sleep. Kim's reading: "So Amy went to bed."

After the reading, Ann commented positively on Kim's reading and then turned back to page 12. The following conversation ensued after the child was invited to reread the page.

> *Kim*: (Reading) "So Amy went to bed." That's not right!
> *Ann*: Good, I'm glad you noticed. So what are you going to do?
> *Kim*: (Reading) "So Amy went to bed."
> *Ann*: That's a good try. It could be bed. That makes sense. But look at the word.
> *Kim*: (Looks at word and then at picture.) Sleeping. "So Amy went to sleep."
> *Ann*: Were you right? Is that what was she doing in the picture?
> *Kim*: Yes, sleeping.
> *Ann*: And does that word look like sleep?
> *Kim*: She's sleeping.
> *Ann*: That's right; that was the picture. What about the word?
> *Kim*: /sl/ (making the first sounds of the word)
> *Ann*: Yes, you did it. Is that what sleep begins with?
> *Kim*: Yes.
> *Ann*: It sure is. You did a nice job with that book. Looking at the picture and knowing how "sleep" starts helped you figure it out.

This conversation supported Kim's increasing use of multiple cues (sources of information) to check on her own reading and problem-solve as she read. The teacher drew the child's attention to the picture (meaning cues) and then to the word. Kim initiated the sounding of the first letters, a productive use of visual information going beyond the first letter. The teacher acknowledged the child's success in using two sources of information.

Figure 17.2
Kim's Writing Pages

Wake

Woke   woke

wake   they   like

They   always Wake

up.

In the writing portion of the lesson, the teacher-child conversation begins with the composition of the child's message. Sometimes, children use their reading books as resources; or they may write about their own experiences. After the story is generated by the child, the child writes the message on an unlined piece of paper, word by word, with the teacher's support. Conversation usually centers around how to construct each word needed to complete the message. There is opportunity for discussion of the details of written language, including sound-letter correspondence as well as letter formation and spelling conventions.

In this lesson, Kim composed the sentence, "They always wake up" (Figure 17.2). This message was about her baby brother and sister waking up in the night and represented a continuation of a story written over several days. She wrote the word "they" independently and the "al" for always, with the teacher finishing the word. After Kim reread what she had written so far, the teacher decided to assist the child in hearing the sounds in the word "wake."

In RR, teachers often use a technique adapted from Elkonin (1973); see also Clay (1985). This technique, called "hearing sounds in words," is carried out using another piece of paper, called the "practice page." The teacher draws a series of connected boxes, one for every sound in the word to be worked out. Early in lessons, the child is invited to push counters into the boxes while slowly articulating the word and trying to think about the letters that represent the sounds. Letters the child hears are accepted and recorded in the appropriate boxes in whatever order is identified by the child. The result is a word in standard spelling, but the child has brought his or her own constructive powers to bear on it in a way similar to "inventing" spelling in the emergent writer. Kim and Ann were working on the next word in the sentence, "wake." The teacher used this opportunity to draw the child's attention for the first time to aspects of words that are visually recognized rather than heard. The following conversation took place while working on the word.

Kim: Is that three sounds?
Ann: It is three sounds but four letters. I'm going to show you how to do that today. "Wake" (said slowly). What do you hear?
Kim: **k**
Ann: Where does it go? "Wake" (said slowly).
Kim: Wake (said slowly). (Writes **k** in the last sound box). **A**
Ann: Where does it go?
Kim: In the middle? (Writes the **a** in the second sound box.)
Ann: Yes. Now the hard part is at the beginning. "Wake" (said slowly).
Kim: **W**
Ann: I like the way you worked that out. Now say the whole word.
Kim: Wake (said slowly).
Ann: You got it to sound right and it has three sounds. But I'm going to show you something new. I'm going to put a dotted line in the last box and I'm going to make it look right. It needs an **e** to make it look right. Just like the word "like" that you know. You know how to spell "like."

The child takes on as much of the task as she can easily and successfully. Each example shows Kim articulating the word, showing the place for the letter, and writing in the letter that she knew. The teacher focuses on having the child operate as independently as possible. What the child cannot produce, the teacher fills in, and the entire message is collaboratively constructed and read many times. Following the completion of the sentence, it is written on a sentence strip and cut apart for the child to reassemble. Thus, the student-generated sentence in the writing activity is returned to a reading task, and the child has an opportunity to work with written language in another way.

For the new book portion of the lesson, a book is selected by the teacher, taking into account the characteristics of the individual reader, with information drawn from the running record and other observations. Besides being an interesting story, the text should be well within the child's grasp and present a minimum of new things to learn. But this requirement does not mean that the vocabulary is controlled; instead, the teacher considers the language of the text and the concepts involved. Before the new book is attempted, the teacher provides an oral orientation to the story. In this beginning conversation, the teacher and child discuss the ideas of the whole story. The child has an opportunity to hear some of the language that he or she will encounter in the text and also may be asked to locate one or two new and important words. The main elements here, as Clay (1985) says, are "recency" and "familiarity." Clay contends that "every child is entitled to an orientation" (1991, p. 331) before attempting a first reading of new material. This conversation weaves an oral language framework that supports the problem-solving needed to read more challenging texts.

Here is an excerpt from Ann's and Kim's conversation during the orientation to *Baby's Birthday* (King 1989a), a book about a young child who prefers to play with candles, wrapping paper, ribbon, and boxes rather than the presents she receives. During the orientation, Ann and Kim talked about all of the pictures in the book and the meaning of the whole story. Kim also was asked to predict and locate one word. The examples do not capture the entire orientation but provide a sense of the interaction:

Ann: I thought you'd like this one., It's called *Baby's Birthday*. You have a baby at home, don't you? Look at baby. What does she have?
Kim: She has a box on her head.

Ann: And ribbon around her shoulders. Oh, look at what she is doing to
   the candle!
Kim: She's sucking it!
Ann: Yes, she's eating it!
Kim: (Laughs)

The example above illustrates that the conversation can also take place
on the nonverbal level. The teacher learns about the child's interests
and appreciation for the story through responses such as laughter,
smiles, or animated comments.

Ann: Do you think she is doing the things she is supposed to be doing?
Kim: No.
Ann: No. This is *Baby's Birthday*. There is baby and it's her birthday
   and she got a book. And what did she do?
Kim: She played with the wrapper.
Ann: Yes, she played with the paper.

Ann responded to Kim's observation of the picture and inserted the
word "paper," the word used in the text, to help the reader have in her
head a new word that she will need when cued by the text.

Ann: She got a cake. What do you think she is going to do?
Kim: Eat it.
Ann: Well, we would eat the cake, but look what that baby's doing.
Kim: She's playing with the candle.
Ann: Yes. She's really a funny baby. Now she's very tired.
Kim: She went to sleep . . . with all those presents?
Ann: With all those presents, yes.
Kim: She seems very funny.

After this exploration of the story, Kim extended her response by
commenting on how odd it would be to go to sleep after receiving all
those presents. As in the beginning of the orientation, the teacher and
child interaction provided a bridge between the text and Kim's own
experiences. This connection supported her ability to take on the new
text, with meaning in the foreground. After the orientation, Kim read
the new book, with ongoing supportive conversation.

Kim: (Reading) We all sang to her.
Ann: You read, "We all sang to her." That's what they did.
   But you know the words "to" and "her." Try it again.

In the above conversation, Ann took the opportunity to draw Kim's attention to some known words. At this point in Kim's program, these "anchor" words are useful to the child in checking on herself while reading. As Clay (1991) says, "they are islands of certainty in a sea of print." As such, they have strategic value for the reader well beyond the word recognition level.

> *Kim*: (Reading) We all sang (long pause).
> *Ann*: What do you sing at a birthday party?
> *Kim*: (Reading again) We all sang happy birthday.
> *Ann*: Were you right?
> *Kim*: Happy birthday.
> Ann: Good. Go on and finish the story.

Kim continued to the end of the story. The reading included a discussion about how the pictures can help us in reading. Prior to this lesson, Kim tended not to productively use pictures to predict and confirm meaning. One of Ann's goals was to help her strategically use all of the information sources, including meaning gained through pictures.

ASSISTED LEARNING

The lesson framework provides organized routines within which teachers can assist children's learning. A group of English researchers (Her Majesty's Chief Inspector of Schools, 1993) who investigated the program in New Zealand, described the RR lesson as "a highly organised, intensive and, it must be stressed, enjoyable occasion" and as "both highly structured and closely differentiated, according to the needs of the individual child" (p. 5). Researchers at Ohio State (Pinnell, Lyons, DeFord, Bryk, & Seltzer, in press) found, further, that the intimate situation with an adult and child participating together in reading and writing provides the setting within which teachers can structure their interactional moves to meet the student where he or she is in learning.

In RR, teaching is designed to support the young learners' construction of critical knowledge about literacy. Research in language and literacy learning supports the idea that children construct for themselves the internal strategies needed for independent reading and writing (Cazden 1972; Harste, et al. 1984). This theoretical position has sometimes been mistakenly interpreted to diminish the role of teaching. Tharp and Gallimore (1988) contend that "in American classrooms, now and since the 19th century, teachers generally act as if students are supposed to learn on their own" (p. 3). Clay, however, makes a strong argument for teaching, broadly defined; she suggests that there is no reason to make children discover things without assistance (Clay 1991).

Detailed studies of caregivers and children indicate ritualized and game-like routines through which infants begin to learn conventions such as social turn taking (see Cazden 1983, 1986). As they interact with their babies, many mothers support children's minimal, nonverbal interactions with a flow of conversation that enables the child to participate while expanding language knowledge. The interactions between mothers and children change with time; as children talk more, mothers relinquish the controlling role and more balanced interchange is evident (Snow 1977). In RR lessons this shift in interaction and responsibility over time is a key element in developing the learner's independence.

This shared problem solving, involving an active learner participating with a more skilled partner, has been likeneded by Rogoff (1990) to an apprenticeship. She stresses several features of guided participation: (1) the importance of routine activities; (2) tacit as well as explicit communication; (3) supportive structuring of novices' efforts; and (4) gradual transfer of responsibility to novices. In RR, teachers and children engage in a set of predictable activities focused on reading and writing whole texts. The routines exist, but as noted earlier, for each child the lesson is uniquely tailored. Teachers, too, are assisted in learning through conversations about their work with colleagues and others who share common understandings. RR provides opportunities for ongoing interactions that support teacher development. The following section addresses the staff development aspects of RR.

STAFF DEVELOPMENT: BECOMING AWARE OF THE POWER OF CONVERSATIONS

A hallmark of the RR training program is that teachers in training have ample opportunity to observe and discuss lessons with peers (Clay & Watson 1982). Regularly scheduled lessons taught behind one-way glass are viewed and discussed by RR teachers-in-training during the year-long training program. RR teacher leaders' visits to observe RR lessons at school sites are another on going facet of RR staff development. During these visits, teacher leaders observe lessons, may demonstrate specific teaching techniques, and provide constructive feedback to the teacher. During the initial training year, the RR teacher in training always has an expert available. Subsequently, teacher leader visits continue to provide expert guidance and insights about teaching that support and extend the teacher's own ability to learn from teaching.

Continuing contact sessions four to six times a year in the years following training are a third source of support for RR teachers. Teacher leaders conduct these sessions, which focus on various topics of interest to the teachers. Often, a sample lesson is observed and discussed in depth. One of the greatest benefits of continuing contact sessions is the interaction among RR teachers who problem-solve together. These sessions also become a vehicle for refining teaching procedures that have evolved as research in RR proceeds. Networking occurs as RR teachers regularly invite other RR teachers to observe their teaching. RR teachers are encouraged to videotape sample lessons to share with colleagues.

Reading Recovery Institutes sponsored annually in many locations are another avenue for advancement in understanding the complex nature of teaching, learning, and conversing with children. Expert teacher leaders, university trainers, and experienced RR teachers conduct sessions on teaching, research, and topics of interest to RR teachers and other interested educators. Seminars and in-depth study sessions carefully examine vital issues. Additionally, RR teachers have opportunities to discuss their own questions with teachers from other parts of the country who face similar problems.

Becoming Aware of Conversations in the Classroom

In this chapter, we have been talking about conversation as a support to learning in RR lessons, and our examples have been drawn from conversations between RR teachers and children. Instructional conversations are central to assisted learning in elementary classrooms as well (see Chapter Fifteen, this volume), and the teachers in those classrooms profit from awareness of how their interactions support and extend children's learning. The challenge is to create a culture that provides opportunities for classroom teachers to talk about and analyze their work by providing time for teacher interactions with others who can assist them. A few of these opportunities are beginning to surface. In some schools, peer collaboration has begun to support teachers' abilities to learn from one another. Some districts have established mentor systems for novice teachers, but seldom is mentoring provided for experienced teachers. The Kamehameha Elementary Education Program (KEEP), a private school, developed a model system of teacher assistance (Tharp & Gallimore, 1988). Despite the aforementioned efforts to foster teacher development and expertise, there are still far too few opportunities for most teachers at every level to receive substantive feedback and assistance.

One forum for peer assistance that has emerged in recent years is the Teachers Applying Whole Language (TAWL) groups through which whole-language teachers meet to talk and share ideas. Additionally, the International Reading Association is encouraging the Teachers As Readers Program, in which teachers form study groups to read and discuss professional articles and books. The National Council of Teachers of English Research Foundation has sponsored many teacher-inititiated projects. Teachers who want to become more aware of their teaching conversations with children often audio- and videotape their own lessons for later self-evaluation. Ideally, combinations of other-assisted and self-assisted learning need to be integrated into school environments so that teachers can continue as learners.

NOTE

[1] KEY: Child's Word=accurate reading; substitution; or repetition. A=appeal; SC=self-correction; YT="you try"; T=told; E=error.

18

Designing a Collaborative Model of Family Involvement in Literacy: Researchers, Teachers, and Parents Work Together

Patricia A. Edwards, Kathleen L. Fear, and Deborah L. Harris

THE IMPORTANCE OF FAMILY INVOLVEMENT

Much has been written about the benefits of involving families in their children's literacy development (France and Hager 1993; Handel 1992; Edwards 1991a). A major focus of this work has centered around the question of how educators and families can better understand, cooperate, and communicate with each other in order to more effectively work together to support children's acquistion of literacy learning. One of the most important themes that has surfaced in the literature is the need for improving current structures for family involvement in schools (Edwards 1991b; Edwards, Boles, & Dunham, in press). A second important theme is that families need to be heard—they need to be given time as well as opportunity to share their ideas, questions, and insights with teachers and administrators (Lynch 1992).

As part of a collaborative Professional Development School (PDS) project, the authors of this chapter met over a period of three years with eight kindergarten through second-grade teachers at Kendon Elementary School. In this chapter, we describe both the processes involved in this collaboration and the projects that developed as a result. We then share our insights and suggestions for others interested in working together with parents to improve literacy learning.

Parent Involvement at Kendon Elementary School

Before this project began, the existing parental involvement activities at Kendon varied in substance and duration, much like the conventional activities described in the literature (Delgado-Gaitan 1991; Epstein 1987; Hess and Shipman 1965; Lareau 1989). At Kendon, when teachers solicited parental participation in classrooms, they often wanted parents to perform mechanical tasks such as typing, editing, or binding children's stories. Annual open houses and biannual parent-teacher conferences provided time for parents to see their child's classroom and get a brief overview of subject matter covered in a specific grade level.

Teachers and administrators had set up PTA/PTO meetings, held parent-teacher conferences, made home visits, and encouraged parents to attend field trips and student performances. While these events brought families and teachers together, they did not necessarily bring them together around specific literacy events, or involve families in ways that would enable them to support children's literacy learning (Edwards et al. in press).

Parent involvement is an integral part of the PDS philosophy, so this was part of the "package" that parents had signed on for. They were well acquainted with what the PDS was trying to accomplish. The teachers seemed to make every attempt to contact all parents during regularly scheduled parent-teacher conferences. One approach employed by the principal—a strong advocate of parent involvement—was to ask the Kendon teachers to make special efforts to hold parent conferences in the inner city for the parents of children who were bussed to school. This proved successful, because 98 percent of the parents usually attended conferences held in neighborhoods surrounding the school and in the inner-city site. In another attempt to contact parents, the principal rode the school bus on regular weekly intervals to share brief comments and see parents in the community. She also took student teachers on these visits to acquaint them with students' homes and living situations. While these parent-teacher interactions were valuable, the teachers unanimously expressed a desire for more substantive and more frequent interaction. They joined the family involvement project specifically seeking alternative means to involve families in childrens' school lives, particularly in terms of understanding and supporting childrens' literacy growth.

We began discussions about parent involvement by defining specific principles that would drive our practices. For example, we were determined that the needs and interests of Kendon's parents and teachers would shape the structure and content of this family involvement project. Rather than simply imposing a preset or previously designed parent involvement program on the existing school structure, we wanted to create opportunities for the parents and teachers to talk together about their needs and goals. We held numerous meetings to discuss the goals and possibilities for a family involvement program. We developed and implemented the project as we attempted to develop partnerships with teachers. Although it took almost an entire school year, we eventually developed a plan that involved families at three grade levels. The projects were cogenerated with both teachers and parents (see Fear & Edwards 1992). We describe below project activities for kindergarten, first, and second grades.

SHARING TIME—KINDERGARTEN PROJECT

Project researchers (the researchers of this paper) asked Kendon kindergarten teachers how they wanted families to be more involved in their children's literacy growth. Teachers immediately thought of soliciting family involvement in their student's sharing time. Sharing time (also called "show and tell") is a recurring classroom language activity, where children are called upon to give a formal description of an object or a narrative account about some important past event (Michaels 1981, 425). The teachers believed that sharing time could be an occasion to develop children's self-confidence, self-esteem, and oral expression. Like Michaels (1981), the teachers viewed sharing time as oral preparation for literacy. However, they acknowledged that in actual practice, sharing time outcomes contrasted with sharing time goals. Mutual interest and respect for children's ideas was a problem for teachers and students because children made unkind remarks to each other. The teachers commented that they couldn't stand another year of looking at student toy collections, fashion shows, or travel logs. Students who possessed many material items always had something to show and tell. Students who didn't have anything to show showed the same item over and over again and were teased by other students. We knew we had to do something different with sharing time or abandon it altogether. We always hoped to find new ways of introducing sharing time.

As a consequence, one of the kindergarten teachers began searching in bookstores for ideas to help her improve sharing time in her classroom. The teacher found a commercially produced show and tell program. She piloted the program with her summer kindergarten and first-grade students. She then shared the program with her teaching partner and together they began to implement the program with their kindergartners during fall 1990.

The initial approach they used for changing sharing time was developed by Williams and Lewis (1988). The program, a workshop approach entitled *Show and Tell,* contains 19 activities and parent letters designed to help kindergarten teachers implement a structured oral language program in their classrooms. For example, a list of some the activities suggested by Williams and Lewis for show and tell include: This is Me, This is My Family, My Neighborhood, I Found a Leaf, Mystery Tastes, Mystery Smells, My Favorite Color, Things to Feel and Guess, Bookmarks, and Nature Hunt. They also predicted that, this workshop approach to show and tell would stimulate new ideas, motivate students to organize their thoughts, speak in complete sentences, and encourage parent involvement.

Introducing the New Sharing Time Experience to Parents

Initially, the teachers used the topics suggested by Williams and Lewis, but they soon reorganized the topics into larger thematic units and added some of their own topics. They decided to assign one particular topic each week. They also requested that parents help their children focus their comments and think about what they were going to say prior to sharing their thoughts with teachers and students in the classroom. The teachers believed that this new approach would allow parents to more fully understand the purpose of requiring their children to participate in sharing time.

Parents were informed of the day that their child would be participating in sharing time and the topic that their child would discuss. They also received a letter introducing the new sharing approach .

The teachers assumed that the parents would be pleased by the new routine. Contrary to the teachers' expectations, parents responded to the letter with varying degrees of confusion and frustration. For parents, the new approach provoked concern about how well their children performed in class. Others expressed interest in classroom events. A few parents suggested changes in the topic and frequency of the assignments. The notes below received by one kindergarten teacher represent the variation in parent responses:

Is Steven's show and tell day Wednesday or is it Friday? Your note said Wednesday, but the large envelope said return on Friday.

Please do not hold it against Lindsay for not turning in her show & tell sheet because I explained it incorrectly to Lindsay and wondered if Lindsay could have another chance at it.

Would it be possible for Mike to bring his homework on Fridays. I work from 10:00 p.m. to 7:00 a.m. or later. My husband works the night shift and sleeps in the afternoon and early evening. So during the week we don't have the time needed to help Mike with all of his home-work. If this can be arranged it would be a big help to both of us and Mike. Thanks.

I love to help my children with all of their work. You might give them an activity every two weeks. Thanks.

Mavrogenes (1990) warned that "sending home a ditto of 'good ideas' tends to be ineffective" (p. 5). Even though the teachers received notes from parents like the ones above, these notes and comments only represent the views of a few parents. Teachers decided to send four follow-up letters to parents explaining the new sharing time activity. However, parents continued to express the same concerns. One teacher described a parent who came to school to find out about her son's participation:

Matthew's mom visited his class to see if Matt had done his show and tell on Thursday because she had worked with him on his sheet only to find it was still in his backpack when he came home.

Teachers began to ponder other ideas for getting parents involved in substantive ways in sharing time because of parent queries like the one above.

Creating Parent Informant Literacy Groups

The teachers began to work more closely with the researchers in order to better understand parent responses. The researchers pointed out that parents are rarely invited to have discussions with teachers about a specific literacy event such as sharing time, and thus some confusion was understandable. Consequently, the researchers sug-gested that a parent informant literacy group could be created to provide a forum for parents and teachers to discuss their kindergartners' literacy growth. This parent informant literacy group would be a vehicle for encouraging parents to share with teachers their perceptions of their children as learners. It could also be used to reveal to teachers the parents' interpretation of specific literacy activities assigned by teachers, since written communication alone had not been effective. The researchers suggested that the confusion surrounding the written communication might be eliminated if teachers met with parents and explained what they hoped to accomplish and how the parents could help with this literacy activity.

Both the researchers and the teachers incorporated suggestions by Mavrogenes (1990) and Joyce and Showers (1980) in order to structure more worthwhile parent meetings. Joyce and Showers (1980) contend that meetings for parents must include an affective component as well as theory, demonstration, practice, and feedback. For example, the affective aspects should include the following:

- Greeting all parents as they arrive
- Name tags to help parents communicate
- Group exercises to unify and relax parents
- Some kind of refreshments

In addition to incorporating the above affective elements in the parent meetings, teachers and researchers stressed demonstration, practice, and feedback. Mavrogenes suggests that "teachers and schools must make suggestions come alive for parents" (1990, p. 5). Casanova (1987) believes that "Parents are most likely to become involved if they see how contributing helps." Consequently, she suggests the need to "Let parents know their help is not just incidental but vital to their child's success" (p. 20).

The first parent informant literacy meeting was held at noon with one-third of the parents attending. The excitement in the group was evident and many parents said that they were pleased to have been invited to school to participate in this new approach to sharing time. For instance, one father wondered if his son actually shared in class everything they prepared together. Another father was not sure why we asked all the questions on the sheet and if he was to answer all the questions. In fact, he asked, "what if the student didn't include all the information in the presentation?" Several of the parents informed us that they liked receiving the sharing time topics on Friday because they could work with their children over the weekend.

We felt that the parents left the first meeting with a better understanding of the concept of sharing time and what our expectations were for this activity. Additionally, we felt after the first meeting that the parents were beginning to support the new approach to sharing time as well as the parent informant meetings. For example one mother said:

> I have a hearing impaired child in a special school where they [teachers] have meetings like this with parents. In these meetings, parents share ideas as well as receive ideas from teachers and other parents. I'm very excited to see this happening for regular education students and especially for all kindergarten parents.

Other parents echoed this mother's sentiments and decided that the parent informant literacy meetings were helpful and should be continued. At the conclusion of the first meeting, the next meeting date was set, additional meeting topics were suggested, and parents volunteered to serve on specific committees such as telephone, refreshment, transportation, and childcare. The teachers, in turn, left the meeting with a much clearer understanding of the parents' perspective regarding what was confusing or difficult about the assignment, and how children responded to parental participation and support. It was also more evident to the teachers after these informant meetings what parents found valuable about this new approach.

FIRST-GRADE PROJECT

We asked first-grade teachers to describe their perceptions of parent involvement. First-grade teachers were frustrated because they said that parents lacked respect for their children's gradual movement toward becoming readers and writers. One first-grade teacher expressed her frustration with parents by stating:

> We need parents to believe that when their kids work on something three days in class that they shouldn't take it off the refrigerator and throw it away. Some of the kids were coming back saying my momma threw that activity away and then the kids were sort of disappointed that

they were trying so hard in school and the parents were not supporting what they were doing at home.

The teacher continued by saying that:

Parents don't understand what we're trying to say to them when we're talking to them about reading and writing. For example, several parents have said to me: "Yeah when they bring that home there's not a word spelled right. There's no capitals. There's no periods. I can hardly read a thing, my kid reads it pretty good and tells me the story and I think gosh this is what they're doing all day. And it went in the garbage."

After several discussions with the first-grade teachers, we (the researchers) were able to help them understand the importance of closely examining their conversations with parents around reading and writing. We were also able to help teachers see that they needed to figure out specific ways to help parents understand what was happening in first grade. We reminded the teachers that the children were trying to construct an understanding of reading and writing. However, it was important to help their parents construct an understanding of how their children were developing as readers and writers.

Our advice to first-grade teachers was consistent with the advice given by other researchers. For example, Edwards (1993) points out that "it is important to note that when children enter school not only are they affected by the new school environment, but their parents are as well" (p. 1). Fletcher (1966) reminds us that :

Education is simply not something which is provided either by teachers in schools or by parents and family members in the home. It must be a *continuing* cultivation of the child's experiences in which *both* schools and families jointly take part. (p. 189)

Lightfoot (1978) makes clear that first-grade parents are greatly concerned about their childrens' academic development. She states that:

First grade is considered the critical period of family-school contact—when mothers [and fathers] are most distressed about releasing their child to the care of a distant person; when school is no longer a world of sand boxes and Playdough but a place for learning to read and write; where parents fear the external judgments made about the quality of their parenting during the first five years of the child's life; and when the child experiences the inevitable trauma of moving from a relatively egocentric, nurturant home environment to the more evaluative, social experience of school (pp. 86-87).

We informed teachers that we believe that a good relationship between parents, child, and teacher should be a priority. Potter (1989) echoed our position by arguing that:

Teachers have the important responsibility of working with and relating to families, not just children. Of course, the teacher's role with the child is different from that of the parent. The teacher has a more achievement-oriented approach where performance will be evaluated, but this cannot be done fairly if the teacher has no knowledge of the family relationships of the child. The teacher should strive to develop an environment where there is a *participatory role* for the family which facilitates the parent-teacher-child relationship and so enables the teaching and evaluation of the child by the teacher to be appropriate and just. (p. 21)

The project evolved as researchers, teachers, and parents worked together to develop a more participatory role for the family, much like Potter described.

Creating a First-Grade Parent Informant Group

We helped the first-grade teachers organize a parent informant literacy group. The purpose of this group was to provide an opportunity for teachers, parents, and researchers to participate in conversations that would facilitate parental understanding of how their children were developing as readers and writers.

At the first meeting, we wanted to give the first-grade teachers the opportunity to lead the discussion with parents. We were disappointed, however, that the teachers were giving the parents global statements when they asked specific questions. Often, the answers teachers gave were only remotely related to what the parents asked.

For the next meeting, parents requested that the meeting focus on child development. They wanted some specific examples of emergent literacy. Some of the discussion at our next meeting is highlighted below:

A lot of us have grown up with this paradigm where everybody drew the same bunny, everybody wrote the same kind of Mother's Day card.

> We now accept all kinds of writing from the kids. If your child was
> born in January and you have, I guess another child that's born in
> September in the same classroom, would you expect the child born in
> September to be doing exactly the same thing that the child is doing
> that's born in January?

Parents all looked at each other and said "No." It made sense to them
that children all enter the class at different levels and with different
amounts of experience. Therefore one cannot expect all of these children to be writing, reading, or moving at the same pace.

Some of the parents were starting to say "Wow, no wonder his (or
her) little face just drops when I throw his (her) papers away." They
realized that children were getting conflicting messages: "My teacher
thinks this is fantastic; my mother, my grandmother, my older brother
and sister they don't think it's good." This began a lively conversation
in which teachers, researchers, and parents all shared stories of children's development. One of Pat's stories seemed to strike parents as
especially significant:

> You know, all of you had this baby who was eight, nine months old
> and when that child looked at a cup and said cup-cup or said cracker or
> said momma. You didn't say No, excuse me this is a cup that we drink
> out of, this is a cracker, this is an oreo cookie and if you want some-
> thing to eat or drink you have to pronounce everything perfectly. When
> your child was in kindergarten, first grade, second grade, they write a
> story and everything isn't a journal and a thesis you don't stop your
> child and say wait a minute dog is d-o-g it isn't d-o-s. You know what
> I mean?

By the end of that meeting, many made comments along the lines of:
"Yeah maybe some of the things they've been bringing home I really
need to praise."

SECOND-GRADE PROJECT

The second-grade teachers were unsure of how they wanted to involve parents in the literacy support of their children. Teachers
struggled to find ways to connect parent involvement activities to the
curriculum in their classrooms. Consequently, two second-grade
teachers, two researchers, and the reading specialist met during

Professional Development School release time to study and discuss parent involvement. In these study group discussions, the second-grade group decided to develop and initiate the program started by a student teacher. She had learned about an integrated reading and writing curriculum for a year during a three-course literacy sequence that preceded student teaching. At the beginning of the school year, the student teacher assessed her students' development as readers and writers and began to implement the integrated curriculum approach she had studied. The teachers decided to work with her, because they saw writing as an important curriculum component and the school had participated in in-service activities three years prior to this experience.

The parent component grew out of changes in the literacy curriculum initially initiated by the student teacher and two events that occurred simultaneously. During regularly scheduled parent-teacher conferences several of the parents talked with the student teacher about the writing that their children were working on at home. Although students were not assigned writing homework per se, they were preparing written pieces at home to share with their classmates in school. The student teacher explained the writing that students were generating in school and shared student portfolios at these conferences. She also described students' responses to each others written pieces. During the same week that parent conferences were held, the study group met to begin to establish a plan for involving parents in literacy instruction. One of the teachers shared with the study group an article by Rodriguez (1991) that described a project that involved encouraging children to write by furnishing writing supplies that were sent home in a "traveling writer's briefcase." The timing of these two events led to the following important first steps. These second-grade teachers decided to follow up on the successes reported during parent conferences and reach out to more parents and students.

The second-grade team extended conventional parent involvement practices by exchanging information at parent-teacher informant meetings. At these meeting the Kendon second-grade PDS team shared portfolios of children's writing and videotapes of writing instruction with parents. The student teacher, teachers, and researchers focused on children's growth and their successes, while parents informed the group of their children's responses to school writing instruction. They also began to raise questions about the writing curriculum. The student teacher began to read examples aloud and to discuss children's interests, successes, struggles, and uses of writing at school. Some parents joined in to affirm their children's growth and to describe their children's writing initiatives at home, while other raised concerns about their children's reticence and lack of initiative. Teachers shared their work, plans, questions, and uncertainties about differences in students' development as writers.

Rather than simply receiving information from teachers about their children's achievements, the parents contributed information of their own and raised specific questions in a public forum. In response to the group's remaining questions, the team planned a second meeting to discuss student progress. In addition, the teachers asked parents to share rides with additional interested parents, and they supplied six briefcases full of supplies for children to use at home. The success of these strategies led to the second activity that substantively changed the level of family involvement.

PARENT INFORMANT JOURNALS

During the second informant meeting, parents began to raise questions about how they might respond to their children's writing, topic selections, and mechanical errors. These questions added a new level of complexity in writing instruction. These children in the second-grade classroom had developed as very different writers and gained expertise in several different writing genres. For example, one student wrote a fantasy story that included a dialogue between a fork and a spoon, another student wrote about his goals as a cub scout, and another wrote about how he cared for his "pet slug." In response to parent questions, the team designed a method to show parents how teachers responded in school to children, depending on the child's development and writing purposes.

The teachers began to audiotape conferences with individual students during their regular classroom writing conferences. These tapes were sent home in the "traveler's briefcases" with a brief message to the parent at the end of the tape. A tape recorder and tape were taken home by each child for three days on a rotating basis. Parents could hear examples of how teachers were responding to their child, as well as the contents and mechanics in their child's writing. A parent journal was also sent home with the tape, and parents were encouraged to respond to the child's writing and also to the teacher's conference either orally or in writing or both, depending on their preferences.

The impact of these changes reached the parent community and the teachers and had an effect on the entire Kendon staff. In response to the information and questions shared in the informant journals and meetings, additional times were scheduled, attendance increased, and parents began to ask more questions. Parents asked the team to continue the project with their children during the next year in third-grade. The reading specialist and principal discussed the project with the third-grade teachers and a student teacher was assigned to one of the third grade classrooms to facilitate this project.

A COMPARISON OF CONVENTIONAL AND NON-CONVENTIONAL INVOLVEMENT

The conventional parent involvement efforts were important because they brought parents and teachers together to discuss unilateral needs. Both parents and teachers saw the need for more frequent and content-focused communication. However, conventional parent involvement efforts were well-accepted, traditional practices that participants had not questioned or explored together. The schools' conventional efforts to involve parents were organized in order to quickly and efficiently meet with parents. Increasing the percentage of conferences held, rather than improving the contents of the conference, was the primary goal, with little incentive for either parents or teachers. In many cases, a short conference was perceived as a good conference because the information from the school focused on learning deficits.

In contrast, information exchanges during parent-teacher informant meetings and in ongoing parent/teacher journals focused on children's developmental growth and progress in literacy. The informant meetings and the audiotaped journals were both a means of fulfilling parent's expectations for more instruction and frequent communication and a means of fulfilling teachers' desires for more interest and support from parents.

The informant meetings established a predictable structure for parents to communicate information about how their child was responding to instruction in school. Parents not only became more knowledgeable about the school curriculum, but they also contributed information about their children's struggles, concerns, and progress. They, as well, began to inform other parents and teachers about their children's desires and they made sense of topics, audiences, and kernel issues in children lives. Many parents gave each other ideas about how they wrote with their children and what ideas had stirred their children's curiosity.

Parents became more than recipients and overseers of assignments. Their creative responses also changed the dynamics of the informant group. There was a mutual sense of pride and enjoyment, shared by parents and professional educators alike, in reading the children's writing and explaining life situations and humorous events such as how a garage sale treasure (a plastic fruit-covered hat) became a critical component in a story. They also shared a mutual frustration over students who refused to write or share their work with their classmates. Rather than just expediting the meetings, teachers reaped rewards by openly sharing their struggles as well as hearing from parents about the positive effects of their teaching. For example, one parent publicly praised the work of his child's teacher and described his responses to a relative who criticized the public schools within the district. Other parents described their child's excitement about writing with friends as a sleep-over activity. Parents received support from the school and also from other parents.

Parents were truly involved in the group and the group process. The curriculum was not simply handed out and parent were not just told about how their children were learning reading, writing, English, grammar, and spelling. The informant meetings in conjunction with the audiotapes, videotapes, invitations to the classroom, and journals created an organizational structure for parent interpretation and expression. Parents could listen in on how their child's interests and problems were addressed during in-school writing conferences. More importantly, the videotaped instruction helped parents visualize and consequently discuss the community of readers and writers that teachers were attempting to build within the classroom. By changing the organizational structure of parent meetings and allocating resources to help parents gain access to information about the school, parents participated in more meaningful ways. They contributed and developed an interpretation of their child's reactions to school assignments, classmates, and their teacher as they developed a strong parent-school and parent-parent relationship.

INSIGHT GAINED FROM THESE THREE COLLABORATIONS

Our primary goal over the three-year project had been to learn ways to promote better understanding, cooperation, and communication between teachers and families. We found out that in this process we were also learning a great deal about what it means to understand, communicate, and cooperate with each other. This discovery occurred between teachers at both the same and different grade levels, between researchers, and between teachers and researchers, and most importantly between parents and professional educators. While, in the end, all participants were pleased with the projects that had been designed and had a much greater appreciation for each other's contributions to the success of the projects, the collaborative process itself was time-consuming, often frustrating, and at times highly stressful for everyone involved. We believe it is important to share some of these feelings and experiences for the benefit of others interested in this type of work.

As mentioned earlier, the researchers were adamant that the Kendon program be designed by and for its constituents—that to import or impose a program developed for another school would be a mistake. For a long time, then, no one had a clear sense of what the Kendon program would, or could, become. After a number of meetings passed with no tangible program or plan of action in place, some of the teachers began to express their concern and commented that the project was going nowhere. Not being accustomed to collaborative projects with university-based personnel, many of the teachers expected—despite our statements to the contrary—that the researchers should get on with the implementation of a previously designed parent involvement program. One teacher commented:

> I think all of the teachers could learn very quickly if we had a workshop . . . it would be important that you bring that to us and two or three of us could watch you go through the program and after that we are trained. You have the program—we don't have the program.

The perception that the researchers had the program, which the teachers would simply carry out, influenced the way teachers viewed their own (and the researcher's) roles. They saw themselves as contributing to the project when they provided information about the school, students, and curriculum, or when they described their goals. They believed that the researchers, in turn, would contribute to the project by tailoring another program to their school population and training them in how to implement it.

Similarly, after several months had passed, some of the researchers began to express feelings of frustration with the lack of progress, and commented that the teachers needed to take on a more active role in the project design. The researchers defined their role in the project as facilitators and as coinventors. They believed they could contribute by linking relevant research findings to the teachers' goals and making suggestions about possible project plans and means of implementation.

Finding a common language and an acceptable style in which to share these different perspectives was often difficult, as well. The school culture called for teachers to take a polite, often indirect approach to airing and mediating disagreements, whereas the researchers, coming from a different culture, viewed disagreements as opportunities for interesting discussions. Their directness and willingness to take on an opposing point of view was often perceived by teachers as confrontational and nonsupportive.

That the participants were able to push through these difficulties to find a productive and mutually satisfying working relationship is evident in the success teachers of the three projects developed. We believe that several factors contributed to the projects' eventual success: First having the opportunity to work together often, over an extended period of time; second, having a structure in place that supported this work (in terms of released time, money, and materials); third, and most importantly, having a common commitment to promote and support childrens' literacy learning.

NOTE

Special thanks to Diedra A. Boles, Nadine L. Dunham, Jan Baker, Gina Bennett, Jan Murchison, Bonnie Lacey, Annie Williford, and Jo Nelson of Kendon Professional Development Elementary School.

Bibliography

Ada, A. F. (1988). The Pajaro Valley experience: Working with Spanish-speaking parents to develop children's reading and writing skills through the use of children's literature. In T. Skutnabb-Kangas & J. Cummins (Eds.), *Minority education: From shame to struggle.* (pp. 223-238). Philadelphia: Multilingual Matters, LTD.

Adams, M. J. (1990). *Beginning to read: Thinking and learning about print.* Cambridge, MA: MIT Press.

Adler, J. C., et al. (1989, October). *A middle school experiment: Can a token economy improve reading achievement scores?* Paper presented at the annual meeting of the Midwestern Educational Research Association, Chicago. (ED 312620)

Allen, J. B., & Mason, J. (Eds.). (1989). *Risk makers, risk takers, risk breakers: Reducing the risks for young literacy learners.* Portsmouth, NH: Heinemann.

Allexsaht-Snider, M. (1991). Family literacy in a Spanish speaking context: Joint construction of meaning. *Quarterly Newsletter for the Laboratory of Comparative Human Cognition, 13* (1), 15-21.

Allington, R. L. (1991). Children who find learning to read difficult: School responses to diversity. In E. H. Hiebert (Ed) *Literacy for a diverse society* (pp 237-252). New York: Teacher's College Press.

Altwerger, B., Diehl-Faxson, J., & Dockstader-Anderson, K. (1985). Read-aloud events as meaning construction. *Language Arts, 62* (5), 476-484.

AMS (1993, July) The National Swedish Labour Market Board. Stockholm: Public Relations Department.

Anderson, A. B., & Stokes, S. J. (1984). Social and institutional influence on the development and
practice of literacy. In H. Goelman, A. Oberg, & F. Smith (Eds.),
Awakening to literacy (pp. 24-37). Exeter, NH: Heinemann.

Anderson, A. B., Teale, W. H., & Estrada, E. (1980). Low-income
children's preschool literacy experiences: Some naturalistic observations. *The Quarterly Newsletter of the Laboratory of
Comparative Human Cognition, 2,* 59-65.

Anderson, R. C. (1978). Schema directed processes in language
comprehension. In A. Lesgold, J. Pelligreno, S. Fokkema, & R.
Glaser (Eds.), *Cognitive psychology and instruction* (pp. 67-82).
New York: Plenum.

Anderson, R. C., Hiebert, E. H., Scott, J. A., & Wilkinson, I. A. (1985).
*Becoming a nation of readers: The report of the Commission on
Reading.* Washington, DC: National Institute of Education.

Anderson, R. C., Wilson, P. T., & Fielding, L. G. (1988). Growth in
reading and how children spend their time outside of school.
Reading Research Quarterly, 23, 285-303.

Arkansas State Department of Education. (1991). *HIPPY: Home instruction program for preschool youngsters. Final Report.* Little
Rock,AR: Division of Vocational and Technical Education.

Atwell, N. (1987). *In the middle.* Montclair, NJ: Boynton/Cook.

Auerbach, E. (1989). Toward a social contextual approach to family
literacy. *Harvard Educational Review, 59,* 165-181.

Baghban, M. (1984). *Our daughter learns to read and write.*
Newark, DE: IRA.

Bailey, D. B. (1987). Collaborative goal-setting with families: Resolving differences in values and priorities for services. *Topics in
Early Childhood Special Education, 7* (2), 59-71.

Barker, R. G. (1968). *Ecological psychology.* Stanford, CA: Stanford
University Press.

Barker, R. G., Wright, H. F. (1955). *Midwest and its children.* New
York: Harper & Row.

Bayley, N. (1969). *Bayley scales of infant development.* New York:
The Psychological Corporation.

Bean, R. M., Southworth, H., Koebler, S., & Fotta, B. (1990). *The
Beginning with Books gift book program: Effects on family and
child literacy.* Paper presented at the 40th annual meeting of the
National Reading Conference, Miami.

Bergin, D. A., Hudson, L. M., Chryst, C. F., & Resetar, M. (1992). An afterschool intervention program for educationally disadvantaged young children. *Urban Review, 24,*
203-217.

Berman, R., Slobin, D., Bamberg, M., Dromi, E., Marchman, V., Neeman, Y., Renner, T., & Sebastian, E. (1986). *Coding manual: Temporality in discourse* (rev. ed.). Cognitive Science Program, University of California, Berkeley.

Bernstein, B. (1962). Social class, linguistic codes and grammatical elements. *Language and Speech, 5,* 31-46.

Bernstein, B. (1971). Class, codes and control. Vol. 1. *Theoretical studies towards a sociology of language.* London: Routledge & Kegan Paul.

Bernstein, B. (1972). Social class, language, and socialization. In P. P. Giglioli (Ed.), *Language and social context* (pp. 157-178). Harmondsworth, England: Viking Penguin.

Berrueta-Clement, J. R., Schweinhart, L. J., Barnett, W. S., Epstein, A. S., & Weikart, D. P. (1984). Changed lives: The effects of the Perry pre-school program on youths through age 19. Ypsilanti: *Monographs of the High/Scope Educational Research Foundation,* No. 8.

Bissex, G. (1980). *GNYS AT WORK: A child learns to read and write.* Cambridge, MA: Harvard University Press.

Björck-Åkesson, E. (1992). *Communicative interaction between young non -speaking physically disabled children and their primary caregivers—A longitudinal study.* Göteborg, Göteborgs Universitet.

Bower, G. H. (1976). Experiments on story understanding and recall. *The Quarterly Journal of Experimental Psychology, 28,* 511-534.

Bradley, L., & Bryant, P. E. (1983). Categorizing sounds and learning to read—A causal connection. *Nature,* 301, 419-521.

Branscombe, A. (1991). "But it ain't real!": Pretence in children's play and literacy development. In J. F. Christie (Ed.), *Play and early literacy development* (pp. 91-118). Albany, NY: SUNY Press.

Bransford, J. D., Stein, B. S., Nye, N. J., & Perfetto, G. A. (1982). Differences in approaches to learning: An overview. *Journal of Experimental Psychology: General, 3,* 390-398.

Bright, J., Hidalgo, N., San-Fong, S., Swap, S., & Perry, T. (1993, April). *Student success and ethnicity: patterns of family and com-*

munity support. Symposium held at annual meeting of American Educational Research Association.

Bronfenbrenner, U. (1979). *The ecology of human development: Experiments by nature and design.* Cambridge, MA: Harvard University Press.

Bronfenbrenner, U., & Crouter, A. C. (1983). The evolution of environmental models in developmental research. In P. H. Mussen (Ed.), *Handbook of child psychology.Vol. 1. History, theory and methods.* (pp. 357-414). New York.

Bruner, J. (1983). *Child's Talk: Learning to use language.* New York: Oxford University Press.

Bruner, J. (1984). Language, mind and reading. In H. Goelman, A. Oberg, & F. Smith (Eds.), *Awakening to literacy* (pp. 193-200). Portsmouth, NH: Heinemann.

Bryant, P. E., Maclean, M., & Bradley, L. (1990). Rhyme, language, and children's reading. *Applied Psycholinguistics, 11* (3), 237-252.

Burke, B. (1990). *Running Start: Final evaluation report.* Toledo: Toledo Public Schools.

Burke, B. (1991)*Running Start: Final evaluation report.* Toledo: Toledo Public Schools.

Bus, A. G. (1989, April). *Storybook reading, attachment and emergent literacy: some experimental studies with children from lower socio-economic status families.* Paper presented to the biennial meeting of the Society for Research in Child Development, Kansas City.

Campbell, R. (1985). When children write nonwords to dictation. *Journal of Experimental Child Psychology, 40,* 133-151.

Carnegie Foundation for the Advancement of Teaching, School Choice (1991). Princeton, NJ.

Carraher, T. N. (1987). Illiteracy in a literate society: Understanding reading failure in Brazil. In D. A. Wagner (Ed.), *The future of literacy in a changing world* (pp. 95-110). Oxford: Pergamon.

Casanova, U. (1987). Parents can be great summer tutors. *Instructor, 97* (3), 20-21.

Case, R. (1985). *Intellectual development: A systematic reinterpretation.* New York: Academic Press.

Cazden, C. B. (1972). *Child language and education.* New York: Holt, Rinehart, & Winston.

Cazden, C. B. (1983). Peekaboo as an instructional model: Discourse development at school and at home. In B. Bain (Ed.), *The socio-genesis of language and human conduct: A multi-disciplinary book of readings* (pp. 330-358). New York: Plenum.

Cazden, C. B. (1986). Classroom discourse. In M. E. Wittrock (Ed.), *Handbook of research on teaching* (3rd ed.) (pp. 432-463). New York: Macmillan.

Cazden, C. B. (1988). *Classroom discourse: The language of teaching and learning.* Portsmouth, NH: Heinemann.

Cazden, C. B. (1992). *Whole language plus.* New York: Teacher's College Press.

Cederström, A. (1990). *Children in foster care and their adaptation— Issues of the relationship with the natural parent. About the placement in foster homes of 25 children aged 4-12.* Stockholm: University of Stockholm.

Chandler, J., Argyris, D., Barnes, W. S., Goodman, I. F., & Snow, C. E. (1986). Parents as teachers: Observations of low-income parents and children in a homework-like task. In B. B. Schiefflin and P. Gilmore (Eds.), *The acquisition of literacy: Ethnographic perspectives* (pp. 402-444), Norwood. NJ: Ablex.

Chomsky, C. (1981). Write now, read later. *Childhood Education, 47,* 296-299.

Christie, J. F. (1987). Play and story comprehension: A critique of recent training research. *Journal of Research and Development in Education,, 21* (1), 36-43.

Christie, J. F., & Enz, B. (1991, April). *The effects of literacy play interventions on preschoolers' play patterns and literacy development.* Paper presented at the annual meeting of the American Educational Research Association, Chicago.

Cipielewski, J. And Stanovich, K. E. (1992) Predicting growth in reading ability from children's exposure to print. *Journal of Experimental Child Psychology.* 54(1) 74-89.

Clark, M. M. (1976). *Young fluent readers.* London: Heinemann

Clark, M.M. (1984). Literacy at home and at school: Insights from a study of young fluent readers. In H. Goelman, A. Oberg, and F. Smith (Eds.), *Awakening to literacy* (pp. 122-130). Portsmouth, NH: Heinemann, Inc.

Clark, R. M. (1983). *Family life and school achievement: Why poor black children succeed or fail.* Chicago: University of Chicago Press.

Clay, M. M. (1966). *Emergent reading behaviour*. Unpublished doctoral dissertation, University of Auckland.

Clay, M. M. (1975). *What did I write?* Auckland: Heinemann.

Clay, M. M. (1979). *Reading: The patterning of complex behavior*. Portsmouth, NH: Heinemann.

Clay, M. M. (1985). *The early detection of reading difficulties* (3rd ed.). Portsmouth, NH: Heinemann Educational Books.

Clay, M. M. (1991). *Becoming literate: The construction of inner-control*. Portsmouth, NH: Heinemann.

Clay, M. M., & Cazden, C. (1990). A Vygotskian interpretation of Reading Recovery. In L. Moll (Ed.), *Vygotsky and education: Instructional implications and applications of sociohistorical psychology* (pp. 206-222). New York: Cambridge University Press.

Clay, M. M. & Watson, B. (1982). An inservice program for Reading Recovery teachers. In M. M. Clay (Ed.), *Observing young readers* (pp. 192-200). Portsmouth, NH: Heinemann.

Cochran-Smith, M. (1986). Reading to children: A model for understanding texts. In B. B. Schiefflin and P. Gilmore (Eds.), *The acquisition of literacy: Ethnographic p erspectives*. (pp. 35-54). Norwood, NJ: Ablex.

Cole, M., & Griffin, P. (1986). A sociohistorical approach to remediation. In S. deCastell, A. Luke, K. Egan (Eds.), *Literacy, society and schooling* (pp. 101-31). Cambridge: Cambridge University Press.

Coleman, J. S. (1987). Families and schools. *Educational Researcher 16*(6); 32-38.

Connell, R. W., Ashenden, D. J., Kessler, S., & Dowsett, G. W. (1982). *Making the difference*. Sydney: George Allen and Unwin.

Cowley, J. (1987). *Spider, spider*. San Diego: Wright Group.

Crain-Thoreson, C. & Dale, P.S. (1992). Do early talkers become early readers? Linguistic precocity, preschool language, and early reading. *Developmental Psychology 28*, 421-9.

Dahl, K., & Freepon, P. (1991). Literacy learning in whole language classrooms: An analysis of low socioeconomic urban children learning to read and write in kindergarten. In J. Zutell & S. McCormick (Eds.), *Learner factors/teacher factors: Issues in literacy research and instruction* (pp. 149-158). Chicago: National Reading Conference.

Davey, B., & Macready, G. B. (1985). Prerequisite relations among inference tasks for good and poor readers. *Journal of Educational Psychology, 77,* 539-552.

De Casper, A. J. & Spence, M. J. (1986). Prenatal maternal speech influences newborn's perceptions of speech sounds. *Infant Behavior and Development, 9,* 133-150.

DeFord, D. E., Lyons, C. A., and Pinnell, G. S. (Eds.). (1991). *Bridges to literacy: Learning from Reading Recovery.* Portsmouth, NH: Heinemann.

Delgado-Gaitan, C. (1990). *Literacy for empowerment: The role of parents in children's education.* New York: Falmer.

Delgado-Gaitan, C. (1991). Involving parents in the schools: A process of empowerment. *American Journal of Education, 100* (1), 20-46.

Delgado-Gaitan, C. (1992). School matters in the Mexican-American homes: Socializing children to education. *American Educational Research Journal, 29,* 495-516.

De Loache, J. S. (1984). What's this? Maternal questions in joint picture book reading with toddlers. *Quarterly Newsletter of Comparative Human Cognition, 6,* (4.), 87-95.

De Loache, J. S., & Mendoza, O. A. P. (1985). *Joint picture book interactions of mothers and one-year old children* (Technical Report No. 353). Urbana, IL: University of Illinois, Center for the Study of Reading. (ED 274 960.)

Dickinson, D. K. (1989) Effects of a shared reading program in one Head Start language and literacy environment. In J. Allen & J. Mason (eds) *Risk makers, risk takers, risk breakers* [pp125-153]. Portsmouth, N.H. Heinemann

Dickinson, D. K. (1991). Teacher stance and setting: Constraints on conversation in preschools. In A. McCabe & C. Peterson (Eds.), *Developing narrative structure* (pp. 255-302). Hillsdale, NJ: Lawrence Erlbaum.

Dickinson, D. K., & Snow, C. E. (1986). Interrelationships among pre-reading and oral language skills in kindergarten for two social classes. Technical report. (ED 272 860)

Dickinson, D. K., & Snow, C. E. (1987). Interrelationships among prereading and oral language skills in kindergartners from two social classes. *Early Childhood Research Quarterly, 2,* 1-26.

Dickson, S. (1972). *Sing, spell, read, and write. Raceway book:* Virginia Beach, VA: Sing, Spell, Read & Write.

Dolan, L. J. (1992). *Project self-help: A first-year evaluation of a family literacy program.* Baltimore: Center on Families, Communities, Schools & Children's Learning.

Duranti, A., & Ochs, E. (1986). Literacy instruction in a Samoan village. In B. B. Schiefflin & P. Gilmore (Eds.), *The acquisition of literacy: Ethnographic perspectives* (pp. 213-32). Norwood, NJ: Ablex.

Durkin, D. (1966). *Children who read early.* New York: Teachers College Press.

Dyson, A. H. (1982). Reading, writing, and language: Young children solving the written language puzzle. *Language Arts, 59*, 204-214.

Dyson, A. H. (1986). Transitions and tensions: Interrelationships between the drawing, talking and dictating of young children. *Research in the Teaching of English, 20* (4), 379-409.

Dyson, A. H. (1988). Negotiating among multiple worlds: The space/time dimensions of young children's composing. *Research in the Teaching of English, 22* (4), 355-390.

Dyson, A. H. (1992) *Whistle for Willie,* lost puppies, and cartoon dogs: The sociocultural dimensions of young children's composing. *Journal of Reading Behavior, 24*(4), 433-462.

Eastman, P. D. (1960). *Are you my mother?* New York: Random House.

Edelsky, C. (1990). Whose agenda is this anyway? A response to McKenna, Robinson, & Miller. *Educational Researcher, 20*(8), 7-11.

Edelsky, C. (1991) *With literacy and justice for all.* Philadelphia: Falmer.

Edelskey, C., Altwerger, B., & Flores, B. (1991). *Whole language: What's the difference?* Portsmouth, NH: Heinemann.

Edwards, P. A. (1989). Supporting lower SES mothers' attempts to provide scaffolding for book reading. In J. Allen & J. Mason (Eds.), *Risk makers, risk takers, risk breakers* (pp. 222-250). Portsmouth, NH: Heinemann.

Edwards, P. A. (1991a). Fostering early literacy through parent coaching. In E. Hiebert (Ed.), *Literacy for a diverse society: Perspectives, programs, and policies* (pp. 199-213). New York: Teachers College Press.

Edwards, P. A. (1991b, May). *Differentiated parenting or parentally appropriate: The missing link in efforts to develop a structure for parent involvement in schools*. Paper presented at the third annual Roundtable on Home-Community-School Partnerships, Chicago.

Edwards, P. A. (1993, Dec). *First grade parents' perspectives on emergent literacy: The missing voices*. Paper presented at the annual meeting of the National Reading Conference, San Antonio.

Edwards, P. A., Boles, D. A., & Dunham, N. L. (in press). Using parents as literacy informants: An ethnographic account of how two kindergarten teachers involved parents in sharing time. In L. Brobst, A. Boehm, & J. Black (Eds.), *Intergenerational literacy: Developing literacy skills of children and adults*. New York: Teachers College Press.

Ehri, L. (1978). Beginning reading from a psycholinguistic perspective: Amalgamation of word identities. In F. B. Murray (Ed.), *The development of the reading process* . (Monograph No. 3) (pp. 1-33). Newark, DE: International Reading Association.

Ehri, L. (1991). Development of the ability to read words. In P. D. Pearson, R. Barr, M. L. Kamil, & P. Mosenthal (Eds.), *Handbook of reading research* (Vol. 2, pp. 383-417). New York: Longman.

Elardo, R., Bradley, R., & Caldwell, B. (1975). The relation of infants' home environments to mental test performance from six to thirty-six months: A longitudinal analysis. *Child Development, 46*, 71-76.

Eldridge-Hunter, D. (1992). Intergenerational literacy: Impact on the development of the storybook reading behaviors of Hispanic mothers. In C. K. Kinzer & D. J. Leu (Eds.), *Literacy research, theory and practice: Views from many perspectives* (pp. 101-110). Chicago: National Reading Conference, Inc.

Elkins, J. & Spreadbury, S. (1991, November) *Family literacy practices from pre-school to grade 1*. Paper presented at the annual conference of the Australian Association for Research in Education, Surfers's Paradise, Queensland.

Elkonin, D. B. (1973). U.S.S.R. In J. Downing (Ed.), *Comparative reading* (pp. 551-580). New York: Macmillan.

Elley, W. B. (1992). How in the world do students read? IEA study of reading literacy. Hamburg: IEA.

Eneskär, B. (1978). Children's language at four and six. :A longitudinal and multi-variable study of language abilities among children. :Lund: Liber. Epstein, J. (1991) Effects on sutdent achievement of teacher's practices of parent involvement. In

Silverin, S. B. (Ed.), *Literacy through family/community and school interactions* (pp. 261-276). Greenwich, CT: JAI.

Epstein, J. L. (1991). Effects on student achievement of teachers' practices of parent involvement. In S. B. Silvern (Ed.), *Literacy through family community and school interactions*. Greenwich, CT: JAI.

Erazmus, T. R. (1987). *The effect of a recreational reading program on standardized test scores*. Unpublished master's thesis, Olivet Nazarene University. (ED 294 169)

Fear, K. L., & Edwards, P. A. (1992). *Teachers' learning about organizational leadership from the action science perspective*. Paper presented at the annual meeting of the American Educational Research Association, San Francisco.

Fein, G. (1984). The self-building potential of pretend play or "I got a fish, all by myself." In T. D. Hankey & A. D. Pellegrini (Eds.), *Child's play: Developmental and applied*. Hillsdale, NJ: Erlbaum.

Feitelson, D., & Iraqui, J. (1990). Story book reading: A bridge to literary language. *Reading Teacher, 44* (3), 264-265.

Feitelson, D., & Goldstein, Z. (1986). Patterns of book ownership and reading to young children in Israeli school-oriented and non-school oriented families. *Reading Teacher, 39* (9), 924-930.

Feldman, S., Wentzel, K., Weinberger, D., & Munson, J. (1990). Marital satisfaction of parents of preadolescent boys and its relationship to family and child functioning. *Journal of Family Psychology, 4,* 213-234.

Ferdman, B. M. (1990). Literacy and cultural identity. *Harvard Educational Review, 60,* 181-204.

Fernie, D. (1985). The promotion of play in the indoor play environment. In J. L. Frost & S. Sunderlin (Eds.), *When children play*(pp. 285-290). Wheaton, MD: Association for Childhood Education International.

Ferriero, E., & Teberosky, A. (1982). *Literacy before schooling*. Exeter, NH: Heinemann.

Fishman, A. R. (1990). Becoming literate: A lesson from the Amish. In A. A. Lunsford, H. Moglen, and J. Slevin, (Eds.), *The right to literacy,* (pp. 29-38). NY: Modern Language Association.

Fitzgerald, J., Spiegel, D. L., & Cunningham, J. W. (1991). The relationship between parental literacy level and perceptions of emergent literacy. *Journal of Reading Behavior, 23,* 191-214.

Fletcher, R. (1966). *The family and marriage in Britain.* Harmondsworth, England: Penguin.

Flood, J. S. (1977). Parental styles in reading episodes with young
children. *Reading Teacher, 30,* 864-867.

France, M. G., & Hager, J. M. (1993). Recruit, respect, respond: A
model for working with low-income families and their preschoolers. *The Reading Teacher* 46(7), 568-572.

Freire, P. (1970). Cultural action for freedom. In *Harvard Education
Review* (Monograph Series Number 1), Cambridge, MA.

Gadamer, H. (1986). *Truth and method.* New York: Crossroad.

Galda, L., & Cullinan, B. E. (1990). Literature for literacy: What
research says about the benefits of using tradebooks in the
classroom. In J. Flood, J. Jensen, D. Lapp, & J. Squire (Eds.),
*Handbook of research on the teaching of the English language
arts* (pp.528-535). New York: Macmillan.

Galda, L., Pellegrini, A. D., & Cox, S. (1989). A short term longitudinal study of preschoolers' emergent literacy. *Research in the
Teaching of English, 23,* 292-309.

Gambrell, L. B., & Koskinen, P. S. (1991). Retelling and the reading
comprehension of proficient and less-proficient readers. *Journal
of Educational Research, 84,* 356-62.

Genesee, F. (1985). Second language learning through immersion: A
review of U. S. programs. *Review of Educational Research, 55,*
541-561.

Goldenberg, C. N. (1989). Making success a more common occurrence for children at risk for failure: Lessons from Hispanic first
graders learning to read. In J. Allen, & J. M. Mason, (Eds.),
Riskmakers, Risktakers, Riskbreakers (pp. 48-79). Portsmouth,
NH: Heinemann.

Goldenberg, C. N., & Gallimore, R. (1991). Local knowledge, research knowledge, and educational change: A case study of early
Spanish reading improvement. *Educational Researcher, 20* (8),
2-14.

Goldenberg, C. N., Reese, L., & Gallimore, R. (1992). Effects of literacy materials from school on Latino children's home experiences
and early reading achievement. *American Journal of Education,
100,* 497-536.

Goldfield, B., & Snow, C. E. (1984). Reading books with children:
The mechanics of parental influence on children's reading
achievement. In J. Flood (Ed.), *Understanding reading compre-*

hension (pp. 204-218).   Newark, DE: International Reading Association.

Goldman, R. (Ed.).   (1968). *Breakthrough*. London: Routledge & Kegan Paul.

Goodlad, J. (1984). *A place called school*. New York: McGraw-Hill.

Goodman, K. (1986). *What's whole in whole language?* Porstmouth, NH: Heinemann.

Goodman, K. (1989). Whole language research: Foundations and development. *Elementary School Journal, 90,* 207-220.

Goodman, K., & Goodman, Y. (1976). *Learning to read is natural.* Paper presented at the Conference on Theory and Practice of Beginning Reading Instruction. Pittsburgh.

Goodman, K. S. & Goodman, Y. (1979) Learning to read is natural. In L. B. Resnick and P. Weaver (Eds.), *Theory and practice of early reading*. Hillsdale, N. J.: Earlbaum.

Goodman, Y. (1984). The development of initial literacy. In H. Goelman, A. Oberg, & F. Smith (Eds.), *Awakening to literacy*. Exeter, NH: Heinemann.

Goodman, Y. (1986). Children coming to know literacy. In W. H. Teale & E. Sulzby (Eds.), *Emergent literacy: Writing and reading* (pp. 1-14). Norwood, NJ: Ablex

Goodsitt, J., Raitan, J., & Perlmutter, M. (1988). Interaction between mothers and preschool children when reading a novel and familiar book. *International Journal of Behavioral Development, 11,* 489-505.

Goody, J. (1977). *The domestication of the savage mind.* Cambridge: Cambridge University Press.

Goody, J. (1987). *The interface between the written and the oral.* Cambridge: Cambridge University Press.

Gordon, C. J., & Braun, C. (1982). Story schemata: Metatextual aid to reading and writing. In J. A. Niles & L. A. Harris (Eds.), *New inquiries in reading research and instruction. Thirty-first yearbook of the National Reading Conference* (pp. 262-268). Rochester, NY: National Reading Conference.

Gordon, I. J., & Guinagh, B. J. (1974). *A home learning center approach to early stimulation.* Unpublished manuscript, University of Florida Institute for the Development of Human Resources, Gainesville.

Goswami, U. (1988). Children's use of analogy in learning to spell. *British Journal of Developmental Psychology, 6,* 21-33.

Goswami, U., & Bryant, P. E. (1990). *Phonological skills and learning to read*. East Sussex, England: Erlbaum.

Gough, P. B., & Tunmer, W. E. (1986). Decoding, reading, and reading disability. *Remedial and Special Education, 7,* 6-10.

Graesser, A., Golding, J. M., & Long, D. L. (1991). Narrative representation and comprehension. In R. Barr, M. L. Kamil, P. Mosenthal, & P. D. Pearson (Eds.), *The handbook of reading research* (Vol. 2, pp. 171-205). New York: Longman.

Graff, H. J. (1986). The legacies of literacy: Continuities and contradictions in western society and culture. In S. deCastell, A. Luke, & K. Egan (Eds.), *Literacy, society and schooling,* (pp. 66-68) Cambridge: Cambridge University Press.

Graves, D. H. (1983). *Writing: Teachers and children at work*. Portsmouth, NH: Heinemann.

Green, J. L. (1983). Exploring classroom discourse: Linguistic perspectives on teaching-learning processes. *Educational Psychologist, 18,* 180-199.

Green, J. S., & Wallat, C. (1987). In search of meaning: A sociolinguistic perspective on lesson construction and reading. In D. Bloome (Ed.), *Literacy and schooling* (pp. 4-31). Norwood, NJ: Ablex.

Griffin, P. (1989) *Literacy profile*. Melbourne: Ministry of Education.

Griffiths, R. (1954). *The abilities of babies*. London: University of London Press ARICD.

Griffiths, R. (1970). *The abilities of young children*. London: Child Development Research Center.

Gump, P. (1975). Operating environments in schools of open and traditional design. In T. G. David & B. D. Wright (Eds.), *Learning environments*. Chicago: University of Chicago Press.

Gump, P. (1989). Ecological psychology and issues of play. In M. Bloch & A. Pellegrini (Eds.), *The ecological context of children's play*. Norwood, NJ: Ablex.

Gumperz, J. (1981). Conversational inference and classroom learning. In J. Green & C. Wallat (Eds.), *Ethnography and language in educational settings*. Norwood, NJ: Ablex.

Hale, C., & Windecker, E. (1993, March). *Influence of parent-child interaction during reading on preschooler's cognitive abilities*. Paper presented at the biennial meeting of the Society for Research in Child Development, New Orleans.

Hall, N. (1991). Play and the emergence of literacy. In J. F. Christie (Ed.), *Play and early literacy development* (pp. 3-25). Albany: SUNY Press.

Handel, R. D. (1992). The partnership for family reading: Benefits for families and schools. *ReadingTeacher, 46*(2), 117-126.

Hannon, P. (1987). A study of the effects of parental involvement in the teaching of reading on children's reading test performance. *British Journal of Educational Psychology, 57*, 56-72.

Hannon, P. & James, S. (1990). Parents' and teachers' perspectives on pre-school literacy development. *British Educational Research Journal, 16* (3), 259-272.

Hannon, P., Weinberger, J., and Nutbrown, C. (1991). A study of work with parents to promote early literacy development. *Research Studies in Education, 6*, 2, 77-97.

Harkness, F., & Miller, L. (1982). *A description of the interaction among mother, child and books in a bedtime reading situation.* Paper presented at the Seventh Annual Boston Conference on Language Development.

Harste, J. C., Woodward, V. A., & Burke, C. L. (1984). *Language stories and iteracy lessons.* Portsmouth, NH: Heinemann.

Harty, S. (1979). *Hucksters in the classroom: A review of industry propaganda in schools.* Washington, DC: Center for the Study of Law.

Havelock, E. A. (1976). *Origins of Western literacy.* (Monograph Series 14). Toronto: The Ontario Institute for Studies in Education.

Hayden, H., & Fagan, W. (1987). Keeping it in context: Strategies for enhancing literacy awareness. *First Language, 7*, 159-171.

Heath, S. B. (1989). Oral and literate traditions among black Americans living in poverty. *American Psychologist, 44*, 367-373.

Heath, S. B. (1982) What no bedtime story means: Narrative skills at home and school. *Language in Society, 11*, 49-76.

Heath, S. B. (1983).*Ways With Words.* Cambridge: Cambridge University Press.

Heath, S. B. (1986a). Critical factors in literacy development. In S. deCastell, A. Luke, K. Egan (Eds.), *Literacy, society and schooling* (pp. 209-229) Cambridge: Cambridge University Press.

Heath, S. B. (1986b). The functions and uses of literacy. In S. deCastell, A. Luke, K. Egan (Eds.), *Literacy, society and schooling* (pp. 15-26). Cambridge: Cambridge University Press.

Heath, S. B. (1986c). Separating "things of imagination" from life: Learning to read and write. In W. H. Teale & E. Sulzby (Eds.), *Emergent Literacy* (pp. 156-172). Norwood, NJ: Ablex.

Heath, S. B. (1990). The children of Trackton's children. In J. W. Stigler, R. A. Shweder, & G. Herdt, (Eds.), *Cultural psychology* (pp. 496-519). New York: Cambridge University Press.

Heberle, J. (1992). PACE: Parent and Child Education in Kentucky. in T. G. Sticht, M. J. Beeler, & B. A. McDonald, (Eds.), (pp. 136-148) *The Intergenerational transfer of cognitive skills Vol. 1.* Norwood, N. J.: Ablex.

Her Majesty's Chief Inspector of Schools. (1993). *Reading Recovery in New Zealand.* London: HMSO.

Hess, R. D., & Holloway, S. D. (1983). Family and school as educational institutions. In R. D. Parke (Ed.), *Review of Child Development Research: Vol. 7. The Family.* Chicago: University of Chicago Press.

Hess, R. D., & Shipman, V. (1965). The socialization of cognitive modes in children. *Child Development* 36, 869-85.

Hiebert, E. H. (1981). Developmental patterns and interrelationships of pre-school children's print awareness. *Reading Research Quarterly, 16,* 236-260.

Hirst, K. & Hannon, P. (1990). An evaluation of a pre-school home teaching project. *Educational Reaearch, 32,* 33-9.

Holdaway, D. (1979). *Foundations of literacy.* Portsmouth, NH: Heinemann.

Holmes, B. C. (1987). Children's inferences with print and pictures. *Journal of Educational Psychology, 79,* 14-18.

Hyder, B. P., & Brown, C. S. (1982). *Neighborhoods and communities.* Glenview, IL: Silver Burdett.

Iaccoca, L. (1989, September 18). Get books into the homes, get parents involved and the kids will read. Syndicated column, *Los Angeles Times.* C 12.

Irwin, O. C. (1960). Infant speech: Effect of systematic reading of stories. *Journal of Speech and Hearing Research, 3,* 187-190.

Isenberg, J., & Jacob, E. (1985). Playful literacy activities and learning: Preliminary observations. In J. Frost & S. Sunderlin (Eds.),*When children play* (pp. 17-22). Wheaton, MD: Association for Childhood Education International.

Iverson, B. K. Brownlee, T. and Walberg, H. J. (1981) Parent-teacher contact and student learning. *Journal of Educational Research, 74*, 6.

Iverson, B. K. and Walberg, H. J. (1982). Home environment and school learning: A quantitative synthesis. *Journal of Experimental Education, 50*, 144-151.

Jacob, E. (1984). Learning literacy through play: Puerto Rican kindergarten children. In H. Goelman, A. Oberg, & F. Smith (Eds.), *Awakening to literacy*, (pp. 73-83). Portsmouth, NH: Heinemann.

Jencks, C. (1972). *Inequality.* New York: Basic Books.

Jencks, C., & Bartlett, S. (1979). *Who gets ahead.* New York: Basic Books.

Jonsson, G. (1969). *Det sociala arvet.* Stockholm: Tiden.

Joyce, B., & Showers, B. (1980). Improving inservice training: The messages of research. *Educational Leadership, 37*, 379-382.

Juel, C. (1988). Learning to read and write: A longitudinal study of fifty-four children from first through fourth grade. *Journal of Educational Psychology, 80*, 437-447.

Juel, C. (1991) Beginning reading. In R. Barr, M. L. Kamil, P. Mosenthal, & P. D. Pearson (Eds.), *The handbook of reading research, Vol. 2*, (pp. 759-788). New York: Longman.

Kamberelis, G. (1992). Markers of cognitive change during the transition to conventional literacy. *Reading and Writing: An Interdisciplinary Journal, 4* (4), 365-402.

Kamberelis, G., & Sulzby, E. (1988). Transitional knowledge in emergent literacy. In J. E. Readance & R. S. Baldwin (Eds.), *Thirty-seventh yearbook of the National Reading Conference* (pp. 95-106). Chicago: National Reading Conference.

Karmiloff-Smith, A. (1985). Language and cognitive processes from a developmental perspective. *Language and Cognitive Processes, 1*, 61-85.

Katz, L. G. (1982). Contemporary perspectives on the roles of mothers and teachers. *Australian Journal of Early Childhood Education, 1*, 3-6.

Keats, E. J. (1966). *Jennie's hat.* New York: Harper & Row.

Keats, E. J. (1962). *The snowy day.* New York: Penguin Books.

King, S. (1989a). *Baby's birthday.* Crystal Lake, IL: Rigby Education.

King, S. (1989b). *Go back to sleep.* Crystal Lake, IL: Rigby Education.

Kintsch, W., & Greene, E. (1978). The role of culture-specific schemata in the comprehension and recall of stories. *Discourse Processes, 1*, 1-13.

Kuhn, T. (1970). *The structure of scientific revolutions* (2nd ed.). Chicago: University of Chicago Press.

Laboratory of Comparative Human Cognition (1983). Culture and cognitive development. In W. Kessen (Ed.), *Handbook of child psychology*, (Vol. 1, pp. 295-356). New York: Wiley.

Labov, W. (1987). *Sociolinguistics patterns*. Oxford: Blackwell.

Lakatos, I. (1970). Falsification and the methodology of scientific research programmes. In I. Lakatos & A. Musgrave (Eds.), *Criticism and the growth of knowledge* (pp. 91-196). Cambridge: Cambridge University Press.

Lancy, D. F. (1983). *Cross-cultural studies in cognition and mathematics*. New York: Academic Press.

Lancy, D. F. (1993). *Qualitative Research in Education*. White Plains, NY: Longman.

Lancy, D. F. (in press). Anthropological study of literacy and numeracy. Chapter In T. Husen & T. N. Postlethwaite et al. (Eds.). *International Encyclopedia of Education*. London: Pergamon.

Lancy, D. F. (in prep). *Playing on the mother ground: Cultural routines for children's development*. New York: Guilford.

Lancy, D. F., Draper, K. D., & Boyce, G. (1989). Parental influence on children's acquisition of reading. *Contemporary Issues in Reading, 4* (1), 83-93.

Lancy, D. F., & Nattiv, A. (1992). Parents as volunteer storybook readers/listeners. *Childhood Education 68*(4), 208-212.

Langer, J. A. (1986). *Children reading and writing: Structures and strategies*. Norwood, NJ: Ablex.

Langer, J. A. (1987). A sociocognitive perspective on literacy. In J. Langer (Ed.), *Language, literacy and culture: Issues of society and schooling*. Norwood, NJ: Ablex.

Langer, J. A. (1989). NAEP Report. Urbana, IL: National Council of Teachers of English.

Lareau, A. (1989). *Home advantage: Social class and parental intervention in elementary education*. New York: Falmer.

Lass, B. (1982). Portrait of my son as an early reader. *Reading Teacher, 36*, 20-28.

Lazar, I. (1984). Emerging models of infant development and their implications for infant care. Presented at the symposium *Models of fostering infant development in families and in society*, Berlin.

Lazar, I., & Darlington, R. B. (1982). Lasting effects of early education: A report from the consortium for longitudinal studies. With commentary by Craig T. Ramey. *Monographs of the Society for Research in Child Development, 47*, 2-3, 195.

Leverich, K. (1978). *The hungry fox and the foxy duck.* New York: Parents Magazine Press.

Levin, P. F. , Brenner, M. E., & McClellan, J. M. (1993). The social context of early literacy in Hawaiian homes. In Roberts, R. N. (Ed) *Coming home to preschool: The sociocultural context of early education* (pp. 195-219). Norwood, NJ: Ablex.

Lewin, K. (1935). *A dynamic theory of personality.* New York: McGraw-Hill.

Lightfoot, S. L. (1978). *Worlds apart: Relationships between families and schools.* New York: Basic Books.

Lindfors, J. W. (1987). *Children's language and learning* (2nd ed.). Englewood Cliffs, NJ: Prentice-Hall.

Little, L. J., & Greenfield, E. (1978). *I can do it by myself.* New York: Thomas Crowell.

Lubeck, S. (1984). Kinship and classrooms. *Sociology of Education. 57*, 219-232.

Lundberg, I., Frost, J., & Petersen, O. P. (1988). Effects of an extensive program for stimulating phonological awareness in preschool children. *Reading Research Quarterly, 23*, 264-284.

Luria, A. (1984). The development of writing in the child. In M. Martlew (Ed.), *The psychology of written language* (pp. 237-278). Chichester, England: John Wiley & Sons.

Lynch, A. (1992). The importance of parental involvement. In L. Kaplan (Ed.), *Education and the family.* Boston: Allyn and Bacon.

Lyons, C. A., Pinnell, G. S., & DeFord, D.E. (1993). *Partners in learning: Teachers and children in Reading Recovery.* New York: Teachers College Press.

MacDonald, K., & Parke, R. (1984). Bridging the gap: Parent-child play interaction and peer interactive competence. *Child Development, 55*, 1265-1277.

Maclean, M., Bryant, P., & Bradley, L. (1987). Rhymes, nursery rhymes and reading in early childhood. *Merrill-Palmer Quarterly, 33* (3), 255-281.

Mandler, J. M., & Johnson, N. S. (1977). Remembrance of things parsed: Story structure and recall. *Cognitive Psychology, 9*, 111-151.

Manning, M. M., and Manning, G.L. (1984). Early readers and non-readers from low socio-economic environments: What their parents report. *Reading Teacher, 4*, 32-4.

Many, J. E. (1988). Interactions About Text and Pictures: A Discourse Analysis. Paper presented at AERA, April in New Orleans.

Markman, E. M. (1979). Realizing that you don't understand: Elementary school children's awareness of inconsistencies. *Child Development, 50*, 643-655.

Martin, J. H. (1986). *Writing to read.* New York: Warner.

Martini, M., & Mistry, J. (1993). The relationship between talking at home and test-taking at school. In R. N. Roberts, (Ed.) *Coming home to preschool: The sociocultural context of early education* (pp. 167-194). Norwood, NJ: Ablex.

Mason, J. (1982, April). *A description of reading instruction: The tail is wagging the dog.* (Technical Report No. 35) Urbana, IL: Center for the Study of Reading.

Mason, J. & McCormick, C. (1983, March). *Intervention procedures for increasing pre-school children's interest in and knowledge about reading.* paper presented at annual meeting, American Educational Research Association , Montreal.

Mavrogenes, N. (1990). Helping parents help their children become literate. *Young children, 45* (4), 4-9.

McCormick, C. E. and Mason, J. M. (1986). Use of Little Books at Home: A minimal intervention strategy that fosters early reading" Urbana, IL: Center for the Study of Reading, Technical Report No. 388.

McCormick, C. E. and Mason, J.M.(1989). Fostering reading for Head Start children with little books. In J. B. Allen & J. Mason, (Eds.), *Risk-makers, Risk-takers, Risk-breakers.* Portsmouth, NH: Heinemann.

McCormick, C. E., Kerr, B. M., Mason, J. M., Gruendel, E. (1992). Early start: A literacy-rich pre-kindergarten program for children academically at-risk. *Journal of Early Intervention, 16* (1): 79-86.

McCormick, S. (1992). Disabled readers' erroneous responses to inferential comprehension questions: Description and analysis. *Reading Research Quarterly, 27*(1), 55-77.

McCully, E. A. (1984). *Picnic.* New York: Harper & Row.

McGonigel, M. J., & Garland, C. W. (1988). The individualized family service plan and the early intervention team: Team and family issues and recommended practices. *Infants and Young Children, 1* (1), 10-21.

McLoyd, V. (1980). Verbally expressed modes of transformation in the fantasy and play of black preschool children. *Child Development, 51,* 1133-39.

Melser, J. (1990). *Two little dogs.* Bothell, WA: The Wright Group.

Michaels, S. (1981). "Sharing time": Children's narrative styles and differential access to literacy. *Language in Society, 10,* 423-442.

Michaels, S., & Cazden, C. B. (1986). Teacher/child collaboration as oral preparation for literacy. In B. B. Schiefflin, & P. Gilmore (Eds.). *The acquisition of literacy: Ethnographic perspectives,* 132-154. Norwood, NJ: Ablex.

Mikulecky, L. (1990). National adult literacy and lifelong learning goals. *Phi Delta Kappan,* 72, 304-9.

Miller, P., Nemoianu, A., & DeJong, J. (1986). Early reading at home: It's practice and meaning in a working class community. In B. B. Schiefflin & P. Gilmore (Eds.), *The acquisition of literacy: Ethnographic perspectives* (pp.3-15). Norwood, NJ: Ablex.

Miller-Rodriguez, K. (1991). Home writing activities: The writing briefcase and the traveling suitcase.*Reading Teacher, 45*(2), 25-26.

Moffett, J., & Wagner, B. J. (1992). *Student-centered language arts and reading (4th Ed.).* Portsmouth, NH: Boynton/Cook.

Morais, J., Bertelson, P., Carey, L., & Alegria, J. (1986). Literacy training and speech segmentation. *Cognition, 24,* 45-64.

Morris, C., Harris, A. J., & Averbach, I. T. (1971). The reading performance of disadvantaged early and non-early readers from grades one through three. *Journal of Educational Research, 65,* 23-26.

Morris, D. (1981). Concept of word: A developmental phenomenon in the beginning reading and writing processes. *Language Arts, 58* (6), 659-668.

Morrow, L. M. (1985). Retelling stories: A strategy for improving young children's comprehension, concept of story structure, and oral language complexity. *Elementary School Journal, 85*(5), 647-661.

Morrow, L. M. (1986). Effects of structural guidance in story retelling on children's dictation of original stories. *Journal of Reading Behavior, 18*(2), 135-152.

Morrow, L. M. (1990). Preparing the classroom environment to promote literacy during play. *Early Childhood Research Quarterly, 5*, 537-554.

Morrow, L. M., O'Connor, E. M., & Smith, J. K. (1990). Effects of a story reading program on the literacy development of *at risk* kindergarten children. *Journal of Reading Behavior, 22*(3), 255-276.

Morrow, L. M., & Weinstein, C. S. (1986). Encouraging voluntary reading: The impact of a literature program on children's use of library corners. *Reading Research Quarterly, 21*, 330-346.

Neill, S. (1982). Experimental alternations in playroom layout and their effect on staff and child behavior. *Educational Psychology, 2*, 103-109.

Nell, V. (1988). *Lost in a book: The Psychology of Reading for Pleasure*. New Haven, CT: Yale University Press.

Neuman, S., & Roskos, K. (1990). Play, print and purpose: Enriching play environments for literacy development. *Reading Teacher, 44*, 214-221.

Neuman, S., & Roskos, K. (1992). Literacy objects as cultural tools: Effects on children's literacy behaviors in play. *Reading Research Quarterly, 27* (3), 202-225.

Newell, A., & Simon, H. A. (1972). *Human problem solving*. Englewood Cliffs, NJ: Prentice-Hall.

Nickse, R. S. (1989). An intergenerational adult literacy project: A family intervention/prevention model. *Journal of Reading, 31*, 634-642.

Nickse, R. S. (1990). *Family and intergenerational literacy programs: An Update of The noises of literacy*. Columbus, Ohio: ERIC Information Series no. 342.

Nickse, R. S. (1992). Family and intergenerational literacy practices at the Family Learning Center. In T. G. Sticht, M. J. Beeler, & B. A. McDonald, (Eds.), *The intergenerational transfer of cognitive skills* (Vol. 1,pp.122-135). Norwood, NJ: Ablex.

Nickse, R. S. & Quezada, S. (1993). *Community collaborations for family literacy.* New York: Neal-Schuman.

Nieto, S. (1992). *Affirming diversity: The sociopolitical context of multicultural education.* New York: Longman.

Ninio, A. (1980). Picture-book reading in mother-infant dyads belonging to two sub-groups in Israel. *Child Development, 51,* 587-590.

Ninio, A., & Bruner, J. S. (1978). The achievement and antecedents of labeling. *Journal of Child Language, 5,* 5-15.

Norman-Jackson, J. (1982). Family interactions, language development and primary reading achievement of black children in families of low income. *Child Development, 53,* 349-358.

Nuckolls, M. E. (1991). Expanding students' potential through family literact. *Educational Leadership, 49,* 45-46.

Oakes, J. (1985). *Keeping track: How schools structure inequality.* New Haven, CT: Yale University Press.

Office of Pre-Schools and Child Care, Victorian Government. (1992). *Annual report.* Melbourne: Government Printing Service.

Ogbu, J. U. (1988) Literacy and schooling in subordinate cultures: The case of Black Americans. In Kintgen, E. R., Kroll, B. M., & Rose, M. *Perspectives on Literacy.* Carbondale, IL: SIU Press,227-311.

Ogbu, J. U. (1993). Variability in minority performance. In E. Jacob and C. Jordan (Eds.), *Minority education: Anthropological perspectives.* Norwood, NJ: Ablex.

Olson, D. (1979). From utterance to text. *Harvard Educational Review, 47,* 257-281.

Olson, D. R. (1984). See! Jumping! Some oral language antecedents of literacy. In H. Goelman, A. A. Oberg, & F. Smith (eds.). *Awakening to Literacy.* (pp. 185-192) Portsmouth, NH: Heinemann.

Oyemade, U. J., Washington, V., & Gullo, D. F. (1989). The relationship between Head Start parent involvement and the economic and social self-sufficiency of Head Start families. *Journal of Negro Education, 58,* (1), 5-15.

Pappas, C. C., & Brown, E. (1987). Learning to read by reading: Learning to extend the functional potential of language. *Research in the Teaching of English, 21,* 160-184.

Park, R. J. (1992). Commentary on three programs for the intergenerational transfer of cognition. In T. G. Sticht, M. J. Beeler, &

B. A. McDonald (Eds.), *The intergenerational transfer of cognitive skills*, (Vol. 2, pp. 159-166). Norwood, NJ: Ablex.

Parke, R., MacDonald, K., Burks, M., Bhavnagri, N., Barth, J., & Beitel, A. (1989). Family and peer systems: In search of linkages. *Family systems of lifespan development* (pp. 65-92). Hillsdale, NJ: Erlbaum.

Parsler, R. M. (1979). Some social aspects of embourgeoisement in Australia. *Sociology, 5*, 95-112.

Pearson, P. D., & Fielding, L. (1991). Comprehension instruction. In R. Barr, M. L. Kamil, P. Mosenthal, & P. D. Pearson (Eds.), *The handbook of reading research* (Vol. 2, pp. 815-860). New York: Longman.

Pellegrini, A. D. (1983). The sociolinguistic context of the preschool. *Journal of Applied Developmental Psychology, 4*, 397-405.

Pellegrini, A. D. (1984). The social-cognitive ecology of preschool classrooms. *International Journal of Behavioral Development, 7*, 321-332.

Pellegrini, A. D. (1985). The relations between symbolic play and literate behavior. *Review of Educational Research, 55* (1), 107-121.

Pellegrini, A. D., & Galda, L. (1982). The effects of thematic-fantasy play training on the development of children's story comprehension. *American Educational Research Journal, 19*, 443-452.

Pellegrini, A. D. & Galda, L. (1991) Longitudinal relations among prescooler's symbolic play, metalinguistic verbs and emergent literacy. In Christie, J. F. (Ed.) *Play and Early Literacy Development.* (pp47-67) Albany: SUNY Press.

Pellegrini, A. D., Galda, L., Dresden, J., & Cox, S. (1991). A longitudinal study of the predictive relations among symbolic play, linguistic verbs, and early literacy. *Research in the Teaching of English, 25*, 219-235.

Pellegrini, A. D., Perlmutter, J., Galda, L., & Brody, G. (1990). Joint reading between black Head Start children and their mothers. *Child Development, 61*, 443-453.

Perfetti, C. A. (1985). *Reading ability.* New York: Oxford University Press.

Perry, M., & Kamberelis, G. (1993). *The function of gesturing during the transition to conventional literacy.* Unpublished manuscript.

Piaget, J. (1962). *Play, dreams and imitation in childhood*. NY: Norton.

Pinnell, G. S. (1991). Teachers' and students' learning. In D. E. DeFord, C. A. Lyons, & G. S. Pinnell (Eds.), *Bridges to literacy: Learning from reading recovery*. Portsmouth, NH: Heinemann.

Pinnell, G. S., Fried, M. D., & Estice, R. (1990). Reading Recovery: Learning how to make a difference. *Reading Teacher, 43*, 282-95.

Pinnell, G. S., Lyons, C. A., DeFord, D. E., Bryk, A., & Seltzer, M. (in press). Instructional models for the literacy education of high risk first graders. *Reading Research Quarterly*.

Plessas, G. P., & Oakes, G. (1964). Pre-reading experiences of selected early readers. *Reading Teacher, 17*, 241-245.

Potter, B. (1902). *The tale of Peter Rabbit*. New York: F. Warne & Co.

Potter, G. (1989). Parent participation in language arts program. *Language Arts, 66* (1), 29-43.

Proshansky, E., & Wolfe, M. (1975). The physical setting and open education. In T. G. David & B. D.Wright (Eds.), *Learning environments* (pp. 31-48). Chicago: University of Chicago Press.

Purcell-Gates, V. (1988). Lexical and syntactic knowledge of written narrative held by well-read-to kindergartners and second graders. *Research in the Teaching of English, 22*, 128-160.

Purcell-Gates, V. (1991a, May). *Emergent Literacy in a non literate home: Problems and issues*. Paper presented at the Conference on Family and School Support for Early Literacy, Toledo. OH.

Purcell-Gates, V. (1991b). Written language knowledge held by low SES inner city children entering kindergarten. In J. Zutell & S. McCormick (Eds.), *Cognitive and Social Perspectives for Literacy Research an Instruction* (pp. 95-105). Chicago: National Reading Conference.

Purcell-Gates, V. (in press). Roots of response. *Journal of Narrative and Life History*.

Purcell-Gates, V., & Dahl, K. (1991). Low-SES children's success and failure at early literacy learning in skills-based classrooms. *Journal of Reading Behavior: A Journal of Literacy, 23*, 1-34.

Putnam, L. (1983). *A descriptive study of two philosophically different approaches to reading readiness, as they were used in six inner city kindergartens*. (Grant No. 0-0202). Washington, DC: National Institute of Education. (ED 220 807)

Quintero, E., & Huerta-Macias, A. (1990). All in the family: Bi-
    lingualism and biliteracy. *Reading Teacher, 44*(4): 306-312.
Quintero, E., & Veralde, M. C. (1990). Intergenerational literacy: A
    developmental, bilingual approach. *Young Children, 45*(4): 10-
    15.
Ramey, C. T., & Campbell, F. A. (1991). Poverty, early childhood
    education and academic competence: The Abecedarian experi-
    ment. In: A. C. Huston (Ed.) *Children in poverty. Child develop-
    ment and public policy,* (pp. 190-221). Cambridge: Cambridge
    University Press.
Ranard, D. A. (1989). Family literacy: Trends and practices. *Perspec-
    tives on Refugee Resettlement,* 7, 2-7.
Read, C. (1986). *Children's creative spelling.* London: Routledge &
    Kegan Paul.
Reading is Fundamental. (1989). *Running Start handbook.*
    Washington, DC: RIF, Inc.
Reder, S., & Green, K. R. (1983). Contrasting patterns of literacy in
    an Alaskan fishing village. *International Journal of the Sociology
    of Language, 42,* 9-39.
Réger, Z. (1990). Mother's speech in different social groups in
    Hungary. In G. Conti-Ramsden, & C. E. Snow (Eds.) *Children's
    Language* (Vol. 7 pp. 197-222), Greenwich, CT: JAI.
Reich, R. B. (1991). *The work of nations: Preparing ourselves for
    21st centurycapitalism.* New York: New York Times Books.
Resnick, D. P., & Resnick, L. B. (1977). The nature of literacy: An
    historical explanation. *Harvard Education Review, 47*(3), 370-
    85.
Roberts, R. N., & Barnes, M. L. (1993). Quality and quantity of
    maternal-child interaction. In R. N. Roberts, (Ed.), *Coming home
    to preschool: The sociocultural context of early education* (pp.
    145-166). Norwood, NJ: Ablex.
Robinson, S. S. & Naumann, J. (1993). *Effects of literacy-based
    parent training on impoverished children.* Paper presented at the
    A.E.R.A. 1993 Annual Meeting, Atlanta.
Robson, C. & Whiteley,G.(1989). Sharing stories: Parents' involvement
    in reading with inner-city nursery children. *Reading, 23,* 1.
Rogoff, B. (1990). *Apprenticeship in thinking: Cognitive develop-
    ment in social context.* New York: Oxford University Press.
Rogoff, B. (Ed.) (1991, Winter). U.S. children and their families.
    SRCD Newsletter, pp. 1-3.

Rosenthal, B. L. (1973). An ecological study of free play in the nursery school. (Doctoral dissertation, Wayne State University, Detroit.) *Dissertation Abstracts International, 34*, 4004A.

Roskos, K. (1987). *The nature of literate behavior in the pretend play episodes of four and five year old children.* Unpublished doctoral disseration, Kent State University, Kent, OH.

Roskos, K., & Neuman, S. B. (1993). A typology of young children's literacy activities in play. *Play Theory and Research,1*(1), 17-25.

Rumelhart, D. E. (1980). Schemata: The building blocks of cognition. In R. J. Spiro, B. C. Bruce, & W. F. Brewer (Eds.), *Theoretical issues in reading comprehension* (pp. 35-58). Hillsdale, NJ: Erlbaum.

Sameroff, A. J., & Fiese, B. (1990). Transactional regulation in early intervention. In S. J. Meisels, & J. P. Shonkoff (Eds.), *Handbook of early childhood intervention.* (pp 119-149). New York: Cambridge University Press.

Sams, J. (1992, November). Beginning babies with books. Paper presented at annual conference, American Society of Directors of Volunteer Programs, American Hospital Association, Boston.

Sarason, S. B. (1983). *Schooling in America: Scapegoat and salvation.* New York: Free Press.

Sartre, J. P. (1964). *The words* (B. Frechtman, Trans.). Greenwich, CN: Fawcett.

SCB. (1992). Statistical Yearbook of Sweden Stockholm: Official Statistics of Sweden, Volume 79.

Schmandt-Besserat, D. (1978). The earliest precursors of writing. *Scientific American, 238*, 38-47.

Schroeder, H., Driver, M., & Streufert, S. (1967). *Human information processing.* New York: Holt, Rinehart & Winston.

Schweinhart, L. J. & Weikart, D. P. (1983). The effects of the Perry pre-school program on youths through age 15—a summary. In Consortium of Longitudinal Studies, *As the twig is bent... Lasting effects of pre-school programs*, (pp. 71-101). Hillsdale, NJ: Erlbaum.

Schweinhart, L. J., Weikart, D. P., & Larner, M. B. (1986). Consequences of three pre-school curriculum models through age 15. *Early Childhood Research Quarterly, 1*, 15-45.

Scollon, R., & Scollon, S. B. K. (1981). *Narrative, literacy and Race in interethnic communication.* Norwood, NJ: Ablex.

Scott-Jones, D. (1984). Family influences on cognitive development and school achievement. *Review of Research in Education, 11.*

Scott-Jones, D. (1987). Mother-as-teacher in the families of high- and low-achieving, low income black first graders. *Journal of Negro Education, 56,* 21-34.

Scott-Jones, D. (1992). Family and community interactions affecting the development of cognitive skills in children. In T. G. Sticht, M. J. Beeler, and B. A. McDonald (Eds.). *The intergenerational transfer of cognitive skills* (Vol. 1, pp. 84-108). Norwood, NJ: Ablex.

Scribner, S., & Cole, M. (1981). *The psychology of literacy.* Cambridge, MA: Harvard University Press.

Seaman, D., Popp, B., & Darling, S. (1991). *Follow-up study of the impact of the Kenan Trust Model for family literacy.* Louisville, Kentucky: National Center for Family Literacy.

Seidenberg, M. S., & McClelland, J. L. (1989). A distributed, developmental model of word recognition and naming. *Psychological Review, 96,* 523-568.

Shefataya, L. (1990). Socioeconomic status and ethnic differences in sociodramatic play. In E. Klugman & S. Smilansky (Eds.), *Childrens' Play and Learning* (pp. 137-155). New York: Teacher's College Press.

Short, E. J., & Ryan, E. B. (1984). Metacognitive differences between skilled and less skilled readers: Remediating deficits through story grammar and attribution training. *Journal of Educational Psychology, 76*(2), 225-35.

Siegler, R. S. (1986). *Children's thinking.* Englewood Cliffs, NJ: Prentice-Hall.

Siegler, R. S. (1989). Mechanisms of cognitive development. *Annual Review of Psychology, 40,* 353-79.

Siegler, R. S., & Crowley, K. (1991). The microgenetic method: A direct means for studying cognitive development. *American Psychologist, 46*(6), 606-620.

Simmons, H. D., & Murphy, S. (1986). Spoken language strategies and reading acquisition. In J. Cook-Gumperz (Ed.), *The social construction of literacy* (pp. 185-206). Cambridge: Cambridge University Press.

Slade, A. (1987). A longitudinal study of maternal invovlement and symbolic play during the toddler period. *Child Development, 58,* 367-375.

Slaughter-Defoe, D. T. (1992). Forward to the past: Black and white American families, literacy and policy lag. In T. G. Sticht, M. J. Beeler & B.A. McDonald, (Eds.). *The intergenerational transfer of cognitive skills* (Vol. 2, pp. 69-83). Norwood, NJ: Ablex.

Sleeter, C. E., & Grant, C. A. (1987). An analysis of multicultural education in the United States. *Harvard Educational Review, 57,* 421-44.

Smilansky, S. (1968). *The Effect of sociodramatic play on disadvantaged pre-school children.* New York: Wiley.

Smith, F. (1988). *Understanding reading* (4th ed.). Hillsdale, NJ: Erlbaum.

Smith-Burke, M. (1989). Political and economic dimensions of literacy: Challenges for the 1990s. In S. McCormick and J. Zutell (Eds.), *Cognitive and social perspectives for literacy research and instruction.* The thirty-eighth yearbook of the National Reading Conference. Chicago: The National Reading Conference.

Snow, C. E. (1977). The development of conversation between mothers and babies. *Journal of Child Language, 4,* 1-22.

Snow, C. E. (1983) Literacy and language. *Harvard Educational Review, 53,* 165-189.

Snow, C. E. (1990). The development of definitional skill. *Journal of Child Language, 17,* 697-710.

Snow, C. E., Barnes, W. S., Chandler, J., Goodman, I. F., & Hemphill, L. (1991). *Unfulfilled expectations: Home and school influences on literacy.* Cambridge, MA: Harvard University Press.

Snow, C. E., Cancino, H., De Temple, B. & Schley, S. (1991). Giving formal definitions: A linguistic or metalinguistic skill? In E. Bialystok (Ed.), *Language processing and language awareness by bilingual children.* New York: Cambridge University Press.

Snow, C. E., Cancino, H., Gonzalez, P., & Shriberg, E. (1989). Giving formal definitions: An oral language correlate of school literacy. In D. Bloome (Ed.), *Classrooms and literacy* (pp. 233-249). Norwood, NJ: Ablex.

Snow, C. E., & Goldfield, B. A. (1982). Building stories: The emergence of information structures from conversation. In D. Tannen (Ed.), *Analyzing discourse: Text and talk* (pp. 127-141). Washington, DC: Georgetown University Press.

Snow, C. E., & Goldfield, B. A. (1983). Turn the page please: Situation-specific language acquisition. *Journal of Child Language, 10*, 551-569.

Snow, C. E., & Ninio, A. (1986). The contracts of literacy: What children learn from learning to read books. In W. H. Teale & E. Sulzby (Eds.), *Emergent literacy: writing and reading* (116-138). Norwood, Ablex.

Söderbergh, R. (1986). Acquisition of spoken an written language in early childhood. In: I. Kurcz, G. W. Shugar, & J. H. Danks (Eds.), *Knowledge and language*. Amsterdam: North-Holland.

Söderbergh, R. (1990, July). *Literacy from infancy: Informal reading education in a changing society*. Paper presented at the 13th World Congress of IRA, Stockholm.

SoS (1991). The National Swedish Social Welfare Board Barnomsorgen i siffror 1990. SoS-rapport 1991:28. Stockholm: Socialstyrelsen.

Spencer, B. R., & Afflerbach, P. P. (1988). Young children's explanations of spaces between words in written text. In J. E. Readance & R. S. Baldwin (Eds.), *Thirty-seventh yearbook of the National Reading Conference* (pp. 69-76). Chicago: National Reading Conference.

St. Pierre, R., Swartz, J., Nickse, R., & Gamse, B. (1991). *National Even Start evaluation: Overview*. Cambridge, MA: Abt Associates.

Stanovich, K. E. (1991). Word recognition: Changing perspectives. In P. D. Pearson, R. Barr, M. L. Kamil, & P. Mosenthal (Eds.), *Handbook of reading research* (Vol. 2, pp. 418-452). New York: Longman.

Stedman, L., & Kaestle, C. F. (1987). Literacy and reading performance in the U.S. from 1880 to the present. *Reading Research Quarterly, 22*(1): 8-46.

Stein, N., & Glenn, C. (1979). An analysis of story comprehension in elementary school children. In R. Freedle (Ed.), *New directions in discourse processes* (Vol. 2, pp. 53-120). Norwood, NJ: Ablex.

Sternberg, R. J. (1984). The mechanisms of cognitive development: A componential approach. In R. J. Sternberg (Ed.), *Mechanisms of cognitive development* (pp. 163-186). New York: Freeman.

Sticht, T. G. (1988-89). Adult literacy education. *Review of Research in Education, 13*, 59-96.

Stock, B. (1983). *The implications of literacy.* Princeton, NJ: Princeton University Press.

Strickland, D., & Cullinan, B. (1990). Afterword. in M. J. Adams (Ed.),*Beginning to Read* (pp. 425-434). Cambridge, MA: MIT Press.

Sullivan, H. & La Beaune, C. (1971). Parents: Summer reading teachers. *Elementary School Journal, 71*(5), 279-285.

Sulzby, E. (1981). *Kindergartners deal with word boundaries.* Paper presented at the 31st annual meeting of the National Reading Conference, Dallas. (ED216 333)

Sulzby, E. (1985). Children's emergent reading of favorite storybooks: A developmental study. *Reading Research Quarterly, 20,* 458-481.

Sulzby, E. (1989). Assessment of writing and of children's language while writing. In L. Morrow & J. Smith (Eds.), *The role of assessment in early literacy instruction* (pp. 83-109). Englewood Cliffs, NJ: Prentice-Hall.

Sulzby, E. (1990). *Writing and reading instruction and assessment for young children: Issues and implications.* Paper commissioned by the Forum on the Future of Children and Families of the National Academy of Sciences and the National Association of State Boards of Education.

Sulzby, E., Barnhart, J., & Hieshima, J. (1989). Forms of writing and rereading from writing: A preliminary report. In J. Mason (Ed.), *Reading and writing connections* (pp. 31-63). Norwood, NJ: Ablex.

Sulzby, E. & Teale, W. (1985). Writing Development in early childhood. *Educational Horizons, 64* 8-12.

Sulzby, E. & Teale, W. (1991). Emergent literacy. In R. Barr, M.L. Kamil, P. Mosenthal, & P.D. Pearson (Eds.), *Handbook of reading research* (Vol. 2, pp. 727-758) White Plains, NY: Longman.

Sundelin Wahlsten, V. (1991). *Development and survival. A study of children at risk living in adverse psychosocial milieu.* Stockholm: Stockholm University.

Sutton-Smith, B. (1986). Play interactions and developmental processes. In A. Gottfried & C. Brown (Eds.), *Play Interactions.* Proceedings of the Eleventh Johnson & Johnson Pediatric Round Table (pp. 313-321). Lexington, MA: Lexington Books.

Svensson, A-K. (1989). *Book Teddy—evaluation of a language stimulation project. Pedagogisk-psykologiska problem,* (Malmö: Lärarhögskolan), Nr 526.

Svensson, A-K. (1993). *Early language stimulation for children.* Stockholm: Almqvist & Wiksell.

Swift, M. (1970). Training poverty mothers in communication skills. *Reading Teacher, 23,* (4), 358-367.

Swinson, J. (1985). A parental involvement program in a nursery school. *Educational Psychology in Practice, 1,* (1), 19-22.

Sylva, K., Roy, C., & Painter, M. (1980). *Childwatching at play group and nursery school.* London: Grant McIntire.

Taylor, D. (1983). *Family literacy.* Portsmouth, NH: Heinemann.

Taylor, D., & Dorsey-Gaines, C. (1988). *Growing up literate: Learning from inner-city families.* Portsmouth, NH: Heinemann.

Teale, W. H. (1978). Positive learning environments for learning to read: What studies of early readers tell us. *Language Arts, 55,* 922-932.

Teale, W. H. (1981). Parents reading to their children: What we know and need to know. *Language Arts, 59,* 555-570.

Teale, W. H. (1984a). Reading to young children: Its significance for literacy development. In H. Goelman, A. A. Oberg, & F. Smith (Eds.), *Awakening to Literacy* (pp. 110-21). Portsmouth, NH: Heinemann.

Teale, W. H. (1984b). *Learning to comprehend written language.* Paper presented at the 74th annual convention, NCTE, Detroit. (ED 255 871)

Teale, W. H. (1986). Home background and young children's literary development. In W. H. Teale & E. Sulzby (Eds.), *Emergent literacy: Writing and reading* (pp. 173-206). Norwood, NJ: Ablex.

Teale, W. H. (1987, April). Factors related to reading performance. Emergent literacy: Reading and writing development in early childhood. Paper presented at the sixth annual University of Wisconsin Reading Symposium on Factors Related to Reading Performance, University of Wisconsin—Milwaukee.

Teale, W. H., Estrada, E., & Anderson, A. B. (1981). *How preschoolers interact with written communication.* Unpublished manuscript, University of California, Laboratory of Comparative Human Cognition, San Diego.

Teale, W. H. & Sulzby, E. (1986). *Emergent Literacy: Writing and Reading.* Norwood, NJ: Ablex.

Teale, W. H. & Sulzby, E. (1987). Literacy acquisition in early childhood: The roles of access and accomodation in storybook reading. In D. A. Wagner (Ed.), *The future of literacy in a changing world.* (pp. 111-130) Oxford: Pergamon.

Tharp, R. G., & Gallimore, R. (1988). *Rousing minds to life: Teaching. learning, and schooling in social context.* New York: Cambridge University Press.

Thistlethwaite, L. (1983). Teaching reading to the ABE student who cannot read. *Lifelong Learning, 1,* 5-7, 28.

Thorndyke, P.W. (1977). Cognitive structures in comprehension and memory of narrative discourse. *Cognitive Psychology, 9,* 77-110.

Tizard, B., Blatchford, P., Burke, J., Farquhar, C. & Plewis, I. (1988). *Young children at school in the inner city,* London: Lawrence Earlbaum.

Tizard, B. & Hughes, M. (1984). *Young children learning,* London: Fontana.

Tizard, J., Schofield, W.N., Hewison, J. (1982). Collaboration between teachers and parents in assisting children's reading. *Educational Psychology, 52,* 1-15.

Toomey, D. M. (1983). Parent participation and involvement in schooling: The La Trobe Parents and Reading Project. Paper presented at the 1983 annual conference of the Sociological Association of Australia and New Zealand, Brisbane.

Toomey, D. M. (1986). Involving parents in their children's reading. *Collected Original Research in Education, 10* (2), 1-69.

Toomey, D. M. (1988). Linking class and gender inequality: The family and schooling in Australia. Paper presented at the 2nd research conference of the Australian Institute of Family Studies. Melbourne.

Toomey, D. M. (1989a). Linking class and gender inequality: The family and schooling. *British Journal of Sociology of Education, 10* (4), 389-402.

Toomey, D. M. (1989b). How home-school relations policies can increase educational inequality: A three-year follow-up. *Australian Journal of Education, 33* (3), 284-298.

Toomey, D. M. (1993a) Parents hearing their children read, A review: Rethinking the lessons of the Haringey project. *Educational Research, 35* (3),

Toomey, D. M. (1993b). Effects of a home visit based book-lending program for preschool children of disadvantaged families. Unpublished paper.

Toomey, D.M., Keck, K., & Atkinson, P. (1987). Early literacy—An intervention program in a disadvantaged locality. *Australian Journal of Early Childhood, 12*, (4), 32-40.

Toomey, D. M. & Sloane, J. A. (1991). Developing emergent literacy for children of low socio-economic status: A preschool-based progam. *Australian Journal of Reading, 14* (1), 40-49.

Toomey, D. M. & Sloane, J. A. (1993). The interaction between a pre-school based booklending program for disadvantaged families and children's family environments. Unpublished paper.

Toomey, D. M. & Sloane, J. A. (in press). Reaching out to help low income parents foster their young children's literacy competencies. In D. Dickinson (Ed.), *Bridges for literacy*. Oxford: Basil Blackwell.

Topping, K. & Wolfendale, S. (Eds.). (1985). *Parents and their children's reading*. Beckenham, Kent: Croom Helm.

Torrance, N., & Olson, D. R. (1985). Oral and literate competencies in the early school years. In D. R. Olson, N. Torrance, & A. Hildyard (Eds.), *Literacy and language learning* (pp. 256-284). New York: Cambridge University Press.

Torrey, J. (1969). Learning to read without a teacher: A case study. *Elementary English, 46*, 550-556, 658.

Varenne, H., & McDermott, R. P. (1986). "Why" Sheila can read: Structure and Determinancy in the Reproduction of Familial Literacy. In B. B. Schiefflin, & P. Gilmore (Eds.), *The acquisition of literacy: Ethnographic perspectives* (pp. 188-210). Norwood, NJ: Ablex.

Various (1991). *Fortune*. (12), 121.

Villaume, S. K. (1988). Creating context within text. *Research in the Teaching of English, 22* (2), 161-182.

Vukelich, C. (1989). *Materials and modeling: Promoting literacy during play*. Paper presented at the National Reading Conference, Austin,TX.

Vygotsky, L. S. (1962). *Thought and language*. Cambridge, MA: MIT Press.

Vygotsky, L. S. (1978). *Mind in society*. Cambridge, MA: Harvard University Press.

Vygotsky, L. S. (1981). *Psykologi och dialektik*. Hydén, L. C. (Red.) Stockholm: Nordstedt.

Wachs, T. D., Uzgiris, I. C., & Hunt, J. M. (1971). Cognitive development in infants of different age levels and for different environmental backgrounds: An exploratory investigation. *Merrill-Palmer Quarterly, 17,* 283-318.

Wagner, D. A., Messick, B. M., & Spratt, J. (1986). Studying literacy in Morocco. In B. B. Schiefflin & P. Gilmore (Eds.). *The acquisition of literacy: Ethnographic perspectives* (pp. 233-260). Norwood, NJ:Ablex.

Walker, G. H., & Kuerbitz, I. E. (1979). Reading to preschoolers as an aid to successful beginning reading. *Reading Improvement, 16,* 149-154.

Weinstein, C. S. (1979). The physical environment of the school: A review of the research. *Review of Educational Research, 49,* 577-610.

Weinstein, G. (1984). Literacy and second language acquisition: Issues and perspective. *TESOL Quarterly, 18,* 471-484.

Wells, G. (1981). Some antecedents of early educational attainment. *British Journal of the Sociology of Education, 2,* 2, 181-200.

Wells, G. (1985a). *Language, learning and education*. Philadelphia: NFER-Nelson.

Wells, G. (1985b). Preschool literacy-related activities and success in school. In D. R. Olson & N. Torrance (Eds.), *Literacy, language and learning* (pp. 229-255). Cambridge: Cambridge University Press .

Wells, G. (1986). Learning through interaction: The study of language development. Cambridge: Cambridge University Press.

Wendorf, J., & Heland, V. (1990). *Running Start: Preliminary report*. Washington, DC: RIF.

Wendorf, J., & St. Clair, W. (1990). *Running Start: Results of the first year*. Washington, DC: RIF.

Wertsch, J. V. (1985a). *Culture, communication and cognition*. New York: Cambridge University Press.

Wertsch, J. V. (1985b). *Vygotsky and the social formation of mind*. Cambridge, MA: Harvard University Press.

Whaley, J. F. (1981). Readers' expectations for story structures. *Reading Research Quarterly, 17*(1), 90-114.

Whaley, J. F. (1982, March). *Improving children's reading comprehension through instruction in schematic aspects of narratives.*

Paper presented at the annual meeting of the American Educational Research Association, New York.

White, K. R. (1982). The relation between socio-economic status and academic achievement. *Psychological Bulletin, 91*(3): 461-81.

Whitehurst, G., Falko, F., Lonigan, C., Fischel, J., DeBaryshe, B., Valdez-Menchaca, M., & Caulfield, M. (1988). Accelerating language development through picture book reading. *Developmental Psychology, 24,* 552-559.

Williams, A. (1990, April). *Variations in home reading contexts.* Paper presented at the 15th annual conference of the Australian Reading Association, Canberra.

Williams, R., & Lewis, S. L. (1988). *Show and tell: Structured oral language activities.* Cypress, CA: Creative Teaching Press.

Williams, T., Long, M., Carpenter, P., & Hayden, M. (1993). *Higher education: Participation and access in the 1980's.* Hawthorn, Melbourne: Australian Council for Educational Research.

Wilson, M. M. (1979). The processing strategies of average and below average readers answering factual and inferential questions on three equivalent passages. *Journal of Reading Behavior, 11,* 235-45.

Wilson, R. A. (1992). *Toledo Even Start year three report.* Toledo Public Schools, Toledo.

Wirth, A. G. (1992). *Education and work for the year 2000: Choices we face.* San Francisco: Jossey-Bass.

Wolf, D., (1988). Beyond A,B,C: A broader and deeper view of literacy. In A. D. Pellegrini (Ed.), *Psychological bases for early education* (pp. 122-151). Chichester, England: John Wiley & Son.

Wood, D., Bruner, J., & Ross, G. (1976. The role of tutoring in problem solving. *Journal of Child Psychology and Psychiatry, 17*(2), 89-100.

Yopp, H. K. (1988). The validity and reliability of phonemic awareness tests. *Reading Research Quarterly, 23,* 159-177.

Zimiles, H., & Kuhns, M. (1976). *A developmental study of the retention of narrative material.* New York: Bank Street College of Education. (ED 160 978)

Index

About the Contributors

Jackie Aldridge is an Instructor in the Toledo Public Schools Family Life Department. She teaches basic, life, and computer skills in adult classes. Her background includes teaching high school English and tutoring international students. Jacqueline has worked with various at-risk groups.

Diane E. Beals is an Assistant Professor of Education at Washington University. Her research interests include the development of discourse and language and literacy development. She teaches courses in development and in methods of teaching reading. She has taught special education for eight years in both public and private schools. She holds a B.A. degree in general science and elementary education from Seattle Pacific College, an M.Ed. degree in developmental reading from the University of Washington, and an Ed.D. degree in human development and psychology from Harvard University.

Christi Bergin is a part-time faculty member in the Department of Educational Psychology, Research, and Social Foundations at the University of Toledo. She was a coordinator of the UT Literacy Corps. Dr. Bergin received her Ph.D. in child development and early education from Stanford University. Her research interests center on family influences on child development.

Eileen M. Carr is an Associate Professor of Reading and Language Arts at the University of Toledo. She conducts research on literacy development and comprehension instruction and is extensively involved in working with school districts to restructure their language arts programs.

Carolyn F. Chryst recently completed a Master's degree in the Department of Educational Psychology, Research, and Social Foundations at the University of Toledo where she coordinated the Hilltop Emergent Literacy Program, Ms. Chryst's professional studies focus on constructivist teaching and learning, culturally responsive pedagogy, and teacher education.

David K. Dickinson received his B.A. from Oberlin College in 1971 and then taught elementary school in the Philadelphia public schools. While teaching he completed a master's degree in elementary education at Temple University. After teaching for five years he entered the doctoral program at Harvard's Graduate School of Education. His central research interest is the language and literacy development of children from low-income homes. He is particularly interested in the nature of support for language and literacy development provided in early childhood classrooms and in the contributions of parents to children's development.

Kelly D. Draper worked as an elementary reading specialist for nine years and taught undergraduate and graduate level language arts and literacy courses for teachers at Arizona State University. Currently she coordinates preschool and primary grade at-risk programs at Machan School in Phoenix and serves as a consultant to schools in the Phoenix area in the area of whole language and reading instruction. She has co-authored numerous articles in journals such as *Anthropology and Education Quarterly*.

Patricia A. Edwards is an Associate Professor of Language and Literacy and a Senior Researcher at the Center for Teaching & Learning at Michigan State University. She is also the author of two nationally acclaimed family literacy programs—*Parents as Partners in Reading: A Family Literacy Training Program* and *Talking Your Way to Literacy: A Program to Help Nonreading Parents Prepare Their Children for Reading*. Her research includes topics in family/intergenerational literacy and emergent literacy, with a special focus on semiliterate and illiterate parents and children. Her recent research agenda involves collaborating with teachers in a Professional

Development School and helping them to create a structure at their specific grade level for parents to be involved in the literacy support of their children. Recent publications include a book chapter "Fostering Early Literacy Through Parent Coaching" in E. Hiebert, *Literacy for Diverse Society: Perspectives, Programs and Policies,* a 1991 Teachers College Press publication, and an article "Involving Parents in Building Reading Instruction for African-American Children" in the Autumn 1992 issue of *Theory into Practice.*

Kathleen L. Fear is an Assistant Professor in the Department of Education at Albion College. She is program coordinator for the elementary education program and teaches literacy methods courses. She received her doctorate in teacher education at Michigan State University, where she worked on the Cognitive Strategies in Writing project and the Michigan Partnership for New Education. She continues to conduct research in Professional Development School settings and is interested in examining literacy instruction and collaborates with teachers.

Lee Galda is a Professor in the Department of Language Education at the University of Georgia, where she teaches courses on children's literature. Her research interests include response to literature, play, and narrative.

Deborah L. Harris is a doctoral candidate in the Department of Teacher Education at Michigan State University. Her doctoral dissertation, *Composing a Life as a Teacher: Stories from a Beginning Teachers' Literacy Sharing Group,* examines how a group of novice teachers construct their personal and professional identities. She has been a research assistant, and has taught literacy courses at Michigan State University, at the University of Michigan-Flint, and at the University of Hawaii. Prior to beginning her doctoral studies, Deborah was a demonstration teacher at the Kamehameha Schools in Honolulu, Hawaii.

Lynne M. Hudson is a Professor and Chairperson of Educational Psychology, Research, and Social Foundations at the University of Toledo. She is also the director of the Hilltop Emergent Literacy Program. Dr. Hudson received her Ph.D. from Wayne State University and completed a NIMH postdoctoral fellowship at Harvard University.

She co-authored *Child Development: An Introduction* with Robert Biehler and has written numerous articles in the areas of social cognitive development, culturally responsive pedagogy, and teacher preparation, with an emphasis on urban education.

George Kamberelis is an Assistant Professor in the Department of Speech Communication, the Department of Curriculum and Instruction, and the Center for Writing Studies at University of Illinois at Urbana-Champaign. He has conducted research on cognitive reorganization during the transition to conventional literacy, young children's understanding and use of the conventions of oral and written genres, and the relationships among reading, writing, and the construction of self.

Patricia R. Kelly is an Associate Professor in the Department of Elementary/Bilingual Education at California State University, San Bernardino. She has conducted research and published articles in the areas of reading and language arts, including reader response, promising classroom practices, and Reading Recovery. She received her doctorate in education with an emphasis in reading and language development from the Claremont Graduate School/San Diego State University Joint Doctoral Program. She is currently a trainer of teacher leaders at the CSUSB Reading Recovery center.

Adria F. Klein is a Professor of Reading Education at California State University, San Bernardino. She has written several books and published articles on a variety of topics including emergent literacy, reader's theater, integrated language arts, staff development, and technology. She is the editor of the California Reading Association's quarterly journal, *The California Reader,* and Vice-President-Elect of CRA. She has taught all levels from kindergarten through graduate school. Her doctorate is in reading and English as a Second Language from the University of New Mexico. She is a Reading Recovery trainer of teacher leaders at the CSUSB Reading Recovery center.

David F. Lancy is a Professor of Anthropology in the Department of Sociology, Social Work, and Anthropology at Utah State University. His primary research focus has been on the cultural context of children's development. He has done fieldwork among the Kpelle in

Liberia, several societies in Papua New Guinea, and on family/school literacy practices in the United States. He authored *Cross-cultural Studies in Cognition and Mathematics* in 1983 and is presently working on another book, *Playing on the Mother Ground: Cultural Routines for Children's Development.*

Susan Neuman is an Associate Professor in the Department of Curriculum, Instruction and Technology in Education at Temple University. She received her doctorate at the University of the Pacific, Stockton, California. Dr. Neuman's research focuses on literacy and technology, and early literacy development. Her most recent book, coauthored with Kathy Roskos, is *Language and Literacy Learning in the Early Years: An Integrated Approach.* In addition, she has written many articles in journals, including *American Education Research Journal, Reading Research Quarterly* and *Journal of Educational Research.*

Jeanne R. Paratore is an Associate Professor of Education at Boston University. She directs the Intergenerational Literacy Project, a university/school partnership with the Chelsea Public Schools. In addition to family literacy, current research interests include implementation of heterogeneous grouping plans for literacy instruction in elementary classrooms and portfolio assessment.

A. D. Pellegrini is a Professor in the Department of Elementary Education and a Research Fellow of the Institute for Behavioral Research at the University of Georgia. He teaches courses on play, early education, and research methods. His research interest is in children's play and ethological methods.

Michelle Perry is an Assistant Professor in the Departments of Educational Psychology and Speech Communication at the University of Illinois at Urbana-Champaign. Her major research interests include the acquisition of new knowledge—especially during moments of transition—and various cognitive, social, and cultural factors that influence the acquisition of new knowledge.

Gay Su Pinnell is Professor of Theory and Practice at Ohio State University, where she teaches courses on language development, literacy, and children's literature. She was formerly a primary school teacher and now teaches children daily as part of the Reading Recovery program. Her books include *Teaching Reading Comprehension, Discovering Language with Children, and Teachers and Research: Language Learning in the Classroom*. She has also authored articles on language and literacy learning. With colleagues at O.S.U. she has been responsible for implementing Reading Reco-very and conducting a research program, which resulted in the recent books, *Bridges to Literacy: Learning from Reading Recovery and Partners in Learning: Teachers and Children in Reading Recovery*. She is principal investigator for the Early Literacy Research Project, sponsored by the John D. and Catherine T. MacArthur Foundation.

Victoria Purcell-Gates is an Associate Professor of Language and Literacy at the Harvard Graduate School of Education. She also directs the Harvard Literacy Lab, where graduate student tutors work with children experiencing problems with reading and writing. Dr. Purcell-Gates received her Ph.D. in language and literacy from the University of California/Berkeley in 1986 where she began her research program focusing on emergent literacy issues. She is particularly interested in the knowledge about written language brought by young children to beginning formal literacy instruction and the ways in which that knowledge influences the children's interpretations of instruction and their success at school. Before entry into the world of research and academia, Dr. Purcell-Gates taught learning-disabled children and children assigned to remedial reading classes.

Lynne Putnam is an Associate Professor of Reading at George Washington University. She works with inner-city teachers in the development and implementation of whole language curricula that feature dramatization as a primary form of response to fiction and nonfiction. She is also interested in the impact of various early literacy curricula on the child's acquisition of a story schema and his/her vocabulary growth.

Dianna Reamsnyder is a master's student in the Department of Educational Psychology, Research, and Social Foundations, University of Toledo. She teaches kindergartners in the Toledo public schools and at the Hilltop Emergent Literacy Program. Her interests include developmentally appropriate practice, culturally responsive pedagogy, and teacher education.

Kathy Roskos is an Associate Professor and Chair of the Department of Education at John Carroll University, where she also teaches undergraduate and graduate courses in language arts and reading. She received her Ph.D. from Kent State University, specializing in early literacy development and reading instruction. Her research interests include young children's literacy development, relationships between literacy and play, and reading pedagogy. She coauthored *Language and Literacy Learning in the Early Years* with Susan Neuman and is currently an associate editor of *The Reading Teacher*.

Judith Sloane is an experienced primary school teacher and researcher. Judith has taught in primary and secondary schools, universities and in adult education. She has for a number of years worked as a researcher and has provided professional development services for teachers through Resourse Education Consultants, her own business.

Ann-Katrin Svensson had been a preschool teacher for seven years before earning her doctorate in 1993 from the University of Lund. Her specialty is the role of parent-child speech in children's language development. She is a lecturer in the teacher preparation program at the University of Jönköping.

Susan D. Talley holds a bachelor's degree in recreation administration and has worked in this field for a number of years. Presently she is pursuing a master's degree in Family and Human Development while working on research in the area of emergent literacy.

Derek Toomey is Senior Lecturer in Education, Centre for the Study of Community and Education, La Trobe University, Australia. A specialist in the study of families, communities, and schooling, Dr. Toomey has, for some twelve years, been researching parental involvement in intergenerational programs with families of parents weak in literacy skills. He has been a school teacher and has worked in a number of universities in Australia, the United Kingdom, and the United States.

Ruth A. Wilson is an Assistant Professor at Bowling Green State University in Bowling Green, Ohio. She works in the Department of

Special Education and serves as the coordinator of the early childhood special education program. Dr. Wilson has also worked as a regular education teacher and a special education teacher with the public schools, and has coordinated several state and federally funded projects. Dr. Wilson's research and publications have focused primarily on language development in young children and program development for young children with special needs. Dr. Wilson served as the evaluator with the Toledo Even Start project from 1989 through 1993.

Ann Burke Zupsic holds bachelors and masters degrees in elementary, early childhood, and special education. She has been involved in two innovative programs in the Toledo public schools. Presently, she is the lead teacher for a program at Riverside School where heterogeneous—age and ability levels combined—grouping is the rule. The program also includes a parent involvement/home literacy component.